Seeing the Psalms

SEEING THE PSALMS

A Theology of Metaphor

William P. Brown

Westminster John Knox Press
LOUISVILLE • LONDON

Scripture quotations marked NRSV are from the New Revised Standard Version of the Bible, copyright © 1989 by the Division of Christian Education of the National Council of the Churches of Christ in the U.S.A., and are used by permission. Translations of the Hebrew are the author's.

Book design by Sharon Adams
Cover design by Pam Poll
Cover photo: Harald Sund/Getty Images

First edition
Published by Westminster John Knox Press
Louisville, Kentucky

This book is printed on acid-free paper that meets the American National Standards Institute Z39.48 standard. ♾

PRINTED IN THE UNITED STATES OF AMERICA

02 03 04 05 06 07 08 09 10 — 10 9 8 7 6 5 4 3 2 1

Library of Congress Cataloging-in-Publication Data is on file at the Library of Congress, Washington, D.C.

ISBN 0-664-22502-2

Contents

Illustrations

Preface

Two years ago at a small adult Sunday school class, the topic for discussion was how God works in and through people. Near the end of the hour Curtis, a disabled African American Vietnam vet who had suffered a stroke, stood up with some difficulty and delivered what amounted to a conversation stopper: "God's not a microwave, but a Crock-Pot." Without expounding on the remark, he sat down, and a moment of rapt silence ensued, followed by some chuckles and affirmations of agreement. As an eyewitness to this event, I found myself captivated not only by what the speaker meant but also by the moment of silence that followed as the metaphors worked their magic to prompt reflection. This event confirmed a lingering suspicion, namely, that a striking image or metaphor can prompt certain levels of discernment that no proposition or formula, however precise, can ever evoke. And so began my search for those images in Scripture that stir both heart and mind, a search that sent me headlong into Psalms.

While form criticism has been the staple of Psalms research for over a century, scholars have by and large overlooked the Psalter's use of imagery at great theological cost. More so than any other corpus in Scripture, the Psalter contains discourse that is as visceral as it is sublime. In the psalms, pathos is wedded to image.

Performative by nature, the psalms find their relevance primarily in what they *evoke* rather than in the countless ways they can be dissected and categorized.

With the exception of the Introduction, which lays the hermeneutical groundwork for the study, each chapter in this book treats a particular class of metaphors or images prominently featured in the Psalter. The final chapters focus on images of God, both personal and impersonal. Far from an exhaustive survey, this study attempts to build a bridge between ancient iconography, on the one hand, and the psalmist's sophisticated use of metaphor in poetic discourse, on the other. Previous studies have explored either one or the other. Many provide a veritable catalog of images, but without sustained literary and theological reflection. Particularly lacking is the concerted effort to determine how the images interact and provide structure and meaning in the psalms. Driving this study is the conviction that familiarity with *both* the ancient context and contemporary poetics is essential to understanding the Psalter's theological landscape.

This study would not have been possible without the generous six-month leave I received from Union Theological Seminary and the Presbyterian School of Christian Education in the fall of 2000. Coupled with that was the opportunity to give the 2000 J. J. Thiessen Lectures at the Canadian Mennonite University in Winnipeg on October 17–18. My thanks go to Gordon Zerbe, Waldemar Janzen, Gerald Gerbrandt, Gordon Matties, George Schillington, Pierre Gilbert, Adelia Wiens, Sheila Klassen-Wiebe, Daniel Epp-Tiessen, Ingrid Peters-Fransen, Dietrich Bartel, Harry Huebner, and Irma Dueck for their gracious hospitality and stimulating conversation. CMBC Publications published the lectures with the title *God and the Imagination: A Primer to Reading the Psalms in an Age of Pluralism* (2001), my first foray and point of departure for the current study. I express my gratitude to CMBC for permission to present adapted excerpts from my earlier work.

On the production side, I am indebted to the resourceful staff of Westminster John Knox and particularly to Carey C. Newman, former senior editor, whose guidance and encouragement proved invaluable in helping this study see the light of day, and to Julie Tonini, who diligently saw the project to its completion. Thanks also go to Mengistu Lemma, a doctoral student from Ethiopia, for reviewing earlier drafts and checking references, as well as to Lou McKinney, who digitized and adapted the pictures in this volume.

Finally, I dedicate this work to Dr. John G. Davies, the former pastor of my home church in Tucson, Arizona (Trinity Presbyterian Church), who helped cultivate in me both a desire for knowledge and a passion for God during my high school years.

N.B.: Although the translations of the Hebrew are the author's, the biblical citations are drawn from the versification of the NRSV (and related English translations) rather than from the Masoretic Text for the sake of the general reader's accessibility.

Abbreviations and Symbols

[ ]	Literary material added for the sake of clearer English translation of the Hebrew
AB	Anchor Bible
ACORP	American Center of Oriental Research Publications
AEL	*Ancient Egyptian Literature*
	M. Lichtheim. 3 vols. Berkeley, Calif., 1971–80
AfOB	Archiv für Orientforschung: Beiheft
ANEP	*The Ancient Near East in Pictures Relating to the Old Testament.* Edited by J. B. Pritchard. Princeton, 1954
ANET	*Ancient Near Eastern Texts Relating to the Old Testament.* Edited by J. B. Pritchard. 3d ed. Princeton, 1969
AnOr	Analecta orientalia
AOAT	Alter Orient und Altes Testament
AR 1	*Assyrian Rulers of the Third and Second Millennia BC (to 1115 BC).* Edited by A. K. Grayson. Toronto, 1987
AR 2	*Assyrian Rulers of the Early First Millennium BC I (1114–859 BC).* Edited by A. K. Grayson. Toronto, 1991

ARAB	*Ancient Records of Assyria and Babylonia.* D. D. Luckenbill. 2 vols. Chicago, 1926–27
ARE	*Ancient Records of Egypt.* Edited by J. H. Breasted. 5 vols. Chicago, 1906–07, 1962
ASOR	American Schools of Oriental Research
BAR	*Biblical Archaeology Review*
BDB	Brown, F., S. R. Driver, and C. A. Briggs. *A Hebrew and English Lexicon of the Old Testament.* Oxford, 1907
BHS	*Biblia Hebraica Stuttgartensia.* Edited by K. Elliger and W. Rudolph. Stuttgart, 1983
BTB	*Biblical Theological Bulletin*
BZAW	Beihefte zur Zeitschrift für die alttestamentliche Wissenschaft
CBQ	*Catholic Biblical Quarterly*
CBQMS	Catholic Biblical Quarterly Monograph Series
ConBOT	Coniectanea biblica: Old Testament Series
HALOT	*The Hebrew and Aramaic Lexicon of the Old Testament.* Koehler, L., W. Baumgartner, and J. J. Stamm. Translated and edited under the supervision of M. E. J. Richardson. 4 vols. Leiden, 1994–99
HAR	*Hebrew Annual Review*
HO	Handbuch der Orientalistik
HSM	Harvard Semitic Monographs
HSS	Harvard Semitic Studies
HTR	*Harvard Theological Review*
HUCA	*Hebrew Union College Annual*
IBC	Interpretation: A Bible Commentary for Teaching and Preaching
IBHS	*An Introduction to Biblical Hebrew Syntax.* B. K. Waltke and M. O'Connor. Winona Lake, Indiana, 1990
IDB	*The Interpreter's Dictionary of the Bible.* Edited by G. A. Buttrick. 4 vols. Nashville, 1962
Int	*Interpretation: A Journal of Bible and Theology*
IRT	Issues in Religion and Theology
ISBL	Indiana Studies in Biblical Literature
JAOS	*Journal of the American Oriental Society*
JBL	*Journal of Biblical Literature*
JNES	*Journal of Near Eastern Studies*
JR	*Journal of Religion*
JRE	*Journal of Religious Ethics*
JSOT	*Journal for the Study of the Old Testament*
JSOTSup	Journal for the Study of the Old Testament: Supplement Series
JTS	*Journal of Theological Studies*
KAT	Kommentar zum Alten Testament

KBL	Koehler, L., and W. Baumgartner, *Lexicon in Veteris Testamenti libros*. 2d ed. Leiden, 1958
KTU	*Die keilalphabetischen Texte aus Ugarit*. Edited by M. Dietrich, O. Loretz, and J. Sanmartín. AOAT 24/1. Neukirchen-Vluyn, 1972. 2d enlarged ed. of *KTU: The Cuneiform Alphabetic Texts from Ugarit, Ras Ibn Hani, and Other Places*. Edited by M. Dietrich, O. Loretz, and J. Sanmartín. Münster, 1995
LCC	Library of Christian Classics. Philadelphia, 1953–
LCMA	*Law Collections from Mesopotamia and Asia Minor*. M. T. Roth. Atlanta, 1995
LXX	Septuagint Text (Old Greek)
MT	Masoretic Text
NCB	New Century Bible
NJPS	*Tanakh: The Holy Scriptures: The New JPS Translation according to the Traditional Hebrew Text*
NRSV	New Revised Standard Version
OBO	Orbis biblicus et orientalis
OTL	Old Testament Library
PEQ	*Palestine Exploration Quarterly*
RB	*Revue biblique*
RSV	Revised Standard Version
SBLDS	Society of Biblical Literature Dissertation Series
SBLMS	Society of Biblical Literature Monograph Series
SBLWAWS	Society of Biblical Literature Writings from the Ancient World Series
SJOT	*Scandinavian Journal of the Old Testament*
SCSS	Septuagint and Cognate Study Series
SWBA	Social World of Biblical Antiquity
ThT	*Theology Today*
UF	*Ugarit-Forschungen*
VT	*Vetus Testamentum*
VTSup	Supplements to Vetus Testamentum
WBC	Word Biblical Commentary
WMANT	Wissenschaftliche Monographien zum Alten und Neuen Testament
ZAH	*Zeitschrift für Althebräistik*
ZAW	*Zeitschrift für die alttestamentliche Wissenschaft*

Introduction

A Poetics of the Psalmic Imagination

No one is more unimaginative than an interpreter who speaks too neatly and readily of the imagination.[1]

With all due respect to the apostle Paul, there is good reason to call the book of Psalms the "Romans of the Old Testament." Luther himself, while lecturing on the Psalter for twenty years (1513–33), found among the psalms both the theological recovery of the Old Testament and the very themes of Reformation theology, crystallized in the doctrine of justification "by faith alone."[2] If not the theological center of the Old Testament, the Psalter is at least Scripture's most integrated corpus. On David's many-stringed lyre, as it were, there can be heard almost every theological chord that resounds throughout the Hebrew Scriptures, from covenant and history to creation and wisdom. In the Psalms, the God who commands is also the God who sustains. The God of royal pedigree and the God of the "poor and needy," the God of judgment and the God of healing, God's hidden face and God's beaming countenance: all are profiled in the Psalter. It was not without justification that Luther called the Psalter "the little Bible."[3]

But that is not all. Such an eclectic portrayal of the divine is consonant with an equally thick profile of the human self. Whether or not the Psalter is the most theological book of the Hebrew canon, one thing is certain: it is the Bible's most introspective book, the one that most intensely probes the "inward zone of the spirit."[4] The public and private spheres, corporate worship and inner devotion, find their nexus in the Psalms. From anger to adulation, the various psalms cover the gamut of human emotion and response to God's presence in the world, or lack thereof. All that is humanly experienced is related to God. Knowledge of self and knowledge of God, to utilize Calvin's categories, are inseparably bound. With its jagged edges yet luminous intensity, the Psalter presents the rich mosaic of faith, pieced together from Israel's turbulent history and cultural diversity.[5]

Nevertheless, the attraction the Psalter has gained throughout the history of interpretation cannot simply be attributed to its wide scope and variety. The power of Psalms lies first and foremost in its evocative use of language. The psalms at once caress and assault the soul. They orient, disorient, and reorient;[6] they scale the heights of praise as well as plumb the depths of despair. The anguished cry, "My God, my God why have you forsaken me?" (22:1a) is matched by the joyful summons, "Make a joyful noise to God, all the earth!" (66:1). The poetry oscillates between anguish and joy, righteous protest and personal confession. Rife with the pathos of praise and the ethos of agony, the book of Psalms captures better than any other corpus of Scripture the "bi-polar" life of faith.

As poetry, the psalms do not simply express; they also impart and teach. The language of ancient verse does more than glorify itself, in distinction perhaps from much modern poetry. Biblical poetry is poetry with a purpose. Paul Ricoeur's observation of the formative dimensions of biblical language pertains especially to the psalms: "The [biblical] word *forms our feeling* in the process of expressing it."[7] By giving voice to unspeakable pathos, the Psalter shapes the life of faith, no less, forming the memory and thus the identity of a people. The psalmist, moreover, declares time and again that such "meditation," however anguished, is devoted to God.[8] Only in the Psalter is God's glory conveyed so personally and lyrically. Rich in metaphor and raw in texture, the various psalms strike the resonant yet dissonant cadences of faith. To read the psalms is to *hear* their rhythms; to hear them is to *behold* the rich imagery they convey; to behold the psalms is to *feel* them in all their pain and promise; and to feel them is, ultimately, to "taste and see that the LORD is good" (Ps 34:8a). The psalmists' anguished voices, jubilant cries, and instructive words together shape the reader's affections and posture *coram deo*. Together, they direct the deepest desires of a people *ad deum* and away from anything less than worthy of praise—and worthy of lament. The psalms offer palpable prayer to the affectively deprived, prayer that, as the rabbis defined it, is a "service of the heart" (*b. Ta'anit*, 2a). Poetry, the discourse of the heart, is the stuff of psalms.

This study is aimed at recapturing the imaginative and affective power of psalmic poetry, particularly the power of imagery, in order to uncover something of the psalms' claim about what is truly real and theologically compelling.[9] All too frequently, however, in the progress of Western thinking, including Western theology, the imagination and the real have been related only antithetically. Yet, in almost every generation since the Enlightenment, voices in the wilderness have called theology back to its poetic roots. From the Romantics[10] to the present,[11] certain interpreters have privileged the language of poetry in theological reflection. Even the distinctly North American brand of biblical scholarship continues to regard the *poetic* casting of a hypothesized "Hebrew Epic"[12] as typologically, and thus theologically, primary to prosaic formulation.[13] By way of introduction to this investigation of the poetic, specifically metaphorical, contours of ancient Israel's faith in the Psalms, a remarkable quote, given its source, is worth retrieving:

> The study of theology ought to begin these days with a study of poetry. This is not merely to hand a rose to the poets, but to advocate a sane program of theological rehabilitation, certainly of theological repatriation. Theology seems to have gone awhoring after the scientific fleshpots of Egypt. It has wandered so far afield that it has forgotten the well springs of its infancy. The antidote must be potent enough to restore sight to the blind and hearing to the deaf. Perhaps modern poetry is sufficiently strong medicine to enable the queen to shake off her torpor.[14]

Establishing the link between theology and poetry, however, is not unique to this writer, Robert Funk, the impressario of the Jesus Seminar. The eminent Spanish biblical scholar Luis Alonso Schökel makes the following claim: "If theo-logy is speaking about God, the biblical poets constructed a proto-theology."[15] Investigating the contours of a "proto-theology" demands, according to Schökel, the exercise of a certain faculty that is all but lost in contemporary scholarship: "[I]n biblical exegesis there is a lack of imagination and perception rather than a surfeit. . . . What has been written with imagination, must also be read with imagination, provided the individual has imagination and it is in working order."[16]

Current theological scholarship has largely ignored Schökel's harsh assessment. Nevertheless, theology cannot afford to abandon its poetic roots in the name of scientific accuracy or dialectical precision.[17] Needed in the art of exegesis, particularly in interpreting psalms, are ways of investigating the most basic building block of poetry, even perhaps of the linguistic imagination itself, the metaphor. "Like a blues song, [the psalms] speak a vividly metaphorical language that is intensely personal and yet not private."[18] Indeed, it is precisely the psalmist's deployment of metaphor that enables the personal language of pathos to be felt and appropriated by readers of every generation.

THE ICONIC METAPHOR

"Images are the glory, perhaps the essence of poetry, the enchanted planet of the imagination, a limitless galaxy, ever alive and ever changing."[19] Though overly effusive, Schökel's statement pertains even to *biblical* poetry. Nevertheless, in modern exegesis the study of imagery has yet to complement the dominant tendency to investigate the verbal or semantic value of words within their particular contexts. Such one-sided attention is in part theologically driven. Gerhard von Rad's comment on the second commandment of the Decalogue is telling:

> Any interpretation which deals in isolation with the impossibility of repre-
> senting Jahweh by an image, and which does not see the [second] com-
> mandment as bound up *with the totality of Jahweh's revelation,* misses the
> crucial point.

The "point" is that Israel's God is a deity of the word, not of the image.[20]

While ancient Israel's legal codes issue a resounding veto on the use of images in worship,[21] Israel's poetic texts are replete with imagery. Scholars, thus, find it paradoxical that despite Israel's iconophobia in the material realm the literary realm of Israel's faith abounds with images for God and the self.[22] Psalm 139, for example, revels in iconic language with utter abandon while, at the same time, pre-senting itself as a defense against idolatry.[23] The poetry of the Psalms achieves a verbal level of iconography that more than compensates for the prescribed absence of images on the material level of ancient orthodox practice. And perhaps that is the point: through the word, icon is made metaphor. Yet armed with the Second Commandment, modern exegetes have tended to overlook the graphic texture of the written word by examining only its linguistic and historical contours. Such is the "tyranny of the word" that has traditionally governed exegesis.[24]

Let it be said loud and clear: Attending to the importance of the text's form-fulness and linguistic background (i.e., its genre, structure, and verbal nuances) does not require neglecting the role that images play in conveying the text's mean-ing. Word and image, form and icon, are indelibly bound together in the for-mative aim of the biblical text, particularly Psalms, as recognized by Athanasius (ca. 293–373 C.E.) in his letter to Marcellinus:

> [I]n the other books one hears only what one must do and what one must
> not do. . . . But in the Book of Psalms, the one who hears, in addition to
> learning these things, also comprehends and is taught in it the emotions of
> the soul, and, consequently, . . . he is enabled by this book to *possess the image
> deriving from the words.*[25]

Athanasius finds the affective language of psalmic poetry to be uniquely instruc-tive. He locates, moreover, the Psalter's pedagogical impact squarely in the psalmist's use of "the image," which for him is "the perfect image for the soul's course of life," a prescriptive yet personal ethos depicted and modeled in imagery.[26] It is the image that enables the reader to see himself or herself in the psalmic prayers; through imagery "these words become like a mirror."[27] To "pos-sess the image," thus, marks the act of comprehension and, consequently, self-recognition by the reader. Only with attention to the image borne by the word, Athanasius implies, is the reader's formation enabled.[28] The psalms, in short, are distinctly "sacramental" in function.[29]

In the Event of a Metaphor

The use of imagery in theological formulation was by no means confined to the biblical authors and their tradents or to later Jewish and Christian commentators on the text. In his investigation of New Kingdom literature, Jan Assmann prefers "icon" over "myth" in characterizing the theology of the Egyptian hymns. His distinctive approach pertains to biblical poetry as well: "I use the term 'icon' in the technical sense as an expression or articulation of content that can be realized in *both* language and image."[30] In Egyptian hymns, "image and language are equivalent, in the sense that either can be used to express 'thought': i.e. to formulate content."[31] So also in biblical poetry.

One class of poetic icon that is particularly evocative of thought is the metaphorical kind. "Metaphors not only communicate suggestive and expressive meanings, but they also become iconic objects through their fusion of sense with sound."[32] In the metaphor, "seeing as" and "saying" converge in powerful ways to stimulate reflection and emotion. The term originally denoted "transference" or "carrying across" ($\mu\epsilon\tau\alpha\phi o\rho\acute{\alpha}$: *meta* "trans" + *pherein* "to carry"), particularly of property. As chief among the tropes, the metaphor signals the transference of meaning from something familiar to something new;[33] it describes one thing in terms of another. For further precision, the following definition by Janet Soskice is as good as any:

> The metaphor is that figure of speech whereby we speak about one thing in terms [that] are seen to be suggestive of another.[34]

In most definitions, at least two components are identified. Most well known is the distinction between the "tenor" and the "vehicle," whose classifications I. A. Richards himself admitted were at best "clumsy."[35] The "tenor" is the "underlying idea," "principal subject," or conceptual meaning signified; the "vehicle" is the mode or figure by which the "tenor" is expressed.[36] Influential as this distinction has been, Richards's classification has its shortcomings. The distinction sets up an unnecessary hierarchy of classification: in hermeneutical practice, the "tenor" easily takes precedence over the "vehicle," which is, thereby, considered secondary or derivative of the "tenor."[37] Such prioritizing is made all the more explicit in Max Black's distinction between "the 'primary' subject and the 'secondary' one."[38] Paul Avis suggests the designations "occasion" and "image," but these, too, offer no improvement in the matter. Moreover, not all metaphors are images. Most importantly, such designations fail to indicate the kind of interaction that takes place between the metaphorical image and its referent or underlying subject in a given communicative context.

Cognitive literary theorists George Lakoff and Mark Turner have made significant gains in delineating how metaphors work, that is, how they communicate knowledge and pervade common language, including rationale discourse, across cultures. Indeed, understanding the function of a particular metaphor in its context requires just that, *understanding* or cognition. The metaphor is not simply a literary ornament or a vehicle of emotive import; it is a means of cognitive mediation.[39] Take, for example, the metaphor "Time is a thief," whereby the abstract category of time is personified. George Lakoff and Mark Turner describe what happens in the deployment of such a metaphor:

> We use a metaphor to map certain aspects of the source domain onto the
> target domain, thereby producing a new understanding of that target
> domain. In this case, part of that mapping superimposes a metaphorical
> understanding of youth as a possession, which carries with it our normal
> feelings about possessions—that we have a right to keep them and that it
> would be unjust for them to be taken away.[40]

The terms "target domain" and "source domain" not only acknowledge a certain
parity of import between the metaphor and its referent but also illustrate more
precisely the *dynamic* that occurs when something is referenced metaphorically,
namely, a superimposing or unilateral "mapping" of one domain on another.[41]
Such "transference" results in a new understanding of the *target* domain, in this
case "time."[42] For a metaphor to work, an understanding of both domains is presupposed. There must be a correspondence between the metaphor and its target
domain that is recognized by both poet and reader; otherwise, the metaphor
remains idiosyncratic and indecipherable. Lakoff and Turner offer the example
"Death is a banana," a metaphor devoid of rhyme and, more importantly, *reason,*[43] an example of catachresis, the improper use of metaphor.[44] The effective
metaphor, by contrast, stands on a common ground of understanding, and builds
on it to elicit new inferences and associations.[45] In short, the metaphor bears a
conceptual power, namely, the power to "*create* structure in our understanding
of life."[46]

The particular associations evoked by a given metaphor can be automatic and
effortless, even unconscious, verging on the trite or literal (as in the so-called
"dead metaphor"[47]), or they can be unconventional and destabilizing. Much of
language consists of dead metaphors.[48] In any case, the metaphor excels in the
art of juxtaposition.[49] The poet is essentially a "match-maker."[50] From a defini-
tional standpoint, the metaphor is not primarily a mental act or an exercise of
the intuition, but a manifestation of language.[51] Yet a consideration of function
is essential to any discussion of how a metaphor *works,* as Soskice points out:

> The purpose of [the] metaphor is both to cast up and organize a network of
> associations. A good metaphor . . . [is] a new vision, the birth of a new
> understanding, a new referential access. A strong metaphor compels new
> possibilities of vision.[52]

Broadly put, metaphors *do* something to enable the reader to perceive something
differently. In the event of a metaphor, two or more modes of perception become
juxtaposed and fused.[53] It marks "an intercourse of *thoughts,* a transaction
between contexts."[54] Yet the kind of intercourse facilitated by metaphor exhibits
focused movement, specifically that of "mapping." A source domain is mapped
onto a target domain, and the reader's perception of the target is irrevocably
altered. At the very least, the metaphor "enables one to see similarities in what
previously had been regarded as dissimilars."[55] Metaphors serve as "grids" or "filters" through which reality is viewed and reconfigured.[56]

It is often the case that the new perception(s) engendered by the metaphor do not come without a degree of dissonance. There is a "dissonance or tension in a living metaphor whereby the terms of the utterance used seem not strictly appropriate to the topic at hand."[57] The metaphor, in other words, exploits an irresolvable incongruity between the target and source domains to generate a "semantic shock."[58] A good metaphor effectively weds together analogy and anomaly.[59] Living metaphors invariably create conceptual and emotional friction by which new meaning is created and the impossible becomes conceivable. The metaphor, thus, is a master of surprise.

Metaphor and Simile

On a grammatical level, it is often thought that metaphors are simply "elliptical similes" in disguise: the latter simply "wear their comparative form on their grammatical sleeves."[60] Rhetorically speaking, however, the difference between metaphor and simile may be anything but negligible. With the simple addition of the term of comparison (e.g., "like" or "as"), one referent is subordinated to the other. Some contend that whereas immediacy, spontaneity, and vividness characterize the metaphor, the simile designates a secondary level of abstraction that diffuses, in effect, the tension between the actual elements of comparison, the source and target domains.[61] Such a global claim, however, needs to be judged on an individual basis. In Song 4:1, for example, the presence or absence of the term of comparison seems to make no appreciable difference:

> How beautiful you are, my love, how very beautiful!
> Your eyes are doves[62] behind your veil;
>   your hair is *like* a flock of goats,
>   moving down the slopes of Gilead.

Despite the fact that the comparative term is reserved only for the second image, "doves" and "a flock of goats" are poetically equivalent comparisons with respect to the facial features of the beloved. Eyes *identified* with doves are no more profound or vivid than hair *likened* to a flock of goats. On the other hand, when the psalmist refers to God as "my rock and my redeemer" (Ps 19:14; see also 18:2), something is lost in the more prosaic statement "my God is *like* a rock" or, worse yet, "God is like my rock." At the very least, the simile represents a form of analogical language that *may* relieve the ambiguity and narrow the interpretive possibilities provoked by the metaphor, but not necessarily. By comparison, the metaphor *may* convey a more evocative level of literary artistry by virtue of the tension it generates for the reader. Given its heuristic nature, the metaphor can initiate the process of imaginative reflection, of discernment and synthesis, that a simile may not match. It is best, then, to classify the simile as a form of metaphor, one that makes explicit the object of comparison, but in so doing *can* limit the range of association.[63] Often, "metaphor and simile, while textually different, are functionally the same."[64] Yet while the simile, like the metaphor, conveys understanding of one thing in terms of another, it often "hedges its bets—it makes a weaker claim" than the metaphor.[65] The metaphor is more a lamp than a mirror (cf. Ps 119:105).

From a lexicographical standpoint, the iconic metaphor is in a class of its own. This "verbal image" is a special kind of word, deployed to evoke an indelible picture in the mind of the reader. The metaphorical image serves as the center of an expanding web of associations and comparisons. Characteristic of the metaphor is a "fullness" of signification that is not evident in other words, a surplus of meaning that extends beyond the semantic restrictions and lexical constraints that define most words. Like a sacred text, the metaphor is *deutungsbedürftig*,[66] that is, continually in need of interpretation. A metaphor, in essence, works by violating language.[67] It is a transgressor that builds bridges across lexicographical divisions. As Jan Assmann notes, the power of the "icon" lies in its facility to bring together "several semantic levels . . . into a relationship of mutual reference: they can be woven together in one icon and various spheres can consciously be 'seen in one.'"[68] The verbal iconography of biblical poetry thus cannot be confined to the "semantics of biblical language."[69]

The metaphor's capacity to generate chains of associations not normally found in other words lies in its "iconic" quality and, more significantly, in its power to bring together various levels of signification. The metaphor is the hinge between multiple lines of associations and manifold worlds of meaning. It is the metaphor's nature to arrest the hearer and to generate enough lexical ambiguity to provoke the reader's imagination into making associations beneath and beyond its semantic surface. In his classic definition of the parable, C. H. Dodd captures well the readerly impact of the metaphor: "a metaphor or simile drawn from nature or common life, arresting the hearer by its vividness or strangeness, and leaving the mind in sufficient doubt about its precise application to tease it into active thought."[70] The metaphor, in short, pushes verbal discourse beyond itself to enrich both language and experience. To those who are more verbally fixated (theologically I am a Calvinist), the focus on metaphor presents new opportunities in biblical interpretation and theology, occasions to mediate between tradition and experience while avoiding, on the one hand, the "idolatry of the new" and, on the other, the "tyranny of the same."[71]

THE POETIC IMAGINATION

The wealth of images and metaphors found in poetry constitutes nothing less than a "a kind of concordance of the imagination."[72] Although "the production of images is the work, *par excellence*, of imagination,"[73] the capacity of the imagination is by no means limited to production. The exercise of imagination is also prompted in the *interaction* between the human subject and the image, which itself is "revealed as a world of dialogue *between* intentional subjects."[74] Like language itself, the linguistic imagination is dialogical by nature. As a figure of speech that cavorts with the visual, the metaphor has its home in the imagination.[75] It instantiates the poetic role of imagining, of saying and seeing one thing in terms of something else, or several things at once, in order to create something new.[76] To talk of literary genres of the imagination is to suggest that the imagination is inextricably tied to language.[77]

If the imagination is crucial for thinking in images, then of all the forms of human discourse, poetry is best suited to make a "raid on the inarticulate," to borrow from T. S. Eliot.[78] "Poetry starts with what is known and from this reaches out to convey the unknown."[79] The art of poetry is "to *conceal* as much as it is to *reveal*."[80] And the leap from sense to transcendence, from the describable to the ineffable, is facilitated by metaphor. The metaphor, according to Paul Ricoeur, introduces the spark of imagination that leads the reader into "thinking more" (*penser plus*).[81] Regarding the moment of faithful discernment, Brian Gerrish observes that it is "likely to be a striking image or metaphor, not an exact formula, that turns the switch: it captures the imagination and stirs the heart, and the intellect has to catch up later."[82] Cast metaphorically, an image need not deny reality. Rather, it can prompt new levels of discernment. Ricoeur refers to the power of the metaphor broaden the horizons of perception as *iconic augmentation*.[83] In the composing and reading of poetry, creation is also discovery. By reinscribing the world, the poetic metaphor expands it.

The power of poetry stems in part from the impact the poetic image makes on the reader. While analytical or critical study is necessary for *understanding* a particular poem, the imagination, Susan Gillingham points out, is essential to *appreciating* the poem.[84] In the former, the reader is the subject "and the poem and the poet are the objects," whereas the reverse is the case in the act of appreciation: "the poem becomes the subject, so that as we allow ourselves to be addressed, the poetry is the active element and we are the recipients."[85] The appreciation of poetry, like music appreciation, requires a *cultivated* receptivity on the part of the reader.[86] To echo Schökel's words: What is written with imagination must also be read with imagination.

The imaginative appreciation of poetry involves "looking *through*" the poem, in addition to "looking *at* it."[87] The power of poetry, specifically biblical poetry, to invite the reader to *look through* and thus *beyond* the written word, beyond its poetic structure and meter, through its symmetry and sonority, presents an irresolvable paradox. "Ancient biblical poetry . . . has a capacity both to stir our memories with things which are strangely familiar, and also to challenge our vision with its depiction of things which will always remain strangely unknown."[88] Owing to its expressive power, biblical poetry makes the familiar strange and the strange familiar.[89]

Image and Idol

As a way of perceiving the world, Scripture embodies and imparts normative patterns for shaping the religious imagination. It is no accident, then, that the Bible is rife with imagery. Yet, in the heat of dispute against Roman Catholicism, John

Calvin roundly proclaimed that "whatever men learn of God from images is futile, indeed false. . . . In short, if it were not true that whatever knowledge of God is sought from images is fallacious and counterfeit, the prophets would not so generally have condemned it."[90] But as poets themselves, the prophets reveled in imagery: Hosea likened God to an "evergreen cypress" (Hos 14:8); Jeremiah was fascinated with the image of the potter and his clay (Jer 18:1–12); and Malachi fashioned the effulgent image of the "sun of righteousness" rising "with healing in its wings" (Mal 4:2a [3:20a Heb.]). In his iconoclastic zeal, Calvin confused image and idol. Is the image merely the signpost on a slippery slope leading ineluctably toward idolatry? Not all images, however, divert the gaze of readers from the beatific vision or from the inspired word. To the contrary, the image can inject new vigor into the written message and aim the word resolutely toward the heavens.

Nevertheless, Calvin's wariness of images does have a place in the hermeneutical imagination. While images, as metaphors, carry a revelatory power that stirs the imagination and enlarges the senses, they are also delimiting in their hermeneutical scope. A metaphor qua metaphor is limited in its transference of meaning. When metaphors, for example, become literalized to the point that they exclude other metaphors for the same subject or target domain, particularly in the case of God, they function as idols. Such has been said of the exclusive use of masculine imagery for God.[91] Put theologically, if any metaphor, no matter how profound, becomes absolutized, as though it were itself considered ultimate, idolatry becomes the norm.[92] Metaphors, particularly those that are theologically oriented, have their own defined scope and shelf life within reading communities. Literarily, an image can become an idol when its connotative force is mistaken for its denotative scope, when the target and source domains are collapsed into one. Theologically, idolatry arises when the deity's power is immanently lodged within the material strictures of the image or source domain, and transcendence, consequently, is eviscerated. Yet to eschew the power of metaphor in theological discourse for fear that idolatry is the unavoidable result would, in effect, sever any connection between God and the world of human perception. The outcome would be an impoverishment of theological discourse. For all his emphasis on the power of the word over the image, Calvin, in the manner of the biblical poets, did not avoid enlisting iconic metaphors drawn even from nature to highlight God's glory and goodness.[93] Such is the *discursive* power of the image.

Approaching Biblical Poetry

The initial contact between the poetic text and the reader is not limited to the poem's meter, structure, or even genre, although these features are crucial to understanding and appreciating the poem. The point of contact lies primarily in what the poem "paints" for the reader via its imagery, the constellation of images that evoke and invite exploration, negotiation, and appropriation through the exercise of the interpreter's informed imagination. Indeed, the poetic image marks nothing less than a *dialogue* between intentional subjects.[94] If genres function to create expectations in the reader that help determine the meaning of the text,[95] then so does the text's deployment of imagery. The inviting and invasive nature of the metaphorical image effectively serves as the bridge that spans the yawning chasm between ancient and (post)modern worldviews and sensibilities. Such is in keeping with the essential role of metaphor, namely, that of "transferring" meaning, and in transference there is reception and, invariably, transformation. In the reader's appropriation of metaphor, the poetic text itself comes to be read in a different way, as *both* understood and appreciated—the two cannot be separated. Archetypal in scope, the most powerful metaphors share a "strangely common" ground between text and interpretation, even between the poet and the reader.[96]

If the language of Scripture is, in varying degrees, "the language of the sanctified imagination,"[97] then it is most evident from the plethora of images and metaphors embedded in it. "All imagination is embodied. Images differ from concepts in the clay that clings to them."[98] One must be careful, however, to guard against the still prevalent notion that images serve only "to dress up ideas."[99] Interpreting Scripture into a more conceptually precise language will not retrieve its original meaning.[100] Such a program, akin to demythologization, dispenses with the image that is so integral to its message, an aberrant form of allegorizing that serves only to tame the text. Scripture is not so much a source of propositions, much less a series of creeds or doctrines, as "a vast collection of interwoven images."[101] Moreover, the imaginative act is not confined to the construction of singular, concrete images. An image is invariably supported by a constellation of images that help to establish an evocative setting or orienting framework. Gordon Kaufman refers to such imaginative constructions as "world-pictures" that provide frames of orientation and worldviews, giving order to the "blooming, buzzing confusion" of life, to quote from William James.[102] As a starting point for exegetical practice intended to discern the "world-pictures" conveyed in Scripture, Luke Johnson makes the following observation:

> The world which the text produces is not simply a haphazard collection of compositions written by various authors speaking from and for diverse communities over a period of centuries, but it is also a complex network of literary interconnections established by the use and reuse of terms that gain depth and richness by means of intricate and subtle allusion. Attention to these interconnections is justified, therefore, because together they create a world of metaphoric structures within which humans can live in a distinctive manner.[103]

That Scripture is the product of the faithful imagination has much to say about the practice of hermeneutics and of "liv[ing] in a distinctive manner." Interpretation is both an epistemological and an ethical issue, a matter of correctness and responsibility.[104] Indeed, acknowledging the moral contours of biblical interpretation is nothing new, and not much, in my opinion, has been (or can be) done to improve upon Augustine's articulation of the aim and limitations of biblical interpretation. In his manual on biblical interpretation, *De doctrina christiana* ("On Teaching Christianity"), the Bishop of Hippo grounds all interpretation in the double love of God and neighbor.[105] The ultimate test of exegetical "correctness," which for Augustine begins with the literal sense, is whether one's interpretation "contribut[es] to the reign of charity."[106] The imaginative power of empathy to identify with the other and to welcome the stranger is in fact the sine qua non of all ethics.[107]

Authentic hermeneutics, thus, is ultimately a hermeneutics of love, and the moral or faithful imagination that undergirds the hermeneutical enterprise is the imagination that drives the moral subject into the world of the Other, into the world of Thou.[108] As the psalmist declares to God, "Whom have I in heaven but you? Nothing on earth is there that I desire other than you" (Ps 73:25). The psalms identify God as the heart's true desideratum and the object of one's moral zeal.

Image and "Incarnation"

Taking seriously the use of imagery in Scripture and, more generally, in theological discourse is not just an academic exercise. Poet and writer Kathleen Norris gives a blistering critique of the way preachers and theologians use words lamely. She notes that the church today has failed to cultivate what she calls "incarnational language," namely, "words that resonate with the senses as they aim for the stars."[109] Such language avoids abstraction and revels in metaphor; it is both visceral and sublime, evocative and intense. It is, in short, biblical. Rejecting the banal verbiage of sound bites, the incendiary speech of ideologues, and the wearying abstractions of academics (including myself), the church must re-present itself as the schoolhouse of God's word if it is to offer an enlivening word, the Word made flesh, the Word made fresh. It need not "reimagine" Scripture, as if Scripture were simply an artifact to be revivified and reshaped in the superior hands of the reader.[110] Re-imagination has its place only when the depth of the Bible's *ancient* imagination has been fully appreciated *and* understood rather than dismissively caricatured. As I hope to demonstrate in the following chapters, there is more than a sufficiency of imaginative vigor within the biblical witness for the "renewing of [our] minds," the conversion of our imaginations (Rom 12:2).[111]

If Octavio Paz is right, that "imagination turns . . . language into rhythm and metaphor,"[112] then the Psalms must be regarded as the font of scriptural imagination, for there is no better place to find rhythm, metaphor, and imagery in Scripture than in the Psalter. Moreover, these poetic features are all pressed into the service of reshaping the reader's worldview.[113] Thomas G. Long aptly notes that the language of the Psalter aims at creating a shift in the basic moral perception of the reader. Psalms operate at the level of the imagination, often swiveling the universe on the hinges of a single image. Sermons based on psalms should also seek to work their way into the deep recesses of the hearer's imagination.[114]

Rife with the language of analogy and anomaly, the Psalter is the schoolhouse of incarnational imagination.

CONTEMPORARY CONTEXT

The need for conducting an iconic analysis of biblical poetry is all the more pressing in light of our contemporary context. More than ever before, Western culture is awash with manipulated images spawned from the corporate world's "imagination," images that, in the words of the female protagonist of a children's classic, "leave so little scope for imagination."[115] We live in an age of media saturation in which an infinite array of competing images circulate for our personal entertainment, fulfillment, and ultimately our enslavement. Such is the iconography of consumption,[116] and it has not left the medium of the text unscathed. Religious reading has become a lost art, reduced to "extract[ing] what is useful or exciting or entertaining from what is read, preferably with dispatch, and then [moving] on to something else."[117] To read religiously, however, is to read the text "as a lover reads, with a tensile attentiveness that wishes to linger, to prolong, to savor, and has no interest . . . in the quick orgasm of consumption."[118] To read theologically is, in part, to linger over the metaphor.

With its own discourse challenged and frequently co-opted by the corrosive rhetoric of consumption and competition, the church finds itself submerged in a corporate-based culture governed by demoralizing images on the one hand, and shallow formulas on the other. The moral challenge, thus, is to reach through the "labyrinth of depthless images to the other."[119] The theological challenge is to relate the other to the One who is related to what is truly real. In their use of depth-filled imagery, the psalms expose the shallowness of contemporary iconography while opening a way for the wholly Other. Against the totalizing discourse of the market, the psalms provide both a bulwark and a bridge. They not only help to set boundaries for the community of faith in its worship of the liberating, covenantal God. The psalms also establish points of contact with the surrounding culture through the use of shared images, redeemed and transformed, as they did in the hands of Israel's poets. The psalms pose with new force a perennial challenge that confronts all communities of faith. Persons of faith must assess the cultural images, symbols, and narratives that saturate their lives and identify counter images and transforming narratives, if only to sustain themselves through the living of these days and invite others to join them in the calling.

MODUS OPERANDI

If the power of biblical poetry stems in part from the poet's evocative use of imagery, then room needs to be made in exegesis for exploring the iconic dimensions of the psalms. In this study, certain central metaphors are selected in terms of the organizing power they wield both within particular psalms and throughout the Psalter as a whole. In accord with the performative value of metaphor, the line of investigation will proceed by identifying the source and target domains in which a metaphor operates. Attention will also be devoted to the particular context, or setting, of the source domain. The iconic metaphor conjures not an *imago ex nihilo,* but one fraught with background, both visual and discursive. Hence, ancient Near Eastern iconography and literature command much of this study's focus.

Just as crucial, however, is the metaphor's foreground, namely, its range of associations within a literary corpus, the psalm in particular as well as the Psalter's larger editorial shape. As a master of surprise, the metaphor may engineer a collision between its background and foreground, a clash between rhetorical convention and innovation as manifested in the specific way it is deployed in a given psalm.

Exploring such matters fills a yawning gap in exegetical practice. Form-critical concerns have traditionally governed critical exegesis of Psalms, and it is only recently that the poetic image has captured the professional exegete's attention. In addition to discerning the formal elements and structure of a given psalm, the exegete must also pay attention to the psalm's "iconic structure" by identifying the various ways particular images and metaphors interact in the text. Driving this study is the conviction that literary and iconic form are mutually informative and indelibly wedded.

Chapter 1

"In the Shadow of *Shaddai*"

The Metaphor of Refuge

Before beginning our search for embedded metaphors, we must first scope out the lay of the land. A map of the Psalter's world is required. To be sure, efforts at uncovering the Psalter's redactional levels, conducting statistical analyses of word distributions, identifying generic components, and ideologically deconstructing individual psalms—lines of analysis unthinkable to the psalmists who produced them and to the ancient readers who recited them—have all helped to illumine the world that shaped the Psalms. Yet, try as they might, such lines of investigation cannot fully account for the unifying shape and purpose of this motley corpus, the "theo-poetic" world the Psalter itself constructs. Statistical studies and the identification of generic components do not, at the end of the day, foster either reverence or righteousness—the Psalter's clear and stated aims. The psalmists were poets, liturgists, lyricists, and musicians. Their hymns and prayers are not simply ideological constructs designed to mask sociological realities or statistical word fields for the lexically inclined. The psalmists were masters of word and image, and their poetry reflects, foremost, the mosaic of Israel's faith.

This chapter and the next identify the Psalter's broadest metaphorical schemas or contexts in which a host of particular images and iconic metaphors have their home. Two in particular are identified as constitutive of the Psalter's theological shape: "refuge" and "pathway." More has been written about the former in recent studies, but to the neglect of the latter. Both root metaphors, moreover, interact mutually in theologically suggestive ways.

INTRODUCTION

The book of Psalms confronts the reader with a bewildering array of images embedded in various prayers, praises, and instructions, all cast in language that is concrete yet stereotypical and open: expressions of conflict and sickness, weakness and strength, security and threat, blessing and distress. Intense and emotive, such language invites appropriation across a wide range of contexts, reaching beyond generic divisions.[1] While form-critical analysis indicates, for example, that Psalm 30 was originally a song of thanksgiving for an individual's recovery from illness, the superscription indicates that it came to be used "at the dedication of the temple," perhaps at the Feast of Dedication (Hanukkah) in 164 B.C.E. The evidence indicates a decisive move from individual application to corporate usage.[2] The very same psalm could thus have an entirely different function depending on the social need and context.[3] Put in modern parlance, the book of Psalms comes without copyright restrictions.

The Psalter as a whole also reflects the opposite direction—a move from cultic or ritual use to personal instruction.[4] One need only note the prominent presence of the so-called wisdom[5] and *tôrâ* psalms, or better designated together "didactic psalms," which stress personal devotion and the appropriation of instruction. With the inclusion of Psalm 1, as well as the development of the Psalter's pentateuchal division,[6] the original *Sitz im Leben* of each individual psalm receives a new functional setting, namely, *tôrâ*-piety or instruction.[7] A literary, didactic setting overlays a liturgical one. The inclusion of the didactic psalms, in effect, transforms Israel's "hymnbook," or symphony of voices,[8] into a book of instruction.

Such literary physics force the issue of the Psalter's overall shape on the reader, not so much to delimit its theological scope as to generate new possibilities for reflection and use, as the early tradents themselves demonstrate. The free application of psalms to settings beyond their generic parameters underscores the expressive power of psalmic poetry. Several studies over the last two decades have made inroads into delineating the Psalter's theological shape and poetic contours.

Past Efforts

One line of investigation, developed by Gerald H. Wilson, focuses on the "seams" or literary junctures among the five books of the Psalter and observes that Books 1–3 exhibit a literary arrangement distinct from Books 4 and 5.[9] The royal psalms seem deliberately placed at the seams of Books 1–3 (i.e., Psalms 2, 72, 89:1–37), each reflecting confidence in royal covenant and thereby establishing a "Davidic framework" for the whole.[10] The latter half of Psalm 89, however, effectively dismantles the Davidic covenant—breached by God—and acknowledges the monarchy's dissolution (vv. 38–51). Book 4, the "editorial center" of the Psalter, responds to this crisis by shifting the focus from the earthly king's reign to God's everlasting rule.[11] The last book concludes the Psalter by exhorting reliance and trust in God alone, culminating with the paeans of praise that comprise Psalms 146–150. The "seams" of Books 4 and 5 (Psalms 90–91, 106, 145) contain sapiential, rather than royal, material and indicate the work of the "wise" in joining Books 1–3 with Books 4–5. According to this view, the shape of the Psalter is conflictive, fraught as it is with "competing editorial frames."[12] The book of Psalms preserves a "tense dialogue" between "royal covenantal hopes" and "wisdom counsel."[13]

Regardless of the editorial tension, however, royal and didactic discourse find their connection at the very outset. Psalms 1 and 2, according to some, serve as a composite introduction to the Psalter.[14] Psalm 1, in particular, constitutes the Psalter's *prooemium* or preface.[15] In addition, the placement of *tôrâ* psalms (i.e., Psalms 1, 19, and 119) alongside psalms of kingship (Psalms 2, 18, 20, 118[16]) appears to be strategic, reflecting an overarching dual focus set by the final editors: God's royal reign and *tôrâ*'s authoritative guidance.[17]

Another fruitful line of inquiry engages the Psalter's outer frame as opposed to its internal junctures. Often noted is that the book of Psalms moves from the theme of *tôrâ* obedience to praise.[18] The movement, however, is not an easy one: the remaining 148 psalms frequently alternate between lament and praise. Psalm 73, it has been argued, constitutes the midpoint of the Psalter, serving both as a bridge from complaint to praise and as a protest against superficial "Torah-piety" and "hymnic praise."[19] Such an investigation has identified another dimension of the Psalter's shape, specifically a movement from a definite point of departure toward a discernible end point, a movement, however, that is most nonlinear. At best, the Psalter "moves" by fits and starts. The oscillating shifts are concomitant to a "dramatic struggle."[20] Like the "tension" reflected in the editorial process, the theological significance of the Psalter is discernible through a largely *sequential* reading of the Psalms. Indeed, the Psalter's own generic identification, *Tehillim* or "praises," suggests something of the aim or end point to which *all* the psalms ultimately point.[21]

A lingering concern in Psalms research, however, remains unresolved, namely the theological coherence and relationship between the respective poles of *tôrâ*, on the one hand, and kingship and cult, on the other. It is one thing to posit an originally cultic ethos that was revised by postexilic scribes intent on advancing *tôrâ*-piety so that wisdom could have "the last word."[22] It is another thing to ask how the reigning motifs of *tôrâ* and kingship cohere in the final shape of the Psalter. The question raised here is not which one came to dominate the other in the editorial shaping of the Psalter—both are unmistakably present—but rather how these motifs are interrelated and mutually inform each other.

A New Line of Inquiry

Shedding new light on the issue of the theological coherence of Psalms is a fresh study conducted by Jerome F. D. Creach, *Yahweh as Refuge*.[23] Although it does not entirely resolve the allegedly "tensive" relationship between kingship and *tôrâ*, it does launch a new direction of promising inquiry.[24] Creach identifies an important root metaphor in the Psalter, "refuge" (*maḥseh*), and charts its distribution, as well as that of its semantic siblings: "secure height" or "retreat" (*miśgāb*), "stronghold" (*mĕṣûdâ*), "place of protection" (*māʿôz*), "hiding place" (*sēter*), "shadow" (*ṣēl*), "rock" (*ṣûr*), and "crag" (*selaʿ*), not to mention a host of verbal forms.[25] The pervasiveness of this word field indicates an "editorial interest . . . [that] spans the entire Psalter."[26] Creach is not about to prove that every psalm contains some reference to "refuge." Indeed, numerous psalms lack the term or anything related to it. His aim is more modest, namely, "to show that the end result of combining these collections has the effect of encouraging readers to seek refuge in Yahweh."[27]

The key phrase in his argument is "the effect of encouraging readers." His analysis effortlessly moves from the world that *codified* the collection of psalms, that is, from reconstructing the editorial dynamics that gave shape to the Psalter, to the world the Psalter itself engenders in interaction with its readers. In so doing, Creach takes the signification of "refuge" to a new level, one that rises above mere lexical distribution and rests ultimately on the conceptual. Refuge is a "common and recurring idea,"[28] a root metaphor. Only as metaphor can "refuge" form an expansive network of associations and forge a pervasive presence within its literary environment to the extent that Creach wants to claim. "Refuge," in essence, is a filter through which the Psalter in its entirety can be viewed theologically.[29]

The litmus test, of course, is whether "refuge," as metaphor, can cover the Psalter's theological spectrum, diverse as it is. Like others, Creach finds an expressly theological home for "refuge" in the image of YHWH as king.[30] But is "refuge" sufficiently comprehensive for the Psalter, particularly in view of the prominent role *tôrâ* assumes in the Psalter? In any case, Creach's study sets the stage for a new look at the Psalter, not for reconstructing the redactional or editorial formation of the collections so much as for determining the basic features that give shape to the Psalter's theological landscape. This, then, is our point of entry in our search for the Psalter's broadest metaphorical contours.

THE REFUGE METAPHOR

As many have noted, the first reference to "refuge" is definitive, setting the tone for the rest of the Psalter. It is found in its verbal form at the conclusion of Psalm 2: "How fortunate[31] are all who take refuge in him (*ḥôsê bô*)" (v. 12b). Although likely a gloss, this beatitude or macarism is no interloper. The psalmist depicts the nations as rebellious and poised to overthrow YHWH's anointed ("son") and his kingdom. But YHWH has a failsafe plan to foil the impending assault. From heaven is decreed, "I have established my king on Zion, my holy hill" (v. 6), a declaration that turns the tables on the conspiring nations and elicits from the mouth of Zion's king the promise of victory and universal dominion such that the nations are reduced to potsherds. The psalm concludes with an ultimatum: either the kings of the earth "serve YHWH with fear" or they can perish in God's wrath (vv. 11–12a). But the last word is reserved for the beatitude. The blessing of "refuge" marks a fitting, albeit abrupt, conclusion to the drama of victory, whose pivot is found in the divine pronouncement to the nations. The setting of God's victory over the nations, the arena by which God foils the nations' plot, is "Zion, [YHWH's] holy hill" (v. 6). Zion is the geographical embodiment of "refuge." To take refuge is to take shelter in Zion amid the swirling chaos and political clamor that threaten to engulf this rock of stability.

Rock

Given its wide range of associations, the "refuge" motif is a metaphorical "schema"[32] or domain populated by a number of concrete images, whose target domain is the protective God: "YHWH my God, in you I take refuge; save me from all my pursuers and deliver me" (Ps 7:1). In that same psalm, God is declared as "my shield (*māgēn*) that delivers the upright in heart" (v. 10). It is precisely the metaphor's theocentric target that generates a variety of related iconic metaphors, which tend to pile up as, for example, in the opening words of Psalm 18:

> I love you, YHWH, my strength (*ḥēzeq*).
> YHWH is my crag (*sela'*), my stronghold (*mĕṣûdâ*),
>   and my deliverer.
> My God is my rock (*ṣûr*), in whom I take refuge (*'ĕḥseh*),
>   my shield (*māgēn*), and the horn of my salvation,
>   my secure height (*miśgāb*).
>   (18:1–2)[33]

These opening lines present a veritable catalog of images that highlight the unassailable security God affords the speaker. Not fortuitously, reference to refuge (cast verbally) is lodged at the center of this litany of epithets, associated most intimately with the riveting image of "rock" (*ṣûr*).[34]

"I say to God, my crag (*sela'*)," the psalmist opens his complaint in 42:9. "Lead me upon the rock (*ṣûr*) that is higher than I; for you are my refuge (*maḥseh*), a strong tower (*migdal-'ōz*) against the enemy" is the psalmist's plea for protection in 61:2b–3. Both protection and deliverance are conjured by this single image: it is a place to which one escapes *and* a place on which one stands firm with feet secured. The "rock" motif, moreover, reflects an intensely personal relationship of the pray-er to God ("*my* rock"), as indicated also by such titles as "my cup" and "my portion" (e.g., 16:5).[35]

Wings

Perhaps the most vividly iconic image associated with refuge and divine protection is that of God's "wings." Though the metaphors are mixed in Ps 61:4, clear reference is made to God's protective wingspan: "Let me abide in your tent forever, find refuge under the shelter (*sēter*) of your wings (*kĕnāpayim*)." A variant expression of the metaphor is found in 63:7: "for you have been my help, and in the shadow (*ṣēl*) of your wings I sing for joy." As a way of extending the sheltering function of the sanctuary (cf. v. 2), God sprouts wings!

A parallel use of such imagery is prominently featured in Egyptian iconography, which frequently depicts a deity with outstretched wings protectively covering an individual, typically the king or another deity.[36] In Egypt, wings were not singularly associated with a particular deity but were attached to various gods and goddesses—some ornithological in form, others not, such as the sun—in order to stress their protective character and function.[37] In the temple of Osiris at Karnak, for example, the protector-goddess Isis is depicted with wings extending from her hips to protect her husband Osiris, who is profiled in mummy form.[38] (See fig. 1.)

Fig. 1: Statue of Isis protecting Osiris from Karnak (26th [Saite] dynasty), dedicated by Sheshonq, chief steward of the "god's wife," Ankhnesneferibre. © Copyright the British Museum. A relief of Isis with outstretched wings is also found on the basalt sarcophagus of Ramses III (20th dynasty), displayed in the Louvre, Paris.

Wing imagery in Egyptian iconography was detachable in the sense that it was not necessarily associated with an ornithological profile of the deity. For all practical purposes, the image pictographically represented "protection."[39] So also in the psalms: the image of the outstretched wing offers a vivid metaphor for divine protection. In a plea for mercy, reference is made in Psalm 57 to "winged" refuge set against outside threat:

> Be gracious to me, O God, be gracious to me,
>   for in you my soul takes refuge (*ḥāsāyāh*).
> In the shadow (*ṣēl*) of your wings (*kĕnāpêkā*) I will take refuge,
>   until the destroying storms pass by.
>
> (57:1)

The urgent plea for mercy that prefaces the references to "refuge" and "wings" suggests that the image of "destroying storms" targets not only the external threat posed by those who "trample on" the psalmist (vv. 3a, 6), but also the ravages of divine judgment.

Another psalm spreads, as it were, God's protective care to near universal breadth.

> How precious is your faithful love (*ḥesed*), O God!
>   [For] all people may take refuge in the shadow of your wings.
> They are well filled with the richness (*dešen*[40]) of your house,
>   and from the river of your abundant provisions (*'ādānêkā*)[41]
>   you give them drink.
>
> (36:7–8)

Divine protection and provision are intimately associated: under God's wings is arranged an abundant feast of food and drink for all the nations. The imagery imparts a sense of spatial breadth and fierce protection to the abundance of divine provision.

The most detailed elaboration of the wing metaphor is found in Psalm 91, where refuge is also prominently featured:

> You who live in the shelter (*sēter*) of *Elyon*,[42]
>   who lodge in the shadow (*ṣēl*) of *Shaddai*,[43]
> will say to YHWH, "My refuge (*maḥseh*) and my fortress (*mĕṣûdâ*);
>   my God, in whom I trust."
> For he will deliver you from the snare of the fowler (*yāqûš*),
>   from the deadly pestilence.
> With his pinions (*'ebrâ*) he will cover you,
>   and under his wings (*kĕnāpayim*) you will find refuge (*teḥseh*).
> His faithfulness is a shield and buckler.
> . . . .
> Because you have made YHWH your refuge,[44]
>   *Elyon* your dwelling place,
> no evil shall befall you;
>   no scourge come near your tent.
>
> (91:1–4, 9–10)

Not only are "shelter" and "shadow" (*sēter* / *ṣēl*) paired synonymously; they are together set in parallel with "refuge" and "fortress" (*maḥseh* / *mĕṣûdâ*). In the larger, metaphorical context, an irony emerges: like a raptor protecting its young, God delivers the supplicant from "the snare of the fowler" (v. 3). Such protection, moreover, extends to the supplicant's own domicile (v. 10), indicating that God's sanctuary presence extends beyond God's own dwelling place, Zion. Here, as elsewhere, refuge is cast as both the setting of God's protection and the object of the psalmist's moral resolve (see below).

The metaphor "God is raptor" and its powerful associations are confirmed in references that lie outside the Psalter. Boaz proclaims to Ruth that under his care she has found "a full reward from YHWH, the God of Israel, under whose wings you have come for refuge!" (Ruth 2:12).[45] In Deuteronomy, the image is pressed into service to highlight God's protective guidance through the hostile wilderness:

> [YHWH] sustained[46] [Jacob] in a desert land,
> . . . .
>   guarded him as the apple of his eye,
> as a raptor[47] stirs up its nest,
>   and hovers over its young;
> as it spreads its wings, takes them up,[48]
>   and bears them[49] aloft on its pinions.
> (Deut 32:10–11)

In a poetic recitation of Israel's history, Moses intones YHWH's incomparable beneficence. Here and in Exodus, the image of the raptor vividly connotes both sustenance and guidance on the part of God. At the foot of Mount Sinai, God instructs Moses to recount the following words to the Israelites: "You have seen what I did to the Egyptians, and how I bore you on raptors' wings (*kanpê nĕšārîm*) and brought you to myself" (Exod 19:4). Within the larger narrative framework of the exodus and conquest, raptor imagery is developed in both passages to illustrate God's *conveyance* of Israel from the house of bondage to God's very self on Sinai (Exod 19:4) or to the highlands of Canaan, the land of Israel's settlement (Deut 32:13).[49]

God's guidance or movable presence is, however, not the primary significance of the metaphor in Psalms. In the Psalter, the image has its home in Zion, God's nest.[50] A closer parallel is found in Isaiah.

> Like birds (*ṣipŏrîm*) hovering overhead;
>   so YHWH of hosts will cover (*yāgēn 'al*) Jerusalem,
> protecting and delivering it,
>   sparing and rescuing it.
> (Isa 31:5)

As in Isaiah, the psalms celebrate not God's *bearing* of Israel from promise to fulfillment, but God's *protection* spread over Zion. The "shadow" of God's wings is cast permanently on Zion, the locus of divine refuge. On Zion, the Eagle has landed, and so has a people.

> How lovely is your dwelling place, YHWH of hosts!
> . . . .
> Even the sparrow (*ṣippōr*) finds a home,
> 　　and the swallow (*dĕrôr*) a nest for herself,
> where she may lay her young,
> 　　at your altars, YHWH of hosts,
> 　　　my King and my God.
>
> 　　　　　　　　　　　　　　　(Ps 84:1, 3)

The analogy is suggestive, moreover, of the procreative function of God's dwelling in Zion, consonant with the figure of Mother Zion profiled in Isa 66:7–9. Indeed, those "born in [Zion]" are "registered" in a list of faithful worshipers (Ps 87:5–7).[51] If refuge under God's "wings" is the locus of Israel's protection, then Zion serves as God's "nesting place" and Israel is her brood (cf. Matt 23:37).

Sanctuary Presence

As "refuge" finds its geographical locus in Zion, God's "holy mountain," so readers are enjoined to examine Zion's imposing presence, however imaginatively, and bask in the security it offers:

> Walk around Zion, go all around it,
> 　　count its towers.
> Consider well its ramparts;[52]
> 　　pass between (*passĕgû*) its citadels,
> 　　so that you may describe it for generations to come.
> For this is God,
> 　　our God, eternal and everlasting.
>
> 　　　　　　　　　　　　　　　(48:12–14a)

Acting as Zion's official tour guide (cf. v. 14b), the composer of this psalm has what one might call an "edifice complex,"[53] a fixation that, however, reaches far beyond historical realia. Through the medium of poetic exhortation, the psalm stirs the imagination to reconstruct Zion's physical majesty, enabling the reader to sense God's presence therein and to walk within it. The psalmist is not so crass as to make God into a building. Rather, the psalmist claims God's saving presence as palpably firm, permanently indwelling, and all-encompassing. The rhetorical effect places the reader squarely in the midst of divine protection.

With the motif of God's "refuge" set in stone, as it were, on Zion, the scope of this metaphorical schema widens considerably as more associations are established throughout the Psalter. Refuge is given cosmic nuance, for example, in the most well known psalm of Zion:

> God is our refuge (*maḥseh*) and strength (*'ōz*),
>   a well-proven help (*'ezrâ*) amid trouble.
> Therefore, we will not fear,
>   though the earth shows flux,
>   though the mountains tumble
>   into the heart of the seas,
>   though its waters roar and foam,
>   [and] the mountains totter at its swelling.
> (46:1–3)

Casting out all fear, refuge marks the locus of divine deliverance. Not only does the metaphor connote immovability amid *cosmic* uproar; it also evokes a dramatic sense of security amid *political* chaos:

> [Yet] there is a river whose channels make glad the city of God,
>   the holiest[54] habitation[55] of the Most High.
> God is in [the city's] midst;
>   [thus] it shall not be moved.
> God will help it at the break of dawn.
> The nations are in an uproar;
>   the kingdoms totter.
> His voice thunders;
>   the earth melts.
> YHWH of hosts is with us;
>   the God of Jacob is our secure height.
> (vv. 4–7)

The psalm's opening reference to "our refuge" (*lānû maḥseh*) finds its corresponding image in "our secure height" (*miśgāb-lānû*) in v. 7. Through metaphor, the saving cosmic power of God, the power of divine deliverance from external threat and the power to render joy and blessing from within, is given spatial, if not fluid, focus. The river is a sign and seal of God's refuge, a salvific order that pulses through the city as flowing streams, the very streams longed for in Psalm 42 and rechanneled in Psalm 1 through the sustaining power of *tôrâ*.[56]

As the "perfection of beauty" (50:2), Zion conveys divine presence and provides a defining context for Israel's faith and conduct. The object of faithful yearning is God's holy dwelling, for there one can "taste and see that YHWH is good" (34:8).[57] Zion symbolizes Israel's sustaining ethos, or proper habitation: "One thing that I asked of YHWH, that I will seek after," declares the pilgrim: "to live in YHWH's house all the days of my life, to behold YHWH's beauty, and to inquire in his temple" (27:4). Or in the concluding words of the so-called Shepherd Psalm: "Only goodness and mercy shall pursue me all the days of my life, so that I may dwell in the house of YHWH my whole life long" (23:6). Such expressions of longing, like the doe that thirsts for flowing streams (42:1), are by no means limited to actual service in the temple. Not everyone who yearns for refuge carries the desire to assume the traditional vocation of the Levite or to be a "doorkeeper" in the temple (see 84:10). Seeking refuge reflects a more general and desperate desire to enter into God's protective presence, established but by no means bounded by Zion's physical parameters. The psalmist's "trust . . . frees itself from the concrete institution [of the sacral sanctuary] and blends the institutional relationship with the symbolic language of prayer."[58]

In the cry of distress, God is made manifest by a *sanctuary presence* that knows no spatial, geographical, or temporal bounds. The king, for example, affirms in the wake of victory: "In my distress I called upon YHWH. . . . From his temple he heard my voice, and my cry to him reached his ears"(18:6). The psalmist places the divine abode in the heavens, from which God descends to deliver the king (vv. 9, 16). By tapping the metaphorical power of Zion's refuge, the psalmist is able to call on God with supreme confidence amid dire straits—"Be a rock of refuge (*ṣûr-māʿôz*) for me, a fortified dwelling (*bêt mᵉṣûdôt*) to save me" (31:2b)—or in rapturous affirmation:

> O Lord, you have been our dwelling place (*māʿôn*)[59]
> in all generations.
> Before the mountains were brought forth,
> or you had formed the earth and the world,
> from everlasting to everlasting
> you are God.
>
> (90:1–2)

Although Zion commands a share of its setting, the refuge schema reaches beyond its geographical locus to point to God as the ultimate object of its signification, Israel's "dwelling place."

In the broadening of God's "sanctuary presence," Zion achieves metaphorical status, embodied as it is by Israel's undivided trust in its redeemer:

> Those who trust in YHWH are like Mount Zion,
> immovable and abiding forever.
> As the mountains surround Jerusalem,
> so YHWH surrounds his people
> from this time on and forevermore.
>
> (125:1–2)

Divine security, signified by Zion, is made efficacious through trust in YHWH. The people take on Zion's defining attribute and its environs ("mountains"): unassailable security. God, in turn, matches Zion's metaphorical expanse by assuming the protective role the mountains provide in surrounding Israel. "Refuge" is *made real,* or embodied, through the community's trust in God and, reciprocally, through God's protective care. Anything less is sinking sand: "It is better to take refuge in YHWH than to place [one's] trust in mortals," even "in princes" (118:8–9). Zion's refuge offers peace to those whose dwellings are found "among those who hate peace" (120:6). Zion offers "rest" to those persecuted and in distress as much as it constitutes God's *own* "resting place," secured by David, who would not rest until "a dwelling place for the Mighty One of Jacob" was found (132:3–5, 14; cf. 95:11). In the imaginative poetry of the psalms, Zion extends far beyond Zion.

Betwixt Pit and Refuge

For all its evocative power as a root metaphor in the Psalter, "refuge" also has its counter metaphor or symbolic opposite: the Pit, or abode of the dead (Sheol).

> To you, YHWH, I call;
>   my rock (*ṣûr*), do not refuse to hear me.
> For if you are silent to me,
>   I shall be like those descending into the pit (*bôr*).
>   (28:1)[60]

As "refuge" marks the object of the psalmist's longing, so "pit" constitutes the domain most feared by the psalmist. Whereas God's "refuge," the "rock" of Zion, is the feature most elevated on the Psalter's theological landscape (61:2b–3), the "pit" marks, as it were, the sinkhole in the psalmist's terrain, into which one descends to death. The "pit" is the grave's metaphor (49:9) as much as "refuge" is Zion's image, the locus of life. Not infrequently, the "pit" is associated with the overwhelming waters, from which the psalmist pleads for deliverance:

> Do not let the flood (*šibbōlet*) rush over me,
>   or the deep (*měṣûlâ*) swallow me up,
>   or the pit (*bě'ēr*) close its mouth over me.
>   (69:15)

To the modern reader, the last two cola constitute an unmistakable case of mixed metaphor. Yet the incongruity is telling and reflects an ancient precedent, for it exposes the pit's identity as death itself by recalling the Canaanite god of death, Mot, whose mouth swallows Baal.[61] As if to preserve the unbridgeable gulf between pit and refuge (and to motivate God to action), the psalmist asks rhetorically, "Do you work wonders for the dead? Do the shades rise up to praise you?" (88:10). The answer is resoundingly negative in 6:5 and 115:17 (but cf. 139:8b–12; Jonah 2:6). Praise in the pit, the antithesis to refuge, is a non sequitur.

Also antithetically related to refuge, God's "hiding place" (*sēter*) for the persecuted,[62] are references to God's "hiding" (√*str*) from the supplicant, evoking an ironic connection to "refuge." The question "Will you hide yourself forever?" marks the culmination of the psalmist's complaint in the face of Jerusalem's destruction and the collapse of the Davidic throne (Ps 89:46). A strikingly contrastive use of this motif is found in Psalm 27. The psalmist proclaims with confidence: "For he will hide me (*yiṣpěnēnî*) in his shelter in the day of trouble; he will conceal me (*yastirēnî*) under the cover (*sēter*) of his tent," and yet also petitions God, "Do not hide (*tastēr*) your face from me" (27:5, 7–9a). The "hiding" of God's "face" casts the problem of unanswered prayer in starkly metaphorical terms.[63] God's "hidden" face denotes a domain of absence set in sharp contrast to God's sanctuary presence, a "shelter" of protection that "hides" the supplicant from impending calamity. A "hidden" God, conversely, entails the supplicant's exposure to danger, both natural and social.

In the anguished language of lament, the psalmist is invariably set between pit and refuge, between God's absence and presence, death and deliverance (see 9:13b–14). It is the psalmist's fervent desire that he be taken from "the gates of death" and brought to "the gates of daughter Zion," from the pit to the Rock of Ages. More often than not, prayer in the Psalter is uttered "out of the depths" (130:1), and finding refuge is invariably its aim. The journey from pit to refuge marks a concomitant shift from lament to praise and, ultimately, instruction.

Zeal for Zion: The Moral Contours of Refuge

For a community dispersed and distanced from its homeland, those psalms that set their sights on Zion aim to provoke the imagination and the heart to action, specifically to reliance on God. In Psalm 62, "rock" and "refuge" imagery signals, in addition to inviolable security, a stance of uncompromising resolve:

> [God] alone is my rock (*ṣûr*) and my salvation,
>   my secure height (*miśgāb*); I shall never be shaken (*'emmôṭ*).
> On God rests my deliverance and my honor;
>   my mighty rock (*ṣûr*), my refuge (*maḥseh*) is in God.
>
> (62:6–7)

On the rock of his salvation, the psalmist declares with stalwart conviction, "Here I stand," as it were. More than a haven of safety, "refuge" is rife with moral potency, as confirmed in the psalm's concluding admonition: "Put no confidence in extortion, and set no vain hopes on robbery" (v. 10). To seek refuge in God is to place one's trust fully in God rather than in any self-procured means of security.

Those who would abide on God's "holy hill" remain anchored in righteousness (15:1, 5; 30:7a). Such holy security evokes confidence amid the world's tumult (46:2; 125:1–2) and at the same time shapes the moral contours of the community (5:7–8; 24:3–4). The yearning for flowing streams is no vague longing; it reflects a motivating "zeal for [God's] house," a consuming jealousy (*qinâ*) for God and God's righteousness (69:9). Psalm 26 specifically correlates "love" of sanctuary with moral conduct:

> YHWH, I love the dwelling place of your house,
>   and the place of your abiding glory.
> Do not sweep me away with sinners,
>   nor my life with the bloodthirsty.
> . . . .
> But as for me, I walk in my integrity (*tōm*);
>   redeem me and be gracious to me.

My foot stands on level ground (*mîšôr*);
in the great congregation I bless YHWH.
(26:8–9, 11–12)

It is in the "great congregation" that the supplicant finds protection and moral conviction. The psalmist moves from *walking* (√*hlk*) "in integrity" to *standing* (√*'md*) "on level ground" in God's abode. With refuge is also pathway (see chapter 2).

That the sanctuary itself is associated with righteousness is confirmed in the processional liturgy of Psalm 118, likely used by pilgrims who have come up to the very gates of the temple seeking entrance:

Open to me the gates of righteousness,
that I may enter through them
and give thanks to YH[WH].
This is the gate of YHWH;
[only] the righteous shall enter through it.
(118:19–20)

The sanctuary is righteous, in part, by its association with the righteous, those qualified to enter its domain (see also 24:3–6). The converse is found in Psalm 11, which reflects the condition of the razed temple (ca. 587–515 B.C.E.). The psalmist's detractors ask, "If the foundations are destroyed, what can the righteous do?" (11:3), to which the psalmist declares, "YHWH is in his holy temple; YHWH's throne is in heaven" (v. 4). Though the earthly temple lies in ruin, righteousness remains inviolable by virtue of God's dwelling in heaven.

In several psalms, the metaphor of refuge is charged with the moral force of economic responsibility and consideration for the poor. Psalm 52 renders judgment against the wicked for their oppressive conduct, specifically for their trust in prosperity, prompting the taunt: "'See the one who would not take refuge (*mā'ôz*) in God, but trusted in abundant riches, and sought protection[64] in wealth!'" (52:7). Taking shelter in God is contrasted with seeking refuge in wealth, a lifestyle conducted at the expense of the powerless and tantamount to distrust of God.[65] Moral character, thus, is defined by one's choice of habitation. While Jesus spoke of the impossibility of serving two masters (Matt 6:24), the psalmist asserts the incompatibility of two kinds of refuge. Refuge is as much a domain of the will as it is God's edifying work. One's source of security grounds one's conduct. Security sets the ethos.

Elsewhere, God's refuge is expressly designed to protect the poor and vulnerable. The psalmist laments the moral decadence of his community, and blames the powerful who "eat up my people as they eat bread" (Ps. 14:4). Leveled against them is the defiant declaration, "You would confound the plans of the poor, but YHWH is their refuge (*mahseh*)" (v. 6). Similarly, Psalm 68 observes,

Father of orphans and protector of widows
is God in his holy abode (*bim'ĕôn qodšô*).

> God enables the desolate to live at home (*baytāh*);
>   he leads out the prisoners to prosperity.
>   (68:5–6a)

God's "holy abode" is bound up with affordable housing, particularly for the homeless. As divine king, God marches through the wilderness from Sinai to sanctuary, and so also do God's people (vv. 16–17, 24).

Refuge of the Cosmic King

Finally, "refuge" turns explicitly cosmic in the Psalter. As motivation for rendering praise to "God, in Zion," Psalm 65 focuses specifically on Zion's abundant provisions to the world. Satisfaction with "the goodness of [God's] house" (v. 4), the psalmist notes, is global in outreach:

> You visit (*pāqadtā*) the earth and give it drink;
>   you greatly enrich it.
> The channel (*peleg*) of God is full of water;
>   you provide their grain,[66]
>   for so you have prepared it.
>   (65:9)

The scene of creation's abundance concludes with a paean of praise proclaimed by the arable land, from the pastures to the fertile valleys (vv. 12–13). The earth itself becomes the worshiper in God's cosmic refuge.

Psalm 147 cements the connection between sanctuary and creation. YHWH's first act of creation is the building up of Jerusalem and the provision of abundance for the "brokenhearted" and "downtrodden" (vv. 3, 6). The cosmos then follows: stars, clouds, rain, grass, and food for the animals (vv. 4, 8–9). Such movement, like expanding ripples in a pond, repeats itself. Zion is commanded to praise God for the provisions it has received—strength and children—as well as for all of creation. The subsequent psalms, not by chance, pick up where Psalm 147 concludes by issuing a command for all creation to give praise (147:12–148:10). The recipient of God's provision, the cosmos is a macrocosm of Zion.[67] As Zion maps the cosmos, so the divine roles of king and creator converge.[68]

The metaphor "God is king," undeniably central in the Psalter,[69] has its home in refuge, monumentalized by Zion and extended cosmically. Psalm 93 opens with the enthronement proclamation, "YHWH reigns (*yhwh mālak*)" and concludes with the observation, "holiness befits your house" (vv. 1, 5). To make a "joyful noise to the rock of our salvation" is to affirm the sovereignty of the "great King above all gods" (95:1, 3). "King" and "refuge" stand on common ground: both connote protection and security for Israel's sake, including the impoverished (e.g., 14:6; 68:5–6; 72:12–14). "Enthroned upon the cherubim," situated in the innermost recess of the temple, YHWH embraces the roles of judge, warrior, and protector (99:1, 4, 8). As king, God executes justice and righteousness on behalf of Israel and the world (99:4). The "world is firmly established," and justice is executed among the peoples, proclaims the psalmist (96:10). "Righteousness and justice are the foundation of [YHWH's] throne" (97:2b), and so also the world's foundation through God's judgment.

In sum, "refuge" is a foundational metaphor or schema in the Psalter. Its associations are wide-ranging and profound. Concretely embodied in the symbol of Zion, the metaphorical schema is powerful enough to incorporate distinctly moral concerns into the fold of divinely wrought deliverance and blessing. The object of deep longing, refuge is emblematic of the person who places complete trust in God. It highlights, moreover, the royal role of God, of the King who is intent on making the world a refuge and provides protection to those in distress. Nevertheless, as defining as it is for the Psalter, the refuge metaphor is by no means the only root metaphor that gives shape to the Psalter's theology. And so we return to the question: Is "refuge" as all-encompassing as some have argued? Such is the topic of the next chapter.

Chapter 2

"I Shall Walk in Freedom"

The Metaphor of Pathway

As noted in the preceding chapter, the metaphor of "refuge" bears not only salvific weight, namely, blessing and protection, but also moral import. God's refuge constitutes both home and destiny for the righteous, and *seeking* refuge connotes trust in and allegiance to YHWH to the exclusion of things that do not warrant ultimate reliance, from idols to riches.[1] Jerome Creach aptly notes:

> In short, those who 'seek refuge in Yahweh', 'trust in Yahweh', 'seek Yahweh', and 'wait for Yahweh' are prototypical believers, ones who perfectly rely upon Yahweh rather than human strength. All such individuals are wise and 'fortunate' (Ps 2:12) because they live in complete trust and humility.[2]

Most important to Creach's argument is his attempt to cement a bond between *tôrâ* and refuge. *Tôrâ* serves as a "surrogate for Yahweh's refuge" in Psalms 94 and 119, "a retreat for the righteous, a hiding place for the pious person."[3] In these psalms, however, *tôrâ* is more than a shelter from external threat. The reference to 94:12–13 is indirect at best: "How fortunate are those whom you discipline, YHWH, and whom you teach from your *tôrâ*, giving them respite (*lĕhašqîṭ*) from days of trouble." Somewhat firmer ground is found in Psalm 119: "You are my hiding place (*sēter*) and my shield (*māgēn*); I hope in your word" (v. 114). Nevertheless, key members of the "refuge" word field are cast as attributes of YHWH, not of *tôrâ*. The psalmist's "hope in [YHWH's] word," a motif that runs throughout the psalm (e.g., vv. 74, 81, 147), establishes at most an indirect link between "word" and "refuge."[4]

THE WAY OF *TÔRÂ*

The encompassing power of the "refuge" motif is strained when pressed to give account of *tôrâ*, in particular, and the Psalter's overall shape, more broadly. The refuge metaphor can be stretched only so far to accommodate the Psalter's *other* defining editorial feature, namely, its prominent *didactic* dimension, as indicated by numerous references to *tôrâ* and sapiential instruction. As the Torah psalm *par excellence,* one that likely concluded an earlier collection, Psalm 119 marks both the limit of the "refuge" metaphor and the scope of its counterpart.

Psalm 119

Tôrâ not only serves as the surrogate for YHWH's refuge; it also marks the *means* by which one lives and moves and has one's being. *Tôrâ* is the preeminent source of *instruction,* and it is within the orbit of a governing metaphor other than "refuge" that the psalmist's moral rhetoric has its home, as is evident in the psalm's opening verses:

> How fortunate are those whose way (*derek*) is blameless,
>   who walk (*hahōlĕkîm*) in the *tôrâ* of YHWH.
> How fortunate are those who keep his decrees,
>   who seek him with their whole heart,
> who also do no wrong,
>   [but] walk in his ways (*bidrākāw*).
> . . . .
> Would that my ways (*dĕrākāy*) be steadfast in keeping your statutes!
>   (vv. 1–3, 5)

The psalmist identifies the righteous as those who are on the move. They "walk" and "seek." This extended macarism—see its summary form in 128:1—provides a suggestive counterpart to the beatitude in 2:12b: "How fortunate are all who take refuge in [YHWH]." The latter implies destination and permanent residence; the former connotes movement and direction. Common to both are the integral values of security and integrity. When it comes to *tôrâ* in Psalm 119, however, the metaphor of "way," both the way of YHWH and the path of the psalmist, predominates:

> How can young people keep their way (*'ōraḥ*) pure?
> By guarding it according to your word.
>   (v. 9)

I delight in the way (*derek*) of your decrees
    as much as in all riches.
                    (v. 14)

I will reflect upon your precepts,
    and fix my eyes on your ways (*'ōrāḥôt*).
                    (v. 15; cf. v. 37)

Make me understand the way (*derek*) of your precepts,
    and I will reflect on your wondrous works.
                    (v. 27)

Put false ways (*derek*) far from me;
    and graciously teach me your *tôrâ*.
                    (v. 29)

I have chosen the way (*derek*) of faithfulness;
    I set your ordinances before me.
                    (v. 30)

I run (*'ārûṣ*) the way (*derek*) of your commandments,
    for you enlarge my understanding.
                    (v. 32)

Teach me, YHWH, the way (*derek*) of your statutes,
    and I will observe it to the end.
                    (v. 33)

Lead me in the path (*nātîb*) of your commandments,
    for I delight in it.
                    (v. 35)

I shall walk (*'ethallēkāh*) in freedom,[5]
    for I have sought your precepts.
                    (v. 45)

I hold back my feet from every evil way (*'ōraḥ*),
    in order to keep your word.
                    (v. 101)

Your word is a lamp to my feet,
    and a light to my path (*nĕtîbâ*).
                    (v. 105)

Each citation features a common metaphor intimately related, in one way or another, to *tôrâ*.[6] Of all the morally legislative terms that populate Psalm 119,[7] only one, "path" or "way" (*derek, 'ōraḥ, nātîb, nĕtîbâ*) is blatantly metaphorical in scope and frequently accompanied by verbs of motion (*hlk, rwṣ*). Poetically speaking, the metaphor of the pathway "maps" both God's *tôrâ*[8] and the speaker's response to *tôrâ*, imbuing them with a sense of dynamic, mutual engagement. Nothing is static about God's commandments and one's adherence to them.

God's "word" is a lamp to illumine the psalmist's "path" (v. 105), and the way of God's precepts is part of God's ongoing "wondrous work" (v. 27).

Other instances of the metaphor in Psalm 119 designate the individual's conduct, whether "pure," "evil," or "false" (vv. 9, 29, 101, 128). This constellation of corresponding metaphors (the "*derek*" word field) is comparable to the "refuge (*ḥāsāh*)" word field. But the statistical distribution of semantic fields is not, in the end, decisive.[9] What is definitive is the range of associations this metaphor, with its numerous attestations, generates. The poetic efficacy of "pathway" matches that of "refuge" in a manner that can more fully account for the shape and theology of the book of Psalms.

Foremost, the metaphor of "pathway" targets *tôrâ* (note esp. v. 1) and, in turn, designates the kind of conduct prescribed by *tôrâ* (vv. 3, 5, 14). The "path" fundamentally illustrates *tôrâ* observance (v. 5). *Tôrâ* is the true "way" among many "false" ones (v. 29). The metaphor, furthermore, points to and binds together a veritable network of poetic references and target domains. In addition to divine instruction, it designates "heartfelt" longing and seeking God without "straying" (vv. 2b, 10, 20, 45, 110b), while the insolent lay snares (v. 110a), dig "pitfalls" (v. 85), and "wander" from the way of God's commandments (v. 21). "Pathway" establishes an indissoluble link between God's "wondrous works" and "precepts" (v. 27). More abstractly, the metaphor points to the import of divine instruction (vv. 12, 29, 33, 102). "Walking the way" reflects enlightened understanding (v. 32). The psalmist directs his "feet" to God's decrees without delay (vv. 59–60), while holding them back "from every evil way" (v. 101). He "pants" for God's commandments while "running the way" (v. 32), but admits elsewhere to having gone "astray" (v. 67).

Finally, the metaphor of "pathway" enhances the psalmist's narrative profile, his *iter vitae* or journey of life: he candidly shares his failures, longings, hopes, and triumphs. The psalmist casts himself as a youth in the crisis of decision (vv. 9, 100); he has "chosen the way of faithfulness" amid various "false ways" (vv. 29–30). Among its many roles, the "pathway" metaphor heightens the personal dimensions of pathos and praise that permeate this psalm. The psalmist tells of his "ways" (v. 26) while keeping a fixed gaze on God's "ways" (v. 15), fixed as it is in the heavens (v. 89) yet accessible and treasured within the heart (v. 11).

Wisdom and *Tôrâ*

As in the Wisdom literature and elsewhere,[10] the "pathway" motif is prominently featured in the Psalter. In his brief dictionary of the Psalter, Jean-Pierre Prévost offers an extended entry on "way (path)," but nothing on "refuge"![11] In the Psalms, both root metaphors are of equal importance. Psalm 1, which orients the reader of Psalms, is deliberately framed by the image of "pathway" (1:1, 6).[12] The righteous and the wicked are distinguished by their respective paths: the way of the righteous is safeguarded by YHWH's protection, but not so that of the wicked. The evocative metaphor of "way" signifies both conduct and destiny. Similarly, Psalm 2 warns the "rulers of the earth" that they "will perish in the way" unless they serve YHWH and acknowledge YHWH's anointed (2:10, 12a).

The moral dimension of "pathway" in the Psalter includes both "wisdom" and *tôrâ*:

> The mouth of the righteous one utters wisdom (*ḥokmâ*).
> . . . .
> The *tôrâ* of his God is in his heart;
> > his steps do not slip.
> > > > (37:30a, 31)

For the righteous, who walk securely, wisdom is practically coextensive with *tôrâ*. Constitutive of conduct and polity, wisdom is the discursive outgrowth of *tôrâ* ingrained in the will or "heart" of the righteous individual (see also 40:8).[13] Though more thematically central in the sapiential rhetoric of Proverbs, wisdom is frequently referenced in the Psalter. As wisdom is taught and imparted,[14] so also is the "way,"[15] as well as *tôrâ* and its precepts, "the way of [God's] statutes."[16] As wisdom establishes creation,[17] so *tôrâ*'s connection to nature in the Psalter cannot be gainsaid.[18]

The inextricable connection between wisdom and *tôrâ* in the Psalms has its precedent or parallel in Deut 4:5–8, which situates the successful appropriation of the "entire law" (*kōl hattôrâ*) in Israel's unprecedented display of wisdom before the nations. Similar to Ps 37:31, obedience to *tôrâ* in Deuteronomy results in a special kind of wisdom, namely, jurisprudence. While Mosaic *tôrâ* is profiled in its particularity in Deuteronomy 4, its significance extends beyond its legislative or constitutional parameters. *Tôrâ* is considered the font of *Israel's* wisdom, incomparable among the nations.

In the Psalms, the special union between *lex* and *sapientia* is metaphorically preserved by the "pathway" image. Indeed, "pathway" exhibits a covenantal scope, as found in one of the most wrenching laments codified in the Psalter. Giving voice to the beleaguered community, the psalmist proclaims Israel's innocence before a negligent God:

> Even though all this has come upon us,
> > we have neither forgotten you,
> > > nor have we been false to your covenant (*bĕrît*).
> Indeed,[19] our heart has not turned back,
> > and our steps have not departed from your way (*'ōraḥ*).
> > > > (44:17–18)

In its larger context, "pathway" unites the ethical import of covenant and the memory of God's gracious deeds (vv. 1–3, 7). Israel has walked according to the way prescribed and ensured by God, the way of covenant. Israel's "way," or moral conduct, and God's "way," or covenantal law, the psalmist contends, are one and the same, and their equivalency forms the basis of bitter accusation.

PATH OF PERIL AND SALVATION

It is no coincidence that *tôrâ,* facilitated by the motif of "way," is profiled in ways that employ sapiential language. Yet this metaphor cannot be limited to either "law" or "wisdom." "Pathway" covers a vast array of connotations, from the ethical to the salutary, and frequently without sharp distinction. The Shepherd Psalm, for example, opens with an evocative bucolic setting imbued with moral nuance in the psalmist's statement: "[YHWH] leads me in the *ma'gĕlê ṣedeq* for his name's sake" (23:3). An ambiguity that verges on double meaning is evident in the untranslated expression. Is the phrase morally prescriptive, in the sense of "paths of righteousness" (so KJV and RSV), or does it refer to "right paths" that ensure safe passage (so NRSV)? Either translation option, however, is reductive, for both senses are clearly meant.[20] The powerful image of the *ṣedeq* path connotes both physical security and moral integrity. As defined by God's instruction, integrity is the path that leads to safety. Within this psalm's structural landscape, the path leads to the "house of YHWH," the object of the psalmist's yearning *and* moral resolve (e.g., v. 6).

Path of Salvation

Unwavering trust in God's salvific character enables one psalmist to "walk before God in the light of life" (56:13). Accompanied by God's providential care, she finds herself safely on the move, even while enemies "stir up strife" and "watch [her] steps" (v. 6). Psalm 37 affirms that the steps of the righteous person "are made firm by YHWH, when [YHWH] delights in his way; though he stumbles, he shall not fall headlong, for YHWH holds him by the hand" (37:23–24). Or, more confidently, "the *tôrâ* of his God is in his heart; his steps do not slip" (v. 31). The path on which the righteous walk is both prescribed and preserved. On the path, the individual is protected from the machinations of the wicked, who are ever poised to ambush the righteous (v. 32). To "fall headlong" on the path can signal both the demise of the righteous at the hands of the wicked and any moral lapse on the part of the righteous. Salvific for the individual is YHWH's firm grip, hoisting and steadying the righteous to continue the trek against all odds. "When I thought, 'My foot is slipping,' your faithful love (*ḥesed*), YHWH, held me up" (94:18). In short, the path of righteousness is also the path of deliverance:

> For you have delivered my life from death,
>   my eyes from tears, my feet from stumbling.
> I walk before YHWH
>   in the lands of the living.
> I have kept faith, even when I said,
>   "I am greatly afflicted."
>
> (116:8–10)

Forged in "the lands of the living," the path is preserved by the psalmist's faith and conduct amid severe affliction. "Pathway" is as much a matter of the psalmist's resolve as it is the outcome of God's act of salvation. It is *on the way* that God's saving presence and the individual's moral mettle intersect.

Path of Peril

Secure as it is, "pathway" also has its share of pitfalls. "They have dug a pit in my path," complains one who had earlier sought refuge "in the shadow of [God's] wings" (57:1b, 6). Similarly, on the brink of despair the psalmist complains:

> When my spirit grows faint,
> you know my way (*nětîbātî*).
> In the path (*'ōrah*) where I walk,
> they have hidden a trap for me.
> Look on my right hand and see—
> no one takes notice of me;
> Escape (*mānôs*) has perished from me;[21]
> no one cares for me.
> I cry to you, YHWH;
> I say, "You are my refuge (*mahsî*),
> my portion (*helqî*) in the land of the living."
> (142:3–5)

The traps and pits laid by unnamed enemies present themselves as obstacles intended to prevent the psalmist from securing refuge (v. 5). Preserved by God's guiding hand, the psalmist "walk[s] amid distress" (138:7).

The wicked, by definition, do not walk the way of the psalmist; they "go astray from the womb; they err from their birth" (58:3) and eventually fall into or dig for themselves a pit (57:6; 94:13). "Let their way be dark and slippery," the psalmist petitions in a prayer of deliverance, "with the angel of YHWH pursuing them" (35:6). In addition, the metaphorical contours of "pathway" find their antithesis in the course of *aimless* wandering:

> Some wandered (*tā'û*) in desert wastes,
> without finding a way (*derek*) to an inhabited town.
> Hungry and thirsty,
> their soul fainted within them.
> So they cried to YHWH in their trouble. . . .
> He led them by a straight way (*derek yěšārâ*),
> until they reached an inhabited town.
> . . . .
> When [the needy] are diminished and brought low
> through oppression, trouble, and sorrow,
> he pours contempt on princes,
> and makes them wander (*yat'ēm*) in trackless wastes.
> But he raises up the needy out of distress,
> and makes their families like flocks.
> (107:4–6a, 7, 39–41a)

The psalmist's path is the "path of life" (16:11), straight and true, protected and prescribed: "Lead me, YHWH, in your righteousness on account of my enemies; make your way straight before me" (5:8). God's deliverance not only elicits the psalmist's praise and gratitude but also awakens the desire to be taught:

> Teach me your way (*derek*), YHWH,
>   that I may walk in your truth.
> [Give me] an undivided heart
>   to revere your name.
> . . . .
> For great is your faithful love toward me;
>   you have delivered my life from the depths of Sheol.
>   (86:11, 13)

Like "refuge," the "pathway" metaphor generates as well as holds together various connotations, from the didactic to the salvific: *tôrâ*, moral conduct, character, destiny, and danger. In the image of the "pathway," conduct and destiny are held as an inseparable unity, pointing to a conceptual schema of moral dynamism that binds together act and consequence.[22]

Pathway and Pathos

In addition to highlighting the didactic dimensions of the Psalter, including the instruction of *tôrâ*, the "pathway" metaphor accounts for an evocative dimension of the Psalter that cannot be fully explicated by "refuge," its counterpart, namely, pathos.[23] Many psalms plunge the reader into the arena of hostile conflict. Though saturated with the themes of "refuge" and *tôrâ*, most of the psalmic prayers are not uttered "in the mystical half-light of a gothic cathedral, or in the well-ordered psalmody of monastic oases, or in the silent chambers of the soul."[24] Or, to borrow from the psalmist's own hyperbole, such prayers are not given from *under* the shadow of God's wings or *within* God's mighty fortress, but rather "out of the depths" (130:1) and "from narrow straits" (118:5). The laments are prayers from *outside* the locus of God's protective care and from *within* the crucible of conflict and affliction. The psalmists find themselves pursued, hunted down (even by God [38:2]!), and attacked; they take to flight like a "bird" (124:7; cf. 11:1), praying that they may be led "on a level path" (27:11), while at the same time finding their feet slipping on a path filled with hidden traps laid by the wicked (94:18; 142:3).

The metaphor of "pathway" lends itself to conveying the struggles the prayer faces within a world ravaged by chaos in all its manifestations as he or she seeks a way *through*, as well as a way *out*, a way to preserve one's dignity, hope, sanity, and even one's life amid demoralizing and debilitating forces. Such is the path of pathos. Such also is the path of righteousness. And yet the path of affliction is no *via negativa;* it is a path the psalmist would gladly abandon for the "path of life" on which God's beaming countenance fully shines. The path is well worn with struggle because it has been laid by the "bloodthirsty" who hold the reins of power over the "poor and needy" (e.g., 40:17). The psalmist's only hope and recourse is that the One "from Sinai" will come to rescue Israel (e.g., 68:8, 17). *God's* "path," thus, is equally crucial to the theological framework of the Psalter (see below). Without God's path, without God's struggle for justice on the community's behalf, the beleaguered psalmist is without a prayer.

PATHWAY AND REFUGE

The "pathway" motif is as strongly associated with divine protection and deliverance as the "refuge" metaphor is with ethos and moral conduct. But are they one and the same? No—the one cannot subsume the other. Given the parameters of their respective source domains, "refuge" and "pathway" have their distinctive contexts and respective associations. A path, by definition, is something on which one walks and is on the move. Refuge is a domain into which one enters and where one, God willing, remains.

Like wisdom or *tôrâ*, "path" is something taught (Ps 27:11), studied (101:2), and revealed (16:11). "Teach me the way (*derek*) I should go. . . . Teach me to do your will, for you are my God. Let your good spirit lead me on a level path"[25] (143:8b, 10). The psalmist appeals for authoritative (and hence divine) guidance. Through *tôrâ*, the psalmist's prescribed "way" and God's salutary "will" find convergence. The psalmist petitions that his will be redirected toward and modeled after the divine will and "spirit." Most detailed is the admonition conveyed in Psalm 32, most likely from God.

> I will instruct you and teach you the way you should go;
> I will counsel you with my eye upon you.
> Do not be like a horse or a mule, without understanding,
>   whose gallop[26] must be curbed with bit and bridle,
>   else it will not stay near you.
>
> (32:8–9)

As beasts of burden require instruments of force to keep them on the way and focused on the tasks at hand, so the implied reader of this psalm requires directive teaching in order to be "led" on the right path at the right pace (cf. 23:4). "Refuge," by contrast, is neither revealed nor taught; it is, rather, a domain of existence established by and identified with God. The "pathway" motif, thus, lays claim to the didactic dimension of the Psalter to which "refuge" alone cannot.

Within the psalmist's arsenal of metaphors, "refuge" is no more central in the Psalter than "path" is peripheral, and vice versa. Together, "pathway" and "refuge" cover the gamut of the psalmist's theological and existential concerns, from the sapiential to the cultic. Particularly telling is how these two root metaphors engage each other. The following examples are representative.

Through the metaphor of "pathway," the psalmist proclaims her ethical integrity in one breath, "My steps hold fast to your paths (*ma'gĕlôt*); my feet have not slipped," and in the next makes petition for refuge: "Wondrously show your faithful love, savior of those who seek refuge (*ḥôsîm*) from [their] adversaries at your right hand" (17:5, 7). The connection between "pathway" and "refuge" is more tightly (and subtly) drawn in the previous psalm: "You show me the *path of life*, the fullness of joy in your *presence*" (16:11a, emphasis added). The revealed "path" runs parallel to God's sanctuary presence, which is bound up with refuge (v. 1). In Psalm 5, the petitioner requests, "Lead me, YHWH, in your righteousness" while also expressing his resolve to "enter your house" and "bow down toward your holy temple" (vv. 8, 7).

This last cited psalm, in particular, suggests a natural connection by which both "pathway" and "refuge" are integrally related. The latter lends directional nuance to the former. It is no accident that the one who is led in the "paths of righteousness" is also the one who traverses the "darkest valley" and resolves "to dwell in the house of YHWH" (23:3b, 4, 6). For all its pastoral imagery, the so-called Shepherd Psalm charts the harrowing journey of an individual pursued by unnamed enemies yet led and protected by God.[27] Bound together, path and refuge make their indelible mark on the landscape of this psalm, "the prototype of the pilgrimage psalm."[28]

> YHWH is my shepherd,
>   [from whom] I lack nothing.
> In meadows of grass he lets me lie;
>   to waters of repose he leads me, refreshing my soul.
> On account of his name,[29] he leads me on the secure paths
>   of righteousness.[30]
> Even as I sojourn in the darkest valley, I fear no danger,
>   for you are with me;
>   your rod and your staff—they give me comfort.
> You arrange before me a table in the presence of my enemies.
> You anoint my head with oil;
>   my cup is well filled.
> [From now on] only[31] goodness and kindness will pursue[32] me
>   all the days of my life;
> So that I may dwell[33] in the house of YHWH[34]
>   as long as I live.[35]
>
> (23:1–6)

Having reached the sanctuary, the psalmist jubilantly proclaims that instead of his enemies, only "goodness (*ṭôb*) and kindness (*ḥesed*)" are in hot pursuit to hunt him down, as it were, from which there is no escape (v. 6). Avenging enemies give way to personified blessings.

Echoing the language of Psalm 23, the theme of guidance is intimately related to refuge in Psalm 31:

> You are indeed my crag (*sela'*) and my fortress (*mĕṣûdâ*);
>   for your name's sake lead me and guide me.

> Take me out of the net that is hidden for me,
>> for you are my refuge (*mā'ôz*).
> . . . .
> You have set my feet in a broad place (*merḥāb*).
>> (31:3–4, 8b)

The direction of the "pathway" is set resolutely toward "refuge," the locus of divine protection. Psalm 84 is particularly evocative in its use of metaphor to highlight this connection:

> How lovely is your dwelling place, YHWH of hosts!
>> My soul yearns, indeed it faints, for the courts of YHWH.
> . . . .
> How fortunate are those who live in your house, ever praising you.
> How fortunate are those whose strength is in you,
>> with the roadways[36] [to Zion] set in their hearts.
> They pass through the valley of Baca,
>> which they transform into a spring;[37]
>>> indeed, with blessings the early rain will envelop it.[38]
> They go from strength to strength;
>> to see the God of gods in Zion.[39]
>> (84:1–2a, 4–7)

While drawing its imagery from nature and theophany, this pilgrimage song integrates both movement and residence: those who set their face toward Zion to dwell in its courts are identified with those who "walk uprightly" (v. 11b). Indeed, the pilgrimage to Zion is a journey of the heart, within which is set the sanctuary route. As they "go from strength to strength," sustained along the way by the fructified land, they reach their final destination. The journey to Zion is rooted in both the will and emotive depth of one's being. The metaphor of the "pathway" effectively directs desire, conjoins body and soul, and prepares the heart to enter God's domain.

Given its directional nuance, "pathway" connotes guidance, whose connection with "refuge" is tightly drawn in Psalm 43, a prayer for vindication:

> Vindicate me, O God, and defend my cause. . . .
> For you are the God of my refuge (*mā'ôz*). . . .
> Send out your light and your truth;
>> let them lead me.
> Let them bring me to your holy hill
>> and to your dwelling.
>> (43:1a, 2a, 3)

Like the "rod" and "staff" of Psalm 23, "light" and "truth" are the instruments— personified as guardians, no less—by which the supplicant is led in righteous conduct, led to none other than Zion. Psalm 61 similarly conveys the plea of one who calls to God "from the end of the earth":

> Lead me to the rock
>   that is higher than I;
> for you are my refuge (*maḥseh*),
>   a strong tower (*migdāl*) against the enemy.
>   (61:2b–3)

The path to the rock is uphill, not because it is necessarily fraught with hardship in Psalm 61, but because it leads to an unassailable position that towers above the fray of conflict. Vertically, the path is one that leads from death's door to Zion's gate (9:3b–4). God's leading of the psalmist on the path is also a "lifting." "Pathway," in short, transforms the search for "refuge" from aimless wandering into a pilgrimage, a theme that underlies many of the psalms, if not the Psalter itself.[40] The metaphor, furthermore, heightens the intensely personal nature of the journey, both for the psalmist and for God. The Psalter, thus, features not only life *coram deo*, "before God," but also life, with all its struggle and desire, *ad deum*, "toward God."

Via Dei

Like the psalmist who journeys to the sanctuary to stand before God, God is portrayed in the Psalter as both indwelling *and* on the move. In addition to God's sanctuary presence on the holy hill, providing refuge for those in distress or falsely accused, there is also God's "way," which like the psalmist's "way" indicates orientation: God resolutely sets God's face to Zion, to a people in need.

As a prayer for restoration, Psalm 85 vividly showcases the metaphor of "pathway" from the standpoint of the deity.

> Faithful love (*ḥesed*) and faithfulness (*'ĕmet*) will meet;
>   righteousness (*ṣedeq*) and peace (*šālôm*) will kiss.
> Faithfulness will spring up from the land,
>   and righteousness will look down from the sky.
> YHWH will give what is good,
>   and our land will yield its increase.
> Righteousness will go before him,
>   and will make a path (*derek*) for his steps.
>   (85:10–13)

God's attributes are personified as servants or emissaries who operate in consort (v. 10) and act as agents that ensure the land's fructification (vv. 11–12). Righteousness in particular serves as God's vanguard, forging the way for God's march as royal warrior (v. 13). As for the direction of God's "path," the psalm is explicit: God is oriented toward Israel's salvation and restoration to make possible God's indwelling of the land (v. 9), as once was the case (vv. 1–3). Had God abandoned Israel? And if so, where was God? The psalmist does not openly address these questions. Nevertheless, he discerns a transition in the life of God, a journey of the heart more than of the feet: the trek from anger to forgiveness (vv. 2, 5), driven by covenantal compassion (*ḥesed*). The "distance" crossed marks a change in orientation, from judgment to promise, a journey that also involves Israel and its move toward repentance (v. 8).[41]

The salvific import of God's way is well developed in the so-called historical psalms:

> I will reflect upon all your work,
>   and meditate on your mighty deeds.
> Your way (*derek*), O God, is holy.
>   What god is so great as our God?
> . . . .
> Your way (*derek*) was through the sea,
>   your path (*šĕbîlkā*),[42] through the many waters;
>   yet your footprints left no trace.[43]
> You led your people like a flock
>   by the hand of Moses and Aaron.
>   (77:12–13, 19–20)

As an encompassing metaphor, God's "way" collectively refers to God's mighty acts in history (vv. 12–13), concretized in the exodus, the paradigmatic event or "root experience"[44] of divine deliverance. Here, God's "way," moreover, is unlike any other mode of activity. It reflects YHWH's incomparability as High God, unsurpassable in strength and unwavering in concern for a people: God's path is traceless amid the "many waters," yet tangibly embodied in the leadership exercised by God's earthly representatives, Moses and Aaron. Psalm 78 reveals the goal and destination of such leadership: "to his holy hill, to the mountain that his right hand had won" (78:54).

As vividly depicted in the hymn of praise in Psalm 68, God's path is both a victory march and a ceremonial procession. Although the motif of "pathway" is not used, its significance is readily evident in the following depiction of God on the move:

> O God, when you went out before your people,
>   when you marched through the desert,
> the earth quaked, the heavens poured down rain
>   at the presence of God, the One from Sinai.
> . . . .
> With mighty chariotry, twice ten thousand,
>   thousands upon thousands,
> the Lord came from[45] Sinai into the holy place.
> You ascended the high mount,
>   leading captives in your train.
> . . . .
> Your solemn processions are evident, O God,
>   the processions of my God, my King,
>   into the sanctuary.
>   (68:7–8a, 17–18a, 24)

God's victory march leads to Zion, the home of the King, "[God's] holy throne" (47:8; cf. Exod 15:17). God's path takes up Israel's path and leads home for both King and people.

As the poetic historiographers depicted the historical sweep of God's deliverance, so one psalmist pleads to God to remember "your congregation, which you acquired long ago" (Ps. 74:2a) and to renew the history of deliverance for the present:

> Remember Mount Zion, where you came to dwell.
> Direct your steps to [its] perpetual ruins;
>   the enemy has destroyed everything in the sanctuary.
>
> (74:2b–3)

God is charged not simply to hold in view the ruins of the sanctuary but to make tracks back to the scene of the crime, to what is left of God's erstwhile, earth-bound domicile, and to make possible its reinhabitation. Later, the psalmist exhorts, "Rise up, O God, plead your cause" (v. 22a). To rise up is to return and to restore.

God's "path" is salutary not only for the psalmist but also for the land. Psalm 65 renders in cosmic form the "goodness of [God's] house" (v. 4).

> You crown the year with your bounty;
>   your wagon tracks (*ma'gālêkā*)[46] overflow with richness.
>
> (65:11)

God's "wagon tracks" have their counterpart in God's victory procession, complete with "mighty chariotry," to Zion (68:17), which in other psalmic contexts causes the earth to quake under God's theophanous power (e.g., 97:4–5; 114:3–8).[47] In Psalm 65, however, fructification rather than dissolution takes place within the natural realm. The earth is not ravaged but revived by God's "coming," and a royal, military metaphor is transformed into a natural, life-sustaining one. In either scenario, God is on the move.

The *via dei* leads not only to victory but also to judgment, against both Israel and Israel's enemies, as well as the world: "Our God comes and does not keep silence, before him is a devouring fire, and a mighty tempest all around him" (50:3). Judgment is rendered against the misuse of sacrifice. More globally, Psalm 98 depicts YHWH as "coming to judge the earth . . . with righteousness, and the peoples with equity" (v. 9). Judgment rendered is justice established, and God's "coming" marks the eve of its execution.

Whether explicitly profiled or implicitly presupposed, the "pathway" metaphor, as it is applied to God, articulates a basic confession that, in fact, precedes the enthronement cry of God's reign: "YHWH comes." God comes to save and to judge, to deliver and to preserve, as well as to indwell and reign. In a world of struggle and injustice, God's "coming" is the *necessary* complement to God's "reigning," for it affirms that all is not yet right with the world. God's "path" and "refuge," thus, signal two complementary poles of divine activity: God's movement and God's indwelling, God's advent and God's enthronement, a dynamic, sometimes elusive, presence. Divine movement finds its destination in Zion the same way the psalmist yearns to find the path and have his or her steps directed toward God's sanctuary. Both moral and salvific significance erupt in the convergence of these two paths. At the juncture where God and the individual meet, the following pronouncements issue forth:

> You gave me room (*hirḥabtā*) when I was in narrow straits (*ṣār*).
> (4:1b)

> You gave me room (*tarḥîb*) for my steps under me,
>   and my feet did not slip.
> (18:36; cf. v. 19)

> You have set my feet on a broad place (*merḥāb*).
> (31:8b)

> From narrow straits (*hammēṣar*) I called to YHWH;
>   and YH[WH] answered me with a broad place (*merḥāb*).
> (118:5)

> I shall walk in a broad space (*bārĕḥābâ*),[48]
>   for I have sought your precepts.
> (119:45)

The psalmist is no longer entrapped, enclosed in a pit, pursued by enemies, or suffering the sore straits of a harsh journey. She has received breathing space, room to live secure, freed from the fear of "falling" and the ravages of op*pression* (cf. 38:16–17). The ground beneath the psalmist's feet is made firm; "narrow straits" are widened into open vistas. With such language, an intrinsic connection is made clear: by God's saving guidance, the psalmist's "pathway" is broadened into a "refuge."

God's search and rescue of the psalmist, God's "way" of salvation, carries an additional dimension: it is deemed holy and thus obligatory for a consecrated people: "Our heart has not turned back, nor have our steps departed from *your* way" (44:18, emphasis added). The way that Israel is prescribed to follow is bound up with God's victorious deeds, making possible Israel's existence and faithful governance in the land. Through the initiative of divine approach ("coming"), God claims Israel as its sovereign Lord *and* Israel makes claim on God as its deliverer and sustainer (vv. 1–3). What is more, God's glorious deeds of yore set a precedent for the present. The psalmist expresses the desire to motivate God to take further action in accord with the past and, thus, to be led in God's new march to Zion (78:52–53). Divinely wrought salvation manifests itself in the preservation of the one who "walk[s] in the midst of trouble" (138:7), whose steps are made secure (40:2), as he or she is led to "the rock" (61:2). With the *tôrâ* of God as lamp and guide, the "steps [of the righteous] do not slip" (119:105;

37:31). Such guidance is identified with none other than the *via dei* (119:3, 27, 32, 33, 35, 37).

The Landscape of History

If "among the Hebrews history itself is properly poetry,"[49] then it comes as no surprise to find the metaphors of "pathway" and "refuge" shaping the contours of such history, uniting the one and the many. The individual's salvation and refuge are bound up with Israel's historical deliverance and secure identity. The psalmist's path runs parallel with Israel's trek through history. Both encounter distress and persecution and experience deliverance. Both are instructed. Through the "pathway" metaphor, the individual is construed as Israel in miniature, and vice versa. Together, "pathway" and "refuge" delineate the course and purpose of historical existence, both corporate and personal.

A survey of the so-called historical psalms bears this out.[50] Psalm 77, for example, begins with an urgent prayer—cast initially in the third person—for help amid distress (vv. 1–3) and moves toward contemplation of God's wondrous deeds in history, concluding with specific focus on the exodus event (vv. 15–20). The movement is matched by greater use of the direct address, signaling a gradual transition from the proclamation of prayer to actual prayer. God's mighty deeds are identified with God's holy "way" (v. 13), historically exemplified by the deliverance at the sea (v. 19). The path continues, however, under the leadership exercised by Moses and Aaron (v. 20). Fraught with cosmic significance (cf. Exod 15:4–10), the exodus event is retold not for its own sake, much less to satisfy the reader's antiquarian interests, but to effect rescue from "the day of my trouble" (Ps 77:2a). God's deliverance and guidance of *Israel* with a "strong arm" (v. 15) serves as both precedent and motivation for the *individual's* petition for rescue and sustenance. The strikingly cosmic yet personal focus turns the Red Sea into the abyss of chaos: Israel's plight is lodged in the "many waters," the waters of chaos (vv. 16, 18). Such a cosmic connection serves also to highlight the individual's own distress, described as an inundation by the waters.[51]

Similarly, the extensive recitation of Israel's deliverance "from the hand of the foe" and of the people's intransigence in Psalm 106 is bracketed by the psalmist's cry for rescue both for his sake and for Israel's (vv. 4–5, 47a). Moreover, Israel's deliverance and the individual's rescue coincide in the psalmist's plea, "Help me when you deliver them" (v. 4b). As God is said to have "regarded [Israel's] distress" with covenantal compassion (v. 44), so the psalmist pleads that he be saved from present affliction. History is the arena in which the Israel of the past and the Israelite of the present join their voices in common petition. Israel's history of rebellion serves as the impetus for the psalmist's beatitude: "How fortunate are those who observe justice, who do[52] righteousness at all times" (v. 3). The historical sweep of Israel's apostasy and God's deliverance is internalized. Like Israel of the past, the psalmist walks the path of Israel's ancestors in confession and in trust that rescue is at hand.

The personal and communal appropriation of history is given an expressly didactic cast in Psalm 78, which binds together *tôrâ* obedience and history. Beginning where the previous one ends, this psalm opens the recital of God's salvific deeds with the divided sea and Israel's trek through it (vv. 12–13). God's guidance and sustenance accompany Israel in its journey through the wilderness to God's "holy hill," Zion (vv. 54, 68). But the journey is marred by Israel's persistent refusal to keep the covenant (vv. 10, 22, 32, 37, 40–42, 56–58). Only by God's forbearance is Israel spared the fate suffered by Egypt, against whom a sure "path" is made for God's wrath (v. 50). God's marvelous deeds are matched but not defeated by Israel's mighty resistance. The psalmist's historical recitation serves to instruct a people "to walk according to [God's] *tôrâ*" (v. 10). As remembering God's works of the past enables observance of the commandments, so the history of Israel's sin and preservation, of *Heil und Unheil*, equips the community of faith to live in gratitude and obedience, on Zion.

Israel's fickle history with a steadfast God, in addition, establishes the motivation for the community's praise, as evinced in Psalms 105, 106, and 136. The recital of God's gracious deeds in Psalm 105, from the Abrahamic covenant through the ancestors' "wandering from nation to nation" (v. 13a) to Israel's departure from Egypt and settlement in Canaan, is bracketed by commands to praise God (vv. 1–3, 45b). An inner envelope is also formed by the command to "seek YHWH" (v. 4) and the result clause, "that they might keep his statutes and observe his laws" (v. 45a). The destination of Israel's journey from bondage constitutes the setting that sustains the community's obedience and praise. Yet the command to "seek YHWH" still rings true *even* in the land of provision. The path to God continues to wind its way *in* "refuge."

Though not to be included in the historical psalms per se, Psalm 107 presents a litany of historically credible scenarios that open wide the efficacy of God's salvation, a *Heilsgeschichte* without the particularity of Israel's *Geschichte*. As a hymn of thanksgiving, the psalm presents four divergent scenarios of distress (i.e., wandering in the desert, imprisonment, sickness, and peril at sea) and recounts how God has come to save the afflicted in each situation. The wanderers are "led by a straight way (*derek yĕšārâ*), until they reach an inhabited town" (v. 7); the prisoners are "brought . . . out of darkness and gloom" (v. 14); the sick are delivered from the "gates of death" (vv. 18, 20); and those who face storms at sea are "brought . . . to their desired haven" (v. 30). In their various situations of distress, the afflicted are the objects of divinely initiated movement; they are delivered *from* their oppressive situation and restored *to* safety and security by God. Each scenario uniquely exemplifies the "needy" whom God "raises up . . . out of distress" (v. 41). The princes, by contrast, are singled out for divine contempt: God causes them to "wander in trackless wastes" (v. 40). The psalm concludes on a specifically instructive note: "Let those who are wise give heed to these things, and consider YHWH's faithful love" (v. 43). *Ḥesed* is the driving force behind the path making.

In short, the metaphorical force of "pathway" and "refuge" can be felt even in the historical psalms, thereby uniting the psalmist's personal situation with that of corporate Israel. The psalmist's personal path from affliction to restoration has its historical counterpart in Israel's corporate experience out of bondage to redemption. Whether God comes from Sinai or *šemayim* ("heaven"), whether the individual emerges from the sinking depths or arrives in pilgrimage from Kedar (120:5), whether Israel journeys from bondage or is spared the ravages of wrath, the destination featured in the Psalter's landscape is a shared one: God's dwelling place, the community's refuge, the psalmist's security. Given this common destination, it is no surprise to find the various paths converging along the way. The psalmist who admits to slipping, owing to his envy of the arrogant, declares,

> Nevertheless, I am continually with you;
>   you hold my right hand.
> With your counsel you guide me,
>   and afterward you will receive me [with] honor (*kā bôd*).[53]
> (73:23–24)

The comparable declaration of confidence in Psalm 23, "You are with me" (v. 4), is the proclamation of a beleaguered refugee seeking safe haven. Israel, too, bears witness to God's guidance and forbearance. With God, the psalmist has gone "from strength to strength" (84:7). "May your way be known upon earth, your saving power among all nations" is the joyful cry (67:2). "Give me life in your ways," proclaims another, to "walk in the *tôrâ* of YHWH" (119:37b, 1b). The metaphor of "pathway" effectively melds the soteriological and the tropological, the salvific and the moral, into a single, formative ethos.

Habit and Habitation

That the concluding beatitude of Psalm 2 ("How fortunate are all who take refuge in [YHWH])" is matched by the opening macarism of Psalm 128 ("How fortunate is everyone who . . . walks in his ways") suggests that a metaphorical dyad, rather than a single all-embracing schema, governs the Psalter. "Refuge" and "pathway," I have argued, best capture the broad contours of the Psalter's metaphorical landscape. Geometrically speaking, the Psalter is more an ellipse than a circle; it has two foci rather than a single center. These two metaphorical schemas adequately capture the dynamic, paradigmatic whole that frames the Psalter as both a pilgrimage of prayer and a sanctuary of praise. Given the myriad voices of praise and prayer that reverberate through its ancient hallways and across time, the Psalter is no sanctuary of silence. Indeed, the sanctuary is also a schoolhouse.

In the Psalms, the didactic and the cultic, devotion and royal dominion, all coexist quite happily. Those who focus on the royal psalms, particularly in Book 4,[54] identify divine rule as the central metaphor for God and, consequently, the Psalter's theological *Mitte*. The result, however, marginalizes the role and theological implications of *instruction*, specifically *tôrâ* and wisdom. The Psalms codify a balance of concerns, as is evident at the outset: whereas Psalm 2 features the Lord's anointed, the king, with God at his side on Zion, Psalm 1 highlights the character of *anyone* with *tôrâ* at his or her side.[55] The Lord reigns *and* the Lord teaches; the psalmist renders praise *and* is instructed. That the Psalter is expressly *instructive*[56] is confirmed by the "pathway" metaphor. "Pathway" and "refuge" effectively integrate the cultic and the didactic, and they provide, respectively, the *mode* and *setting* for faithful living, life directed *ad deum* and established *coram deo*. The psalmists seek God within the fray as much as they find themselves in God's presence beyond it.[57]

By developing these metaphors as governing motifs, the psalmists and their editors inseparably related the didactic and cultic dimensions of the Psalter within a fundamentally shared context. Such features need not constitute a tension-based polarity, as some have suggested.[58] To the contrary, they indicate a complementarity that powerfully evokes a yearning for God's presence through prayer and worship, on the one hand, and the thirst for righteousness and wisdom, on the other. (And woe to anyone who would split them asunder!) The metaphor of "refuge" lends specific orientation or direction to the "path of life," and, by extension, conveys divine support, even solidarity, in the quest for faithful obedience. "Refuge," in nuce, underscores the telos of right conduct. "Pathway," in turn, imbues "refuge" with a sense of process and greater moral nuance, as well as pathos. It ensures that "dwelling in" thanksgiving and praise is ethically dynamic and ongoing, in short, a matter of praxis. The psalmist's request—"Teach me your way, YHWH, that I may walk in your truth"—is embedded in praise from one who has already taken refuge (86:11, 13). Moral integrity, conversely, is admission into God's presence: "YHWH, who may abide in your tent? Who may dwell on your holy hill?" asks the psalmist in priestly fashion, to which the response is given, "Those who walk in integrity (*tāmîm*) and do what is right" (15:1–2a; see also 24:3–4). The "paths of righteousness," in short, lead to the "gates of righteousness" (23:3; 118:19).

Something of the distinctive nuance "pathway" and "refuge" receive in the Psalter can be discerned from a comparison with the didactic literature of Proverbs 1–9, in which wisdom and *tôrâ* are also inextricably bound.[59] Both Proverbs and Psalms utilize the motif of the "two paths": the path of the wicked and the path of the righteous or wise.[60] Beyond that, however, the similarities break down. Proverbs focuses intensely on the moral quality or nature of the path: "For human ways are under the eyes of YHWH, who examines all their paths" (Prov 5:21). The way of wisdom is straight (3:6; 4:26): it embodies justice (2:8; 8:20), righteousness (8:20; 11:5), uprightness (2:13; 4:11), peace (3:17), security (3:23; 10:9), wisdom (4:11; 28:26), discipline (6:23), and insight (9:6). By contrast, the way of the wicked is "crooked" (2:15): it is deemed evil (1:16; 2:12; 8:13) and dark (2:13; 4:19) and leads to death (5:5–6). But nowhere in Proverbs 1–9 is specific reference made to God's refuge or sanctuary.[61] Rather, another destination is indicated. The "pathway" metaphor in Proverbs targets the ongoing quest for wisdom,[62] which showers the "student" with the blessings of prosperity and long life, "tree of life" that she is (3:13, 16–18). Wisdom, too, has her habitation, which she has built for her students' edification (8:34; 9:1–6). By comparison, the Psalter dwells relatively less on the specific contours of "pathway"—its straightness and moral direction (although it is presupposed)—and more intently on its destination, God's habitation. In Proverbs, the sapiential counterpart to God's dwelling place is wisdom's domicile.

Together, Psalms and Proverbs offer two complementary yet distinctly different metaphorical landscapes through which the "path" of conduct winds its way. Both paths lead to their respective destinations. Further comparison can also be made between their respective "antipaths." While the Psalter contends that the way of the wicked leads to death (Ps 1:6), the destination of the fool or the wicked is given sharper and more elaborate focus in Proverbs. The end point on the "crooked path" (Prov 2:15) is an abode in its own right. As the Psalter depicts "refuge" as YHWH's dwelling place on Zion, Proverbs yields an equally evocative picture of Sheol or the pit as the abode of "woman stranger" or "woman folly."

> Her house is the way (*dĕrākîm*[63]) to Sheol,
>   descending into the chambers of death.
>   (Prov 7:27; cf. 2:18)
>
> She sits at the door of her house,
> . . . .
>   calling to those who pass by,
>   who have made straight their way (*mĕyaššĕrîm 'ōrĕḥôtām*).
> . . . .
> But they do not know that the shades (*rĕpā'îm*) are there,
>   that in the depths of Sheol her guests [reside].
>   (9:14a, 15, 18)

This mythic figure serves as the antitype to the sapiential occupant of the abode of life in Proverbs; she is the antisophia. The Psalter, by contrast, lacks any comparably vivid figure to occupy the pit or Sheol and to serve as the antipersona of the divine resident of "refuge."

To summarize: In both Proverbs and Psalms we find a necessary and essential connection between "pathway" and "refuge." These two motifs help define the Psalter's deep structure. The didactic dimension, connoted by "pathway," is contextualized within the sacred parameters of "refuge," concretized by Zion. At the same time, "refuge," via "pathway," constitutes the *telos* of learning and moral conduct, as well as the *locus* of divine presence and activity. Together they evoke a powerful setting for the praxis of faithful living, for righteousness and reverence, obedience and worship. By comparison, the metaphorical landscape of Proverbs lacks by and large a cultically defined notion of the "refuge" that accommodates God's presence. Standing in its place is a distinctly sapiential model of "refuge": "wisdom's house," the locus of learning. The Psalter's "refuge," however, is not without its didactic dimension any more than the house of learning in Proverbs is empty of soteriological force, the protective care that wisdom extends to her would-be disciples. Zion's edifice is edifying, and wisdom's house is salutary.

THE "RITUAL" OF HABITATION

Despite its variegated context and content, one unifying characteristic of Psalms is its performative value: each psalm cries out to be prayed, sung, recited, studied, and appropriated. This feature, in and of itself, makes the Psalter the literary embodiment of *ritual*, whereby even meditation or devotional reading constitutes a form of ritualized activity, a life-forming discipline.[64] It is no accident, then, that a theologian of liturgy, Tom F. Driver, finds the two motifs of "pathway" and "refuge" essential to ritual itself:

> To ritualize is to make (or utilize) a *pathway* through what would otherwise be uncharted territory. . . . As a particular act of ritualizing becomes more and more familiar, as it is repeated so often that it seems to circle round upon itself, it comes to seem less like a *pathway* and more like a *shelter*. These two images—*pathway* and *shelter*—reflect the tension in ritualization between the verb and the noun. Some ritualizations have become in the course of time such elaborate shelters that they are like architecture, and indeed often have impressive buildings dedicated to their performance. What once were newly blazed *pathways* are now old forms invested with rich symbolic content and carefully guarded by explicit traditions and rules. These are the great liturgies and ceremonies of stable institutions. . . . They both *guide* and *shelter* the passing of generations.[65]

Driver aptly notes the fundamental ritual setting, or performative context, in which these two "images" operate and inform each other. Like those who discern a "tensive dialogue," or competing editorial frameworks, between *tôrâ* or wisdom, on the one hand, and cult or royal covenantal hope, on the other, Driver discerns a fundamental "tension" between refuge and pathway. Nevertheless, the grammar suggests a tight coherence between the "noun" and the "verb" of ritual activity. Metaphorically, the tension pales into a partnership. "Shelter" cannot exist apart from "pathway," and vice versa. Regrettably, Driver's definition of ritual "shelter" as a frozen pathway is insufficient. Each having its own integrity, these two metaphors are complementary and mutually related. Together, "pathway" and "refuge" establish a stabilizing yet dynamic ethos that binds together habit and habitation. As metaphor, "refuge" constitutes a necessary component in Psalms for various reasons, not least of which is the theme of conflict and danger: the individual is beset by enemies; the community is oppressed by foreign powers. Thus, the psalmist's cry of deliverance and vindication resounds in refuge.

The "refuge" metaphor conveys a zone of safety, respite, and even empowerment for a community besieged by the powers and principalities of this world.

But "refuge" is no isolated haven in a world bent on self-destruction. "Refuge" creates the possibility for an enclave of praise that ultimately extends outward to transform the very sources of hostility and conflict, of persecution and oppression, into vehicles of praise. Even enemies can be reconciled within the protective setting of "refuge," "the house of YHWH" (23:5–6). Matching the psalms of imprecation are those that embrace the world within a horizon of universal praise, all uttered from God's cosmic refuge (e.g., Psalm 148). But whether exhorting all the world to praise or appealing to God to vanquish the enemy, the psalmists agree that God remains a rock and stronghold. Under the guise of *tôrâ*, "refuge" provides "respite from days of trouble" (94:13).[66] The retreat and respite that "refuge" provides are foundational to worship, rooted as they are in a theology of Sabbath.

The notion of "pathway" is equally crucial.[67] The world-creating power of path making is characteristic of the Psalter's performative power. Indeed, "pathway" denotes the *ongoing* process of refuge making by which the psalmist can ultimately leave behind the cry for vengeance in favor of the call to praise, a move illustrated by the general movement of the Psalter as a whole.[68] As Psalm 1 lays out the "path" of righteousness, the journey is not complete without entrance into "refuge," the world-embracing setting for thanksgiving and praise, as conveyed in Psalms 146–150. A veritable rite of passage, or more precisely a "rite of incorporation,"[69] is created by which the user of psalms is incorporated into the all-encompassing *communitas* of God's favor, identified with the "congregation of the righteous" and "the assembly of the faithful."[70] "Out of the depths," from the mire of the "pit," to the "rock" and "wing" of God, the psalmist traverses the path toward deliverance *and* edification. But "refuge" is not only a destination, just as "pathway" is not merely a liminal state of transition. On the one hand, the pray-er of psalms who embarks on the "pathway" seeks to be enclosed within the protective walls of God's "refuge." On the other hand, the psalmist's journey is by no means concluded once refuge is taken. Both "pathway" and "refuge" are continually at work in the psalmist's words. This, in fact, is the goal of ritual:

> While it is the business of literature to give names (the right descriptive words), that of ritual is to give "local habitation." Performance makes present. Because it is performance and not verbal description or exhortation, ritual brings the faraway, the long-ago, and the not-yet into the here-and-now.[71]

Prayed, sung, and studied, the Psalms "perform" for the community of faith. They construe a world full of risk and refuge, of order and chaos. Prayer establishes refuge and forges a path; it is world making and conduct forming. Praying the psalms prepares "place" by creating "pathway," while blazing a "path" by establishing "place." As ritual in general "teaches us to seek a created order in the world,"[72] so "pathway" and "refuge" are the benchmarks of a dynamic sacred order, one that rests on trust in God and is fulfilled, ever partially, by a life led in reverence and integrity. "Pathway" and "refuge" define the narrative of the self in the landscape of faith.[73] By joining "refuge" and "pathway," the warp and woof of the Psalter's variegated tapestry, the psalmists reorient the reader on the way *toward* God, while discerning God's path *into* the fray of human existence. In the convergence of "pathways," true *communitas* is formed and refuge is found, embodied in a community of worship enabled to reflect on God's presence, to sing in praise, to pray in trust, to live with understanding, and to work for justice and righteousness. It is a community on the move toward and at the same time in communion with God.

The Psalms, in short, limn a *sanctuary movement* in every sense: the psalmist's sojourn to God and God's journey toward the psalmist. "Pathway" and "refuge" are the tectonic plates that give coherent shape to the Psalter's rugged landscape, much in the same way they continue to inform and shape communities of faith today. Do not persons of faith today think of themselves as on a journey, one having a destination they call "home" that is not entirely of this world? Yet do they not also find themselves linked together in community, "at home" with each other, as they continue to live and grow in faith? Indeed, how is a path formed except by the passage of *many* feet by those who have gone before? And what is a sanctuary without the gathering community? The journey of faith is filled with painful wrenchings, yet surprising gifts. The Psalms imagine a world that is at once relentlessly real and stridently hopeful, a journey *within* the fray that is also "homeward" bound.

While supplying the contours of psalmic discourse, these two root metaphors by no means exhaust the Psalter's storehouse of tropes and images. They merely outline the map in which the vividly concrete images that populate the Psalter find their place. On the winding path, the reader of Psalms encounters various signposts and markers along the way, beginning, most auspiciously, at the trailhead, Psalm 1.

Chapter 3

The Transplanted Tree
Psalm 1 and the Psalter's Threshold

Everybody does not see alike. The tree which moves some to tears of joy is in the Eyes of others only a Green thing that stands in the way.

William Blake[1]

Psalm 1 stands as the Psalter's hermeneutical entry point,[2] and for good reason. It lacks a superscription, contains a number of lexical links to the following psalms, and underscores certain themes that resonate throughout the Psalter. Together with the following psalm,[3] Psalm 1 introduces the Psalter and, thereby, guides the reader's appropriation of subsequent psalms. Its orienting power is generated, in part, by metaphor and image. The purpose of this chapter is not to highlight every link the psalm establishes with the Psalter as a whole, but to determine how its central metaphor, which stands at the Psalter's threshold, serves to orient the reader of Psalms.

TRANSLATION

1   How fortunate[4] is the one who neither walks in the counsel of the wicked,
     nor stands in the path of sinners,
     nor sits in the seat of scoffers;

2   but rather finds delight in the *tôrâ* of YHWH,[5]
    and reflects upon[6] his *tôrâ* day and night.

3   He will be[7] like a tree transplanted[8] by channels of water,
    yielding its fruit in due season,
        and whose leaves do not wither.
    Everything that he does will prove efficacious.

4   Not so with the wicked:
    they are, rather, like chaff,
        which the wind drives away.

5   No wonder[9] they do not stand up in judgment,
    nor sinners in the congregation of the righteous.

6   Surely,[10] YHWH knows the way of the righteous,
    but the way of the wicked will perish.

The psalmist is a cultivator of images. The deployment of metaphor, along with the pacing of the poetry, highlights the import of *tôrâ*-piety. The poet lingers over the stately, arboreal profile of the righteous individual, who remains in a state of continual study and blessed constancy, while passing over the "wicked," who are only hastily described as wind-driven chaff. Tantamount to nothing, the "wicked" require little poetic reflection; they are gone with the wind. Not so with the "righteous": they steadily flourish under the poet's lavished attention. The contrast could not be more sharply drawn: the wicked are purely passive, driven away, while the image of the righteous commands the position of subject. Whereas the chaff is blown away by the winds of judgment, the tree not only has standing; it bears fruit.

As often noted, the contrast between the righteous and the wicked appears to be one of motion, or lack thereof. The righteous distinguish themselves in their "ability to stand still and reflect upon true things,"[11] in contrast to the wicked, whose "frenetic activity is a dance down the path to oblivion."[12] And yet by cultivating the image of the tree, the poet grants the righteous a modicum of movement. With his green thumb, the psalmist cultivates righteousness as a matter of gradual, steady growth. Well rooted and productive are the righteous, whose "way" is steadily upward and outward.

The structure of the psalm is, in part, informed by the psalmist's arrangement of particular images, as illustrated in the following outline:[13]

A   Description (and fate) of the righteous: **path**   1–2
    B   Metaphor for the righteous: **tree**   3a–b
        C   Objectifying conclusion: success   3c
        C' Objectifying introduction: lack of success   4a
    B' Metaphor for the wicked: **chaff**   4b
A' Description (and fate) of the wicked: **path**   5–6

The psalm reflects a concentric arrangement framed by certain images designed to distinguish the righteous from the wicked. Its tightly wrought structure and evocative use of imagery set the psalm's message in sharp relief, which grafts together will and fate as inseparable features of human conduct. While the image of the pathway highlights ethical choice, the horticultural metaphors underscore the nature and destiny of opposing "ways." As the rhetorical focus moves from pathway to community, both that of the wicked and that of the righteous, the psalm's overall design influences the reader's moral choice—to read or not to read *tôrâ*—and reveals what is ultimately at stake: life and death.

From the path of the wicked in v. 1 to the way of the righteous in v. 6, the reader encounters several signposts: *tôrâ* as the source of delight, a tree flourishing beside flowing channels, and wind-driven chaff. Such images and motifs are deployed to leave an indelible stamp on all subsequent psalms. They serve to guide the reader through the densely populated, tensive world of the Psalter. The mortal threats made by bloodthirsty enemies are blown away like chaff, and the dissonant cries of the oppressed find resolution in the cadences of certain vindication. The pathos of praise, moreover, is redirected toward *tôrâ*. From this opening psalm, thus, an edifying ethos maps the Psalter's pain and praise—its "bipolar" character—with the template of righteousness, and the following psalms thereby become readable as lessons for the learned. The psalmist's anguish becomes an object of reflection; her pain is transformed into an edifying word.[14] The pathos of praise and protestation is mediated by instruction and study. Moreover, the opening psalm instills a measure of hope, even assurance, that righteousness will prevail, while blazing a pathway into the fray whose end is blessing: "How fortunate is the one . . ." Psalm 1 begins the pilgrimage and anticipates the destination.

TREE AND *TÔRÂ*

The conceptual framework for the psalm's central images is *tôrâ*, the supreme object of desire and the focus of diligent reflection. For all the relative lack of pathos in this opening psalm, the poet speaks of ultimate "delight" (*ḥepeṣ*, v. 2).[15] With image and word, the poet cultivates the reader's desire, indeed passion, for *tôrâ*, whose parameters extend beyond civil legislation or cultic prescription. As the governing verb *hgh* ("reflect, meditate") in v. 2b suggests elsewhere, *tôrâ* is all-embracing in its scope.[16] The object of the psalmist's "reflection" includes God (63:5–7) and God's "work" or "deeds" (77:11–13). God's work in history, both salvific and judgmental, is incorporated into *tôrâ*. As YHWH's word is "firmly fixed in heaven" (119:89), so *tôrâ* is given cosmic expanse.[17] Moreover, God's *tôrâ* is shot through with the pathos of *poesis,* for to "reflect" also entails "lyrical intent" (see 49:3–4).[18] Psalm 1, in short, weds the psalmists' words of praise and pain with God's word, deed, and creation. With its fivefold division, the Psalter is, ultimately, a reflection of Pentateuchal Torah and deemed authoritative. Revelatory word, narrative account, cosmic order, and human need are seamlessly united under the shelter of *tôrâ*. Informing and sustaining the righteous, *tôrâ* defines the very essence of the Psalter as a composition *of* the heart, both human and divine, that also *instructs* the heart.[19]

As *tôrâ* lays the conceptual foundation for Psalm 1 (and thereby for the Psalter as a whole), so the "tree" constitutes the psalm's most central metaphor. Designating the wicked, "chaff" serves as an apt antitype. Both images are drawn from a common source domain that casts human character in botanical terms. The arboreal image, mapped onto righteous character, connotes various associations such as cultivation, growth, and well-rootedness, which ethically speaking point to enduring success, maturity, and steadfastness in conduct. As the "leaves" of this tree do not wither, so the individual's integrity remains constant and efficacious. As the tree bears fruit "in due season," so the individual knows the right time in which to act and speak, as well as to find success.[20]

The juxtaposition of tree and *tôrâ* evokes a profound, albeit subtle, connection. As the righteous individual reaps joy and continual guidance from *tôrâ*, so the tree gains its sustenance from the ever-flowing "channels of water" beside which it is transplanted. Grammatically, the prepositions "in" and "on" (identical in Hebrew: *bĕ*) in v. 2, which denote the individual's relationship to *tôrâ*, find their counterpart in the preposition "by" (*'al*) of v. 3a, indicating the tree's proximity to and dependence on the water channels. That the tree specifically targets the righteous individual lends further confirmation to this subtle association and generates the related underlying metaphor, "*Tôrâ* is nourishing water."[21]

TRUE TREE: POSITIVE CONNOTATIONS

With the psalm's poetic foreground accounted for, the stage is set to unpack the soil in which this arboreal image was cultivated and to examine its ancient Near Eastern roots. The tree of Psalm 1 does not stand isolated from its iconic environment, devoid of background and attendant associations. Much more lies underneath the surface. In fact, the psalmist's use of the metaphor reflects a degree of controversy, as indicated by the positive and negative connotations this image bears in various contexts. This tree, in other words, has good standing only in certain plots.

Tree of Life

The power and range of this riveting metaphor cannot be fully grasped without examining its stature in antiquity, both biblical and extrabiblical, literary and iconographic.

Literary Associations

In biblical, specifically prophetic, tradition, the power of this arboreal image assumes mythic proportion.

Consider Assyria,[22] cedar of Lebanon,
> beautiful of branch and forest shade,
>> and of great height [with] its top among the clouds.
The waters made it great;
> the deep made it grow tall,
making its rivers flow[23] around where it was planted,
> sending forth its streams to all the trees of the field.
No wonder it towered high above all the trees of the field;
> its boughs grew large and its branches long,
>> from abundant water[24] in its shoots.
. . . .
It was beautiful in its greatness,
> in the length of its branches;
>> for its roots extended down to abundant water.
The cedars in the garden of God could not rival it;
> nor could the fir trees match its boughs.
The plane trees were nothing like its branches;
> no tree in the garden of God was like it in beauty.
I made it beautiful with its mass of branches,
> the envy of all the trees of Eden in the garden of God.
>> (Ezek 31:3–5, 7–9)

Drawing from the garden mythos, Ezekiel profiles certain elements that resonate with Psalm 1. The tree's unprecedented stature stems from the "abundant water" that flows underground (v. 7b). The tree's profile of Psalm 1 likely draws from such arboreal majesty. Moreover, a strong connection is evident between the prophet's temple vision of the mythic grove planted by the sacred river and the psalmist's tree:

> On the banks, on both sides of the river, will grow all kinds of trees for food. Their leaves will not wither and their fruit will not fail. Rather, they will bear fresh fruit every month, because their [source of] water will flow from the sanctuary. Their fruit will be for food, and their leaves for healing. (Ezek 47:12)

Such preternatural fertility, evinced by the lush orchards of deciduous trees whose leaves do not wither and that bear an unending harvest of fruit, is due to a singular source, the river of Zion, God's holy sanctuary. Thus, one can speak of Eden as the "archetype for the temple," as does Dexter Callender in his pertinent survey of ancient Near Eastern literature.[25] Like the psalmist, the prophet takes pains to establish the necessary connection between the life-giving waters, issuing from the temple, and the miraculous flourishing of arboreal life. Slightly different, however, is Ezekiel's vision of the tree's *uninterrupted* fruit bearing. The psalm reflects the more sapiential (and realistic) nuance of *seasonal* activity.[26]

As the tree draws its sustenance from subterranean streams, so it represents life in all its potency. The life-giving efficacy of the tree image is on full display in the evocative description of wisdom in Proverbs 3, whose precursor is likely the 'ăšērâ cult image (see below).[27]

> How fortunate (*'ašrê*) is the one who has found wisdom.
> . . . .
> Long life is in her right hand;
>   in her left hand—riches and honor (*kābôd*).
> Her ways are pleasant,
>   and all her paths are peace.
> A tree of life is she to those who grasp her;
>   those who hold her fast are deemed fortunate.[28]
> (Prov 3:13a, 16–18)

As the tree of life, wisdom is the font of blessing, and it is no accident that both this passage from Proverbs and Psalm 1 begin with a beatitude of blessing. Whereas the tree is "grasped" by the student of wisdom, the righteous individual and the tree coalesce in the psalm, suggesting that the psalmist identifies wisdom with *tôrâ*. In any case, the image of the tree in Psalm 1 bears some connection to the mythic tree of life. In Mesopotamian lore, one finds repeated references to a special tree or plant that imparts renewal and rejuvenation, that is, "long life." In the Epic of Gilgamesh, for example, the tragic hero has in his grasp the "plant of renown," named "When an Old Man Grows Young (Again)," but loses it when a snake snatches it while the tragic hero is resting from his taxing journey.[29] Shedding its skin, the snake, in turn, acquires new life, but immortality is irretrievably lost to Gilgamesh.[30]

The tree of life is also associated with Gilgamesh's intended destination, a mountain on which stands a "lapis lazuli tree . . . in full fruit and gorgeous to gaze on."[31] The life-giving efficacy of the tree is matched by the tree's striking appearance (Gen 2:9). Undergirding this motif in ancient lore is the tree's distinctive relationship to the cult. In Eridu, the sanctuary of Enki, the god of water and wisdom (Akkadian Ea), stands a tree whose "appearance is lapis-lazuli, erected on the *Apsu*," or the watery abyss.[32] Utterly removed from human encroachment, this scene corresponds to the sacred grove in Enki's holy temple. In his survey of Mesopotamian texts, Geo Widengren traces the "tree of life" motif and finds it typically situated within a "garden of paradise" at the mouth of the two rivers. This sacred grove is recognized by a special cult tree, planted in a grove near the sanctuary, described in one text as "the House of the Plant of Life, the holy dwelling."[33]

As a fruit tree whose "leaves do not wither," the central metaphor of Psalm 1 bears some connection to the "tree of life" in mythopoeic lore. As the tree situated in the garden of God served to confer everlasting life to the primal couple, so the psalmist's tree is the sign and symbol of prosperity and success for the individual. Similar connection is found in the apothegmatic sayings in Proverbs, in which the motif signifies everything from fulfilled desire (13:12) to healing speech (15:4). Proverbs 11:30 explicitly associates the tree of life with righteousness. Psalm 1, thus, effectively combines the benefits of shalom and righteousness into a single figure, a natural connection within sapiential thought, and leaves the tree for the reader to *self*-appropriate. The psalmist has pruned the mythic tree down to its barest limbs, while finding a new entrance back into the garden, making accessible the tree's promise for life, even if that promise is only a vestige of its primordial potency. The individual who follows the path of righteousness is, in turn, elevated to mythic stature. Gone are the cherubim and flaming sword, the guardians of the tree of life. All that is required is the desire for righteousness. The student of *tôrâ* and the tree have become one.

Iconographic Parallels

In addition to the literary, mythopoeic associations evoked by this image, iconographic parallels and precedents abound. On the textual surface, the tree of Psalm 1 connotes the blessed life of the righteous individual. Its visual roots can be traced to the countless images found on material remains as early as the Middle Bronze Age.[34] One finds, for example, among numerous seal impressions, tomb reliefs, and statues, images of goats and caprids eating the leaves or buds of trees: from the ornate "golden goat" statues of a Sumerian grave at Ur (ca. 2650 B.C.E.)[35] to the crudely simple seals and seal impressions in Syria-Palestine, as well as an elaborate drawing on a storage jar or pithos from Kuntillet 'Ajrud.[36] Among them all, the figure of the tree assumes a prominent, frequently central, position. Shown here are two representative examples: the drawing from Kuntillet 'Ajrud (fig. 2) and an obsidian scaraboid from Tell el-Far'ah (south) (fig. 3).[37]

Fig. 2: Plant drawing on Pithos A from Kuntillet 'Ajrud. Reprinted with permission from *Tel Aviv*, published by the Institute of Archaeology in Tel Aviv and currently edited by David Ussishkin. The storage jar was discovered by Ze'ev Meshel, the excavator of Kuntillet 'Ajrud, and the drawing is featured in Pirḥiya Beck, "The Drawings from Ḥorvat Teiman (Kuntillet 'Ajrud)," *Tel Aviv* 9 (1982): 7 (#4).

Fig. 3: Scaraboid of a plant flanked by two ibexes from Tell el-Far'ah (south). Reprinted with permission from Othmar Keel and Christoph Uehlinger, *Gods, Goddesses, and Images of God in Ancient Israel*, trans. Thomas H. Trapp (Minneapolis: Fortress, 1998), 216 (#222b). Courtesy of the Department of Biblical Studies, University of Fribourg.

Fig. 4: Ivory carving of a goddess flanked by two ibexes from Ugarit. Reprinted with permission from Othmar Keel, *Song of Songs: A Continental Commentary* (Minneapolis: Fortress, 1994), 55 (#11). Courtesy of the Department of Biblical Studies, University of Fribourg. The artifact is displayed in the Louvre, Paris.

From the Middle Bronze to the Iron Age, the figure of the tree was evidently associated with a goddess who was "venerated as a creator of vegetation, if not of life itself."[38] Figure 4 is an ivory carving from Minet el-Beida near Ras Shamra (Ugarit) that depicts what appears to be an example of such a goddess flanked by two ibexes or goats (see above).

Tree and goddess were portrayed interchangeably. In at least two instances, the figure of the tree was associated with the genitalia of a goddess. Particularly striking is a terracotta fragment discovered at Tel Harassim in the Shefela, dated to the fourteenth or thirteenth century B.C.E., which displays the pudenda of a goddess held open by her hands (see fig. 5). On each thigh, facing inward, is a stylized tree with a caprid eating its top.[39] Graphically clear is the association of the tree with the divinely wrought blessing of fertility.

Also revealing is the well-known tenth-century terracotta cult stand from Taanach, which stands approximately sixty centimeters in height. It features four friezes or registers, two of which bear some association with the tree and goddess. The third register from the bottom (see fig. 6) depicts a stylized tree flanked by caprids, which in turn are flanked by two lions. The bottom register (see fig. 6, bottom) depicts a nude female standing between two lions, in the likeness per-haps of the goddess Asherah, known as "the Lion Lady" in West Semitic epigra-phy. On the very same cult object, tree and goddess find tight correspondence.[40] In certain contexts, thus, the tree represents the "goddess of Earth, of Plant Life, of Sexuality and Prosperity."[41]

Variations on this theme are discernible in the Iron Age in Syria-Palestine. Ter-racotta shrine models from the eleventh and the tenth centuries whose entrances are flanked by naked goddesses correspond to entrances depicted in similar mod-els of the ninth century that are flanked by stylized palm trees.[42] This motif undoubtedly lies in the background of the *"yākîn"* and *"bōʿaz"* pillars that flanked the vestibule of Solomon's temple: two massive freestanding bronze columns adorned with pomegranate designs and capitals and decorated with carvings of palm trees and flowers.[43] Although the precise significance of their names is not certain (the former could be rendered "he [God?] establishes"[44]), they served to demarcate sacred space by conveying a sense of divine presence, the source of the temple's holiness. "The twin pillars loomed large at the entry to the temple, pro-viding the visual link to the unseen grandeur within."[45] Much like the terracotta shrine models, the twin pillars of the Solomonic temple, in addition to marking the boundary between the profane and the holy, represented the "paradisiacal life-giving aspect of the sanctuary."[46]

Also of note from a cultic context is the garden paradise that is vividly depicted on the wall paintings of an early eighteenth-century palace at Mari, located on the banks of the Euphrates in modern Syria.[47] (See fig. 7.) In a courtyard that once led into a vestibule in front of the king's throne room, a mural scene features a royal ceremony—perhaps the annual induction of the statue of the goddess Ishtar or, less likely, the investiture of a king—set within a luxuriant orchard inhabited by fantastic creatures. The setting is easily

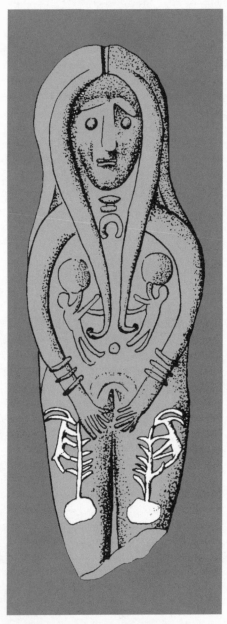

Fig. 5: Composite drawing of a terracotta plaque of a fertility goddess from fragments found in Palestine (Afek, Kibbutz Revadim, and Tel Harassim). Reprinted with permission from Othmar Keel, *Goddesses and Trees, New Moon and Yahweh: Ancient Near Eastern Art and the Hebrew Bible* (JSOTSup 261; Sheffield: Sheffield Academic Press, 1998), Part I, #52. Courtesy of the Department of Biblical Studies, University of Fribourg.

discernible: a paradise garden populated with winged sphinxes (or cherubim), griffins, and bulls.

Flanking the royal scene that depicts the king, presumably Zimri-Lim, are stylized trees and date palms, whose fruits are harvested by human figures. One theory suggests that the actual courtyard enclosed live trees, in the middle of which an artificial palm tree stood with a wooden core plated with bronze and silver leaf.[48] In any case, the Mari mural provides a vivid parallel to Solomon's temple, whose architectural and decorative features are indicated in the biblical witness. The doors and interior walls of the Solomonic temple were similarly adorned with gilded carved-wood reliefs of cherubim, ornamental palms, and calyxes or open flowers. Ezekiel describes the temple walls

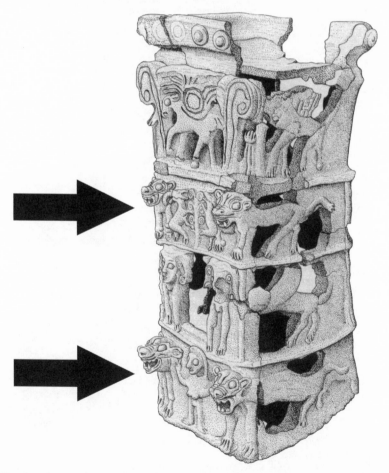

Fig. 6: Cult stand from tenth-century Taanach with registers 1 and 3 designated. Reproduced with permission from Mohr Siebeck and featured in Kurt Galling, ed., *Biblisches Reallexikon*, HAT 1,1 (2d ed.; Tübingen: J. C. B. Mohr, 1977), 191, #45 (3).

Fig. 7: Wall painting from Zimri-Lim's palace in Mari. Reprinted with permission from Othmar Keel. *Die Welt der altorientalischen Bildsymbolik und das Alte Testament. Am Beispiel der Psalmen* (Cologne: Benziger Verlag / Neukirchen-Vluyn: Neukirchener Verlag, 1972), 125 (#191). Courtesy of the Department of Biblical Studies, University of Fribourg.

as decorated with a pattern of "cherubim and palm trees, with a palm between every two cherubim" (Ezek 41:18). Iconographically and architecturally, the temple reflected the garden of God.

The iconographic data are particularly suggestive for the psalm. It is no accident that the Psalter is introduced with the image of the tree, the metaphor of blessing. Standing at the threshold, the tree demarcates the poetic counterpart to the holy sanctuary, whose entrance leads to a cacophony of voices in praise and petition, including the voice from on high, the sound of worship.

Tree and King

That the metaphor of the tree targets the *individual*—specifically the righteous individual—reflects another class of associations that exhibit a distinctly *royal* provenance. In addition to their prowess on the battlefield, kings excelled in horticultural skill. It was altogether common practice among ancient Near Eastern despots, from Egypt to Mesopotamia, to cultivate their gardens with plants taken from foreign lands.[49] Ashurnasirpal II, for example, described his "garden of happiness" in his new capital city of Calah as consisting of over forty varieties of trees, collected and transplanted from recently conquered territories.[50] Tiglath-pileser I took pride in his internationally renowned green thumb: "I took cedar, boxtree, Kanish oak from the lands over which I had gained dominion . . . and planted [them] in the orchards of my land."[51] In their annals, Assyrian kings boasted that the trees and plants of the royal orchards thrived better under their green thumb than in their natural habitats.[52] The exotic garden thus represented the king's dominion over foreign lands. A particularly telling scene can be found in a wall relief of Ashurbanipal's palace in Nineveh (see fig. 8), which portrays a lavishly landscaped garden, complete with lawn furniture and attentive servants. But under close scrutiny, one can discern within this peaceful grove the head of an Elamite king dangling from the top of the left tree.[53] The king's garden was literally a victory garden!

Fig. 8: The so-called "Garden Party" wall relief from Ashurbanipal's palace in Nineveh. © Copyright the British Museum.

Horticulture was also the forte of the pharaohs. Ramses III repeatedly makes mention of the great groves and arbors (lit., "places of chambers of trees"[54]) that he cultivated around his temples. Regarding the restoration of the Horus chapel, he states: "I made to grow the pure grove of thy temple."[55] Such sacred groves were considered the gardens of particular gods, the property of their estates. The existence of sacred trees and groves has been confirmed archaeologically by the discovery of tree pits in Cyprus and Phoenicia.[56] With such widespread precedent throughout the ancient Near East, from Egypt to Mesopotamia, it is not surprising to find references in Scripture to royal gardens in the City of David. In the guise of Solomon, Qoheleth proclaims his royal prowess in his catalog of accomplishments:

> I made great works:
>   I built houses and planted vineyards for myself;
> I made myself gardens and parks,
>   and planted in them all kinds of fruit trees.
> I made myself pools
>   from which to water the forest of growing trees.
>   (Eccl 2:4–6)

Perhaps more historically supported, the Deuteronomistic history refers to the "king's garden," which served as an escape route for Zedekiah when the city walls were breached by the Babylonian army (2 Kgs 25:4; Jer 39:4; 52:7). The garden included the "Pool of Shelah" (Shiloah) or "King's Pool," which was watered by the Gihon spring, east of the fortified city (Neh 2:14; 3:15; see also Isa 8:6–7a). From the time of Solomon to the end of the Davidic dynasty, the Kidron valley consisted of a "cascade of terraced gardens and parks," otherwise known as the "terraces of Kidron."[57] As water source, the Gihon ("Gusher") is also featured in the Yahwist's primordial map of the world as one of the four rivers of paradise (Gen 2:13).[58] The royal garden of Jerusalem, as both the City of David and the City of God, was a replication of, or even the basis for, the primordial garden of Eden in Genesis. As noted above, Jerusalem's garden also served as a basis for the temple's restoration in Ezekiel, in which a great river is depicted issuing from the temple to fructify the land (Ezek 47:3–12; cf. Joel 3:18 [4:18]; Zech 14:8). Not only will this sanctuary stream desalinize the Dead Sea, stocking it with abundant fish, it will also bring forth an infinite variety of trees.

As the king was a warrior, so he was also known as a cultivator. Common to Akkadian and Sumerian rulers were the epithets "gardener" (NU-KIRI$_6$ / *nukarribu*) and "farmer" (ENGAR / *ikkaru*). In the "Legend of Sargon," the king of Agade, abandoned by his mother and placed in a reed basket in the river, was discovered by the gardener Akki and appointed his assistant, attracting the love of Ishtar with his agronomic prowess, and invested as king.[59] In the so-called "Sargon Chronicle," a Neo-Babylonian document, a certain Irra-imitti, king of Isin, is said to have "installed Bel-ibni, the gardener, on his throne as a 'substitute king.'"[60]

Another host of ancient Near Eastern parallels suggest an even more intimate link between tree and king, as indicated in the Sumerian reference: "Šulgi, the king, the graceful lord, is a date palm planted by the water ditch."[61] And of the same ruler: "Like a cedar rooted by abundant water, of pleasant shadow thou art."[62] The king is identified with the towering cedar and fruitful date palm. Biblical examples also abound. Ezekiel likens the king of Judah to a vine "transplanted to good soil beside abundant waters so that it might produce branches and bear fruit" (17:8; cf. v. 5). Similarly, in Ezek 31:3–9, as discussed above, the *arbor mundi*, with its roots sunk deep into the primeval waters and whose beauty and stature rival the "trees of Eden" (v. 9), is representative of a foreign king.

Tree imagery is also enlisted to designate the righteous rule of the king. In the famous passage of Isa 11:1, the Davidic king is depicted as a "shoot" and a "branch," a royal figure to usher in a new age of righteousness and justice (vv. 3b–5). By contrast, the king of Babylon in Isa 14:19 is pejoratively called a "loathed branch" (*nēṣer nitʿāb*). The correspondence between arbor and righteousness is cemented in Jeremiah, where the Davidic king is given the epithet "righteous Branch" (*ṣemaḥ ṣaddîq*, Jer 23:5–6; cf. 33:15). The legitimacy of this new ruler is founded upon the manner of his rule: he is to execute "justice and righteousness" (*mišpāṭ ûṣĕdāqâ*, 23:5). In Zech 3:8 and 6:12, "Branch" is used metaphorically as a messianic title.[63] The latter citation contains a wordplay that adumbrates the king's rise to power and his accomplishments:

> Thus says YHWH of Hosts: Here is a man whose name is Branch (*ṣemaḥ*), for he shall branch out (*yiṣmāḥ*) in his place and build the temple of YHWH. (Zech 6:12)

The original form of this passage most likely referred to Zerubbabel, one of the leaders of the return from exile, whose name means shoot of Babylon" (cf. Hag 2:20–23).

In both biblical and ancient Near Eastern tradition, thus, the individual most typically identified with a tree is a person of royalty. Firmly planted on YHWH's holy hill, this "righteous branch" wields the power to implement justice and, thereby, bring about peace and prosperity for his people (see Ps 72:2–3). Not coincidentally, the tree of Psalm 1 is also intimately associated with righteousness and prosperity. Moreover, as the reader of psalms is to "reflect upon *tôrâ*," so must also the king. According to Deuteronomic tradition, the king is informed by and held accountable to covenantal law (*tôrâ*), the very charter of Israel's existence as a theocracy, to ensure the proper exercise of the royal office (Deut 17:18–19). Likewise, the protagonist of Psalm 1 embodies righteousness through diligent observance of *tôrâ*. Regardless of the extent to which Deuteronomic *tôrâ* and psalmic *tôrâ* overlap semantically, an indissoluble connection is evident between the reception of authoritative guidance and the exercise of right conduct and faith.

Through the deployment of a common metaphor, the righteous individual of Psalm 1 is given a distinctly royal profile (cf. Psalm 2). The poet has reconfigured royal tradition in order to render an expansive and edifying profile of the reader of Psalms. As one finds in other late biblical traditions, the psalmist has, in effect, democratized the image of the king as tree by applying the arboreal image to every righteous reader.[64] As the king is to become a student of *tôrâ,* so also must the reader, whose ultimate desideratum is the law and, by extension, God. The reader's character is thus infused with the image of the king through the image of the tree. As the king is to execute righteousness and be an instrument of blessing, so must the reader, made in the image of God, informed by *tôrâ,* and sustained by the flowing channels that "make glad the city of God" (Ps 46:4). In Deuteronomy, the king becomes the model Israelite; in Psalm 1, the Israelite becomes the model king.

Tree and Community

In addition to its specifically royal and life-giving connotations, arboreal imagery is applied collectively to Israel, as one finds in certain remnant passages of Isaiah.

> The surviving remnant of the house of Judah shall again take root downward and bear fruit upward; for from Jerusalem a remnant shall go out, and from Mount Zion a band of survivors. The zeal of YHWH of hosts will do this. (Isa 37:31–32)

Such imagery is connected specifically to Zion's reestablishment, Israel's "refuge" (see Isa 4:2–5).

In Isaiah 41, the "prophet" of the exile ("Deutero-Isaiah") employs arboreal imagery to convey the inclusive expanse of the restored community and its miraculous nature:

> I will open rivers on the bare heights,
>   and fountains in the valleys;
> I will turn the wilderness into a pool of water,
>   and the dry land into springs of water.
> I will put in the wilderness the cedar,
>   the acacia, the myrtle, and the pine;
> I will set in the desert the fir tree,
>   the plane, and the cypress together,
> so that all may see and know,
>   all may consider and understand,
> that the hand of YHWH has done this;
>   the Holy One of Israel has created it.
>   (vv. 18–20)

The various trees, many of which do not flourish naturally in the same environment, underscore the diversity of the new community, the nursery of a nation cultivated by God, the divine warrior *and* gardener.[65] The last verse recalls the ancient victory hymn that commemorates Israel's deliverance from Pharaoh's army in Exod 15:1–18, which concludes:

You brought them and planted them (*wĕtiṭṭā'ēmô*)
   on the mountain of your heritage,
The place for your dwelling that you made, YHWH,
   the sanctuary, LORD, that your hands have established.
                                 (Ex 15:17)

The "place" of God's planting is Sinai or Zion.[66] But regardless of the destination, Israel is no mere "pleasant planting" (cf. Isa 5:7). It is God's victory garden over the forces of chaos and oppression, a sacred grove off limits to foreign encroachment. The collective force that sustains the arboreal image in various traditions lends further nuance to the tree image in Psalm 1, thereby tightening the bond between individual and community already evident in the psalm (vv. 5–6). The collective background of arboreal imagery, moreover, explicitly identifies the agency behind the "transplanting" in Psalm 1 (see below).

KNOTTY TREE: NEGATIVE CONNOTATIONS

In much of the Pentateuchal and Deuteronomistic literature, particular trees and groves were considered evocative of divine presence. Such arboreal settings were thought to provide settings for theophany, an encounter with the deity.[67] Abraham, for example, builds an altar to YHWH near Hebron at "the Oaks (*'ēlōnîm*) of Mamre" and lives there (Gen 13:18; 14:13). There, his encounter with the divine in the form of three mysterious visitors takes place (Gen 18:1–2). At Beer-sheba, Abraham plants a tamarisk (*'ēšel*) and calls "on the name of YHWH" (Gen 21:33). At the beginning of his sojourns, Abraham is said to have "passed through the land to the place at Shechem, to the Oak (*'ēlôn*) of Moreh," where YHWH appeared to him (Gen 12:6–7). The name of this oak literally means "teacher" or perhaps "oracle giver" (√*yrh*). It is also referred to as the "diviners' oak" in Judg 9:37 (cf. v. 6).[68] Finally, in the ratification of the covenant at Shechem, Joshua "wrote these words in the book of the law of God; and he took a large stone, and set it up there *under the oak in the sanctuary of YHWH*" (Josh 24:26, emphasis added).[69]

Yet within the purview of Israel's cultic polity and practice not every tree or grove had good standing "in the sanctuary of YHWH." Isaiah held a particular disdain for sacred groves:

Zion shall be redeemed by justice
   and those in her who repent, by righteousness.
. . . .
For you shall be ashamed of the oaks (*'êlîm*) in which you delight;
   and you shall blush for the gardens you have chosen.
For you shall become like an oak (*'ēlâ*) whose leaf withers,
   like a desiccated garden.
The strong shall become like tinder,
   and their work like a spark.

> They and their work shall burn together,
> without anyone to quench them.
>
> (Isa 1:27, 29–31)

A source of shame rather than delight (cf. Ps 1:2), the trees of Zion are portrayed as desiccated and destined for burning, and so also the people. Instead of assuring success in all matters of work and conduct, misplaced desire ("delight" and "choice") will invariably result in total lack of fulfillment, even outright destruction. According to the prophet, might cannot hold a candle to righteousness. Oaks being singled out by the prophet may reflect the fact that the Hebrew term for "oak" or "terebinth" (*'ēlâ*), an impressive tree in its own right, resembles the feminine form of the word that denotes divinity (*'ēl*).[70] In any case, the prophet condemns such sacred groves as pagan cult symbols. Similar condemnation is also found in Isaiah 17.

> For you have forgotten the God of your salvation,
> and have not remembered the Rock of your refuge.
> Therefore, though you plant pleasant plants,
> and set out shoots of an alien [god] (*zĕmōrat zār*),
> though you make them grow on the day that you plant them
> and make them blossom in the morning that you sow,
> the harvest will flee away in a day of grief and incurable pain.
>
> (Isa 17:10–11)

Although prized for their beauty and fruitfulness, the result of careful cultivation, the "pleasant plants" will only disappoint. The cause of their demise is clear: the plants are redolent of apostasy (*zār*). The cultivation of groves for cultic practice, specifically as settings for sacrifice, evidently continued well into the Persian period, despite the prophet's and his literary successor's indictments (Isa 65:3).

The Bane of Asherah

As perceived by Isaiah and the Deuteronomists, the popularity of sacred trees and groves posed a grave challenge to centralized worship. Deuteronomy mandates the destruction of "all the places where the nations whom you shall dispossess served their gods, upon the high mountains and upon the hills and under every green tree (*'ēṣ ra'ănān*)" (Deut 12:2). The danger is particularly clear in a terse prohibition against cultic impurity:

> You shall not plant for yourself an *'ăšērâ*, any tree,
> besides an altar of YHWH your God.
>
> (Deut 16:21)

Translated as "sacred pole" in the NRSV, the *'ăšērâ* was evidently a stylized tree (real or artificial),[71] most likely related in some way to the iconographic portrayals found in Palestine and elsewhere, as discussed above. The biblical description is also suggestive: the cult object is planted, built, or erected. When destroyed, it is cut down, plucked up, uprooted, overturned, burned, or broken into pieces.[72] Some association with a goddess is evident, though to what extent remains debatable.[73] As the consort of the progenitor deity and high god El of Ugaritic lore, Athirat (Hebrew Asherah) was regarded as the fertility goddess par excellence, the creatress of the gods.[74] Although the extrabiblical literature nowhere connects Asherah specifically with a tree, the arboreal image most certainly symbolizes fertility and vegetation, which the goddess represents iconographically.[75]

Either the tree was planted beside the altar or the altar was constructed in open areas under a luxuriant tree, perhaps in part for its protective shade (see Judg 6:25). Perhaps the oldest condemnation of such practice is attested in Hosea:

> My people make inquiry with a piece of wood,
>   and their divining rod delivers oracles to them.
> For a fornicating spirit has led them astray,
>   and they have played the prostitute, forsaking their God.
> They sacrifice on the tops of mountains
>   and make offerings upon hills,
> under oak, poplar, and terebinth,
>   because their shade is good.
>
> (Hos 4:12–13)

The tree, consulted perhaps for oracles (see 2 Sam 5:24), is reduced by the prophet to its material "lifeless" quality: "wood" (see also Isa 44:13–17; Jer 2:27; 3:9). Hosea indicts his audience for conducting worship under such trees because of their shade ($ṣēl$). Whether as living tree, artificial object, or goddess image, the tree's presence within sacred space not only provoked the ire of the Deuteronomist,[76] but also warranted harsh condemnation from the prophets.[77] Such trees had to be cut down and destroyed, along with their accompanying altars and pillars ($maṣṣēbôt$; see Exod 34:13; Deut 7:5; 12:3).

Though ambiguous, the epigraphical evidence from Kuntillet 'Ajrud and Khirbet el-Qôm suggests that the '$ăšērâ$ cult object was associated with YHWH worship in popular, non-Deuteronomic form.[78] Whether simply a cult object ("his asherah") or the image of a full-fledged goddess or consort of YHWH ("his[79] Asherah"),[80] the stylized tree was deemed anathema by orthodox Yahwism. It seems that the Deuteronomists did associate '$ăšērâ$ with a goddess,[81] although many references could refer to a cult object or statue, not necessarily to the goddess herself.[82] Whether correctly or incorrectly, the Deuteronomists polemically impugned the stylized tree with Asherah worship, a case of guilt by association that elicited nothing less than outright condemnation.[83] The Chronicler, moreover, reflects direct awareness of the connection between the cult object and the goddess.[84] Perhaps, then, the polemically inspired mandates of the prophets, historiographers, and legalists were not without warrant.[85]

All in all, trees in proximity to the sanctuary held an ambivalent place in ancient Israelite faith and cultic practice. Their standing within the cult depended on the precise signification they had vis-à-vis the established Yahwistic worship.[86] If tree symbolism underscored YHWH's creative power to bless, recalling the shalom of the primordial garden, then its legitimacy was secure. Rejection was warranted, however, if the image of the arbor was at all suggestive of another deity or an alternative mode of worship. Even this criterion is not entirely clear, however, for it is uncertain whether the 'ăšērâ tree eventually condemned as heterodox by the Deuteronomists actually signified the veneration of a goddess or was simply a nonsignifying (but not insignificant) accoutrement to Yahwistic worship. In any case, a tree flourishing in the precincts of the Lord was a matter of grave contention.

A Tree in the Temple Precincts?

With all the bad press trees receive from orthodox Yahwism, particularly in association with the 'ăšērâ cult symbol, it seems rather daring that the opening psalm of the Psalter develops arboreal imagery at all (Ps 1:3). The poet's specific commendation of tôrâ, moreover, suggests some awareness of Deuteronomic legislation against the use of trees in Israel's cultic life. Deuteronomic law, coupled with prophetic condemnation, makes it highly unlikely that the poet behind Psalm 1 was naive enough as to tread blindly on theologically suspect ground. The boldness of the poet's use of arboreal imagery is all the more apparent in light of the tree's theological landscape. Possibly dependent on Ezek 47:12, which describes a feature of the prophet's grand temple vision, the rhetorical setting of the tree image in Psalm 1 has its traditio-historical home within the temple or on Zion. The special reference to *channels* of water (*palgê mayim*) in Psalm 1:3 suggests some relationship to Zion, the sanctuary of God,[87] in contrast to the parallel in Jer 17:8. Psalm 46:4 is particularly suggestive, as also 36:7–9 and 65:9, each of which employs related imagery. In each citation, river and stream are inextricably linked to Zion (cf. 65:1, 4), the mountain of God, suggesting that the reference to "channels of water" in Psalm 1 also reflects a distinctly cultic setting.[88] But in none of these passages is specific mention made of trees,[89] although the soil's fertility is most certainly implied, as in Psalm 36.[90]

Not so with Psalm 1. In light of the strident critique issued elsewhere in biblical tradition, a *Baum* within the bulwark of God is provocative. Again, given the lateness of the text and its central reference to *tôrâ*, some familiarity on the part of the poet with the negative assessment of trees in proximity to the sanctuary is reasonable to assume. Psalm 1, thus, provides an ingenious solution, proffered already in the Psalter (see below), to this intractable matter of contention. By turning the arboreal image into a metaphor, the psalmist has delimited certain possibilities of association, while generating others. The tree is not an 'ăšērâ pole or any stylized tree; it connotes rather the righteous individual who desires to "enter" into the psalmist's world of worship and study, a literary sanctuary in effect. The didactic poet has turned a controversial cultic object into an evocative metaphor, an image of apostasy transformed into an icon of righteousness.[91] The tree has taken on the identity of the worshiper, the character of one whose delight is in *tôrâ,* the reader of Psalms. Rather than indicating goddess, earth, or even the power of fertility, the tree featured at the threshold of the Psalter is *reflexive of the reader* who chooses to grow in righteousness and thereby bask in God's blessing. Not only is this tree permitted within the sphere of the holy; its presence is mandated.

THE ARBOR IN THE PSALTER'S LANDSCAPE

By choosing this evocative image—the figure of the tree with its wide range of associations—the poet has drawn deeply from the well of mythopoeic tradition to orient the reader of Psalms. The psalmist has, in effect, placed a tree at the entrance to the Psalter, at the threshold of its refuge and the head of its pathway. Perhaps most significantly, the Psalter's opening "chapter" serves to shape the Psalter *as a book,* as a sacred deposit of devotion, worship, and authoritative guidance, in short, *tôrâ.* Like the freestanding tree-pillars that flank the entrance to the temple, demarcating the sanctuary as inviolably holy, so the opening psalm delineates the Psalter as wholly instructive and comprehensively cultic in its scope. Psalm 1 replaces temple with *tôrâ.* The psalms, in effect, serve as the temple's surrogate. Moreover, like Solomon's temple, adorned with elaborate carvings of flora on its walls and doors, the tree standing at the entrance of the Psalter is a powerful image that sets in relief the plethora of botanical figures featured in the subsequent psalms, including images of withering and flourishing,[92] as well as fertility.[93] The power of the metaphor lies not only in its traditio-historical *background,* but also in its literary *foreground,* specifically in the presentations of botanical imagery featured throughout the Psalter, to which Psalm 1 orients the reader.

Of Psalms and Date Palms

Most akin to Psalm 1 and its central metaphor are two striking references to trees flourishing in the temple found elsewhere in the Psalter. As chaff is separated out from the edible grain on the threshing floor, so on Zion—the former threshing floor of Araunah, the Jebusite (2 Sam 24:18–25; cf. Isa 41:14–16)—stand the righteous as flourishing trees.

> The righteous one sprouts (*yiprah*) like a date palm (*tāmār*),
> and grows like a cedar (*'erez*) in Lebanon.
> They are transplanted (*šĕtûlîm*) in the house of YHWH;
> in the courts of our God they flourish.
> In old age they still produce;
> fat and fresh they remain,
> declaring that YHWH is upright;

> he is my rock,
>> in whom there is no unrighteousness.
>> (Ps 92:12–15)

As the most fertile place on earth, Zion is where the righteous flourish. The date palm symbolizes the vitality that defies even old age, much in contrast to the image of withering grass and mortality conveyed in Psalms 90 and 103. But woven into such a testimony of physical potency, sustained and nurtured in the garden temple, is a distinctly moral fiber. Like *tôrâ* in Psalm 1, Zion in Psalm 92 constitutes the setting or ethos for the cultivation of righteousness. Zion points to the "rock" of righteousness. God has delivered the psalmist from mortal danger, vindicating him in the presence of "evil assailants" (vv. 10–11). The source of righteousness, however, comes not from the psalmist's initiative, but from divine deliverance and beneficence. "Flourishing" in the house of YHWH is a sign of grace.

Psalm 52 features similar imagery to underscore vindication of the one who has sought "refuge in God" (v. 7):

> But I am like a leafy olive tree (*zayit ra'ănān*)
>> in the house of God.
> I trust in God's faithful love
>> forever and ever.
> I will forever thank you
>> for what you have done.
> In the presence of the faithful,
>> I will proclaim[94] your name, for it is good.
>> (52:8–9)

The psalmist, like the poet of Psalm 1, draws from imagery that is found to be suspect elsewhere in biblical tradition: the term *ra'ănān* ("leafy, fresh") is most frequently associated with pagan worship in the formula "leafy tree" (*'ēṣ ra'ănān*).[95] Again, righteousness is cultivated not as an initiative on the part of the psalmist but as a matter of divine grace and, specifically in this psalm, of *trust* in God's enduring, covenantal favor.

Both Psalms 52 and 92 find their closest analogue to Psalm 1, making explicit what is already implicit in the opening psalm, namely, that the righteous, *as trees*, have their home in Zion. As the king is set on Zion, God's holy hill, in order to bring about victory and dominion over the foreign nations that conspire "against YHWH and his anointed" (Ps 2:1–6), so the righteous are firmly planted within the temple, which serves as both a refuge and (botanical) conservatory, metaphorically a "hothouse" for growth in righteousness.

Transplantation

Finally, crucial to the message of Psalm 1 and of the Psalter as a whole, is a term shared in common by 1:3 and 92:13, "transplant" (√*štl*). The tree is not planted from seed but "*trans*planted" as a branch or shoot,[96] that is, transported from a nonspecific location into a well-specified surrounding for it to thrive. As the ancient Near Eastern kings boasted of their horticultural abilities in transplanting exotic plants from their newly conquered territories, so the psalmist speaks of God, the divine gardener, delivering and cultivating the righteous. The historical analogue to the language of horticulture is found in Psalms 44 and 80.

> We have heard with our own ears, O God,
>   our ancestors have told us,
> what deeds you performed in their days,
>   in the days of yore:
> You with your own hand drove out the nations,
>   but them you planted (*tiṭṭā'ēm*).
> You afflicted the peoples,
>   but them you set free.
>   (44:1–2)

Israel's deliverance culminates with Israel's "planting." Here, God's deed of deliverance is set in stark contrast to, and at the expense of, the nations. Israel is planted, whereas the nations, like weeds, are uprooted and cleared out. Israel is literally "set loose," while the nations suffer affliction. Similar, but more vivid, is the historical recitation and botanical construal of Israel's destination in Psalm 80.

> You brought a vine out of Egypt;
>   you drove out the nations and planted it (*tiṭṭā'ēhā*).
> You cleared the ground before it;
>   it took deep root, filling the land.
> The mountains were covered with its shade,
>   the mighty cedars with its branches.
> It sent out its branches to the sea,
>   and its shoots to the river.
>   (80:8–11)

This psalm in particular illustrates Israel's "transplanting" in graphically historical terms, encompassing within its purview the exodus, wilderness wandering, and conquest of Canaan. In its cultivation, Israel flourished to became a refuge for all the land, surpassing even the mighty cedars (literally "cedars of God ['*ēl*]") and spreading to the Euphrates to the east and the Mediterranean to the west. But, as the psalmist laments by bringing Israel's history painfully up to date, the vine turned grove has been ravaged, its walls torn down, its fruit plucked (vv. 12–13), and its wood cut down and burned as if it were an '*ăšērâ* (cf. v. 16). Greater, verdant Israel is no more. The psalmist, in effect, pleads that God once again wield a garden spade and recultivate Israel on its holy hill.[97]

The historical casting of Israel's "cultivation" elicits a new understanding of the Psalter's opening psalm, as well as its offshoots, Psalms 52 and 92. The righteous individual "transplanted" on Zion's soil is paralleled with Israel's historical passage from bondage to deliverance and, ultimately, its constitution in the land.[98] Typical of the lament psalms, wrenching descriptions of personal affliction, persecution, and physical debilitation convey realities from which the psalmist pleads to God for relief. Such conditions, too, are brought into correspondence with communal bondage and national demoralization, now individualized and personalized. In most cases, the psalmist petitions for a way to safety and restoration, culminating in a peal of praise cast within the sanctuary itself. By employing the technical term "transplanting," the poet of Psalm 1 echoes Israel's own pilgrimage of release and fulfillment, applying it to the plight of the individual, now restored and sustained by "channels of streams." In so doing, the opening psalm adumbrates the end and culmination of the Psalter itself: praise given by a restored member of the community, vindicated and vouchsafed by God.

CONCLUSION

The opening psalm, in sum, initiates a dramatic movement that contributes to the overall shape of the Psalter. The tree is transplanted beside waters that issue forth from the Psalter's (i.e., *tôrâ's*) sanctuary (1:3), marking the entrance. In Psalms 52 and 92, the tree has gained full entrance into the precincts of YHWH, flourishing within the temple itself. The righteous, moreover, have aged, reaching full maturity yet still "full of sap" and bearing fruit (92:14). Near the end of the Psalter, nestled amid peals of praise, botanical imagery has spread its shoots, as it were, to envelop the family and nation of Israel (Psalms 128, 144), while the wicked wither away like "grass on the housetops" (129:6). The psalmist's enemies, indeed all those who impede the supplicant from treading the path of life toward God's refuge, have vanished within the ever-expanding world of praise.[99] The growth of botanical imagery in the Psalter reflects the general movement of the psalms toward unobstructed reverence to God, both within and beyond the inviolable walls of God's refuge. Psalm 1 profiles, in effect, the beginning reader of Psalms as a seedling whose stalk may bend *but not break* before the God-awful wind that drives away the chaff. With continued sustenance from both stream and soil, from the life-giving power of *tôrâ*, the sapling can grow to unprecedented heights of moral maturity and blessedness. In the poet's earth-clotted hands, the declaration of blessing (*'ašrê*) has replaced the adoration of *'ăšērâ*, while the blessings associated with *'ăšērâ* are directly transferred to the one deemed *'ašrê*.[100] Put another way, by shifting the arboreal metaphor's target domain from deity to *tôrâ's* disciple, the psalmist rejects the *'ăšērâ* association while retaining the metaphor's *'ašrê* significance. An image of apostasy is, consequently, transformed into an icon of righteousness. The metaphor is transferred, and a tree is transplanted.

The palm tree of Ps 92:12, too, has its way, its journey, held in God's palm and carried from danger and desiccation to the fertile land of peace and flowing streams. The tree is planted in shalom—in the blessing of Zion and, so in Psalm 1, in the sustenance of *tôrâ*—cultivated to cover the mountains under its protective shade, as the waters cover the sea (80:10–11; cf. Isa 11:9). So let the reader understand, the psalmist beckons, and choose the path of life that leads to the sanctuary garden, to *tôrâ*.

Chapter 4

The Sun of Righteousness

Psalm 19 and the Joy of Lex

It was not without good reason that C. S. Lewis considered Psalm 19 to be "the greatest poem in the Psalter and one of the greatest lyrics in the world."[1] Bursting at the seams with hymnic power, the psalm limns a world rife with myth and metaphor in order to advance a particular theological agenda, namely, the elevation of *tôrâ*. As in our investigation of Psalm 1, attention will be focused on identifying the psalm's central image and mapping the web of associations it generates both within and beyond this psalm.

TRANSLATION

To the leader, a psalm of David:

1 The heavens are telling the glory of God;
    and the firmament is proclaiming his handiwork.
2 Day to day discharges speech;
    and night to night imparts knowledge.
3 Though there is no speech, nor are there words

—their sound cannot be heard—
4 yet throughout all the earth their "lines"[2] extend outward,[3]
   so also their words to the end of the world.
For the sun, [God] has set a tent in the heavens.
5 Like a bridegroom, it bursts out of its wedding canopy;
   like an athlete, it rejoices in sprinting [its] course.
6 From one end of the heavens is its rising,
   and its circuit is complete at the other.
There is nothing hidden from its heat.

7 The *tôrâ* of YHWH is complete (*tĕmîmâ*),
   reviving the soul.
The testimony of YHWH is sure (*ne' ĕmānâ*),
   imparting wisdom to the simple.
8 The precepts of YHWH are straight (*yĕšārîm*),
   gladdening the heart.
The commandment of YHWH is lucid (*bārâ*),
   giving light to the eyes.
9 Reverence of YHWH is radiant (*ṭĕhôrâ*),
   enduring forever.
The ordinances of YHWH are firm (*'ĕmet*),
   altogether righteous.
10 They are more desirable than gold,
   more than abundant fine gold,
      sweeter also than honey, the drippings of the honeycomb.

11 Indeed, your servant is enlightened (*nizhār*) by them;
   in observing them there is great reward.
12 Who can discern [my] errors?
   From hidden sins clear me!
13 Even from presumptuous thoughts[4] deliver your servant;
   let them not gain mastery over me.
Then I will become blameless (*'êtām*[5]),
   and innocent of great transgression.

14 May the words of my mouth be a pleasing offering;
   and the meditation of my heart be acceptable to you,
   YHWH, my rock and redeemer.

Psalm 19 is easily divisible into three sections according to theme, style, and meter. Verses 1–6 depict creation as the cosmic medium of God's glory, whereas vv. 7–10 identify the moral and salutary contours of *tôrâ*. The final verses, signaled by the language of direct address, offer a petition. The psalm's very divisibility has caused many a biblical scholar to wonder about its literary integrity. Not unexpectedly, the case has been made that these parts were originally two, if not three, discrete pieces, the first adapted from an ancient Canaanite hymn to the sun, and the second, an ode to *tôrâ* culminating with a prayer.[6]

Such an accounting of the psalm's formation is plausible enough, but it would be a mistake to claim from such a diachronic reading that these discrete parts have been *artificially* linked.[7] To the contrary, the choice of metaphor and terminology suggests a remarkably tight coherence that cuts across the literary divisions and, at the same time, undercuts the modern, rational tendency to bifurcate nature and law.[8] Elsewhere in the Psalter, one finds cosmos and *tôrâ* inseparably bound together (e.g., 119:89; 147:15–20). In Psalm 19, however, it is a single cosmological image that holds the key to the psalm's unity and message, which can be demonstrated in the following outline and analysis:

I.   God's Cosmic Discourse: **Celestial Glory**   Verses 1–6
     A.   The Celestial Glory of God   1–4a
          1.   Heavens   1
          2.   Day and Night   2
          3.   Emanating speech   3–4a
     B.   The Trek of the **Sun**   4b–6
          1.   Abode   4b
          2.   Course   5–6a
          3.   Heat   6b

II. God's Instructive Discourse: **Tôrâ**   Verses 7–10
     A.   Moral Nature   7aα, 7bα, 8aα, 8bα, 9aα, 9bβ, 10
     B.   Salutary Effects   7aβ, 8aβ, 7bβ, 8bβ

III. Prayer for Purgation   Verses 11–14
     A.   Benefits of Instruction   11
     B.   Petition for Purgation   12–13
     C.   Petition for Prayer   14

The psalm progresses from the top down, beginning with the heavenly realm, and concludes with an earthly petitioner. The heavens and the firmament—the realm of transcendence bounded by the domed sky—erupt with discursive power, proclaiming God's glory. Cosmic speech runs unceasingly as day addresses day and night speaks to night. The kind of discourse the psalmist records is not the background hiss of microwave radiation emanating from outer space. True contact, rather, is established by the veritable explosion of communication that occurs on a daily basis, no less. Such discursive drama is conveyed phonetically in the first part of v. 2b: *yôm lĕyom yabbîaʿ* ("day-to-day discharges")! The verb literally means to "gush forth." In the case of the fool's discourse, it describes the fool's mouth "belching forth" folly (Prov 15:2; cf. v. 28). More akin to an erupting geyser than to background static, cosmic speech is "discharged," and the "lines" or rays that emanate throughout all creation constitute the medium of communication. The primal divisions of time itself (cf. Genesis 1) erupt with testimony of God's glory (*kābôd*). Day and night, the heavens and the firmament, all have a "voice" in bearing witness to God's praiseworthy presence.

Yet such discourse, the psalmist acknowledges, is inaudible. There is speech, but unlike anything within earshot. The celestial voices are perceived *visually*.

Creation's voice cannot be heard; it is beheld. This paradox of the visual, yet silent voice begs the question: What is the vehicle for this nonverbal discourse of the cosmos that issues forth to the ends of the earth?[9] The answer is given in Ps 19:4–6, where the psalmist focuses on a single image, one that, in fact, has all to do with the regular rhythm of day and night. Literarily the sun constitutes the psalm's central, governing image. It serves as a bridge that unites the various literary components, thereby conjoining the discursive rhythms of the cosmos with the moral contours of *tôrâ*. In its perceived revolutions, the sun constitutes the vehicle of cosmic discourse, most evocatively cast in metaphor: like a bridegroom and an athlete, the sun bursts out of its wedding chamber to run its course across the sky (v. 5). The fiery orb explodes upon the scene with virility and joy as it arcs from one end of the heavens to the other, penetrating all hidden things. The day is its victory lap; the night is its sabbath. Yet the question remains: What kind of discourse is transmitted by the sun? Whatever it is, it is an inaudible voice turned vibrant and visual.

DEUS PRAESENS: THE BACKGROUND OF SOLAR IMAGERY

Requisite to examining the psalm's iconic texture is familiarity with the contextual milieu of its most central image. Although the sun's prominence in this *tôrâ* psalm may seem peculiar to modern readers, the presence of solar imagery in religious discourse is hardly innovative, particularly in light of other psalmic and ancient Near Eastern testimonies.

Solar Presence in the Psalms

In psalmic tradition and elsewhere, the *deus praesens* is typically depicted as an effulgence of light or solar theophany.[10] Several psalms, for example, associate "seeing God" or "God's face"[11] with light or shining.[12] In addition to storm imagery, deployed to convey the dramatic, fear-inspiring experience of the *mysterium tremendum*,[13] light, too, bears an intimate association with God, as seen in the following examples:

> YHWH is my light (*'ôr*) and my salvation;
>   whom shall I fear?
> YHWH is the stronghold of my life;
>   of whom shall I be afraid?
>
> (27:1)

> Send out your light (*'ôr*) and your truth;
>   let them lead me.
> Let them bring me to your holy hill
>   and to your dwelling.
>
> (43:3)

> You are clothed with honor and majesty,
>> wrapped in light (*'ôr*) as with a garment.
>> (104:1b–2a)

In Psalm 43, God's "light" is given didactic nuance in its pairing with "truth," both of which are personified as guardians of the wayfarer. Evocative also is the poetic juxtaposition of God's "garment" and "light" in Psalm 104. Psalm 63, moreover, contains a wordplay that gives a radiant cast to God's sanctuary presence:

> O God, my God you are; I seek you (*'ăšaḥărekā*).
>> My soul thirsts for you.
> . . . .
> So I have looked upon you in the sanctuary,
>> beholding your power and glory.
>> (63:1a, 2)

In this pilgrim psalm,[14] the verb "to seek" (√*sḥr*) is the verbal denominative form for the noun "dawn" (*šaḥar*), identifying the break of day as the rhetorical setting for the psalmist's longing for God.[15] Similarly, in an ancient snippet of coronation liturgy, the Judean king is instructed by a court prophet to go forth "out of the womb, toward the dawn" (110:3), that is, into the presence of God for investiture by the divine King.[16] Such a rendering of this difficult verse has broad Canaanite precedent. In a letter written in Ugaritic, a certain Talmiyanu recounts his visit to the king: "My mother, you must know that I came before the Sun (*šapš*), and the face of the Sun shone on me greatly."[17] The image of the sun was versatile enough to target both heavenly and earthly kings.[18] Finally, it is no accident that Psalm 46, a Zion psalm, associates God's saving presence with the dawn:

> God is in the midst of [the city];
>> it shall not be moved.
> God will help it at the break of dawn (*lipnôt bōqer*).[19]
>> (46:5)

From the psalmist's perspective, the image of the sun heralds, if not bears, God's deliverance of Jerusalem/Zion.[20] Similarly, from the pious perspective of an individual in a pilgrimage to the temple, the speaker of Psalm 17 associates divine epiphany ("face") with the psalmist's awakening:

> Rise up, YHWH, confront them,
>> overthrow them!
> By your word deliver my life from the wicked.
> . . . .
> As for me,
>> in righteousness I shall behold your face (*'eḥĕzeh pānêkā*);
> when I awake (*bĕhāqîṣ*),
>> I shall be satisfied with your likeness (*tĕmûnâ*).[21]
>> (17:13, 15)

Whether from the standpoint of the pilgrim or from the corporate voice of the nation, God's saving presence is conveyed by the sun's dawning light. In such texts, solar imagery evokes the luminescent embodiment of divine presence that dispels the chaos of darkness.

Many, if not all, of the psalms cited above presuppose a sanctuary setting.[22] To the list one can add Psalm 80, which enlists solar imagery to illumine the innermost recess of the temple, the *dĕbîr*, with God's effulgent presence:[23]

> Listen, O Shepherd of Israel,
>   you who lead Joseph like a flock!
> You who are enthroned upon the cherubim,
>   shine forth (*hôpî'â*)[24] before Ephraim, Benjamin,
>   and Manasseh.
> Stir up your might and come to save us!
>   Restore us, O God.
> Let your face shine (*hā'ēr*) that we may be saved.
>   (80:1–3)

Emanating from the temple, God's epiphany is invoked by the psalmist to bring about Israel's deliverance from the "boar . . . that ravages" Israel (v. 13a). God's solar power is salvific and just. Emblazoned with light, the "God of vengeance" is called on to "shine forth" to punish the wicked (94:1). As "the perfection of beauty, God shines forth (*hôpî'â*)" from Zion to execute justice (50:2).

Conveying the psalmist's deep longing for an experience of God in Zion, Psalm 84 unapologetically solarizes YHWH.

> For a day in your courts is better
>   than a thousand elsewhere.
> I would rather be a doorkeeper in the house of my God
>   than live in the tents of wickedness.
> For YHWH God is Sun and Shield (*šemeš ûmāgēn*);[25]
>   he bestows favor and honor.
> No good thing does YHWH withhold
>   from those who walk uprightly.
>   (84:10–11)

The solar imagery directly "targets" the protective deity (v. 11a). Nearly an epithet, "Sun" operates on much the same rhetorical level as the more frequently attested metaphor for God, "rock" (see chapter 1). The association of the sun with divine presence, in short, has its home in royal temple theology.

Sun Worship in Israel?

Critical confirmation of a solar cult operating within the precincts of the temple can be found in the harsh polemics of the Deuteronomistic history and Ezekiel.[26] Among his various cultic reforms, "[Josiah] removed the horses that the kings of Judah had devoted to the sun . . . ; then he burned with fire the chariots of the sun (*markkĕbôt haššemeš*)" (2 Kgs 23:11; cf. v. 5). Up until the late seventh century B.C.E.,[27] standard royal practice evidently included a display of solar symbols at the entrance to the temple. The image of a solar chariot, derived from the ancient idea that the sun was a wheel turning through the heavens, is already attested in the story of the chariot of fire that carried Elijah up to the heavens.[28] Archaeological remains also attest an apparently related motif: numerous horse figurines with what appear to be a sun disk situated above their heads have been discovered at Iron Age levels in Lachish, Hazor, and Jerusalem.[29]

Also well known is the tenth-century cult stand from Taanach, discovered in a cistern shaft by Paul Lapp in 1968. (See fig. 9.) In its uppermost register or tier is displayed a sun disk situated above the body of a quadruped, most likely a horse. The scene may correspond to the second register from the bottom, which features an empty space flanked by two cherubs, perhaps to convey the invisible deity.[30] In any case, equine and solar imagery are intimately associated. Moreover, if Keel and Uehlinger are correct in contending that all four registers convey a sense of graded holiness from bottom to top, then the top register would most closely represent the inner sanctum or most holy domain (cf. Ps 80:2–3, translated above).[31]

To these attestations of solar iconography can be added various seals and stamps found in Palestine that feature a winged sun-disk, such as the two-sided *šbnyw* seal (shown in fig. 10) and the *lmlk* seals of the eighth and early seventh centuries B.C.E., both of royal provenance.[32] Iconography of the winged sun, moreover, was widespread from Egypt to Mesopotamia, including Phoenicia and, to a lesser degree, Israel.[33] An enameled tile from the reign of the ninth-century Assyrian monarch Tukulti-Ninurta II, for example, depicts the god Assur riding the winged sun-disk with drawn bow aimed, presumably, at the king's enemies.[34] (See fig. 11.)

The reference to YHWH as "Sun and Shield" (Ps 84:11a) evokes a comparable sense of militant might and protection. Furthermore, the motif of divine wings, widespread in the Psalter,[35] may also bear some connection with a solarized, as well as ornithologized, depiction of YHWH.[36]

The other biblical example of a polemic directed against solarized worship is found in Ezekiel. The prophet looks with disgust as he beholds in a vision certain abominable temple practices, including one involving solar worship:

> There, at the entrance of the temple of YHWH, between the porch and the altar, were about twenty-five men, with their backs to the temple of YHWH and their faces toward the east, prostrating themselves to the sun toward the east. (Ezek 8:16)

Typical of Syrian-Palestinian cultic architecture, the east-west orientation of the Jerusalem temple lent itself to such practice,[37] in distinction from the northern orientation of temple sites that seem to reflect storm-god worship, such as Temple H in Hazor.[38] As the sun rose over the Mount of Olives, it invariably struck the temple's main entrance, penetrating and illuminating the gilded interior,

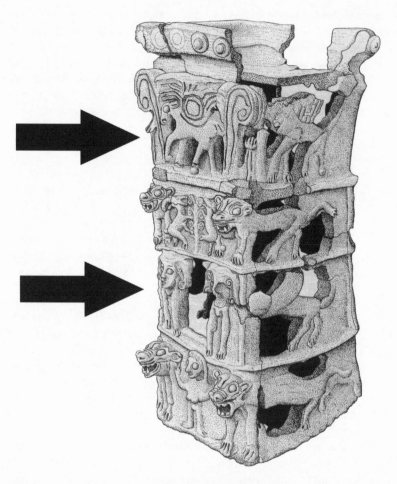

Fig. 9: Cult stand from tenth-century Taanach with registers 2 and 4 designated. Reproduced with permission from Mohr Siebeck and featured in Kurt Galling, ed., *Biblisches Reallexikon*, HAT 1,1 (2d ed.; Tübingen: J. C. B. Mohr, 1977), 191, #45 (3).

marking the dramatic arrival of divine glory. Given its eastern orientation, the temple in effect routinized and enshrined what was historiographically conveyed in the earliest reference to a solar epiphany in the Hebrew Bible:

> YHWH came from Sinai,
>   and dawned (*zāhar*) from Seir upon us.
> He shone forth (*hôpîaʿ*) from Mount Paran.
> With him were myriads of holy ones,
>   at his right, a host of his own.
>   (Deut 33:2)

This hymnic poem, likely predating the existence of the temple, describes YHWH's entrance into Canaan from Sinai across the southeastern highlands of Edom ("Seir") as a solar theophany.

The evidence suggests that the use of solar imagery was indigenous to temple worship during much of the monarchic period. While it fell out of favor under Josiah's reign, it persisted in some form until the temple's destruction and continued among more popular circles through the Persian and Hellenistic periods.[39] The sun, moreover, continued to provide an especially evocative image of God's saving presence, as attested in Malachi:

> But for you who revere my name,
>   the sun of righteousness (*šemeš ṣĕdākâ*)
> shall arise (*wĕzārĕḥâ*) with healing in its wings.
>   (Mal 4:2a [3:20a, Heb.])

Nothing less than a solar theophany is invoked by the prophet, one that confers the salutary benefits of healing and protection on the righteous yet issues searing judgment against "evildoers," a day "burning like an oven" (4:1 [3:19, Heb.]).

READING PSALM 19

While solar imagery in the Psalms and elsewhere in biblical tradition typically presupposes the setting and ethos of the temple, Psalm 19 fails to exploit the connection. The voice of royal temple ideology, so prominent in the psalms of vigil, is mute. Instead, the psalmist redirects the reader's attention to the efficacy of

Fig. 10: Second side of the *šbnyw* seal from Palestine. Reprinted with permission from Othmar Keel and Christoph Uehlinger, *Gods, Goddesses, and Images of God in Ancient Israel*, trans. Thomas H. Trapp (Minneapolis: Fortress, 1998), 263 (#263b). Courtesy of the Department of Biblical Studies, University of Fribourg.

Fig. 11: Enameled brick fragment from Assur of the god Assur riding a winged sundisk. Reprinted with permission from Othmar Keel, *Die Welt der altorientalischen Bildsymbolik und das Alte Testament. Am Beispiel der Psalmen* (Cologne: Benziger Verlag / Neukirchen-Vluyn: Neukirchener Verlag, 1972), 195 (#295). Courtesy of the Department of Biblical Studies, University of Fribourg.

tôrâ. The move from a cosmic to a constitutional frame of reference is hardly abrupt, for solar imagery holds together both thematic frameworks. Moreover, the sun serves as the linchpin that unites two movements of reading: one that maintains the reader's attention to solar imagery in the *tôrâ* section that follows, and one that looks back to the sun through the lens of *tôrâ*. Law and sun, in effect, operate as two distinct yet interrelated filters through which to read and understand the psalm. The first movement involves the normal process of reading "forward" from sun to *tôrâ;* the second entails reading "backward," or rereading solar imagery from the perspective of *tôrâ*. Both indicate reading strategies elicited by the psalm through its creative, interactive use of metaphor. From a poetics standpoint, the psalm offers a dramatic illustration of mutually mapping metaphors.

Reading Forward

Burning brightly and exposing every "hidden" thing at the conclusion of the first section, the sun also shines on *tôrâ*. Illuminating the "law" as its target, solar imagery turns explicitly metaphorical in the second section. As the sun, full of strength and exuding joy, makes its trek across the domed sky, penetrating the darkness with its rays, so *tôrâ* performs an enlivening and purifying function for the reader.

Iconographic Precedents.

The quickening role the sun exercises in Psalm 19 is comparable to the sun's significance in the iconographic and hymnic representations that proliferated during the New Kingdom period in Egypt, as well as in Mesopotamian ritual prayers codified between 1500 and 1000 B.C.E.[40] A cursory glance at the solar iconography commissioned during the reign of Akhenaton ("Effective for Aten"), or Amenhotep IV (ca. 1353–1336), is instructive if only to highlight what is common and at the same time distinctive in the way the psalmist makes use of solar imagery in the psalm. Marking a "demythification" and depersonalization of the divine realm,[41] the "New Solar Theology" developed under the so-called heretic king of Egypt iconographically features a solar disk whose light (Aten) emanates in the form of penetrating rays,[42] each of which terminates in a hand.[43] (See fig. 12.) As can be seen, some of the solar beams hold ankh signs, which symbolize the giving of life.

Fig. 12: Relief of royal family of Amenophis IV Akhenaton from Tell el-Amarna. Egyptian Museum, Cairo, Egypt. Copyright Erich Lessing / Art Resource, New York.

Originally a war god who marched before the king to give him victory, Aten was thoroughly solarized by Akhenaton and conceived as the guarantor of creation's daily renewal. The solar disk embodied a new theology of *creatio continuata,* which found fulsome expression in the Great Hymn to the Aten.[44] Although this hymn primarily celebrates the universal expanse of the sun's rays, imparting life to all creation,[45] the iconographic medium depicts the solar beams extending exclusively to Pharaoh and his family, conferring rejuvenating power. Indeed, Akhenaton often styled himself as the "beautiful child of the living Aten,"[46] an informal title matched by depictions of the childlike king on amulets during this period.[47]

In addition to its life-giving rays, the Egyptian sun god exhibits another defining characteristic comparable to the psalmist's depiction of the sun, namely, *movement.* The Leiden Amun Hymn is most evocative:[48]

> How "passing over" (*ḏ3j*) you are, Harakhty,
>   completing your task of yesterday every day.
> The one who creates the years. . . ,
>   the hours correspond to his stride.
> You are newer today than yesterday,
>   while passing the night you are already set upon the day.
> . . . .
> Swift of stride with shooting rays,
>   who circumnavigates the earth in a moment,
>   all being accessible to him.
>   (Lines 1–3, 13–14)

The sun's movement is characterized by rejuvenating strength and speed, a power that "creates" time itself.[49]

Equal to the dynamic, solar power that irradiates the earth and imparts life through its "shooting rays," solar imagery in Psalm 19 exudes strength and endurance as it sprints across the heavens and casts its heat upon the earth. In the second section, the sun's rays are redirected toward *tôrâ,* the divine word. As the rays or "lines" that emanate from the heavens *communicate* God's glory (v. 4a), so the sun illuminates and enhances the efficacy of *tôrâ,* which imparts wisdom.[50] God's precepts and ordinances reflect, as it were, the communicative power of the celestial world, the sun in particular, thereby enlightening the one who appropriates *tôrâ.*

The Solar Power of Tôrâ

The litany of predicates that structure the second section of Psalm 19 limn the efficacy of *tôrâ.* Under the light of the sun, the distinctly moral qualities ascribed to *tôrâ* are given new focus and more brilliant nuance.[51] The adjective *bārâ* (√*brr*) in v. 8b, for example, connotes moral purity as well as physical cleanness,[52] an appropriate description of codified commandments. But charged with solar imagery, a new level of significance comes to light. Taking on a more cosmic (and pedagogical) scope, *tôrâ* is enabled to impart "light to the eyes" (see LXX *tēlaugēs,*

Vulgate *lucidum*). The same can be said of the semantic equivalent *ṭĕhôrâ* (from √*ṭhr*) in v. 10, which also connotes ceremonial cleanness and moral purity.[53] But here, the term can connote physical luster, as it does also in connection with the gold furnishings of the tabernacle.[54] *Tôrâ*, in short, is irradiated.

Other qualifiers in this section stress *tôrâ*'s "perfection" (*tĕmîmâ*, v. 7a) and reliability (*ne'ĕmānâ*, v. 7b; *'ĕmet*, v. 9b), which become all the more suggestive when underscored by the rhetorical power of solar imagery. *Tôrâ* is as sure and efficacious as the sun's daily rising. *Tôrâ*'s "perfection" lies in its completeness and sufficiency, analogous to the sun's completion of its daily trek (v. 6). Under the light of the sun, *tôrâ* becomes cosmically expansive and totalizing in its scope. Like the sun, nothing is hidden from its purview, as the psalmist declares from a poignantly personal standpoint: "Your servant is enlightened (*nizhār*) by [your ordinances]. . . . From hidden sins clear me!" (vv. 11a, 12b). Indeed, the verb *zhr* functions as a *double entendre*. The psalmist is both "warned" (*zhr* I) and "given light" (*zhr* II), hence, prescriptively *enlightened*.[55] As much as the sun penetrates the world with its all-encompassing light (v. 6), *tôrâ* searches out the dark impulses of the soul, leaving nothing outside its purview, to purify the suppli-cant.

Finally, the divinely ordained precepts are described as "upright" (*yĕšārîm*, v. 8a), a moral quality that also bears a physically dimensional nuance, namely, "straightness" (√*yšr*). The latter characterization is particularly highlighted by *tôrâ*'s cosmic counterpart in the first section, specifically the "lines" that emanate from the celestial bodies that populate the temporal domains of day and night (v. 4a). Straight as a measuring line (*qaw*) are the precepts of YHWH. There is, the psalmist suggests, a distinctly "linear" quality to *tôrâ*. Straight and true is God's guidance, giving direction, as well as imparting life, to those who follow its mandates.

Such correlations between the seemingly disparate parts of the psalm reveal the psalmist's aim to enlist the life-sustaining, directive power of solar imagery for augmenting *tôrâ*'s restorative power, which "revives the soul" (*mĕšîbat nepeš*, v. 7a) and imparts wisdom (*maḥkîmat*, v. 7b). The enlivening function of *tôrâ* is fully consonant with and underscored by the image of the sun profiled in the first half of the psalm. As the sun, cast in the image of an athlete or warrior (*gibbôr*),[56] exudes energy and strength, so *tôrâ* imparts renewed vigor.[57] Through the "law," one is rejuvenated for the task of obedience and empowered to follow the pre-scribed path of righteousness, which is cosmically forged.

Solar imagery, in sum, sheds new light on the attributes of *tôrâ*. Like the sun, *tôrâ* "revives the soul" (v. 7a); its precepts gladden the heart (v. 8a); and its com-mandment "enlightens" the eyes (v. 8b). Israel's *tôrâ* is as lucid and firmly estab-lished in the heart of the community as the sun is radiant and permanently fixed in the heavens. As the dawn's radiance dispels the darkness, making possible even perception itself (Gen 1:3–4), as day and night impart knowledge (Ps 19:2), so *tôrâ* "imparts wisdom" and, more broadly, informs and guides the conduct of the com-munity that reveres its creator (vv. 7, 9). As the sun is superlative in might, ruling the day, so *tôrâ* is a source of moral strength and the supreme object of delight, surpassing material wealth and sensual delights. This law, the psalmist contends, is no burden; it is rendered effulgent with prescriptive, enlivening power. *Tôrâ* quickens the languishing soul and the morally dead. Like the temple's gilded interior reflecting the dawn, *tôrâ* imparts power, figuratively solar power, to the reader of psalms, providing new impetus for *tôrâ*-piety. Analogous to the cosmos, *tôrâ*'s discursive power imparts nothing short of divine glory and strength.

Reading Backward

If reading forward highlights the soteriological and solarized dimensions of "law," rereading the first section of the psalm heightens the moral character of the sun. By explicating *tôrâ* in solarized fashion, the psalmist also turns the tables on the readerly process by inviting reflection on how the sun reflects *tôrâ*'s ethos, prompting a rereading of the first section in light of the second. If the commandment of YHWH gives "light to the eyes," as the psalmist claims (v. 8; cf. 119:105), then all of creation should look different, including even the sun, the cosmic object of the poet's reflection. The distinctly moral qualities ascribed to *tôrâ* in the second section provide some of the brilliant hues with which the sun's image is portrayed in the first.

Iconographic Precedents

The traditio-historical and theological relationship between solar imagery and moral prescription is by no means an innovation on the psalmist's part. The link between sun and law clearly predates the psalm by at least a millennium. In Mesopotamia, the sun god Šamaš was considered the source and preserver of the social order.[58] The famous stele that features the Code of Hammurabi, for example, depicts the Babylonian sun god giving the law (or commissioning its codification) to Hammurabi (ca. 1792–1750 B.C.E.).[59] Šamaš bears the epithet "great judge of heaven and earth" (*dajānum rabîm ša šamê u erṣetim*). In Hammurabi's words, "By the order of Šamaš, the great judge of heaven and earth, may my justice (*mîšarum*) prevail in the land."[60] As a devotee of Šamaš, Hammurabi refers to himself as the "king of justice (*šar mîšarim*), to whom Šamaš committed law."[61] As the god's representative, Hammurabi takes on solar attributes: he is the "sun of Babylon, who causes light to go forth (*mušeṣi nūrim*) over the lands of Sumer and Akkad,"[62] himself rising "like the sun-god Šamaš over the black-headed [people] ... to illuminate the land,"[63] establishing "law and justice (*kittam u mîšaram*)."[64]

Less vainglorious is a bilingual incantation prayer used in the *bît rimki* ("House of the Ritual Bath") series, designed to purify and protect the king from contamination.[65] Although a prayer of purification, legal terminology characterizes much of the petition. The assisting exorcist, for example, proclaims to Šamaš, "You resolve conflicting testimony as if it were one," after which the king implores the deity, "Stand in judgment upon my case this day, illumine my darkness, clear up my confusion."[66] The judicial character of the sun is by no means limited to royal discourse, however. An Akkadian prayer against ghosts proclaims Šamaš as the "judge of heaven and earth," who "judge[s] the case of the oppressed man and woman" and "administer[s] their verdicts."[67] The supplicant, like the king, petitions Šamaš to judge his own case (line 17). In the *Šurpu* ("incineration") incantations, whose purpose is to purge the petitioner of sin, is the following reference to the judicial duties of the sun god:

> Be it released, Šamaš, lord of above and below . . .
> You are the one who deals out justice to the gods;
>   you are king of all lands.
> Through your command let justice be done;
>   may there be justice in his land befo[re you].[68]

In this ritualized petition for personal purity, the solar deity is singled out for praise precisely as the one who exacts justice in the land.

That solar imagery is used to promote justice and righteousness in the land is also a feature of Egyptian royal ideology. Certain throne names, for example, link social order (*m3't*) with the sun god Re.[69] The solar deity, whose strength is displayed in the eviction of evil and darkness from the land,[70] is frequently given the epithet "Lord of justice" (*nb m3't*).[71] In Egyptian lore, the cosmic opponent to the solar deity's salvific activity is Apopis, the monster serpent of the night, who is ever poised to attack Re's barque and prevent his daily rising. The struggle between the sun god and Apopis is not so much an issue over cosmic might as it is a matter of reestablishing justice and order in the land.[72] Within the judicial realm, Amun-Re's beneficence is indicated in the deity's advocacy for the poor:

> Amun-Re, who first was king,
> The god of earliest time,
> The vizier *(ṯ3tj)* of the poor.
> He does not take bribes from the guilty;
> He does not look at him who promises;
> Amun judges the land with his fingers.[73]

As in Mesopotamian religion and lore, the Egyptian solar deity acts as both *Retter und Richter,* savior and judge.[74]

The Prescriptive Power of the Sun

In a similar vein, biblical texts outside the Psalter develop the connection between solar imagery and divine justice or judgment.[75] Particularly dramatic is an indictment in Zephaniah:

> YHWH in [the city's] midst is righteous;
>   he does no wrong.
> Morning by morning he renders judgment,
>   at dawn (*lā'ôr*) without fail.
>   (Zeph 3:5*)

The execution of God's justice is signaled by the sun's daily rising

Though capitalizing on the connection between the sun and divinely wrought justice, the psalmist is far from depicting the sun in the manner found in the iconography of the Hammurabi Code or, more strikingly, in the Sippar Tablet Relief, which commemorates the restoration of the cult of Šamaš during the reign of the Babylonian king Nabu-apla-iddina (885–852 B.C.E.).[76] (See fig. 13.)

The pertinent epigraph of the Sippar Tablet Relief, located above the three small figures on the left side advancing toward Šamaš, reads: "Image of the great lord Šamaš, who resides in the Ebabbara, in the midst of Sippar land." In the middle of the relief is a sun-disk emblem suspended on a stand with four rays and four sets of wavy lines, symbolizing the four quadrants of the earth and/or the four cosmic rivers. Behind the disk stands a canopy, representing the vault of the highest heavens, within which the cult statue, or personified figure of the sun, is magnificently enthroned over the watery abyss (*apsu*). Šamaš is depicted as a bearded figure wearing a tiara with four rows of horns and holding the symbols of Babylonian rulership. Iconographically, the relief distinguishes between the cult image (*ṣalmu*) of the god, enthroned within the canopy, and the sun-disk emblem (*nipḫu*, which is guided by reins held by a two-headed serpent-man, identified as the sun god's chief constable.

Whereas the earthly king Hammurabi assumes the role of lawgiver, installed by the sun god, it is YHWH who is the lawgiver in Psalm 19 and in the Sinai narratives of the Pentateuch.[77] As supplicant, the "servant" of the psalm's final section is the receiver, "enlightened" by *tôrâ*. The psalm, moreover, makes no dis-

Fig. 13: Iconographic relief from the tablet of Šamaš from Sippar. © Copyright the British Museum.

tinction between constable and cult image. It is YHWH who sets the sun in its tent and along its ordained path. In contrast to the Šamaš of the Sippar relief, the sun of Psalm 19 resides only temporarily in a tent for its nocturnal rest and runs its heavenly trek (*'ōraḥ*) literally in the heat of the day.

Nevertheless, the image of the tent connotes much more than simply tempo-rary residence. First noted by Gunkel, the metaphorical background of the sun's tent (*'ōhel*) or canopy (*ḥuppâ*)[78] is likely a vestige of the Mesopotamian myth of the sun-god's repose with his spouse.[79] The psalmist, thus, has charged *tôrâ*-piety with potency, including sexual potency, yet in a radically mixed way. In contrast to the pictorial motif of Šamaš rising from the "great mountain" (*šadû rabû*),[80] with rays emanating from his arms and shoulders, the sun of the psalmist exits a "tent" at the break of dawn. Given the psalm's broader emphasis on *tôrâ*, this image could easily allude to the "tent" of the tabernacle, specifically the priestly *'ōhel hā'ēdut* ("tent of the testimony"),[81] in which the ark and the tablets of the law were traditionally considered to be held. One can only speculate, but it is such speculation that is deliberately provoked by the psalmist's masterful use of metaphor.

In any case, through the filter of *tôrâ*, the sun becomes reinscribed as a cipher of righteousness. As *tôrâ* is solarized, to put it crassly, so the sun is "torasized," that is, recast as an object of moral reflection and a figure of righteousness. The overtly moral language used to describe *tôrâ* as "upright" or "straight" ($\sqrt{yšr}$, v. 8a) and "righteous" ($\sqrt{ṣdq}$, v. 9b) is cosmically illustrated in the *prescribed* move-ment of the sun across the heavens. The reference to the sun's "trek" or "path" (*'ōraḥ*) in v. 6 can connote moral, faithful conduct.[82] Figuratively, the sun mod-els the path ordained by God that all are to follow, as stipulated in the so-called "Psalm of the Law" (Ps 119:3, 15, 37): "How fortunate are those who keep God's decrees . . . who also do no wrong, but walk in God's ways" (vv. 2–3). The sun, thus, provides cosmic inspiration for following, literally, the path of *tôrâ*. More-over, the sun does more than walk its ordained path. It sprints![83] Like the sun, the follower of *tôrâ* displays strength, joy, and penetrating discernment. "I run (*'ārûṣ*) the way (*derek*) of your commandments, for you enlarge my understand-ing," the psalmist boasts to God in 119:32. Like an athlete, the reader is to abide by *tôrâ* with untiring alacrity, rejuvenated by the enlivening spirit—symbolized by the sun—that pulses through every ordinance and precept of God's *tôrâ*. The sun not only evokes the ethos and efficacy of *tôrâ;* it also embodies and models *tôrâ*-piety.

THE PURIFICATION OF THE INDIVIDUAL

Progressing from the cosmic to the social order, Psalm 19 would not be complete without overt reference to the individual, in this case a petitioner. The psalmist is at once illumined and admonished by the precepts of the "law" (v. 11). Such "enlightenment" entails purgation. Following hard on the heels of v. 11 is the psalmist's fervent prayer that he or she be cleared of *hidden* faults (v. 12), recalling the pure radiance of the sun, which penetrates every *hidden* thing (v. 6b).

Iconographic Precedents

The deployment of solar images in the rhetoric of discernment and purgation has strong precedent in certain Mesopotamian prayers and hymns. In an incantation prayer, again from the *bît rimki* series, the king declares that the sun god Šamaš is a "purifier of god and man."[84] In another prayer from the same series, the exorcist highlights the deity's discerning powers:

> O Shamash, you are greatest of leaders,
>   judge of heaven and earth.
> Whatever is (secret) in the heart is spoken out [before you?];
>   all people's passing thoughts speak (as if aloud) to you.
> You strike down instantly the party in the wrong,
>   you single out truth and justice.[85]

The sun's judicial character is evinced in its capacity to expose unspoken thoughts, bringing them into the realm of retribution and, thereby, delivering the victim from affliction or danger.[86] The scrutinizing power of Šamaš, "the penetrator of darkness, illuminator of the wide world,"[87] is as cosmically extensive[88] as it is inwardly discerning, probing the very depths of the human heart. "At the brightness of your light, humankind's footprints become vis[ible]," proclaims the Šamaš Hymn.[89] The imperceptible traces of human activity point to hidden thoughts and desires: "[You] know their intentions, you see their footprints."[90] The light of the sun discerns what is hidden from human sight; the resulting exposure leads to the purgation of the individual.

Finally, the individual's purification is a matter of protection. A large number of incantations that appeal to Šamaš as judge are ritual prayers for protection against evil magic, frequently with the petitioner presenting images or figurines for burning.[91] In the Mesopotamian *Maqlû* ("burning") series is the following prayer against witchcraft:[92]

> Dawn has broken; doors are (now) opened;
> The traveler[93] has passed through the gate;
> [The messenger] has taken to the road.
> Ha! w[i]tch: you labored in vain to bewitch me!
> . . . .
> For I am now cleansed by the light of the (rising) sun.[94]

Purification from the sun symbolically offers protection from black magic. As the dawn overturns the darkness, so cleansing wards off evil conjured against the purified. Further resembling the psalmist's concerns are the *Šurpu* incantations, which focus on the evil *from within* the individual and invoke the sun god Šamaš, or the fire god Girra, to purify the individual.[95]

O Girra, with your pure flame,
You provide light to the House of Shadows.
. . . .
May the limbs of (this) man,
    son of his (personal) god, be purified!
May he be pure as the heavens,
May he be pure as the netherworld!
May he shine like innermost heaven.[96]

The ritual behind the *Šurpu* incantations involves burning various materials, from onion peelings and dates to wool and flour, that symbolize the sin and affliction of the supplicant.[97] The person's cleansing is commended by the "purification-priest," who manages the fire while saying, "May his sin be poured out today, may it be wiped off him, be released for him."[98] The symbolic cleansing of the individual by fire results in a personal luster of purity ("shine").[99]

Exposing the Hidden

Discernment, purity, and protection are also matters of keen interest in Psalm 19. Under the light of the "law," the psalmist is able to discern flaws undetectable by the human will alone. The supplicant's fervent hope is for a purified heart (cf. 51:2, 10), more refined (and lustrous!) than fine gold (19:10),[100] the crowning result of appropriating divine instruction. Compared to the Mesopotamian incantation prayers, Psalm 19 makes an additional interior move: the psalmist petitions that one's *very thoughts* do not "gain mastery" (v. 13).[101] Absolution and protection from *hidden* sins are the psalmist's paramount concern.[102] Through appropriation of the law, the petitioner is made complete, as blameless as *tôrâ* is perfect (v. 13; cf. v. 7).

THE LIGHT OF THE LAW

Through the juxtaposition of sun and *tôrâ,* solarized worship of God is wrapped in the scroll of *tôrâ*-piety; the silent but visual voice of creation is subsumed under the spoken word of YHWH, given voice in *tôrâ.* The psalmist boldly transfers a powerful cosmic image associated with temple worship and lodges it squarely within the ethos of *tôrâ.* Consequently, the verbal discourse of *tôrâ,* with all its ordinances, precepts, testimonies, and commandments, is rendered imagistically. No harsh polemic is at work, as some have tried to claim.[103] Typical is a recent treatment that attributes a polemical edge to the psalm: "Torah is far superior to the revelation offered by the cosmos."[104] It is not, however, the psalmist's intent to elevate the status of *tôrâ by demonstrating the inferiority* of the cosmos. The communicative power of the cosmos is not disparaged or even muted. Rather, the voice of creation is enlisted and transmitted in such a way as to heighten *tôrâ*'s efficacy.

The second part of the psalm, thus, does not serve to correct the first. Both parts, rather, are mutually related.[105] The ethos of *tôrâ* is given cosmic stature, and the mythos of the sun is imbued with ethical force. Glen Taylor notes that ostensible continuity between God and the sun is assumed, not negated, in the psalm.[106] To be sure, the sun is portrayed positively within the realm of divine glory, but Taylor overstates the case: nowhere is the sun actually *identified* with God. The celestial orb is an object of creation that renders profound witness to God's glory and moral order, matched but not surpassed by *tôrâ*. Moreover, the sun serves as a cosmic embodiment of *tôrâ*-piety. The psalmist enlists creation itself in its capacity to communicate God's glory, *not* in order to denigrate nature to ancillary status but to elevate the significance of *tôrâ*, to "transcendentalize" *tôrâ* for the reader and thereby underscore its efficacy for the life of faith. The sun is enlisted to illumine the glory and power of *tôrâ*. *Tôrâ* is not set against the sun to eclipse its brilliance.

As the speaking "servant" of Ps 19:11–14 professes, YHWH's ordinances serve to purge the individual of "hidden sins" and "presumptuous thoughts," thereby rendering new life. As graphic image is incorporated into evocative word, the word becomes transformed into a cosmic image, "giving light" and "reviving the soul" (vv. 7–8). Thus, the cosmos is "heard" through *tôrâ*, and *tôrâ* is "seen" as a veritable element of creation, life-giving and morally directive. But the psalm's final emphasis falls on *tôrâ*, which prompts the question as to why cosmic imagery is used at all. One answer finds plausibility that reaches beyond the narrow search for the traditio-mythological roots of sun and deity and takes seriously the poetics of the psalm: to rejuvenate *tôrâ*. The wonder of the cosmos and its capacity to convey God's glory is nowhere called into question, for it is *constructively* marshaled to enhance *tôrâ's* status and efficacy vis-à-vis the individual and the community. As *tôrâ* is enhanced to "revive the soul," so the sun is enlisted to revitalize *tôrâ* for the reader.

In the case of the arboreal metaphor in Psalm 1, the royal temple setting typically presupposed in the deployment of solar imagery is fused with, or perhaps even replaced by, *tôrâ*. The displacement of the temple by *tôrâ* may suggest a relatively late date for the psalm, reflecting a time or place in which the temple no longer held a centralizing role within Israel's cultic life. What is certain, however, is that *tôrâ*, and not the temple, serves as the social setting for God's glory. Psalm 19 conveys a broad, indeed transcendent, view of *tôrâ*.[107] *Tôrâ* here is by no means limited or even reducible to Pentateuchal legislation, though it most likely includes the ordinances of Mosaic law within its cosmic reach. As Psalm 119 states, the word of God "is firmly established in the heavens" and governs the celestial bodies, including the earth (vv. 89–91). Both psalms, in short, profile a cosmic *tôrâ*.

IMAGE AND ICON: THE SYNAGOGUE MOSAICS

However Psalm 19 was used in the worship life of ancient Israel, it functioned decisively in later Jewish life and practice at a time when the temple was no longer in existence. The floor mosaics of several synagogues, including most notably Bet Alpha and Hammath-Tiberias, give silent, visual testimony that Psalm 19 played a formative role in cultic practice.[108] The most dramatic example, perhaps, is the sixth-century C.E. synagogue mosaic at Bet Alpha (see fig. 14), which displays a breathtaking view of the cosmic order, symbolized by the four seasons and the twelve signs of the zodiac, all framing the sun, flagrantly depicted as the Greek sun god Helios in his chariot.[109] Above the solar representation and nearest to where the Torah alcove stood are the symbols of the cultic order, specifically a Torah ark flanked by two menorahs and guardian lions, as well as two incense shovels, shofars, and other cultic accoutrements associated with temple worship.[110] Unique to the mosaic of Bet Alpha is the lamp that hangs from the gabled roof. The earlier zodiac mosaic of Hammath-Tiberias features Helios holding the globe and a whip in his hand, "the symbols associated with the Roman emperor, deified as *Sol Invictus*."[111]

Fig. 14: Floor mosaic from the Bet Alpha synagogue in Israel. Reprinted with permission from Ugarit-Verlag and featured in Martin Metzger, "Hannaja, Mischael und Asarja auf der Mosakinschrift der Synagogue von En Gedi," in *Prophetie und Psalmen,* ed. Beat Huwyler, et al. (AOAT 280; Munich: Ugarit-Verlag, 2001), 272.

In both floor mosaics, the zodiac wheel, with the figure of Helios at its center, was no doubt offensive to some Jews.[112] The images and arrangement of the solar chariot, zodiac wheel, and personified seasons are taken directly from Greco-Roman iconography, assimilated from Babylonian astrology. Whereas the Babylonian Talmud, for example, disclaims all belief in planetary "luck" in Jewish practice (*Shabbath*, 156a–156b), here on full display is the zodiac in all its astrological glory. Theories abound about whether the zodiac mosaics represent a need to adapt the Hebrew calendar to the solar year or if it represents creeping astrological and magical practices within rabbinic Judaism.[113]

A comparison with Psalm 19 suggests that much more than syncretism or solar intercalation is at work on these ancient synagogue floors. Overlooked in most analyses that attempt to determine the significance of pagan motifs is the larger framework in which these motifs are set. Jacob Neusner, for example, finds no connection between the iconic and the verbal among the synagogue mosaics.[114] I beg to differ. As in Psalm 19, we find on these carpets of stone both sun and *tôrâ* tightly juxtaposed.[115] The psalm sets a biblical precedent for associating the celestial orb and God's authoritative instruction. The same can be said of our mosaicists. The details are pagan (i.e., the zodiac and chariot), but the larger setting is unmistakably biblical. In both the psalm and the mosaics, word and world are bound together.

To be sure, Psalm 19, in contrast to the third panel of the Bet Alpha mosaic, does not allude to the binding-of-Isaac (*Akedah*) story in Genesis 22, even though the dramatic scene is intricately depicted in the third panel of the mosaic. Worthy of note is that the third panel is spatially set apart from the other two panels by a decorative division. Nonetheless, the *Akedah* story does share common ground with sun and *tôrâ:* it provides further background to the temple setting, which the priestly paraphernalia featured in the first panel presuppose. The dramatic narrative in Genesis unfolds on an unnamed mountain "in the land of Moriah" (Gen 22:2), the site that David, according to the Chronicler, acquired from the Jebusites and where Solomon built his temple (2 Chr 3:1). In later biblical lore and rabbinic tradition, the *Akedah* narrative came to serve as a foundational narrative for temple worship.[116] Like the Dura-Europos synagogue mural three centuries earlier,[117] the Bet Alpha mosaic incorporated the sacrificial context of temple worship into the fold of *tôrâ*-piety, which the biblical tradition itself facilitates by identifying Abraham as the exemplar of incomparable obedience and faith (Gen 15:6). Indeed, its inclusion in this cosmic scene completes the same rhetorical movement found in Psalm 19, the movement from the glorious ethos of the cosmos to the moral integrity of the individual.

A more contemporary (?) yet equally dramatic example of the intimate relationship between sun and *tôrâ* is experienced by almost every tourist and pilgrim who has had opportunity to visit the traditional site of Mount Sinai near St. Catherine's monastery in the southern part of the Sinai peninsula. Visitors typically begin the arduous ascent of *Jebel Musa* several hours before daybreak to witness the sunrise from the summit. At the first light of dawn, one invariably hears pilgrims reciting Psalm 19 in various languages as the sun's rays burst upon the rugged landscape where Moses allegedly received the Law.

CONCLUSION

Psalm 19 is a sound-and-light show, a poetic tour de force that brings together image and word and gives witness to the explosive reaction that ensues. If the psalm drew from two (or more) independent compositions, including a Canaanite hymn to the sun, the resulting combination achieves a remarkable metaphorical coherence and theological enhancement of *tôrâ*-piety.[118] Like its more lengthy counterpart (Psalm 119), Psalm 19 integrates comparable legal terminology (*'ēdût, miṣwâ, mišpāṭîm, piqqûdîm*) with cosmic imagery, grounding *tôrâ* in the very structures of creation. Moreover, the psalm exhibits the kind of metaphorical interaction whereby the boundaries that delineate the source domain from the target, the vehicle from the tenor, are deliberately broken down. Sun and *tôrâ* are *mutually* related; one informs and shapes the other. Through the filter of *tôrâ*, the sun is rendered a model of *tôrâ*-piety. At the same time, *tôrâ* receives nothing short of cosmic legitimacy; it is made radiant, transformed into an effulgence of "law." On a more existential level, this double movement at once broadens the horizons of the moral self and familiarizes the realm of the other. The moral integrity of the individual is shown to have cosmic implications, and the realm of the transcendent is found to be intimately related to the faithful conduct of the righteous. As the sun is viewed through the lens of *tôrâ*, word interprets world. And as *tôrâ* is given cosmological grounding, the world, in turn, has a hand in shaping and broadening the word. Like the sun that bursts out from its canopy to cover the extremities of heaven, "Torah shall go forth out of Zion and the word of YHWH from Jerusalem" for all the nations (Isa 2:3).[119]

Through the written word, the world is revealed, to borrow from Calvin, as the theater of God's glory.[120] But one must also add that through the world in all its unsettled glory and continued preservation the word is shown to be the catalyst of creation, both old and new, the genesis of cosmos and community. As the heavens declare God's glory and instruction, so *tôrâ* imparts God's handiwork within the crucible of human identity, a *creatio continuata* in miniature. With the sun traversing its cosmic circuits and *tôrâ* reviving the soul, the community is nurtured, like a tree planted beside flowing streams, basking in the light of the sun in God's cosmic temple.

Chapter 5

The Voice of Many Waters

From Chaos to Community

The psalms feel like a gentle spring rain: you hardly know that it's sinking in, but something good happens.[1]

There are two easy ways to die in the desert: thirst or drowning.[2]

One of the most evocative metaphors in all of Scripture, water is tapped by the biblical poets in various profound ways. Destructive and cleansing, formless yet sustaining, water can convey diametrically opposing nuances even within one verse or line of poetry.[3] Like a flash flood coursing through a desert wadi, the power of water can leave a path of destruction or, like a steady rain, prepare the soil for fertile possibilities. Whether as a hostile force or as a source of sustenance, water is as much a polyvalent image in the Psalter as it is a defining element in the diverse environment of Palestine, a small land of remarkable topographical and climatic contrasts.[4]

As the backdrop for the psalmist's use of water imagery, Palestine's rugged landscape is primarily dependent on rainfall for agricultural production and, thus, subject to extreme climatic conditions, from drought to flood, particularly in the southern regions. Unlike more temperate regions, Palestine's rainfall is of "high intensity," concentrated as it is during the winter season (December to February), which results in increased runoff, flooding, and, consequently, soil erosion.[5] Most streams in Palestine are ephemeral, flowing no more than a few hours after each rain in the Negev or a few days in the Judean highlands or up to a few weeks or months in the northern regions.[6] In the south, as in the highlands of the Negev ("the dry land") and around the "Sea of the Arabah" (the Dead Sea), permanent settlements such as Jericho to the north and Beer-sheba to the south—each receiving no more than two hundred millimeters in mean annual rainfall[7]—were possible only by natural springs and wells.

From the gushing waters that feed the Jordan near the foot of Mount Hermon (e.g., Bāniyās) to the desiccated landscape surrounding the Dead Sea, Palestine's variegated geography is conducive for the various roles water assumes in biblical poetry. Water imagery in the Psalter reflects both geographical and climatic extremes: the metaphor of thirst in a parched land connotes the psalmist's desperate yearning for God's saving presence, and the onslaught of chaos is well illustrated by the roaring power of a flash flood and churning sea during a storm. To capture something of the facility with which the psalmists navigated the full range of this metaphor's power, we begin by examining the various ways water imagery is employed throughout the Psalter, noting the domains that the metaphor "targets" or designates. The chapter concludes with an analysis of a portion of one particular psalm that encapsulates water's expansive range of significance in a radical way.

FEAR OF DROWNING

In their various laments and thanksgiving songs, the psalmists convey the raw, destructive power of rushing water and roiling waves in vivid ways. Of the various scenarios of disaster and deliverance featured in the thanksgiving song of Psalm 107, the most extensive is aquatic by nature:

> Some went down to the sea in ships,
>   doing business on the many waters (*mayim rabbîm*);
> They saw YHWH's deeds,
>   his wonders in the deep (*měṣûlâ*).
> He gave word and stirred up a storm wind (*rûaḥ sě'ārâ*)
>   that raised its[8] waves (*těrômēm gallāw*).
> They went up to heaven;
>   they went down to the depths (*těhômôt*);
>   their hearts[9] melting in such calamity.
> . . . .
> In their distress they cried to YHWH,
>   and he brought them out of their calamity.
> He made the storm (*sě'ārâ*) be still,
>   and their[10] waves (*gallêhem*) were hushed.
> They rejoiced that they had quiet (*yištōq*[11]),
>   [for] he had brought them
>   to their desired harbor (*měḥôz*).[12]
>   (Ps 107:23–26, 28–30)

The poetry evokes the horrifying scene of a ship caught in an almost "perfect storm."[13] Up and down the fragile ship is tossed until YHWH, responding to urgent petition, stills the sea's waves. Storms at sea constitute an occupational hazard for those who do "business on the many waters." YHWH is the storm God who both stirs and stills the waters (cf. Jonah 1:4; Mark 4:35–41). Such imagery is as literal as it is suggestive; the psalmist evokes a world of primal fear by forcibly taking the reader into the precarious world of seafaring. The reader's response is seasickness. Relief is not provided until the final two verses, in which the poet evokes scenes of stillness and safe haven (Ps 107:29–30). Such is the physical drama behind the source domain of the "many waters." As for the mythical drama, much lies below the billowing surface. The danger of drowning is by no means restricted to seafaring merchants.

The Icon of Chaos

The motif of watery chaos is fraught with background. The poets of the Psalter drew from the venerable West Semitic tradition of depicting water as the supreme agent of chaos, a motif so widespread that it made its way into Mesopotamian literature.[14] Such is the dramatic struggle narrated in the Babylonian theogony *Enūma eliš* ("When on high"), otherwise known as the Babylonian Epic of Creation, which depicts the primeval forces of water, Tiamat and Apsu, that must be overcome by the new generation of gods before the world can be created. In Tablets IV and V, the fateful encounter between the Marduk, commissioned by the Anunnaki as their young champion, and the maternal deity of the primeval ocean, Tiamat, is gut-wrenching. Among the various acts of graphic violence, Marduk dispatches a gust of wind to force Tiamat's mouth open and shoots an arrow that "slit[s] her down the middle and . . . her heart."[15] The epic narrator revels in the gore of conquest to affirm that from death, literally out of a corpse, split like a fish, comes the creation of the cosmos. Half of Tiamat's body constitutes the heavens ("roof"). From the lower half are fashioned land and rivers, as the next fragmented tablet describes:

> He placed her head, heaped up [ ]
> opened up springs; water gushed out.
> He opened the Euphrates and Tigris from her eyes,
> closed her nostrils,
> He piled up clear-cut mountains from her udder,
> bored waterholes to drain off the catchwater.
> He laid her tail across, tied it fast as the cosmic bond.[16]

As the epic narrator relates in graphic detail, watery chaos is no amorphous entity. It has a body whose anatomy provides the raw material for creation. The language of combat and creation is telling: the victorious god Marduk defeats Tiamat and fashions creation primarily by dismembering the body parts.

The royal archives of Ugarit also narrate a cosmic battle between the heroic storm god, Baal (*Ba'l*), and *Yamm* or Sea. In this dramatic cycle, the antagonist is given various names and epithets: Tunnan (*tnn* or "dragon"), Litan (*ltn*,

"Leviathan" in biblical tradition), Twisty Serpent (*bṭn 'qlṭn*), Fleeing Serpent (*bṭn brḥ*), Potentate with Seven Heads (*šlyṭ d šb't r'ašm*), and Judge River (*ṭpṭ nhr*).[17] Like Tiamat, *Yamm* represents an inimical cosmic force whose defeat is followed by an account of construction, namely, of Baal's palace. Yet the struggle is so fierce that the protagonist's attempt to defeat watery chaos initially fails. The climactic scene, however, proves otherwise:

> The weapon leaps from Baal's hand,
> [like] a raptor from his fingers.
> It strikes the head of Prince [Yamm,]
> between the eyes of Judge River.
> Yamm collapses and falls to the earth.
> His joints shake,
> and his form collapses.
> Baal drags and dismembers (?)Yamm,
> destroys Judge River.[18]
>
> (*KTU* 1.2.iv.23–27)

As in the Babylonian epic, the use of weapons to defeat the chaos deity plays a crucial role. What Baal does with Yamm's body, however, is unclear.[19]

Historically, the *Chaoskampf* or combat motif of ancient Near Eastern lore served as a means to legitimate monarchic rule in various Semitic cultures of antiquity: Babylonia, Assyria, Mari, and Ugarit, to which one could also add Jerusalem.[20] Although the "waters" do not bear the same mythological weight that they do in the extrabiblical literature,[21] it is no surprise to find in the poetic hyperbole of the Psalter (and elsewhere in Scripture) hints of this literary mythos. The combat motif is most prominently featured in Psalms 89 and 74.[22]

> YHWH God of hosts,
> who is as mighty as you, YHWH?
> Your faithfulness (*'ĕmûnâ*) surrounds you.
> You rule the raging of the sea (*gē'ût hayyām*);
> when its waves rise, you still them.
> You crushed Rahab like a carcass;
> you scattered your enemies with your mighty arm.
> As the heavens belong to you, so belongs also the earth;
> the world and all that is in it—
> you have founded them.
> . . . .
> I will crush [the king's] foes before him,
> and strike down those who hate him.
> My faithfulness (*'ĕmûnâ*) and love (*ḥesed*) shall be with him,
> and in my name his horn shall be exalted.
> I will set his hand on the sea
> and his right hand on the rivers.
>
> (89:8–11, 23–25)

In this preeminently royal psalm, language ascribed to God in praise is mirrored by God's effusive promises to the anointed one, the Davidic ruler (see vv. 19–20). Both God and the king are engaged in mortal combat against the "raging of the sea." Earthly governance, in conjunction with divine rule, necessitates *both* the sea's quelling and the defeat of national enemies: the primeval chaos monster Rahab within the divine arena and the king's national foes on earth. Even so, the earthly king participates in the divine task of subduing primeval chaos ("sea" and "rivers"), symbolic of the extent of his earthly kingdom.[23]

In Psalm 74, God achieves victory over watery chaos through the exercise of royal office:

> Yet God my King is from of old,
>   who works salvation in the earth's midst.
> You divided Sea (*yam*) by your strength;
>   you broke the heads of the dragons (*tannînîm*) of the waters.
> You crushed the heads of Leviathan;
>   you gave him as food for the denizens of the desert.[24]
> You cut openings for springs and torrents;
>   you dried up ever-flowing streams (*nahărôt*).
> Yours is the day, yours is also the night;
>   you established the luminaries and the sun.
> You have fixed all the bounds of the earth;
>   you made summer and winter.
>
> (74:12–17)

Depicting the defeat of watery chaos, this litany is rife with the language of violence and conquest. The sea is not only personified in its own right, but also populated with inimical creatures. Similar to Psalm 89, Psalm 74 provides a classic illustration of the combat myth.[25] Like Tiamat in the Babylonian myth, the sea has a "body" that God divides, breaks, crushes, and cuts open. Following the description of the sea's defeat, potentially positive images of water command the reader's attention: springs and rivers (v. 15a). Such language recalls Marduk's invasive work on Tiamat's corpse to commence the work of creation. The scenario of destruction paves the way for the establishment of a salutary order (vv. 16–17). Divine rule is thus grounded in cosmogony.

The psalm, however, does not conclude with God's forceful imposition of order on natural chaos. References to mythological struggle set the stage for the psalmist's plea to God that his foes be vanquished (vv. 18–23). Chaos lingers in the form of national enemies who "clamor" and "roar" (v. 23). Though the sea is tamed, indeed defeated, human violence haunts the land.

The motif of divine combat with chaos, however, recedes into the misty background elsewhere, as in Psalm 29, a hymn to YHWH, the storm deity.

> The voice of YHWH [thunders] over the waters (*mayim*);
>   the God of glory thunders,
>   YHWH [thunders] over many waters (*mayim rabbîm*).

> The voice of YHWH is powerful;
> the voice of YHWH is full of majesty.
> . . . .
> YHWH sits enthroned over the flood (*mabbûl*);
> YHWH sits enthroned as king forever.
>
> (29:3–4, 10)

Through a highly poeticized arrangement,[26] the psalmist pits the thundering voice of YHWH against the roiling waters. The waters, however, put up no resistance; any hint of struggle between the waters and the deity is entirely absent. Indeed, the waters provide the fundament of YHWH's throne.

Without explicitly invoking the combat mythos, Psalms 114 and 104 depict the sea in flight from God's approaching presence: "The sea saw and fled; Jordan turned back" (114:3);

> At your rebuke (*ga'ărātĕkā*)[27] they fled;
> at the sound of your thunder they took to flight.
> They rose up to the mountains,
> [and] ran down to the valleys
> to the place you set for them.
>
> (104:7–8)

Although God's thunderous "rebuke" or roar—a battle cry, in effect—sends the recalcitrant waters fleeing to their appointed places, cosmic combat prior to creation is nowhere evident in either psalm. The rebuke of the waters is integral to the creative process.[28] Their containment not only ensures the earth's stability; as bodies of water they become sources for springs that course through the valleys. As in Psalm 74, the waters' flight is followed immediately by the formation of streams, which Psalm 104 depicts as a sign and means of God's provision for the animals.[29] God's "victory"—if the term is at all applicable—is strikingly nonviolent.[30]

The scene of the waters' flight from God's thunderous "rebuke" finds its historical correlate in the exodus event, as described in Psalm 106: "He rebuked (*wayyig'ar*) the Red Sea, and it became dry; he led them through the deeps (*tĕhōmôt*) as through a desert" (v. 9). Divine "rebuke" secures Israel's safety, which involves "drying" the Red Sea (*yam-sûp*)[31]—death by desiccation (see also 66:6). Since Psalm 106 is the penitential companion to the preceding historical psalm, a political counterpart to God's rebuke is evident: "[YHWH] allowed no one to oppress them; he rebuked (*wayyôkaḥ*) kings on their account, saying, 'Do not touch my anointed ones; do my prophets no harm'" (105:14–15). As God's people, wandering in the wilderness, are deemed "off-limits" for the kings of the nations,[32] so the engulfing waters of the Red Sea are warded off (and defeated) as Israel is led through the deep. History and myth are inseparably conjoined to highlight God's providential, militant care for Israel.

Other references to the exodus event echo, albeit faintly, the tumult of cosmological struggle, as in Psalm 78, another historical psalm that narrows its focus on the wilderness period.

> He divided (*bāqaʿ*) the sea and let them pass through it,
>   and made the waters stand like a heap.[33]
> . . . .
> He split (*yěbaqqaʿ*) rocks open in the desert,
>   and gave them drink abundantly as from the deeps (*kitěhōmôt*).
> He made streams come out of the rock,
>   and caused waters to flow down like rivers.
>
>   (78:13, 15–16)

Similar to the *Chaoskampf* topos in Psalm 74, the exodus event begins with God *dividing* the Red Sea in two, as if it had a body for dismemberment (cf. 74:13).[34] The same verbal root describes God's provision of water for Israel in the wilderness: God both *divides* the sea to save Israel from drowning and *splits* the rocks to deliver Israel from death by dehydration. In the latter scene, the parallel between "sea" and "rock" is cemented with reference to the "deeps" in v. 15b: the death-dealing cosmic waters become life-sustaining in the desert! The converse is given elsewhere: Israel is led "through the deeps *as through a desert*" (106:9b, emphasis added).[35] The sea's inimical force, however, returns by defeating, literally "covering over" (*kissāh*), Israel's enemies (78:53; see also 106:11).

Finally, one account of the exodus event invokes the language of theophany to highlight the turmoil of the "many waters."

> The waters saw you, God;
>   the waters saw you [and] writhed (*yāḥîlû*);
>   the deeps, moreover, trembled (*yirgězû*).
> The clouds poured out water;
>   the skies thundered;[36]
>   indeed, your arrows flashed all around.
> The clap of your thunder was in the whirlwind;
>   [your] lightnings lit up the world;
>   the earth trembled and shook.
> Through the sea was your way,
>   your path[37] through the many waters (*mayim rabbîm*);
>   yet your footprints left no trace.[38]
> You led your people like a flock
>   by the hand of Moses and Aaron.
>
>   (77:16–20)

Presented in a series of three tricola, this vivid scene resembles the dramatic scenario depicted in Pss 29:3–10; 68:8; and 104:7. The last two verses of Psalm 77, however, lodge this type-scene squarely within the historical context of the exodus event. The vanquishing of chaos is historicized. As much as it helps to establish creation itself, cosmological turmoil also sets the stage for Israel's emergent identity.

The polarization of God and the waters is given subtle nuance in an enthronement psalm that draws from the *Chaoskampf* mythos:

YHWH is king, robed in majesty.
  YHWH is robed, girded with strength.
He established the world,
  [so that] it shall never be moved.
Your throne is established from of old;
  you are from everlasting.
The floods (*nĕhārôt*) have lifted up, YHWH;
  the floods have lifted up their voice;
    the floods lift up[39] their bellowing (*dokyām*[40]).
Greater the voice of the many waters (*mayyim rabbîm*),
  more majestic ('*addîr*[41]) than the breakers of the sea,
    [most] majestic on high is YHWH.
Your decrees are very firm;
  holiness befits your house,
    YHWH forevermore.

(93:1–5)

Typical of royal temple liturgy, the psalm boldly affirms God's cosmic reign to ensure the stability of creation. In contradistinction to ancient Near Eastern lore, the convulsion of creation is not the *prerequisite* for royal rule but the *result* of it.[42] As *royal* warrior, God is poised to subdue any force that would plunge creation into chaos. And, as the second half of the psalm attests, the mighty waters or floods would do just that. In the liturgically adept form of "staircase parallelism,"[43] the psalmist describes the raging floods in a threefold prosodic pattern that escalates in intensity. Through syntactical comparison, the following verse serves to override the sound of aquatic fury and, consequently, affirm God's majesty above the pounding surf. The tricolon rhetorically "shouts down" the preceding one. The crescendo builds to a climax that discloses the subject of comparison. God's majesty exceeds the deafening roar of rushing floodwaters. God's "voice" overpowers all threats of chaos and can be distinctly heard in the divinely wrought decrees, a roar whose reverberations promulgate order over the disabling discourse of chaos.

The Targets of Chaos

Chaos characterizes much of the water imagery featured in the Psalter. Yet the examples cited above do not deploy water imagery in any explicit metaphorical way. At most, water performs metonymically: it *stands* for chaos but is nowhere "mapped" onto another discrete referent, at least on the textual surface. When water imagery, along with its mythopoeic trappings, *is* applied metaphorically, chaos is bound up with the source domain, not the target. In other words, through water imagery the psalmists channel chaos to target various conditions of human and divine distress.

God

The element of chaos, for example, sets in stark relief a striking case of metaphorical usage in the Psalter. In a radical twist of the combat mythos, the most despairing of psalmic laments associates the watery abyss not with a cosmic enemy but with the deity's very self. The metaphor's target is God.

> YHWH, God of my salvation,
> . . . .
>   incline your ear to my cry.
> For my soul is sated with distress,
>   and my life draws near to Sheol.
> I am counted among those who go down to the pit;
>   I am like one who has no help.
> . . . .
> You have put me in the depths of the pit (*bôr taḥtîyôt*),
>   in regions dark and deep (*mĕṣōlût*).
> Your wrath lies heavy (*sāmĕkāh*)[44] upon me,
>   and with all your waves (*mišbārêkâ*) you overwhelm [me].
> . . . .
> Your wrath has swept over me (*'ābĕrû*);
>   your dread assaults destroy me.
> They surround me like waters (*mayim*) all day long;
>   from all sides they close in on me.
> You have caused friend and neighbor to shun me;
>   my companions are in darkness.
>   (88:1*–4, 6–7, 16–18)

God's heavy "wrath" (v. 7a; cf. 32:4) is matched by the pounding waves of God's fury (88:7b, 17). Like a flood, God's anger inundates the psalmist (v. 16). The pit is likened to the watery depths, whose breakers assault and overcome the psalmist (vv. 6–7). Indelibly associated with cosmic conflict or turmoil, the image of raging waters is recast as an image of *divine* rage. In this Job-like complaint, God is the embodiment of chaos, and the psalmist finds himself plunged into the very heart of darkness. In order to heighten the terrifying impact of God's wrath, the metaphor's source domain maps the very contours of divine fury. The enemy, the psalmist has discovered, is God.

Enemies

The watery depths, in addition, frequently connote danger of a more political or social nature in the Psalter. Armed with metaphorical force, water "targets" attacking enemies. The examples are legion, as, for example, in the desperate plea voiced in Psalm 69:

> Save me, O God,
>   for the waters are up to [my] throat (*nepeš*).
> I am sinking in deep mire (*yĕwēn mĕṣûlâ*[45]),
>   where there is no foothold;
> I have entered the watery depths (*ma'ămaqqê-mayim*);
>   the flood (*šibbōlet*) is engulfing me.
> I am weary with my crying;
>   my throat is parched;
>   my eyes are failing from[46] waiting for my God.

> More numerous than the hairs of my head
> are those who hate me for no reason.
> Mighty are those who would annihilate me,[47]
> my enemies who accuse me falsely.
> What I did not steal I must now restore![48]
>
> (69:1–4)

Various designations of water serve to highlight the psalmist's social distress: "waters" "deep mire," "deep waters," and "flood." Colloquially speaking, the psalmist is "sunk"; slander is swallowing him up. The psalm's catalog of water images is matched by the various labels the psalmist ascribes to his detractors, cast in a series of participles in Hebrew: "those who hate me" (*śōnĕ'ay*), "those who would annihilate me" (*maṣmîtay*), and "my enemies" (*'oyĕbay*). As the waters threaten to engulf the psalmist, so a multitude of enemies surround him. To both water and enemy are ascribed certain quantitative dimensions: *many* are the enemies; *deep* are the waters.

The correspondence between water and enemy is established even more tightly elsewhere in the same psalm:

> With your faithful help,
> rescue me from the mire (*ṭîṭ*).
> Let me be delivered from those who hate me (*miśśōnĕ'ay*),[49]
> from the deep waters (*ma'ămaqqê-mayim*).
> Do not let the flood (*śibbōlet*) sweep over me,
> or the deep (*mĕṣûlâ*) swallow me up,
> or the pit (*bĕ'ēr*) close its mouth over me.
>
> (69:13b–15)

"Enemies" and "deep waters" are juxtaposed in fine parallelistic fashion. The psalmist, moreover, complains of being "swallowed up" by the "mouth" (*pî*) of the "deep" or "pit," a graphic depiction of death.[50] In light of such correspondence, other associations emerge in the psalm. In line with the psalmist's focus on the "mouth" of the pit, attention to the discourse of the psalmist's enemies is highlighted: they render false accusation (v. 4), insult (vv. 9, 10, 19–20), and slander (vv. 11b, 12). Because of their accusations, evidently of theft (v. 4b), "shame has covered" the psalmist's "face" as the waters cover the deep (v. 7). The psalmist is drowning in shame. Finding himself helpless before his enemies' accusations, the psalmist prays that he be delivered and his enemies be found guilty of slander (v. 27).

The rich use of water metaphors in Psalm 69 serves to heighten the speaker's defenselessness before the false accusations leveled against him. Like the relentless pounding of waves, slander, insult, and false accusation crush the psalmist, reducing him to an object of scorn. Submerged in shame, the psalmist's only hope is divine vindication, for God alone rescues those caught in the waters and, thus, acts as advocate within the judicial arena.

A political target domain for water imagery is evident in other instances throughout the Psalter. Psalm 124 articulates a communal thanksgiving that credits God for having kept national enemies, and the "raging waters," at bay:

> Had YHWH not been on our side
>> when our enemies ('ādām) rose up against us,
> then they would have swallowed us up alive,
>> when their anger was kindled against us;
> then the waters (mayim) would have swept us away;
>> the torrent (naḥlâ) would have passed over our throats (nepeš);
> then over our throats would have passed
>> the raging waters (hammayim hazzêdônîm).
>
> (124:2–5)

The correspondence between the target and source domains could not be more tightly established. Syntactically, the series of result clauses do not present sequential action; waters, torrents, and raging waters do not signify separate predicaments, one following the other. In each case, the result particle "then" (ʾăzay) signals a new clause that is semantically coextensive with the other clauses that constitute the extended apodosis. That is to say, the image of inundating waters is deployed to heighten the mortal danger posed by Israel's national enemies. Similarity in language is explicit: enemies "swallow up," and the waters "pass over the throat"; enemies are "angry," and the waters are "raging." Indeed, the final qualification of the source image in v. 5 (hazzêdônîm), derived from the root √zyd, can also mean "seethe" and "act presumptuously, rebelliously," as in the case of the Egyptians (Exod 18:11) and Babylonians (Jer 50:29).

Beyond the poetic flourish, the enlistment of water metaphors serves to throw the resolution of Israel's international predicament entirely on God's shoulders. Only God can pull Israel out of the depths, out from the mouth of death and onto solid ground. As God alone can still the billowing waves of the sea, so only God can save a people in the face of military defeat or deliver an individual before the power of any enemy (see Pss 18:16–17; 144:7–8). Water imagery imbues the psalmist's opponents with the attributes of chaos:

> You silence the roaring (šĕʾôn) of the seas,
> the roaring (šĕʾôn) of their waves,
>> the tumult (hămôn) of the peoples.
>> (65:7).

The clamor of enemies is comparable to the bellow of roiling waters. "Roaring" tumult cuts across political and natural domains.[51]

One of the most evocative Zion psalms revels in water imagery of a cataclysmic scale, while conveying the calm assurance of God's saving power amid national threat:

> God is our refuge and strength,
>> a well-proven help amid trouble.
> So we will not fear,
>> though the earth shows flux (bĕhāmîr),
>> though the mountains tumble (bĕmôṭ)
>>> into the heart of the seas (lēb yammîm),

> though their waters roar (*yehĕmû*) and foam,
>   [and] the mountains totter (*bĕmôṭ*) at their swelling.
> There is a river whose channels make glad the city of God,
>   the holiest[52] habitation[53] of the Most High.
> God is in [the city's] midst;
>   [thus] it shall not be moved (*timmôṭ*).
>   God will help it at the break of dawn.
> The nations are in an uproar (*hāmû*);
>   the kingdoms totter (*māṭû*).
> His voice thunders;
>   the earth melts (*tāmûg*).
>
>   (46:1–6)

A picture of stalwart confidence is set against a horrifying scene of cosmic convulsion and political turmoil. The seas roar, and the nations are in an uproar. Mountains totter, and so do kingdoms. Yet amid the chaos, God's city stands firm and its inhabitants unperturbed. The volatile political arena assumes the qualities of swelling seas *and* tottering mountains. As cosmic chaos slides into political mayhem, the metaphorical power of the natural environment, specifically that of water and mountain, is unleashed. While both mountains and nations collapse into the churning sea, indeed as the entire earth dissolves, the city of God remains unmoved, set apart from creation's dissolution. The psalmist marshals such imagery to convey not fear but confidence, even joy. The psalm concludes with a cease-and-desist order against the nations and the cosmos: "Settle down (*harpû*) and acknowledge me as God! Exalted am I among the nations and in the earth!" (v. 10). The command reflects a new reality, an equilibrium established by God's dramatic intervention in which the weapons of war are silenced and chaos subsides.

Though water remains in Psalm 46 the agent of chaos that brings about the land's collapse, its metaphorical range is shared by its natural counterpart, the mountains. Quaking hills and churning seas—both are mapped onto the political realm not merely for dramatic effect. The kingdoms are shown to be both perpetrators and victims of their own chaos: they "roar" and they "totter"; they whip up chaos while collapsing in the very tumult they provoke. As an exercise in suicide, chaos defeats itself.

In an abrupt turnabout, water imagery is deployed also to enhance Jerusalem's preeminence over the nations as a refuge against chaos. Within the city, water is an agent of joy; outside its walls, water both joins and destroys the nations. In the abrupt transition from chaos to sustaining joy, the psalmist channels the water metaphor in a new direction. And metaphor it is, for in the physical world of Jerusalem's environment no mighty river exists. Its historical correlate can be found only in a modest underground spring known as the Gihon, or the "waters of Shiloah."[54] The image recalls the crucial import of a water source, a lifeline no less, in the face of besiegement, which in fact the Gihon supplied during Hezekiah's time.[55] Theologically, the river connotes God's solidarity: as the streams flow throughout the urban landscape, so God is present within the city, supplying its needs and imparting strength and confidence to its inhabitants. The river, thus, is no ordinary channel; it is uniquely a sanctuary stream, one that issues forth from God's holy residence. The city "shall not be moved" because God has taken up residence in the city and a river runs through it. The image of the holy river highlights God's sustaining power on behalf of urban dwellers and sets apart the city from all other political domains. The river is a sign and seal of God's holy habitation in Jerusalem's midst.

A final example associates submergence with national defeat and displacement, but with a remarkable twist:

> But God will shatter the heads of his enemies,
> the hairy crown of those who walk in their guilty ways.
> The Lord declares, "I will bring [them] back from Bashan,
> I will bring [them] back from the depths of the sea (*měṣulôt yām*),
> so that you may bathe[56] your feet in [their] blood,
> so that the tongues of your dogs
> may have their share from the foe."
>
> (Ps 68:21–23)

As divine warrior, God defeats the enemy in battle and rescues Israel from its displaced status. Bashan, a mountainous region in the northern Transjordan (cf. vv. 15–16), is equated with the "depths of the sea." In defeat, Israel is plunged into the heart of chaos (v. 22).[57] God's declaration to rescue Israel from Bashan is a resolve to restore, in effect, a people from national dissolution.

Yet there is more. By "mapping" Bashan with the metaphor of the watery abyss, a vicious irony unfolds. Earlier, Bashan was the "mighty" and "many-peaked mountain" accused of harboring envy over God's towering abode, presumably Zion (vv. 15–16). Now, however, Bashan's height is identified with the watery depths. The imagery, moreover, generates another association, namely, the blood of the vanquished enemy. Bashan will be an abyss of blood in which a delivered people will bathe their feet.[58] An image of horror and hopelessness is transformed into a graphic image of confidence. The depths of chaos have become, as it were, a tub of corpses. Bashan is "sunk."

To summarize: various levels of cosmic turmoil are connoted by water imagery. A topos of mythological lore, this motif lends itself to rhetorically creative applications, from God's hard-won victory over the sea (i.e., Psalms 74 and 89) to God's provoking cosmic convulsion and flight (e.g., Psalms 77, 104). From the metonymical to the metaphorical, the range of water's signification, moreover, cuts across the cosmic, political, and social spheres. It serves to heighten the danger of the psalmist's "personal" enemies, Israel's national enemies, and God's cosmic enemies, as well as to highlight God's role in rectifying situations of distress, however varied. As God requires a worthy opponent to display the deity's unmatchable power in the combat mythos, so national conflict underscores God's solidarity with a covenant people. When the psalmist pleads for deliverance from personal distress, even within a juridical context, God is petitioned to reprise the role of royal warrior, armed with thunderous pronouncements, to vindicate the psalmist and vanquish her persecutors. In one instance, however, associations with chaos are turned on their head: God, specifically God's wrath, *is* chaos personified (Psalm 88).

The Formlessness of Grief

The psalmist's encounter with divine anger elicits another type of water imagery that is distinguishable from, yet not unrelated to, the pounding waves of chaos.

> YHWH, do not rebuke me in your anger,
> or discipline me in your wrath.
> . . . .
> I am weary with my moaning;
> every night I submerge (*'aśḥeh*) my bed;
> with tears (*bĕdimʿātî*) I drench (*'amseh*) my couch.
> My eyes waste away because of grief;
> they grow weak because of all my foes.
> (6:1, 6–7)

The psalmist envisions his bed submerged in a pool supplied by his tears.[59] The second verb (√*msh*) literally means to "dissolve, melt," as in the case of ice (cf. 147:18). Threatening to drown the psalmist, grief over God's wrath brings about its own inundation. Metonymic of sorrow, the image of tears adds a new layer of significance to water's metaphorical repertoire.

Through the medium and metaphor of tears, God's anger against the individual is imbued with a poignancy poetically designed to provoke not chaos but mercy.

> YHWH, God of hosts,
> how long will you be angry with your people's prayers?
> You have fed them with the bread of tears (*leḥem dimʿâ*),
> and given them tears (*dĕmāʿôt*) to drink in full measure.
> You make us the scorn[60] of our neighbors;
> our enemies laugh among themselves.
> (80:4–6)

> All day long my enemies taunt me;
> those who deride me use my name for a curse.
> For I eat ashes like bread,
> and mingle my crying (*bibkî*) with my drink,
> on account of your indignation and anger;
> for you have lifted me up and thrown me aside.
> (102:8–10)

During this time of wrath, the psalmist finds himself and his people force-fed, as it were, with "tears." Or as another psalmist laments, "My tears have been my food day and night, while people say to me continually, 'Where is your God?'"

(42:3). The image of "tears" injects an element of poignancy and personal anguish into the harsh rhetoric of judgment.

Similarly, in a prayer for deliverance from persecution, the psalmist—likely in the role of king (56:1–2, 5–7, 9)—enlists the image of "tears" to prompt divine vindication:

> You have kept count of my convulsions (*nōdî*);[61]
>   put my tears (*dim'ātî*) in your flask (*nō'dekā*).
> Are they not in your book?
>
> (56:8)

The reference to "tears" stored in a "flask" is bracketed by references to accounting or tabulation: "convulsions" are counted (*sāpartâ*) and registered in a "book" (*siprâ*), God's ledger of the psalmist's complaints (cf. 40:7; 69:28; 139:16). Embedded in this context, the image of "tears" constitutes part of God's record, evidence that the psalmist submits as reason for God to exact retribution against his enemies. Here, as elsewhere, this image of grief connotes the psalmist's injuries. More specifically, this metonym for grief is "mapped" onto the psalmist's complaint of persecution, transforming grief into grievance. His "tears" are for the record. By storing tears in a flask, God registers the psalmist's complaint and responds accordingly.

The question remains, however, why the metaphor of tears is deployed at all, for it seems to detract from the overall juridical tenor of the verse. Yet this is no aimless detour: the juxtaposition of "flask" and "book" is deliberate and powerfully suggestive. A "flask" or waterskin is used for storing wine and milk.[62] The implication is clear: to record the psalmist's complaint, God must drink, as it were, the psalmist's tears! Reversing the imagery of grief found in other laments, the psalmist "force-feeds" God with his tears; indeed, the verb is cast as an emphatic imperative (*śîmâ*). By calling for God's vengeance against his enemies, the psalmist commits poetic justice in more ways than one. God is exhorted, albeit indirectly, to drink the full measure of the psalmist's tears to ensure that his grievances will not be passed over but duly digested and, thus, recorded.

Not coincidentally, similar language is found in Psalm 116, except for the additional reference to "tears," suggesting some level of textual dependency between these two psalms.[63]

> For you have delivered my soul from death,
>   my eye from tear (*dim'â*),
>   my foot from stumbling.
> I walk before YHWH in the land of life.
>
> (116:8–9)

As conditions from which the psalmist has been delivered, the shed "tear," "death," and "stumbling" are placed on the same par. Grief is akin to the bondage of death. Life, conversely, is liberation from grief, a "tearless" existence.

In Psalm 69, grief is portrayed as a taxing burden. Weeping depletes one's strength (v. 3a). Moreover, the psalmist not only limns the enervating work of grief, but also conjoins such a picture of affliction with an opposite image: the image of eyes clouded with tears finds its counterpart in the parched throat (v. 3b). The juxtaposition is striking, particularly given the references to the psalmist swallowing tears as drink, noted above (cf. v. 21). Tears do not quench thirst; they are, rather, testimony to deprivation.

A particularly evocative use of "tears" is found in Psalm 126, which gives witness to the transformation of tears from a sign of grief to a fertile vision of hope:

> Restore our fortunes, YHWH,
> like the watercourses (*'ăpîqîm*) in the Negev.
> May those who sow with tears (*hazzōrē'îm bĕdim'â*)
> reap with shouts of joy.
> Those who go out weeping,
> bearing seed for sowing,[64]
> shall come home with shouts of joy,
> carrying their sheaves.
>
> (126:4–6)

Remarkably different from the previous psalms discussed, images of grief are lodged within a distinctly agricultural setting. The passage opens with the transformation of a desert region, the Negev, into a well-irrigated oasis. The land's physical restoration is matched by a concomitant emotional change from grief to joy. Preserving the agricultural context, the latter transformation is depicted, remarkably, on the same canvas. Tears become seeds, watered by tears, and the result is a harvest of joy. Grief, conversely, is a *dry* land. The evocative power of this passage lies in the reversal of imagery. The image of tears reveals an iconic twist. Rather than as a condition from which the psalmist pleads for deliverance (cf. 116:8) or as drink to be avoided, tears of grief become instrumental in precipitating the land's fructification; sorrow becomes the means by which the land is restored. Through divine agency, tears, as water, provide the sustenance for shalom, and lament turns to joy.

Finally, Psalm 22 imbues the rhetoric of grief and affliction with a striking mix of metaphors that include images of dissolution and desiccation:

> Like water I am poured out (*kammayim nišpaktî*),
> and all my bones are disconnected.
> My heart is like wax;
> it is melted (*nāmēs*) within my breast.
> My palate[65] is dried up like a potsherd;
> and my tongue sticks to my jaws.
> You lay me in the dust of death.
>
> (22:14–15)

Wasted with grief, the psalmist enters a state of utter dissolution (cf. 42:4). As spilled water and melted wax exemplify fluidity, so the psalmist's life ebbs away.

Such mixed imagery imbues grief with formlessness. As death approaches, the structures that support and define life dissolve. One's physical frame becomes a bag of disjointed bones. In corresponding manner, life dissolves into nothingness, like wax melting before fire (see 68:2) and water poured out of a pitcher. Life is defined metaphorically as *contained* water. Matching the similes of dissolution are metaphors of death that draw from the opposite source domain, dryness. Like the parched throat in Psalm 69, the mouth is described as dried out, and thus unable to function. Potsherd and dust are the counterparts to images of water and melted wax, all marshaled to map the target domain of death and accompanying grief. Death embraces the images of opposite extremes. The connection is, in part, sequential: as water is spilled, like blood shed, soaked up by the ground, so desiccation sets in. Dissolution leads to dryness, water to dust.

AFFLICTION AS DESICCATION

Several psalms depict distress and lamentation not by inundation but by the distinct *lack* of water. "My heart is stricken and withered like grass," complains the debilitated speaker of Ps 102:4 (cf. v. 11; 90:5–6). Such language taps an entirely different metaphorical schema from the one discussed above, a schema that associates moisture with life and dryness with death.[66] Most prominent is the motif of "thirsting," a metaphor indicating the psalmist's desperate desire for an encounter with God. Psalm 63, for example, deploys this metaphor to map the psalmist's desire for temple worship.

> O God, my God you are,
>   I seek you.
> My soul thirsts (*ṣāmĕ'â*) for you;
>   my flesh faints for you,
>   [as] in a land dry and weary (*ṣîyâ wĕ'āyēp*) without water.
> So I have looked upon you in the sanctuary,
>   beholding your power and glory.
> . . . .
> My soul is satisfied (*tiśba'*) with fat and fatness,
>   and my mouth praises you with joyful lips.
> . . . .
> My soul clings to you;
>   your right hand upholds me.
> But those who seek to destroy my life
>   shall go down into the depths of the earth.
>   (63:1–2, 5, 8–9)

Like the speaker in Psalm 42, the psalmist seeks God amid severe deprivation. With the metaphors of thirst and hunger (63:5), the psalmist limns God as the fulfillment of deep longing, of abundant sustenance amid scarcity. As God is cast as the object of ultimate desire, so the psalmist depicts himself as utterly dependent on God, like a "dry and weary" land (v. 1).[67] In this psalm of trust, the profession of thirst for God construes faith as a matter of desire and dire need, heightened all the more within the arena of conflict, as the last section of the psalm indicates. Fulfillment is found within the temple sanctuary.

Psalm 143 similarly lodges the pray-er's thirst for God within a situation of conflict:

> For the enemy pursues me,
> > crushing my life to the ground,
> > > making me sit in darkness like those long dead.
> Therefore my spirit faints (*tit'aṭṭēp*) within me;
> > my heart within me is appalled.
> I remember the days of old;
> > I reflect upon all your deeds;
> > > I dwell on the works of your hands.
> I stretch out my hands to you;
> > my soul [yearns]⁶⁸ for you like a parched (*'ăyēpâ*) land.
> Answer me quickly, YHWH;
> > my spirit comes to an end (*kālĕtâ*).
> Do not hide your face from me,
> > or I shall be like those who descend into the pit.
> > > > > > > > > (143:3–7)

The drama of conflict in this prayer of deliverance intensifies the psalmist's "thirst." His life is both "crush[ed] to the ground" and desiccated as "a parched land." Trust is met with the hope of sustenance and, thus, deliverance from persecution. Sustaining such hope is the supplicant's remembrance of God's past deeds. Paired with the psalmist's expectation of deliverance (vv. 3, 9) is also his hope for a clear word, a teaching, of God's *ḥesed* "in the morning" (v. 8), reiterated in v. 10: "Teach me to do your will, for you are my God. Let your good spirit lead me on a level path." The psalmist thirsts both for God's saving presence, which establishes "refuge" (v. 9), *and* for instruction that will enable him to walk "the way" (v. 8) and perform God's "will."

REFRESHMENT AND RENEWAL

References to thirst and dryness lead to an entirely different group of water metaphors that invite examination. In addition to featuring water as the defining metaphor of conflict and distress, the Psalter is equally replete with positive images of water, which highlight God's sustaining care and provision for Israel and the world.

God as Water

As the psalmist thirsts for God in a land of lack (e.g., 42:1), so God is frequently associated with nourishing, abundant water.

> YHWH, your faithful love (*ḥesed*) extends to the heavens,
>   your faithfulness (*'ĕmûnâ*) to the clouds.
> Your righteousness (*ṣĕdāqâ*) is like the mighty mountains (*harrê-'ēl*);
>   your judgment (*mišpāṭ*) is like the great deep (*tĕhôm rabbâ*);
>   humans and animals alike you save, YHWH.
> How precious is your faithful love, O God!
>   Indeed, [all] people may take refuge in the shadow of your wings.
> They are well filled from the richness of your house,
>   and from the river of your
>   abundant provisions (*naḥal 'ădānêkā*)[69] you give them drink.
> For with you is the fountain of life (*mĕqôr ḥayyîm*);
>   in your light we see light.
>
>   (36:5–9)

In this hymn of praise, God's *ḥesed* is celebrated with vivid imagery. Mountains and deep illustrate the expansive grace of divine justice, enacted for the sake of all life. From the vastness of creation the psalmist moves into the precincts of the temple ("your house"), cultivated as the new Eden, the garden of abundance. There, God's river flows, the "fountain of life," to sustain all who take refuge (cf. Ps 46:4).[70] The parallelism in the last verse indicates that this "fountain," associated with Zion, designates God as sustainer. As light is God, so also is life. Indeed, the association is not without precedent. Jeremiah employs a similar expression as a divine epithet, "the fountain of living water" (*mĕqôr mayim ḥayyîm*; Jer 2:13; 17:13).[71]

The association of God with fountain is situated, indeed declared, within the setting of temple worship in another psalm.

> Your solemn processions are evident, O God,
>   the processions of my God, my King,
>   into the sanctuary—
> the singers in front, the musicians last,
>   between them girls playing tambourines:
> "Bless God in the assemblies;[72]
>   [Bless] YHWH, you who are
>   of Israel's fountain (*mimmĕqôr yiśrā'ēl*)!"[73]
>   (68:24–26)

As in Psalm 36, the metaphor marks God's sustaining and enlivening power to elicit an eruption of praise. Like solar and arboreal imagery in the Psalter, water has its source and setting within the cultic sphere.[74]

Parallels between water and God are also found in several scenes of theophany. While Psalm 88, as noted above, forges an identity between God's wrath and the sea's pounding waves, such association is also imbued with neutral or positive nuance. In response to urgent appeal from an individual on the brink of death, God approaches in storm:

> [YHWH] bowed the heavens and descended;
>   thick darkness was under his feet.
> Riding upon a cherub, he flew;

> he came swiftly upon the wings of the wind.
> He made darkness his covering around him;
>   his canopy was watery darkness (*ḥeškat-mayim*), thick clouds.
> Out of the brightness before him,
>   there broke [through] his clouds hailstones and coals of fire.
>   (18:9–12)

God's approach is accompanied by cosmic turmoil. Thunderclouds are poised to bombard the land with lightning, like "arrows" (v. 14), delivering, moreover, an onslaught of hail. Meteorological phenomena are marshaled as weapons to bring about the psalmist's rescue and vindication at the expense of his enemies (e.g., vv. 16–19). Dark, thick clouds, laden with precipitation, mark God's saving presence and justice in the face of conflict (see also 97:2–5).

One psalm in particular enlists the imagery of torrential rain within the context of theophany for a distinctly restorative purpose:

> O God, when you went out before your people,
>   when you marched through the desert,
> the earth quaked, the heavens poured
>   at the presence of God, the One of Sinai,
>   at the presence of God, the God of Israel.
> Bountiful[75] rain, O God, you waved[76] abroad;
>   you established your heritage when it languished;
>   your flock found a dwelling in it.
> In your goodness, O God,
>   you provided for the needy.
>   (68:7–10)

As the "Rider of the Clouds" (v. 4),[77] the God of Sinai accompanies the people in the desert. Evoking the wilderness scene of the Pentateuchal narrative, the psalmist draws from the stock language of storm theophany to highlight God's protective guidance. Such imagery, however, is confined to references to rain (vv. 8–9). The reason is clear: the psalmist stresses only the *salutary* dimensions of theophanous aid to a people stranded in a desert. God's rain restores the land as Israel's "heritage." The desiccated land becomes a pasture for Israel, God's flock, and the psalmist suggestively concludes with a general statement about God providing for the needy (v. 10).[78] Distinctive of the language of provision in this psalm is the distinct *lack* of reference to God's drawing water from rock.[79] Rain, instead, is the exclusive means of provision, establishing the land of promise *in* the wilderness. Most unique is the subtle association with sacrificial offering. The language flirts with nomenclature drawn from the cult: the abundant rain is described as a freewill act, showered upon the land like an offering "waved" by a worshiper at the altar.[80] Such language highlights God's beneficence, paradigmatically set within the wilderness experience and witnessed by Israel's securing of the land for its habitation.

Sustenance as Water

As much as water imagery connotes chaos, inimical social forces, and the *mysterium tremendum* of God's presence, it can also signify God's gracious provision for the land and its inhabitants.

> [God] turns a desert into pools of water (*'ăgam-mayim*),
>   a parched (*ṣîyâ*) land into springs of water (*mōṣā'ê mayim*).
> And there he lets the hungry live,
>   and they establish a town to live in.
> They sow fields, plant vineyards,
>   and get a fruitful yield.
> By his blessing they multiply greatly,
>   and he does not let their cattle decrease.
>   (107:35–38)

The transformation of the desert into springs provides the setting for both agriculture *and* urban culture. Previous to this section, the psalmist affirmed that such a scenario of provision can easily be reversed (vv. 33–34). Water, thus, is the sign of God's contingent blessing, of divine provision that is responsive to the conduct of a people and makes possible the cultivation of culture.

Psalm 104, the consummate creation psalm, casts such provision as more gratuitous than contingent.

> You make springs gush forth into the wadis;
>   they flow between the hills,
>   providing drink to every wild animal.
> The onagers quench their thirst.
> By [the streams] the birds of the air find habitation;
>   they sing among the branches.
> From your lofty abode you water the mountains;
>   the earth is satisfied with the fruit of your work.
>   (104:10–13)

Immediately following God's containment of the waters to *protect* the earth, the earth becomes satiated with water to *provide* for the earth's inhabitants, particularly the animals. Here, water is a sign of God's gratuitous care, contingent only on God's continuing joy in creation (v. 31b; cf. Job 38:25–27).

In Psalm 65, the provision of water is evidence of God's "visitation," inaugurating not cosmic destruction, but agricultural bounty.

> You visit (*pāqadtā*) the earth
>   and give it abundance (*wattĕšōqĕqehā*),[81] greatly enriching it.
> The channel (*peleg*) of God is full of water;
>   you provide [the people with][82] grain,
>   for so you have prepared it.
> You water (*tĕlāmêhā*) its furrows abundantly,
>   soaking its ridges,
>   softening it (*tĕmōgĕgennāh*) with showers (*rĕbîbîm*),

and blessing its growth.
You crown the year with your goodness;
   your wagon tracks (*maʿgālêkā*) overflow with richness (*dāšen*).
The pastures of the wilderness overflow;
   the hills gird themselves with joy.
The meadows clothe themselves with flocks;
   the valleys deck themselves with grain.
They shout and sing together for joy.

(65:9–13)

This passage follows on the heels of God's "silencing" of the seas in v. 7a, and in the abrupt transition the waters' role changes dramatically from an inimical force as "seas" (*yammîm*, corresponding to *ʿummîm* [people] in v. 7b) to a channel of blessing as rain and river. Water from on high makes possible the cultivation of the land: the earth is "softened," literally melted (√*mwg*), by rain. Rather than submerging the land in chaos, the earth's "dissolution" sets the condition for agricultural production. And yet within this luxurious scene of the fructification, a lingering image persists that evokes the prior scene of cosmic struggle, namely, God's "wagon tracks." The image is frequently applied elsewhere to refer to the path of peace or right conduct (e.g., Isa 26:7; 59:8; Pss 17:5; 23:3). Here, however, the image is more literal: a path created by a "wagon" or "cart" (*ʿăgālâ*), to which this metaphor is etymologically related.[83] The imagery casts God in the role of farmer, driving a cart whose mighty wheels plow the land. The scene marks a significant shift from the earlier depiction of the warrior God (v. 7). Indeed, in such a scene of cosmic struggle, the "Rider of the Clouds" (68:4)[84] is frequently pictured with a chariot or accompanied by chariotry (√*rkb;* 68:17; 104:3; cf. 76:6). With the shifting role of the waters, God's chariot is transformed into an oxen-driven wagon, and God's sword, in effect, is exchanged for a plow. The praise that is given by all the land, from hill to vale, is as much a celebration of victory as a cry of gratitude.

In a final psalm of praise, various forms of precipitation are outlined and brought together under the rubric of God's word.

He dispatches his speech to the earth;
   his word runs swiftly.
He gives snow like wool;
   he scatters frost like ashes.
He hurls down his hail like crumbs—
   who can stand[85] before his cold?
He sends out his word and melts them (*wĕyamsēm*);
   he makes his wind blow, and the waters flow (*yizzĕlû-māyim*).
He declares his word[86] to Jacob,
   his statutes and ordinances to Israel.
He has not dealt with any other nation in this fashion;
   they do not know his ordinances.
Praise YH[WH]!

(147:15–20)

God's "word" or "command" controls all meteorological phenomena. The waters' place is found in the melting of frozen precipitation (v. 18). Word and wind are poetically joined: God's command stirs up a sirocco or khamsin from the southeast desert to melt the ice, producing flowing streams, the culmination of God's meteorological work. Highly suggestive is the pairing of God's *precipitous* word "to the earth" and God's *constitutional* word (i.e., *tôrâ*) "to Israel" (cf. Isa 55:10–11). The juxtaposition cements the bond between nature and law: as much as the waters sustain and provide life throughout the earth, so God's ordinances and statutes shape and preserve Israel's identity as a nation.

Finally, water imagery, specifically that of rain showers, is deployed in a royal psalm to highlight the stabilizing, moral force of the king's reign.

> O God, give the king your justice,
>   and your righteousness to a king's son.
> May he judge your people with righteousness,
>   and your poor with justice.
> May the mountains yield prosperity for the people,
>   and the hills in righteousness.
> May he defend the cause of the poor of the people,
>   give deliverance to the needy,
>   and crush the oppressor.
> May he live[87] while the sun endures,
>   and as long as the moon throughout all generations.
> May he be like rain (*māṭār*) that falls on the mown grass,[88]
>   like showers (*rěbîbîm*) that irrigate (*zarzîp*)[89] the earth.
> In his days may righteousness[90] flourish (*yiprah*)[91]
>   and peace abound, until the moon is no more.
>   (Ps 72:1–7)

The psalm oscillates between the realms of politics and nature to highlight the king's salutary rule. References to righteousness and justice are matched by scenes of agricultural bounty, including that of steady showers fructifying the land (vv. 3, 5–6). On the aesthetic level alone, the image of green grass glistening from the light of the sun lends potent approbation (and beauty) to the royal office and marks the king as the guarantor of prosperity (see also 2 Sam 23:3–4). The image of steady rain, moreover, targets the constancy and potency of royal rule, its benefits and its promises. The rain sets the stage for the "flourishing" of righteousness and peace, as if the moral order were a crop to be harvested. Likened to rain, the king provides the means for the cultivation of justice. Far from being burdensome or violent, royal rule according to the psalm is as salutary as showers nourishing the soil, a graceful image deployed to promulgate royal ideology, quite contrary to the aphorism, "A ruler[92] who oppresses the poor is a beating rain that leaves no food" (Prov 28:3).[93]

Doxology and Water

In contrast to gentle rain showers, the image of foaming, roiling waters need not connote only destructive chaos. Such imagery can serve as a vehicle of praise. The dissonant "bellowing" of the floods that reverberate in Ps 93:3 is transformed into a chorus of praise elsewhere in the Psalter. Theologically, the step is taken with the expressed affirmation that the seas, traditionally the locus of chaos, is part and parcel of God's good creation:

> For YHWH is a great God,
>> and a great king above all gods.
> In his hand are the depths of the earth;
>> the heights of the mountains are also his.
> The sea is his, for he made it (*'āśāhû*),
>> and the dry land, which his hands have formed.
>>> (95:3–5)

Divine rule is celebrated not because God has proven victorious over hostile forces, be they cosmic or human. Rather, the psalmist affirms God as maker and lord of all creation, an order unthreatened by chaos. God's kingdom is not established in conflict, but constituted in praise. Even the sea, thus, is claimed as fashioned by God.

Whereas Psalm 95 directs its exhortation to praise toward Israel (v. 7), other psalms exhort the seas and mighty waters themselves, giving them unbounded license to roaring and foaming *in praise*.

> Let the heavens be glad and the earth rejoice;
>> let the sea roar (*yir'am*) and all that fills it;
>>> let the field exult and everything in it.
> Then shall all the trees of the forest sing for joy before YHWH;
>> for he is coming;
>>> for he is coming to judge the earth.
> He will judge the world with righteousness,
>> and the peoples with his truth.
>>> (96:11–13)

Or more graphically:

> Let the sea roar (*yir'am*) and all that fills it,
>> the world and those who live in it.
> Let the floods clap their hands;
>> let the hills together sing for joy before YHWH;
>>> for he is coming to judge the earth.
> He will judge the world with righteousness,
>> and the peoples with equity.
>>> (98:7–9)

Both psalms render cosmically what Psalm 67 confines to the political realm (67:4–5). Within the cosmic arena of praise, the sea's "roar"—usually taken as threat—is heard as the sea's song. In the psalmist's cry for a "new song" (*šîr ḥādāš*, 96:1; 98:1), the roaring of the waves is heard anew, namely, as praise rather than battle cry. The old "song" of conflict and violence is gone, displaced by the new song of all-encompassing praise. Just as divine kingship is celebrated by *all* creation in Psalm 96 (see v. 10), the deafening noise of pounding waves is perceived as hand-clapping in celebration of God's victory on Israel's behalf (98:1–3). Given its associations with chaos elsewhere, the image of the roiling sea is the perfect choice as the metonym of universal praise. Concomitant to the sea's praise in Psalm 96 is, moreover, the erasure of all gods, deemed as idols (96:4–5). As the creator of all (including the seas), YHWH is without equal within the divine realm, indeed alone, the psalmist asserts. Stripped of all associations of hostility and conflict, the sea's discourse of praise parallels God's solitary, uncontested reign.

Forgiveness as Cleansing

In addition to its sustaining power, water is cast as a cleansing agent in the well-known Psalm 51.

> Have mercy on me, O God,
>   according to your faithful love (*ḥesed*).
> According to the abundance of your compassion (*raḥămîm*),
>   blot (*měḥēh*) out my transgressions.
> Wash me (*kabběsēnî*) thoroughly from my iniquity,
>   and cleanse me (*ṭahărēnî*) from my sin.
> . . . .
> Purge me with hyssop so that I will be cleansed (*wě'eṭhār*);
>   wash me (*těkabběsēnî*) so that I shall be whiter than snow.
> Let me hear joy and gladness;
>   let the bones you have crushed rejoice.
> Hide your face from my sins;
>   and blot out (*měḥēh*) all my iniquities.
> Create in me a clean (*ṭāhôr*) heart, O God,
>   and put a new and steadfast spirit within me.
>   (51:1–2, 7–10)

Of all the penitential psalms, so designated in Christian tradition,[94] only Psalm 51 employs the language of washing. The imagery is strategic, since it corresponds to a certain metaphorical, albeit conventional, view of sin that is also unique to this psalm.[95] Whereas Psalm 38 regards sin as a crushing weight or burden to be lifted (38:4), Psalm 51 views sin as an intractable stain, "ever before" the psalmist's face, to be washed away or blotted out. The references to hyssop and purgation associate the psalmist's cleansing with ritual purification of the individual who has recovered from a skin affliction, as outlined in Lev 14:4–7. In this procedure, the hyssop is used as an aspergillum, or sprinkler, for applying blood and water, considered cleansing agents, on "the one who is to be cleansed" (14:7). Afterward, the individual's clothes must be washed and he or she must bathe, requisite acts for regaining the status of purity (*ṭāhōr*) and, thus, reinstatement into the community. The metaphor "Sin is stain" is matched by "Purity is spotlessness" and, in turn, "Forgiveness is cleansing."

In Psalm 51, however, there is no priest to bring about or confirm the speaker's cleansing. Only God, the one ultimately wronged, is sought by the psalmist. Designating the act of divine forgiveness is the regnant metaphor of washing. By extension, water targets the divine attributes—or, metaphorically speaking, ingredients—that effect moral cleansing: *ḥesed* ("faithful love") and *raḥămîm* ("compassion"). God's steadfast mercy, thus, would cleanse the psalmist, removing the stain of sin and thereby creating "a clean heart." What water metaphorically offers the contrite spirit is the sustaining, cleansing act of forgiveness.

Community and Sustenance

In a very different vein, liquid imagery is deployed in Psalm 133 to promulgate the value of comm*unity*. The psalmist develops the common image in a series of similes that evoke interrelated settings or source domains:

> See how good and pleasant it is
>   for kindred to live together in unity.
> [It is] like fine oil (*haššemen haṭṭôb*) upon the head,
>   running down upon the beard,
> [upon] the beard of Aaron,[96]
>   running down upon the collar of his robes.
> [It is] like dew (*ṭal*) on Hermon,
>   running down upon the mountains of Zion.
> For there YHWH has ordained the blessing,
>   life forevermore.
>
> (133:1–3)

As the psalmist invites the reader to "see," so the reader beholds three evocative scenes, each painted by metaphor. While the first verse unequivocally identifies the target domain, what follows is a series of two fluid images, oil and dew, that map the topography of community. The first simile, in fact, draws from two source domains. Evoking a sense of refreshment, oil on the head is emblematic of the custom of hospitality (see, e.g., Ps 23:5b). The same image dripping down Aaron's beard and collar suggests, however, an entirely different setting and source domain, namely, that of priestly consecration (Lev 8:10–12; cf. 1 Sam 10:1; 16:13). "Oil" carries the dual role of highlighting the joy and the sacredness of community. But that is not all: the final image of glistening dew on the mountains of Zion paints a picture of abundant fertility and prosperity, in short, shalom. God's blessing in and through community is embodied by the basic gifts of agricultural sustenance. What is more, the particular location of this image is critical: Mount Hermon (over nine thousand feet in elevation) in the far north[97] and Zion in the south (Jerusalem). These geographically extreme points share mountain dew, as it were, and thus common ground. Together, they serve as a call for national unity throughout greater Israel. The shift in imagery and source domain corresponds in part to the psalm's methodical movement from familial to religious to political unity. Dew and oil highlight the sacred blessing and prosperity of a kingdom united.

Instruction and Sustenance

It is appropriate to conclude this survey of such metaphors by taking another look at the psalm that opens the Psalter. Psalm 1 evinces an entirely unique use of water imagery that, in view of its position vis-à-vis the Psalter, helps to determine how all subsequent psalms are to be appropriated.[98]

> How fortunate is the one who
>   neither walks in the counsel of the wicked,
>   nor stands in the path of sinners,
>   nor sits in the seat of scoffers;
> but rather finds delight in the *tôrâ* of YHWH,
>   and reflects upon his *tôrâ* day and night.
> He will be like a tree transplanted by *channels of water*,
>   yielding its fruit in due season,
>   and whose leaves do not wither.
> Everything that he does will prove efficacious.
>
> (1:1–3)

Underlying and supporting the tree metaphor, which commands the iconic structure of the psalm, is the image of water channels. As noted in chapter 3, the images of tree and channeled watercourses recall the setting of the temple sanctuary. Yet in the deft hands of the psalmist, the source domain targets something new. The clue is found in a close structural comparison of vv. 2 and 3. As the righteous individual delights *in* and reflects *on* YHWH's *tôrâ* (v. 2), the tree is planted *by* ever-flowing streams (v. 3). The juxtaposition is deliberate and provocative. If, as the psalmist makes explicit, the arboreal metaphor designates the righteous individual, then the image of flowing channels signifies *tôrâ*, on which the individual reflects. As the tree is nourished by irrigated water, so the psalmist is sustained by *tôrâ*. Without *tôrâ*, the individual would wither, as it were, and dry up like chaff (v. 4).

The manner in which the water metaphor is deployed in Psalm 1 indicates innovative usage. Departing from its traditional association with the temple, water imagery, redirected by the poet, indicates the written and spoken words of *tôrâ*. *Tôrâ* replaces the temple as the sustaining and guiding force for the psalmist. *Tôrâ* becomes the object of deepest desire for those who thirst for God's sanctuary presence. By identifying *tôrâ* with flowing channels, the poet imbues such imagery with unmistakable didactic nuance. The individual is "instructed" as the tree is nourished by water. Authoritative instruction is thereby identified as the psalmist's sole source of sustenance.

It is striking, moreover, that the psalmist has chosen to cast the image of flowing water in the *plural*. Not a solitary stream or river commonly associated with the temple setting, but "channels" of water nourish a *single* tree. A river, indeed the river of God, split into separate channels is suggestive, for the psalmist acknowledges that *tôrâ* is no monolith but a plurality. Does the psalmist have in mind the fivefold division of the Torah and the Psalter? Put more broadly, are there to be heard amid the rush of flowing channels the various voices of the psalms, a "congregation" of voices, words from the righteous in refuge and in distress, in confession and in praise, all for the reader's edification (see v. 5)? Acknowledged also, perhaps, is that even the floodwaters of God's wrath and the fearsome abyss lift up their voice for the reader's *instruction*. One can only imagine. At any rate, the power of a metaphor unleashed provokes the kind of speculation that the psalmist would no doubt welcome. Such is the knowledge of water, knowledge couched in metaphor and revealed in *tôrâ*.

FROM THIRST TO INUNDATION: PSALM 42:1–8

Psalm 42 warrants extended discussion, since it features various images of water interrelated in profoundly evocative ways.[99]

1   As a doe longs for ravines of water (*'ăpîqê-māyim*)
     so my soul longs for you, O God.
2   My soul thirsts (*ṣāmĕ'āh*) for God, for the living God (*'ēl ḥāy*);
     when will I come and behold the face of God?
3   [Instead] my tears have been my food day and night,
     while [my detractors] say to me incessantly, "Where is your God?"

4   These things let me remember as I pour out my soul before me:
     How I passed over the covert of the mighty[100] to the house of God,
       with the cry of jubilation and thanksgiving,
          the din (*hāmôn*)[101] of festival making.
5   Why are you cast down, O my soul?
       Why do you rumble[102] within me?
     Wait upon God, for I shall again praise him,
       the victories of my God's countenance.[103]

6   My soul is cast down before me;
       therefore, I remember you:
     From the land of Jordan and Hermon,
       from Mount Mizar,
7   deep calls to deep at the clamor of your cataracts;
       all your billows and your waves pass over me.
8   By day YHWH commands his faithful love (*ḥesed*),
       and at night his song is with me,
          a prayer to the God of my life.

United by the refrain in vv. 5, 11, and in 43:5, these eight verses open a lament that extends through Psalm 43. Nevertheless, the opening verses form a distinct, coherent unit, in which the psalmist declares her remembrance of two separate episodes that provoke both despair and hope (42:4, 6b). The rhetorical appeal of this section, moreover, stems from the psalmist's evocative use of imagery. The unit is bounded and permeated by various metaphorical references to water.

From dry streambeds to sweeping floodwaters, the poetic parade of water images makes this psalm distinct among psalms. Most remarkable is the psalmist's deliberately ambiguous, if not innovative, use of such imagery. The psalmist seeks God's salutary presence, the "living God" (*'ēl ḥay*) of flowing streams,[104] and the floodgates are opened (v. 7). Like a doe searching for a gushing wadi to quench her thirst, the psalmist yearns to perceive God's presence in the temple, her refuge (43:2). "Streams," thus, signify the sustaining power of God's presence in worship. No other source will satisfy the psalmist's longing. Like many psalms, Psalm 42 plumbs the reader's deepest yearning and directs it toward God.[105] The psalm sets the tone at the outset by identifying God as the sole object of desire; indeed, the psalmist's life hangs in the balance. But no relief is in sight: desperation turns to grief as tears replace the prospect of fresh water. The psalmist must quench her thirst with salty tears shed over God's absence amid the taunts of her detractors.[106] The imagery turns metonymic: through tears the psalmist "pours out" her soul. She is on the verge of dissolution.

Such grief is only heightened by the remembrance of things past. Two quite vivid scenes are recalled: (1) a time when the psalmist sought refuge and became caught up in the clamor of festive worship at the sanctuary; and (2) a recollection of the mighty headwaters at the foothills of Hermon, the source of the Jordan.[107] Zion and the upper Jordan, two different worlds, are interlocked in memory. Contrary to appearances, both scenes share much in common, held together by similar terminology: the din of Jordan's cataracts and the clamor of festive worship, and interlaced throughout is the mournful tumult of the psalmist's soul (v. 5). The juxtaposition cries out for closer comparison. As the psalmist, engulfed by songs and shouts of praise, is caught up in a tidal wave of worship, she finds herself also swept away by the cascading waters of the Jordan-turned-flood. Are these mutually interrelated or diametrically opposing scenes?[108] Is the crush of watery chaos merely the foil for edifying worship and quenched thirst? The psalmist provokes such questions and, at the same time, provides certain clues.

Striking is the psalmist's claim that the overpowering billows are of God, not of chaos. Are the pounding waves, then, the instruments of God's wrath meant to drown the psalmist? Nowhere is reference made to divine judgment (contra Psalm 88). The psalmist exhorts herself to be patient in hope, not contrite or broken in spirit. She is not obliged to render restitution. Sin and judgment find no place in this psalm. Rather, the psalmist discerns something profoundly liturgical about "deep call[ing] to deep," something irresistible in the peals of praise and thanksgiving issuing from the temple. She does not founder before God's mighty waves; to the contrary, she identifies God's billows with *ḥesed* (v. 8)! As God stirs the stormy waves, so God "commands" steadfast kindness. Overwhelmed, the psalmist is at once awestruck and buoyed, however momentarily, by God's faithful love. Swept away by grace, the psalmist proclaims God's "song," voiced by worshipers and intimated by the deep, a song to ease and eventually replace her inward groaning. Worship and roiling waters have taken up the psalmist's inward tumult and borne it away. Through the deployment of metaphor, the voice of many waters and the voices of many at worship blend together.[109]

The clash and resulting transformation of iconic metaphors is well illustrated in this passage, which draws deeply from the rhetoric of sustenance, grief, and chaos to paint a new picture of divine compassion and human pathos. Abstractly put, three controlling, yet interrelating, metaphorical schemas structure this part of Psalm 42.

1. *God as water.* The opening wilderness scene associates water with God, specifically divine sustenance. As flowing streams quench the thirst of wild animals, so "seeing God" satisfies the psalmist's fervent longing. Yet only deprivation is found to be the norm. The metaphor of thirst maps the psalmist's felt lack of divine aid and presence. God is out of sight; water is only a mirage. The taunting question "Where is your God?" reveals the target of the psalmist's figurative thirst. Sustenance obtained is vindication by God (43:1).

2. *Self as water.* Through the metonym of tears, the psalmist identifies herself as water "poured out" in grief. Without God's sustaining presence, without water in the wadi, the psalmist's only resort is tears for "nourishment," salty drops, which fail to quench a parched throat. Yet she is sustained, however fleetingly, in her articulation of grief. With tears shed and consumed, the psalmist remembers and finds hope.

3. *Worship as water.* Amid the psalmist's inward groanings, the roar of cascading waters and the din of festive worship are bound together by poetic hyperbole. Both evince God's *ḥesed* and song (42:8). The psalmist is left inundated, submerged in worship and in memory, with the seeds of hope in hand. The scene of onrushing water, in fact, imbues the refrainlike admonition with special significance: "Wait in God; for I shall again give praise." Even the driest streambeds will once again be charged with rushing water, sweeping away rocks, cleansing the soil, and fructifying a parched land, albeit temporarily.

From a silent, barren wadi to the thunderous roar of flood-borne waves, water finds a way of filtering through the psalmist's complaint and praise in this first section. Indeed, the opening unit marks only the first of several sections in the two psalms that move from despair and complaint to hope and praise. The psalmist's lament ebbs and flows, perhaps to testify not only by image but also in structure that God's sustaining presence flows like a seasonal wadi: it runs dry but will surely roar again, indeed with a vengeance. Such is, the psalmist implies, the bipolar character of faith.

Chapter 6

The Song of Leviathan

God's Theater of Praise

[Y]ou have only to sing, and the rocks will crystallize;
Sing, and the plants will organize;
Sing, and the animals will be born.

Ralph Waldo Emerson[1]

Had I fought with wild animals at Ephesus with only human hopes, what
would I have gained by it?

Apostle Paul[2]

Although references to animals abound in the psalms, their significance for the Psalter's shape and theology has been largely overlooked.[3] Easily classifiable according to their various target domains, many animal metaphors are deployed to target the psalmist's enemies. Fewer in number are those that bear self-referential status: they designate the individual speaker or professing community. Several references, however, do not carry ostensible metaphorical force, as in the creation psalms. Nevertheless, even these are so fraught with contextual background that their significance extends beyond mere zoological classification.

Finally, animals play a climactic role at the Psalter's conclusion: they, along with the human community, give voice to God's praise. An examination of each of these levels of signification reveals something of the Psalter's performative drama and theology.

ANIMALS AS METAPHORS

Most references to animals in the Psalter find a home in the rhetoric of affliction, as in the psalmist's cry for rescue. Evoking a world ravaged by mortal conflict and contention, animal imagery serves to label both the psalmist and the perceived enemy.

Animal as Enemy

The psalms present a virtual taxonomy of dangerous animals to underscore the various threats encountered from *within* the human community: encircling bulls (22:12), scavenging dogs (22:16a; 59:6, 14), sharp-horned wild oxen (22:21b), venomous serpents (58:4–5), a swarm of bees (118:12),[4] a ravaging boar (80:13),[5] and devouring lions (7:2; 10:9; 17:12; 22:13, 21a; 35:17; 57:4; 58:6).[6] In addition, references to mythological creatures such as Leviathan (74:14; 104:26) and Rahab (89:10), though not metaphors proper, evoke by virtue of their cosmic stature certain associations within the psalmist's immediate purview.

Lion

Of all the animal species profiled in the Psalter, the most common is the lion, whose predatory strength was well known among the ancients and highly adaptable for poetic application.[7] The prophets, for example, found the lion to be a fitting image of military aggression.[8] The psalmists, similarly, deployed the image to designate certain unnamed enemies, as in the following plea for deliverance:

> YHWH, my God, in you I take refuge;
>> save me from all my pursuers, and deliver me,
> lest like a lion (*'aryēh*) they[9] rip my throat (*nepeš*),[10]
>> dragging [me] away with no one [around] to rescue.
>>> (7:1–2)

The horror that this scene evokes is graphically shown in an ivory relief from Nimrud, seen in fig. 15, which dates to the late eighth or early seventh century B.C.E. Owing to its rapacious reputation, the lion makes an eminently evocative metaphor for the psalmist's enemies and their abusive use of power. The psalmist, however, is not the only victim. The socially vulnerable are also counted as objects of predatory treatment, in this case by the wicked.

Fig. 15: Ivory plaque of a lion devouring a boy from the palace of Ashurnasirpal II, Nimrud. © Copyright the British Museum. Phoenician in style, a nearly identical plaque is featured in the Iraq Museum, Baghdad.

With cursing is his mouth filled, along with deceit and oppression;
    under his tongue are trouble and iniquity.
He sits in ambush in the villages (*ma'rab ḥāṣērîm*);
    in hiding places he murders the innocent.
His eyes stealthily watch (*yiṣpōnû*) for the unfortunate (*ḥēlĕkâ*);
    he stalks (*ye'ĕrōb*) in secret like a lion (*'aryēh*) in its covert.
He stalks (*ye'ĕrōb*) in order to seize the poor;
    he seizes the poor and drags them off in his net.
He stoops, he crouches,
    and the unfortunate[11] fall by his might.
He thinks in his heart, "God has forgotten;
    he has hidden his face; he will never see it."

(10:7–11)

Although both psalms vividly convey the lion's power to seize and drag, Psalm 10 supplies additional detail that marks the metaphor's limit. The psalmist's enemy seizes by stealth his victims, who are like the weak among the lion's prey (see also 17:11–12). Stress is also laid on the enemy's discourse in 10:7, which corresponds metaphorically to the lion's devouring mouth. The metaphor, however, abruptly changes in v. 9 with reference to "net." Lions, as far as we know, do not cast nets to snatch their prey. Through reference to the net, the psalmist mixes the metaphorical framework and sets the lion's stealth within the larger figurative context of game hunting. While the lion's furtiveness is underscored, the actual attack is conveyed by the image of the hunter who successfully bags his prey. The lion has become "personified," revealing all the more the generative power of the metaphor to establish associations with human character, specifically that of the wicked.

The figure of the lion featured in Psalm 22 is counted as one among several violent animals (i.e., bulls, dogs, and wild oxen) that beset the psalmist (vv. 12, 16, 21). The lion in particular is noted for its ravenous appetite and roar (v. 13), as well as its distinctive weapon of destruction, the mouth (v. 21a), comparable to the deadly horns of the wild ox (v. 21b).

> Many bulls encircle me;
>   strong bulls of Bashan surround me.[12]
> They open wide their mouths against me,
>   a lion (*'aryēh*), ripping and roaring.
> . . . .
> Save me from the mouth of the lion (*'aryēh*)!
> From the horns of the wild oxen you have rescued me.
>   (22:12–13, 21)

As in Psalm 22, the mouth of unnamed adversaries featured in Psalm 35 receives the most attention: the psalmist rails against "malicious witnesses" who mock and gnash the psalmist "with their teeth" (vv. 11, 16). "Rescue me from their ravages, my life from the lions!" is the urgent cry (v. 17). Such focus on the lion's mouth corresponds to the wounds the psalmist claims to have suffered from the abusive discourse of his or her enemies, those "who do not speak peace, but . . . conceive deceitful words against those who are quiet. They open wide their mouths against me" (vv. 20–21a). The enemies' most brutal weapon, the psalmist contends, is their discourse. The violence is verbal. Elsewhere in the Psalter, the tongue of the wicked is "a sharp razor" (52:2); the wicked "love all words that devour" (v. 4). While the sages of Proverbs highlight in general the harmful effects of wicked and foolish speech,[13] the psalmist presents a brutally personal account of discursive abuse.

The "discourse" of the lion receives particular focus in Psalm 57, which vividly describes the psalmist's dire straits:

> I must lie down among lions (*lĕbā'im*),[14]
>   aflame (*lōhăṭîm*)[15] for human beings.
> Their teeth are spears and arrows,
>   their tongues sharp swords.
>   (57:4)

To be the object of the enemies' scorn is to be cast into the lions' den. Again, the devouring mouth commands the lion's share of attention. The remedy is vividly described in the following psalm, a prayer for vengeance: "O God, break the teeth in their mouths; pull out the fangs of the young lions, YHWH!" (58:6). Lions defanged are the wicked "de-potentialized." Backbiting enemies stripped of their malicious discourse are rendered harmless. Without the capacity to devour the righteous by their words, the wicked, backed by the gods (vv. 1–2), will ineluctably "dissolve away" like "the snail (*šabbĕlûl*) into slime" (v. 8), making way for God's justice to reign supreme throughout the land (v. 11).

Various psalmic passages, moreover, invoke the figure of the lion, or comparable metaphor, only indirectly. In Psalm 35, the psalmist complains of "foreigners"[16] who "tore at me without ceasing . . . , gnashing at me with their teeth" (vv. 15–16), and later pleads to God to save his life "from the lions" (v. 17). Elsewhere, the psalmist praises God for not having "given us as prey to their teeth" (124:6). In one instance, the target domain of the metaphor is not the psalmist's human enemy, but God: "Mark this," the psalmist warns, "you who forget God, or I will tear you apart without anyone to deliver" (50:22).[17]

Lion imagery, in short, heightens the psalmist's helplessness before the overwhelming power of the enemy, like prey before the predator. The enemy exhibits a fearsome combination of stealth and aggression. As consummate predators, the wicked are cast as eminently bloodthirsty, reveling in the destruction of the weak. Moreover, the lion's mouth is singled out as particularly dangerous, suggesting that the gravest weapon enemies wield is discursive in nature. Their "devouring" words consist of false accusations and slander, against which the psalmist has no hope for defense except from God, vindicator of victims and lion hunter.

Serpent

In addition to the lion, other deadly species serve to highlight the threatening nature of the psalmist's opponents, including the venomous serpent. As quintessential metaphors for the psalmist's enemies, the serpent and the lion share a natural alliance:

> Surely, [YHWH] will command his angels in your behalf,
>   to guard you in all your ways.
> On their hands they will bear you up,
>   lest you dash your foot against a stone.
> You will tread on the lion (*šaḥal*)[18] and the cobra (*peten*),
>   the young lion (*kĕpîr*) and the serpent (*tannîn*)
>   you will trample underfoot.
>   (91:11–13)

Though the passage conveys their imminent defeat, the psalmist's enemies are as dangerous as lions and serpents. Nevertheless, under God's protection the psalmist need "only look . . . and see the punishment of the wicked" (v. 8).

Psalm 58 gives exclusive attention to the serpentine nature of the wicked, whose "venom" is to be avoided at all costs.

> The wicked are estranged (*zōrû*) from the womb;
>   the spokesmen of deception (*dōbrê kāzāb*) err from their birth.
> They have venom like the venom of a serpent (*nāḥāš*),
>   like the deaf cobra (*peten*) that stops its ear.
> It does not hear the voice of charmers,
>   of the cunning enchanters.
>   (58:3–5)

As with the lion, most feared about the wicked is their mouth. Far from benign, their deceitful words are venomous. Evildoers, complains another psalmist, have "sharpened their tongue as a snake's (*nāḥāš*), and under their lips is the venom of vipers ('*akšûb*)" (140:3).[19] Like a snake that cannot be charmed and thus will strike at whim, the wicked, moreover, are unyielding and unmanageable, indeed untamable. In the psalm, the conflict between the righteous and the wicked begins, at the very least, as a war of words, escalating into violence.[20] Not only do the wicked utter life-threatening pronouncements, they are impervious to the words of the righteous, for they are "deaf."

Dog

Associated with filth and death, "dog" (*keleb*) typically serves as a term of contempt in biblical tradition.[21] Unlike lions and other "beasts of the field," dogs were half wild in ancient times, flourishing as scavengers on the margins of human civilization. In the Psalter, an element of fear is added to the canine's pejorative status. Like the lion and the serpent, "dogs" are noted for their deadly mouth, specifically their bark and bite. Moreover, canine imagery in the Psalms supplies another dimension to the profile of the enemy. As a pack animal, the dog highlights the collective force of the psalmist's foes.

> Each evening they come back, howling like dogs
> and prowling about the city.
> See them bellowing with their mouths,
> with swords on their lips—
> For "Who will hear us?"[22]
> . . . .
> Each evening they come back, howling like dogs,
> and prowling about the city.
> They roam about for food,
> and growl if they do not get their fill.
> (59:6–7, 14–15)

The image of prowling, howling dogs running loose throughout the city expresses the sense of impunity shared by the psalmist's enemies.[23] Nobody can stand up to their ravenous bellowing; they go about wreaking havoc, unheard, as it were (v. 7b). Like the deadly serpent, dogs roaming in packs about the bleak urban landscape are untamable. As with the lion, the danger lies in the "swords on their lips." Deliberately sandwiched between the canine descriptions is attention paid to prideful, hostile discourse:

> [Because of] the sin of their mouths, the words of their lips,
> let them be trapped in their pride.
> Because of the cursing and lies they utter,
> destroy them in wrath.
> (59:12–13a)

With a flair for poetic justice, the psalmist petitions that the devouring dogs be themselves trapped. Although the precise nature of their "words" is irretrievably hidden underneath the metaphorical veneer, the psalmist does offer a clue as to the cause of his or her plight early in the prayer: "For no transgression or sin of mine, YHWH, for no fault of mine, they run and make ready" (59:3–4a). The psalmist's complaint is in part a protestation of innocence in the face of false accusation, from which the psalmist seeks "refuge" in God (v. 16b).

Along with lions and bull, Psalm 22 identifies the dog as an equally fearsome animal:

> Surely, dogs (*kĕlābîm*) are all around me;
> a company of evildoers encircles me.
> . . . .
> Deliver my soul from the sword,
> my life from the power of the dog (*keleb*)![24]
> Save me from the mouth of the lion.
> (22:16, 20–21a)

Like the "strong bulls of Bashan" (v. 12), the image of encircling dogs indicates the collective force of enemies who have it in for the psalmist. Sword, dog, and lion are all rhetorically equated at the conclusion of the psalm's complaint.

In sum, the psalmist's "personal" enemies, as well as the wicked in general, are associated with certain dangerous animals. As the domain of the wild is considered inimical to human culture in ancient Near Eastern lore,[25] so the wicked are considered deleterious to ordered society. More than simply robbing enemies of their humanity,[26] the psalmists' choice to deploy specifically *animal* metaphors within the rhetoric of complaint sets in stark relief the imminent danger the "wicked" pose to society and the innocent individual. Within the psalmist's world, the wicked *qua animalia* are considered subhuman in their penchant for violence and, thus, warrant retribution that is equally inhumane. Descriptions of their just deserts are just as brutal as the drawings of their caricatures. Not surprisingly, such descriptions are occasionally shrouded in the metaphorical cloak of *suffering* animals: the enemies, for instance, are to become "prey for jackals" (63:10) and "like the snail that dissolves away into slime" (58:8). In petition, the psalmist expresses the fervent hope that the predator become the prey.

Nonetheless, such vengeance is fulfilled *not* by anything the psalmist does. He or she does not typically pray for combat prowess, special weapons,[27] or, more metaphorically, theriomorphic transformation as the wicked have undergone via the psalmist's rhetoric. Unlike the theriomorphic self-portraits of many an ancient Near Eastern king, the psalmist is never cast as a predator or hunter poised to pounce on enemy prey. Oriental despots of antiquity, by contrast, frequently portrayed themselves as devouring lions, belligerent bulls, ravenous wolves, venomous serpents, and ferocious dragons consuming their enemies.[28] Not so with the psalmist: only *divine* justice can rectify the psalmist's distress.

Wild Animals

The setting of social conflict reflected in a number of animal references in the Psalter provides critical background to the several references to divine judgment leveled against wild animals per se. The lion and the serpent in 91:13, for example, warrant divine vengeance, not only because they are in fact dangerous but also because they evoke a range of associations beyond their zoological classification: dangers, including *human* danger, that can beset the one who seeks refuge with God. The punishment of the wicked is assured via God's protection of the righteous (v. 8). The broad significance of these animals is no more confined to zoological danger than the "stone" from which God's "angels" protect the psalmist is limited to geological formations and stubbed toes (vv. 11–12). Fraught with social background, these literary figures connote the ever-present danger posed by the wicked, the psalmists' enemies, against the community of the righteous.

In Psalm 68, a composite processional hymn of praise, the following charge is given:

> Rebuke the beast of the reed-thicket (*ḥayyat qāneh*),
> the herd of bulls with the calves,[29] the peoples.
> Trample[30] underfoot those who prize[31] silver;[32]
> scatter[33] the peoples who delight in battles.
> (68:30)

God is exhorted to "rebuke the beast" and at the same time "trample" militant nations. Given the parallelism, considerable semantic overlap is evident between the wild kingdom and oppressive human kingdoms. Although the precise sense of this poetic line is disputed, "bulls" (*'abbîrîm*) and "calves" (*'ăgālîm*) seem to designate human rulers or warriors.[34] Furthermore, reference to "reeds" suggests association with Egypt (see v. 31).[35] The metaphorical scope of these terms is made all the more explicit by the larger context of Israel depicted as a "flock" secured by God's "goodness" and provision (v. 10).

There are, in addition, references to wild animals in the Psalter that do not appear to be metaphorical in scope. Occasionally an animal is just an animal, though rarely so in the Psalter. Even the two examples given above (91:13 and 68:30) are cases in which the boundary between metaphor and zoological reality is deliberately blurred. Although animals *qua animalia* are meant, their connection with human adversaries cannot be altogether severed. Psalm 74 presents a typical example of parallel association:

> Remember how so the enemy scoffs, YHWH,
> and a foolish people reviles your name.
> Do not deliver the soul of your dove (*tôr*) to the wild animal (*ḥayyat*);
> do not forget the life of your poor forever.
> (74:18–19)

The analogy remains in place: the wild animal is to the dove as the enemy is to the psalmist and the "poor." The poetic parallelism suggests both guilt and innocence by association.

Mythological Beasts

More cosmic in scope and, in turn, less metaphorical in degree are references to mythological creatures in the Psalter. The figure of Leviathan in Psalm 74 is exemplary:

> Yet God my King is from of old,
>   who works salvation in the earth's midst.
> You divided Sea (*yam*) by your strength;
>   you broke the heads of the dragons (*tannînîm*) of the waters.
> You crushed the heads of Leviathan;
>   you gave him as food for the denizens of the desert.[36]
> You cut openings for springs and torrents;
>   you dried up ever-flowing streams.
>
>   (74:12–15)

This vivid scene is set within the larger mythological drama of God's battle against chaos and the establishment of creation, reflecting a long and venerable tradition in ancient Near Eastern lore.[37] Yamm, Tiamat, Leviathan, Rahab: each is associated with watery chaos, whose powerful waves assault creation, threatening to overwhelm it. As royal warrior, God vanquishes chaos in order to establish the salutary order of creation. Similar to the Mesopotamian epic of creation, *Enūma eliš,* itself rooted in West Semitic lore, divine conquest leads to creation, including the formation of rivers, celestial spheres, and seasons (vv. 15–17). Psalm 74, in particular, conjoins the defeat of the chaos monsters with the division of the sea (vv. 13–14a). The transition from the waters' defeat to their positive role on earth, alluded to in v. 15a, is abrupt yet not unprecedented (see, e.g., 46:2–4; 104:6–13).

In addition to Leviathan and the sea dragons of Psalm 74 looms another figure spawned from watery chaos among the psalms.

> YHWH God of hosts,
>   who is as mighty as you, YH[WH]?
> Your faithfulness is your surrounding.
> You rule the sea's raging;
>   when its waves rise, you still them.
> You crushed Rahab like a carcass;
>   with your mighty arm you scattered your enemies.
> The heavens belong to you, the earth also is yours;
>   the world and all that is in it—
> You have founded them.
>
>   (89:8–11)

Like Leviathan, Rahab is associated with the "raging" sea, whose defeat is requisite to the establishment of divine rule over the waters and God's incontestable ownership of all creation, both heaven and earth. Like Tiamat's defeat by Marduk, Rahab's demise in Psalm 89 signals the rout of God's enemies. Such cosmic, primordial struggle, however, is not without political significance. God's enemies are considered Israel's enemies, and vice versa. God promises to "crush" the king's foes like Rahab and, thereby, extend Israel's dominion to the "sea" (vv. 22–25; cf. vv. 41–43). Moreover, the fearsome figure of Rahab is often deployed elsewhere as a poetic label or target for Egypt (Ps 87:4; Isa 30:7; 51:9), an association that possibly pertains in Psalm 89 as well.[38] In any case, Rahab is the mythological metonym *and* metaphor for God's enemies, both cosmic and historical.

Conclusion

As this all too brief survey suggests, cosmos and culture are inseparably intertwined within the Psalter's world of image and figurative speech. Animal imagery serves to label and, in turn, dehumanize the enemies of God, of Israel, and of the righteous individual. In addition, the stock of faunal images out of which the psalmists drew for their petitions and laments are scarcely domestic in type; they are thoroughly wild and dangerous, even the scavenging dogs. They pose a dire threat to the livelihood of the individual as well as to the cosmic order. Their defeat, in turn, inaugurates both blessing for the individual and God's life-sustaining rule in behalf of creation.

The connection between cosmos and individual is, in fact, rhetorically strategic. From the psalmist's standpoint, the vindication of the individual vis-à-vis the wicked is enlisted as an integral part of God's cosmic rule, an association made all the more blatant in the one dissonant note sounded in the great hymn of creation of Psalm 104 (see pp. 158–62). Having recounted the grandeur of creation in all its manifold glory, the psalmist concludes with a peal of praise that is interrupted by a single dissonant chord: "Let sinners be finished off from the earth, and let the wicked be no more. Bless YHWH, O my soul" (104:35). Chaos persists, the psalmist observes, not in lions and Leviathan, who are considered bona fide recipients of God's sustaining care and pleasure (vv. 21, 26), but in the wicked, the *truly* wild, untamable part of creation, warranting nothing less than their eradication. Only then, the psalmist implies, will creation be complete.

Self and God as Animal

The agents of chaos and opposition, whether cosmic or human, do not possess a monopoly on faunal images in the Psalter. In addition to castigating the wicked, the psalmist targets himself or herself as an animal within certain polemical contexts.

Bird

The most common animal metaphor that carries self-referential status, attested five times in the Psalter, is ornithological by genus:

> In YHWH do I take refuge;
>> so how can you say to me,
> "Flee to the mountains like a bird (*ṣippôr*);[39]
>> for look, the wicked bend the bow.
> They have fitted their arrow to the string,
>> to shoot in the dark at the upright in heart. . . ?"
>> (11:1–2)

The psalmist is urged to flee before being attacked by the wicked (in the metaphorical guise of fowlers), yet stands firm in the conviction that protection is imminent (vv. 5–6). Refuge, the psalmist confidently declares, is already realized and made available by YHWH's residing in "his holy temple" (v. 4). To flee like a bird is not only rash but a violation of trust in God's care and protection of the righteous (v. 7).

Nothing, however, is shameful in the use of such imagery in the following cry for help:

> My heart writhes (*yāḥîl*) within me;
>> the terrors of death have fallen upon me.
> Fear and trembling befall me,
>> and horror covers me.
> I say, "O that I had wings like a dove (*yônâ*)!
>> I would fly away and be at rest.
> See, I would flee far away;
>> I would lodge in the desert.
> I would hasten to find a place of escape (*miplāṭ*) for myself
>> from the rushing wind, from the tempest."
>> (55:4–8)

The psalmist finds herself in the midst of conflict against "many . . . arrayed against me" (v. 18). But the battle is not waged by distant, anonymous enemies; it is instigated by a "familiar friend" and "companion" (v. 13). Nowhere in this psalm is the companion-turned-enemy cast as a savage animal, as is so often the case elsewhere among the psalms, for such a rhetorical move would subvert the sense of intimacy that once characterized the psalmist's relationship with the other and would thereby dilute the corrosive nature of betrayal. The rhetoric of betrayal requires that the hostile *other* maintain some semblance of human identity, indeed be her familiar equal, while also her bitter nemesis. The language of fraternal violation, rooted in covenant (v. 20b), spills over into the language of discourse: the speech of her betrayer is both "smoother than butter" and "set on war"; it is "softer than oil" yet violent as "drawn swords" (v. 21).

The magnitude of such betrayal is so overwhelming that the psalmist desires only to escape and "be at rest." The image of the dove, the prey of raptors, innocent and vulnerable, provides an evocative means of transporting the psalmist to a wish-filled realm of safety. Such a domain is not to be found, however, within the protective walls of Zion. Rather, into a natural shelter "in the desert," a refuge apart from Refuge, remote from all contact with the cult, must the psalmist flee

(v. 7), while calling on God, "enthroned from of old," to wreak vengeance (vv. 16–19, 22–23). Traditionally associated with danger and chaos, the wilderness is the psalmist's locus of refuge. Why such a move that runs counter to most references to "refuge" in the Psalter? Because the psalmist's betrayer is himself associated with the "house of God" (v. 14)! Finding refuge *within* Zion is no longer an option for the speaker (v. 12); fleeing as far as possible to a distant, uninhabitable place is the psalmist's desideratum. The dove is her vehicle.

Much in contrast to Psalm 55, another bird in the wilderness has found not refuge, but desolation.

> I am like a scops owl (*qā'āt*)[40] of the desert,
>   like a tawny owl (*kôs*)[41] of the waste places.
> I lie awake and cry (*wā'ehyeh*),[42]
>   like a bird, [I am] alone (*bôdēd*)[43] on the housetop.
> All day long my enemies taunt me;
>   those who deride me use me for a curse.
>   (102:6–8)

The imagery is prefaced by the psalmist's physical distress: burning bones and wasted condition (vv. 3–5). Though their precise zoological identities are not certain, these species are classified as unclean in biblical tradition[44] and associated with scenes of devastation.[45] In Arabic lore, the nocturnal owl is the "mother of ruins."[46] Such association raises the level of lament to a new height: the psalmist suffers isolation, even derision. Through metaphor, the psalmist's distress is given a distinctly social nuance insofar as the imagery of unclean birds associated with lamentation is expressive of isolation (both in the wilderness and on the housetop!) and vulnerability. Instead of finding refuge in the wilderness, the psalmist *qua avis* finds only rejection, hence his accusation against God, "[Y]ou have lifted me up and thrown me aside" in anger (v. 10). The owl's plight in the wilderness is not its refuge but its exile. The psalmist's only hope is that Zion be rebuilt and, thereby, provide occasion and setting for YHWH to "regard the prayer of the destitute" (vv. 16–17[47]) and not to kill him at the "mid-point" of his life (v. 24).

Such imagery also finds its nest-home in a hymn of thanksgiving, testifying to YHWH's deliverance amid enemy attack:

> Blessed be YHWH,
>   who has not given us as prey to [our enemies'] teeth.
> We have escaped like a bird (*ṣippôr*)
>   from the snare of the fowlers (*yôqěšîm*);
>   the snare is broken, and we have escaped.
>   (124:6–7)

The metaphors that target both the community and its enemies fit hand in glove to highlight the inequity of power: birds and fowlers. Unlike many psalms, however, there is no talk of vanquished enemies. The occasion for praise is relatively more modest. According to the psalmist, who speaks on the community's behalf, God has enabled Israel to escape the "snare" (*paḥ*) of its enemies. There is no apology for the narrowness of such escape; no shame is associated with the flight of a bird. Rather, the very success of escape is sufficient to provoke petitionless praise.

An ostensibly stronger basis for praise is found in Psalm 103, in which the specific image of the raptor is used to connote the people's strength and rejuvenation.

> Bless YHWH, O my soul,
>   and do not forget all his benefits—
> who forgives all your iniquity,
>   who heals all your diseases,
> who redeems your life from the pit,
>   who crowns you with faithful love and mercy,
> who satisfies you with good as long as you live
>   so that your youth is renewed like the raptor's (*nešer*).
>   (103:2–5)

Reference to the "raptor" (specifically, "griffon vulture"?[48]) is situated at the culmination of God's redemptive work. Beginning with the theme of forgiveness and concluding with enduring sustenance, Israel's rejuvenation marks the climax of this litany of redemption. As in Isa 40:31, the specific image of the raptor expresses renewal of strength in the face of insurmountable challenges. Whereas the prophet identifies the specific experience of exile as occasion for redemptive hope, the psalmist catalogs the more general challenges of sin, disease, death, and danger. In both texts, the image of the raptor marks the community's recovery of strength, a return to what once characterized the flourishing life of the community. Much in contrast to the figures of dove, owl, and bird, the raptor embodies the renewal of strength over and against the enervating powers of chaos.

As discussed in chapter 1, God is also often envisioned as a bird in the Psalter. Of all the animal metaphors that could be used to "target" or "map" the deity, particularly predatory images,[49] only ornithological imagery is explicitly employed.[50] Applied to the psalmist, such imagery frequently connotes vulnerability and flight in the face of adversity. Applied to God, however, such imagery suggests the opposite. YHWH's "wings" and "shadow" afford inviolable protection for those who seek refuge. As God's spirit or wind (*rûaḥ*) "hovered" like a bird over the abysmal waters prior to creation (Gen 1:2; cf. Deut 32:11), so God's presence, *qua avis*, creates a shield of protection on behalf of the needy and afflicted.[51]

Worm

As ornithological imagery can connote either vulnerability or strength, shame or survival, depending on the specific image and context, there is one species of animal that expresses only abject self-debasement and rejection in the Psalter.

> I am a worm (*tôla'at*) and not a human (*'îš*),
>   scorned in public,[52] despised by people.

All who see me mock me;
    they open wide their mouths at me;
    they shake their heads.
        (Ps 22:6–7)[53]

Quite striking in this prayer for deliverance from persecution is the way both the psalmist and her enemies are characterized. The psalmist is no lone voice crying out in the wilderness. She expresses outrage over those who assault her and over the God who remains scandalously aloof. The victim feels robbed of humanity and debased as a lowly worm, a scavenger of corpses. The imagery is set in stark relief to the psalmist's tribute to the maternal care she had received in the womb *and* after birth (vv. 9–10). She lovingly affirms her move from mother to God and petitions that God once again be near to her, as her mother's breast once was in her infancy.

But now, more vulnerable than an infant, the psalmist is nothing more than a worm. Associated with frailty and death, the image serves to heighten the gravity of her distress and abandonment.[54] The speaker of Psalm 22 finds herself far from masterfully made (contra 139:14); she sees herself undone, both physically and morally. Her deprecation is comparable to that of another psalmist, who regards himself as a "grasshopper" (Ps 109:23b). Moreover, she considers her detractors to be equally inhuman; savage animals they all are (22:12–13, 16, 21; see above). The rhetoric of conflict that characterizes vv. 1–21 has reduced *all* human parties to veritable animals, either vicious or vulnerable, setting the stage for a remarkable transition that begins in v. 21b. In thanksgiving for God's deliverance, the psalmist talks of kindred, the "offspring of Jacob," "the great congregation," the "poor" who are satisfied, and "all the families of the nations" worshiping God (vv. 22–27). Consonant with the dramatic yet abrupt movement from complaint to praise, the psalmist is changed from worm to witness, and along with her transformation all humanity is restored, "de-theriomorphized," as it were.

Behemoth

Another self-debasing use of animal imagery is found in Psalm 73, one of several psalms that wrestle with the problem of theodicy.[55]

I was stupid and ignorant;
    [as] Behemoth[56] I was to you (*'immāk*).
Nevertheless, I continue to be with you (*'immāk*);[57]
    you hold me by my right hand.
You guide me by your counsel,
    and afterward you will receive me [in] glory (*kābôd*).
        (73:22–24)

The animal imagery in Psalm 73 is species-specific. The term *běhēmôt*, an apparent plural form for "cattle" elsewhere in Hebrew, likely reflects the proper name found in Job 40:15 and probably in Isa 30:6. Speculation about the precise species of animal has focused on the hippopotamus as a likely candidate. In Job, the creature bears mythic stature and is portrayed as a formidable, lumbering beast (40:15–24). Such imagery serves to capture the psalmist's former self, one who was intransigent and defiant toward God (cf. Ps 32:8–9). The imagery changes dramatically from that of brutish ignorance to the tenderness of a parent holding a child's hand.[58] Earlier, the psalmist confesses his envy of the arrogant (73:3a), plagued as he is with the prosperity of the wicked (vv. 3b–14) and wearied in his attempts to make sense of such undeserved blessing. Only by entering into the "sanctuary of God" is the psalmist granted new sight: "then I perceived their end" (v. 17b). And so the ignorant beast is transformed into enlightened witness, not by dint of intellectual power but by means of God's sustaining guidance, whose telos is sanctuary.

Deer

One of the most familiar psalms opens with the faunal imagery of a deer:

> As a doe[59] longs for ravines of water,
>   so my soul longs for you, O God.
> My soul thirsts for God, for the living God;
>   when will I come and behold[60] the face of God?
> [Instead] my tears have been my food day and night,
>   while [my detractors] say to me incessantly, "Where is your God?"
>   (42:1–3)

As "flowing streams" are associated with Zion, the "house of God" (v. 4),[61] so the image of the thirsty deer conveys most vividly the psalmist's singular yearning for God. Iconographically, the image of the *female* deer, with its head lowered to graze or drink, is a widespread motif among numerous Judean seals and bullae dating to the eighth and seventh centuries B.C.E., like the seal shown in fig. 16.[62]

The image of the grazing doe represents the petitioner in worship and prayer. In Psalm 42, the imagery corresponds to the psalm's focus on the "soul" (*nepeš*), feminine grammatically and referenced throughout, including in the refrain (vv.

Fig. 16: Seal with an engraved doe from southern Palestine. Reprinted with permission from Othmar Keel and Christoph Uehlinger, *Gods, Goddesses, and Images of God in Ancient Israel*, trans. Thomas H. Trapp (Minneapolis: Fortress, 1998), 185 (#200b). Courtesy of the Department of Biblical Studies, University of Fribourg.

4, 5, 11; 43:5). The image of the doe is the projected "soul," the psalmist's personal self. The faunal metaphor defines the soul as the person's existential core, embodied in piety, fully dependent and vulnerable, searching and satisfied by God's salutary presence. The psalmist yearns to behold the face of God, to enter into God's sanctuary presence.[63] Conversely, her distress is heightened by God's absence, and like the doe whose head is stooped as it searches for water, her soul is "downcast."

The psalmist, moreover, feels hunted and mortally wounded by the verbal barbs of her detractors in their relentless questioning: "Where is your God?" (42:3, 10). The enemies' deadliest weapon, as noted in other psalms, is their discourse; their questions shoot forth like arrows that pierce everything that had defined and nurtured the psalmist's very being or "soul" (vv. 4–5, 11). The figure of the doe thus lends a poignant sense of pathos, as well as humble piety, to the profile of the speaker.

Deer imagery is employed most positively in the royal thanksgiving song of Psalm 18, which celebrates the king's victory over national foes.[64] The "refuge" word field is prominent: God is rock, shield, refuge, stronghold, and warrior. It is from God's temple that the king's cry is heard (v. 6). But of all the evocative metaphors in this psalm, only one is reserved for the king, and a modest one at that:

> For who is God except YHWH?
>   And who is a rock besides our God?—
> The God who girds me with strength,
>   and has made my way perfect.
> He sets my feet like the feet of does (*'ayyālôt*),
>   and places me secure on the heights.[65]
> He trains my hands for war,
>   so that my arms could bend a bow of bronze.
> You give me the shield of your salvation,
>   and your right hand supports me;
>   your help[66] has made me great.
> You lengthen my stride beneath me,
>   so that my feet do not slip.
>
>   (18:31–36)

In the context of war, the image of the delicate deer appears woefully out of place. Instead of flowing streams and bucolic meadows is a blood-soaked battlefield. The psalmist revels in graphic descriptions of his successful pursuit and victory over his enemies, who are beat into "dust before the wind" (v. 42). Such a setting, it would seem, requires a different animal metaphor, like the *lion*—an eminently royal, military image in its own right.[67] Both Mesopotamian and Egyptian kings favored the figure of the lion to underscore their prowess on the battlefield.[68] The lion was more than a predator of the wilderness; it was a fitting image for the victorious king. Largely absent in such royal testimonies, however, is the image of the doe. Conversely, the fearsome image of the lion *as a designation for the king or psalmist* is distinctly lacking in the psalms.[69]

Clearly, the psalmist had something else in mind in choosing a less aggressive, fear-inspiring animal image. A clue is found in the psalmist's specific attention to the swift deer's feet, made secure "on the heights" (v. 33), a theme repeated in v. 36. Security of step and swiftness of foot in difficult terrain are evoked, but attention is also directed toward the ground on which such feet tread, namely the "rock" of God (vv. 31, 46). By choosing the deer image, the psalmist gives due credit to God as the one who establishes a secure foothold, an advantage on the battlefield.[70] And yet it is hard to imagine a deer, an herbivore, in swift pursuit of prey. The psalmist does not intend to provoke such a clash of associations. Rather, the image, as in Psalm 42, sets in relief the king's dependence on God, which makes the image of a wild predator in this context highly unsuitable. Typically associated with hunted game, the deer is by nature vulnerable to human encroachment. Many an Assyrian and Egyptian monarch, for example, prided himself on bagging or herding wild game, including deer, gazelles, and ibexes, not to mention lions.[71] Yet in the psalm's "royal" recounting, the hunted is the victor. Victory goes to the fleet of foot on God's ground, not to predatory aggression on human footing.

Sheep

One other prominent metaphor cannot escape notice. Not infrequently in the psalms, Israel is referenced as God's "flock" or "sheep." This eminently domestic image highlights God's guidance and sustaining care of Israel, whether through the hostile wilderness (78:52) or at God's dwelling place, a setting of sustenance for the needy (68:10). As shepherd, God receives the following praise from the flock:

> O come, let us worship and bow down;
>   let us kneel before YHWH, our Maker!
> For he is our God,
>   and we are the people of his pasture,
>   and the sheep of his hand.
>   (95:6–7)

Such imagery provides the basis for praise. Similarly, in Psalm 100, also a hymn of praise and call to worship, the following injunction is given:

> Know that YHWH is God.
> It is he who made us, and we are his;[72]
>   his people, the sheep of his pasture, we are.
>   (100:3)

As God's flock, Israel is established and claimed by God. As the sheep of God's pasture, Israel is lavished with covenantal care (*ṭôb, ḥesed,* v. 5). As Shepherd, God's claim on Israel is a claim of rulership over a subject people. Particularly in Assyrian annals, the label "shepherd" constitutes a stock royal epithet. Tiglath-pileser III, not immodestly, makes reference to himself as the "shepherd of mankind."[73] More vivid is Tukulti-Ninurta I's self-reference: "I set my foot upon the neck of the lands (and) shepherded the extensive black-headed people like animals."[74] But Israel does not celebrate God's sovereignty only for its power; the community sees itself in salutary relation to its Maker, a people subjected not by coercion but by the bounty of divine beneficence. It is with God's rod and staff that the psalmist is comforted and led to safe sanctuary through the valley of darkness (23:4). God's "shepherdship" is a rulership of compassion that constitutes Israel's existence. Israel's identity as God's flock, in turn, enjoys the *succor* of divine kingship. Elsewhere in the Psalter, the metaphor of shepherding provides the model of an earthly king, David:

> [God] chose his servant David,
> and took him from the sheepfolds.
> From tending the nursing ewes he brought him
> to be the shepherd of his people Jacob,
> of Israel, his inheritance.
> (78:70–71)[75]

David's tender beginnings profile the salutary pattern of kingship that Israel is later to enjoy: protection from outside encroachment and sustenance for its flourishing in the land. No more suitable a metaphor is to be found that, according to the psalmists, characterizes the kingdom, dependent as it is on God and God's anointed.

Conclusion

This nonexhaustive survey highlights the various ways in which animal motifs and metaphors are deployed in the Psalter's rhetoric of prayer and praise. Most telling is the use of such imagery to identify both the speaker and the other, usually as foes. More often than not, animal imagery depicts situations of distress that require rectification, prompting a cry for help to God on the part of the individual or community. Less often, but just as significant, such metaphors are used to underscore in a positive fashion either the psalmist's or the community's dependence on God, as in the case of deer and sheep or flock. Only in one instance is animal imagery employed to underscore the psalmist's strength or prowess in a situation of conflict, but it is not the image one would expect. In the setting of battle, the author of Psalm 18 chooses the image of the doe to connote swiftness in battle and dependence on the deity.

The use of animal imagery in Psalms is weighted more toward the figurative than toward zoological realism. Rarely is an animal *just* an animal in the Psalter. In some cases, the delineation between zoological classification and metaphorical significance is not clearly marked. Those psalms that refer to animals *without* explicit metaphorical significance—i.e., those that reflect on the goodness of God's creation (see below)—become indirectly fraught with metaphorical significance by virtue of their association with the vast majority of psalms that do deploy animal imagery figuratively. To read the Psalter as it was codified by the second century B.C.E., that is, to view the Psalms as a *book*, is to imbue *all* references to animals in the Psalter with some degree of connotative force, even in their purely creational contexts, that they would not otherwise have in isolation. This accumulative effect carries forward the interactive process that the metaphor itself initiates, now expanded to include the more "global" literary context of the Psalter as a whole. Moreover, if such a reading strategy is accepted, certain contours of the Psalter's dramatic shape begin to emerge, the shape of an unfolding metanarrative in which animals play an indispensable role in the theology of Psalms.

FROM METAPHOR TO CREATION

In certain creation passages, animals are designated without explicit metaphorical significance.[76] In other instances, animals are simply listed as altogether separate from human beings. After repeated references to enemies as devouring lions earlier in the Psalter,[77] Psalm 34, for example, provides a remarkably different outlook on the king of beasts, this time stripped of human garb:

> Fear YHWH, you his holy ones,
>   for those who fear him have no want.
> The young lions (*kĕpîrîm*)[78] suffer want and hunger,
>   but those who seek YHWH lack no good thing.
>   (34:9–10)

Even at their prime, the psalmist affirms, lions are vulnerable and subject to hunger. Job, too, notes that lions are not self-sustaining; their prey must be *provided* (Job 38:39–40). The psalmist distinguishes between the "holy ones," who revere God, and the lions, which rely on their own prowess. In conjunction with Psalm 23, where a similar declaration of divinely provided sufficiency is given (v. 1b), an implicit contrast is established between the flock, which knows and relies on its provider, and the lion, which devours on its own accord yet lacks sustenance. Like the protagonist in Psalm 23, the speaker of Psalm 34 prescribes dependence on God by encouraging the reader to revere YHWH and, thereby, find sufficiency. Thus, even in its immediate context, the reference to lions (*kĕpîrîm*) is suggestive enough to provoke some degree of association with persons who rely solely on themselves rather than trust in God. By simple poetic juxtaposition, the implication is drawn that "young lions," full of virility and voraciousness, do not revere God. The way of the lion, in short, serves as a negative example for the reader. As the most voracious of beasts is subject to starvation, so the rich "cannot abide in their pomp; they are *like the animals* that perish" (49:20, emphasis added).

Positively, the psalmist exhorts his readers to "seek peace, and pursue it" (34:14), a fitting contrast to lions, which pursue in stealth and violently overtake their prey. As the lions "suffer want and hunger," so the wicked languish and die (v. 21). For the righteous, God and God's ways ("life," "peace," "righteousness") are the worthy objects of pursuit and appropriation: "O taste and see that YHWH is good" (v. 8a). To press the metaphorical analogy to its extreme, God is the "prey" of the righteous, and praise of God is the psalmist's staple: "his praise shall continually be *in my mouth*" (v. 1, emphasis added).

Animals in Situ

Apart from the creation passages to be discussed below, two instances of animal imagery are referenced primarily for what they are and not for what they stand for or connote. First, Psalm 36 vituperates against the wicked, who speak deceitfully, plot mischief day and night, and serve as a fitting contrast to the faithful character of the God who grants vigilant protection to the psalmist:

> Your faithful love, YHWH, extends to the heavens,
> your faithfulness to the clouds.
> Your righteousness is like the mighty mountains;
> your judgments are like the great deep.
> You save human and animal (*bĕhēmâ*) alike, YHWH.
> (36:5–6)

As God's faithfulness extends to infinite depth and height, so the breadth of God's beneficence includes both animals and human beings. The wideness in God's mercy extends to the next section, which attests that "all people may take refuge in the shadow of [God's] wings," to feast and drink in God's house (vv. 7–8). Are the animals, consequently, left behind? Yes and no. No doubt the psalmist means what she says in v. 6, that human and nonhuman life are bound together in God's economy of salvation. Yet the focus narrows in the following section: God's universal claim is on humanity. "*All* people," including, in principle, the wicked, can come to trust God and take refuge. The animals are invoked to underscore the universal embrace of God's covenantal care.

Second, Psalm 50 depicts God from Zion admonishing the people for misconstruing the fundamental aim of sacrifice. God does not desire sacrifice in order to satisfy hunger (v. 13). God's ownership of *all* life precludes such misunderstanding:

> I will not accept a bull from your house,
> or goats from your folds.
> For every animal of the forest belongs to me,
> the cattle on a thousand hills.
> I know every bird of the air,[79]
> and all that moves in the field is mine.
> If I were hungry, I would not tell you,
> for the world and all that is in it belong to me.
> (50:9–12)

Animal sacrifice is not a matter of giving to God something that God lacks, namely, the life of the animal. As creator, God is lord of creation, commanded into existence at the beginning of time (Genesis 1). Bound together under the encompassing expanse of divine ownership, the domestic and the wild, from bulls to birds, represent only relative distinctions. Though the language of mastery is suggestively absent in this taxonomy of animal life, the wild are claimed by God. As their creator and sustainer, God owns the animals by knowing (*yd'*) them (Ps 50:11; cf. Job 38–41).

Nevertheless, despite God's ownership of all creation, the psalm acknowledges the one thing that God does lack and want, thanksgiving (*tôdâ*). Giving thanks is something God cannot coerce from the worshiper, for it is to be rendered freely. And yet God provides ample opportunity for thanksgiving by guaranteeing deliverance to those who "call on me in the day of trouble" (Ps 50:15).

Whether this psalm was intended to dispense with animal sacrifice remains an open question. In any case, the psalm makes clear that satisfying God's *hunger* is not the aim of sacrifice. God is not a carnivore, human or animal, who "eat[s] the flesh of bulls, or drink[s] the blood of goats" (v. 13). Sacrifice, rather, is conducted for the sake of God's *honor,* not appetite (v. 23); it is an expression of thanksgiving. Such a correct understanding of the intent and goal of sacrifice marks more generally the prescribed way of life *coram deo* (v. 23). As a consequence, animals, both wild and domestic, are in principle freed from instrumental status for sustaining the relationship between God and human beings. They, too, have intrinsic standing in God's creation.

Creation

Two psalms of creation—Psalms 8 and 104—in particular feature animals in crucially important roles. As in Psalm 50, references to animals in these psalms do not explicitly bear metaphorical force, as is commonly the case elsewhere in the Psalter. Nevertheless, they do figure significantly in the Psalter's dramatic scope.

Psalm 8

Like Psalm 19, this hymn of praise begins with an acclamation of God's glory. Creation, too, is enlisted as incontrovertible evidence of divine majesty. But as Psalm 19 makes a dramatic turn from cosmos to *tôrâ*, more a horizontal than a vertical move, Psalm 8 plunges the reader from the celestial order to life on earth.

1 YHWH, our LORD, how majestic is your name in all the earth;
    indeed, I extol[80] your glory over the heavens.
2 From the mouth of nursing infants[81] you have established a stronghold;[82]
    but on account of your foes,[83]
        you have utterly[84] vanquished the avenging enemy.[85]
3 When I gaze upon your heavens, the works of your fingers—
    the moon and the stars that you have established—
4 [I ask,] "What are human beings that you call them to mind,

mortals that you care for them?"
5 Yet you have made them a little lower than the divinities,[86]
   with glory and honor you have crowned them.
6 You have given them dominion over the works of your hands;
   you have put everything under their feet:
7 All sheep and oxen, also the beasts of the field,
8 the birds of the air and fish of the sea,
   those that pass along the paths of the sea.
9 YHWH, our LORD, how majestic is your name in all the earth!

The "plot" of the psalm turns on vv. 4–5, from awe over God's celestial creation to wonder over humankind's status within the vast earthly order. The theological pivot, cast as a question, rests on God's attention to and care of human beings (v. 4). The psalmist looks to the heavens only to find finitude and frailty as part of the human condition. Before the towering heights of heaven on which God's splendor rests, humankind shrivels in stature.

A comparable question is posed in Psalm 144:3, a prayer for deliverance, in which equivalent verbs are employed but with a decidedly different response. Psalms 8 and 144 part company over the response to the question regarding God's attentiveness to humankind. The former does not end at the point of consternation or despair *coram mundo*. To be sure, the common question acknowledges the fragile finitude of humankind. Nevertheless, humanity's smallness before the vastness of creation constitutes merely the beginning point for the psalmist's reflection, which successfully moves from humanity's finitude to nobility in Psalm 8. The relative insignificance of human beings is mysteriously matched by an intractable dignity granted to humankind at creation and exercised in dominion over the creative order. What, then, are human beings? They are either fragile, ephemeral creatures, "passing like a shadow" (so 144:4b), or creatures invested with divine power over all creation (so 8:6–8). Neither response, however, identifies the reason behind God's magnanimous attention over humankind.

Both psalms remain on the level of anthropological description, not theological intention. Whereas Psalm 144 is an urgent prayer to God for rescue from national distress, Psalm 8 is a hymn of praise extolling God's beneficence *in* behalf of humankind, which enables humankind to act *on* behalf of God. Psalm 8 suspends itself above the fray of national crisis by addressing the universal matter of human identity and role. The orderly structures of creation replace the vicissitudes of human history. Humanity's role in Psalm 8 is defined in relation to the rest of creation, specifically the animal world. The psalmist does not equivocate: humankind is placed unreservedly at the top of a hierarchy of dominion, analogous to God's relation to the celestial cosmos. As both celestial sphere and human creature are subject to God, so the animal creatures, both domestic and wild (vv. 7–8), are subject to human beings. The analogy is tersely summarized in another psalm: "The heavens are YHWH's heavens, but the earth he has given to human beings" (115:16).

As is often noted, a similar conception of humankind's status in and over creation is conveyed in the first creation story of Genesis, which lodges humankind's
status in the divine image, effecting thereby dominion over all life (Gen
1:26–28). Human beings, both male and female, mirror the image of divinity
("our image").[87] In the same way, human beings in Psalm 8 reflect God's glory
(vv. 2b, 6). Invested with royal prerogative and responsibility, human beings are
"stand-ins" for divine lordship. Such dominion, however, is not won without
struggle, as the preface to the psalm indicates. God's investiture of humanity
comes at the price of victory over unnamed "foes" and the "avenging enemy" (v.
2b), reflecting the ancient mythos of cosmic struggle.[88] Order *follows* conquest;
such is the royal way. Humanity's dominion over nature is lodged in and sustained by God's cosmic stronghold. This note of conflict is also reflected in
humankind's relationship to animal life: as the forces of chaos have been subdued
by God, so all animal life is subjected to human rule. The animal kingdom is
annexed into God's kingdom so that humanity, as the surrogate of the Suzerain,
can flourish. Such a picture resonates with the priestly portrayal of the relationship between human beings and animals, announced at the establishment of
Noah's covenant:

> Be fruitful and multiply, and fill the earth. The fear (*môrā'*) and dread (*ḥat*)
> of you shall rest on every animal of the earth, and on every bird of the air,
> on everything that creeps on the ground, and on all the fish of the sea. Into
> your hand they are delivered. Every moving thing that lives shall be food for
> you; and just as I gave you the green plants, I give you everything. (Gen
> 9:1–3)

The "dread" that is to afflict every animal reflects humanity's lordship over creation. "Fear and dread" is the fitting response to the Suzerain's subject. The status of human beings in the world is, in short, one of royal supremacy, achieved
by God, whether by divine decree or conquest. In either case, Psalm 8 places the
animals "under [the] feet" of humankind as the subjects of humanity's derived
lordship. While a king may speak of enemies falling "under my feet" (Ps 18:38)
or a victorious community proclaim the nations as falling "under our feet" (47:3),
the psalmist casts, analogously, the animal world as a defeated kingdom within
the expanse of God's mythic struggle against chaos.

An implicit assumption runs throughout Psalm 8 that drives a further wedge
between human being and animal, and it concerns the issue of discourse.[89] The
psalm is intensely performative, bursting with the discourse of praise, conveyed
in inchoate form from the mouths of nurslings. The stronghold of God's creation
is not wrought by measured decree (cf. Gen 1:3–28) but by unrestrained babble,
yet babble that adumbrates the proclamation of YHWH's name (Ps 8:2, 9). The
outcome of such discourse, whether infantile or mature, is the same: a world that
places humankind at the pinnacle of the created order. If spoken language in its
most inarticulate form can sustain the divine bulwark, then how much more is
the case with the psalmist's eloquent praise! The psalm is a celebration of God's

grace, a public reminder of a created order in which humankind has been granted unmatchable dominion. As a powerful witness to the efficacy of praise, the psalmist upholds with words the stronghold of God's refuge. Along with babbling infants, the psalmist's praise buttresses the bulwark of God.

The animals in Psalm 8, by contrast, remain mute within the cosmic extent of the psalmist's purview. As objects of human dominion, they are nothing more than an essential source of human sustenance, God's gracious provision for human flourishing. Because they have no facility for speech, animals cannot assume active status within the created order. They are merely instrumental. A very different order, however, is given in the Psalter's quintessential creation psalm.

Psalm 104

Like Psalm 8, Psalm 104 is a cosmic hymn of praise. However, it paints a vastly different picture of the cosmos in general and the animal world in particular. The psalm is sometimes classified as a "sapiential creation hymn" because of its taxonomic approach to creation: it provides a veritable catalog of zoological species.[90] Moreover, Psalm 104 is self-designated as the psalmist's "meditation" (*śîaḥ*), a labor of joy (v. 34), an ode to creation. Both Psalm 8 and Psalm 104 open with effusive praise of God's majesty. But while Psalm 8 presents a thoroughly anthropocentric view of creation, the latter psalm moves toward an ecocentric profile. The distinctiveness of Psalm 104 rests in part on what it defers saying. For the first thirteen verses not a single syllable addresses humanity's place in the created order.[91] Where they *are* mentioned in the following verses, human beings are considered at most coinhabitants with the onagers and the coneys. The pertinent section, vv. 10–31, 35, is translated below. To indicate the psalm's rhetorical movement, references to animals are rendered in italics, whereas references to human beings are underlined. Those references that comprise *both* human and animal are cast in bold, as well as underlined and italicized.

> 10 You make springs gush forth into the wadis;
>   between the mountains they flow,
> 11 giving drink to every *wild animal*;
>   the *onagers*[92] thereby quench *their* thirst.
> 12 By [the streams] the *birds* of the air find habitation;
>   *they* sing among the branches.
> 13 You water the mountains from your lofty abode;
>   with the fruit of your work the earth is satisfied.
> 14 You cause grass to sprout for the *cattle,*
>   and plants for human cultivation,
>   to bring forth grain from the earth,
> 15 and wine to gladden the human heart,
>   oil to make the face shine,
>   and bread to strengthen the human heart.
> 16 The trees of YHWH are sated,
>   the cedars of Lebanon that he planted.
> 17 Where the *birds* make nest,

the *stork*[93] in the fir trees has its home.
18 The high hills are for the mountain *goats*;
     rocks are refuge for the *coneys*.[94]
19 You have made the moon as seasonal signs;
     the sun knows its setting time.
20 You make darkness so that there will be night,
     in which every *animal* of the forest comes creeping out.
21 The *young lions* roar for prey,
     seeking from God *their* food.
22 When the sun rises, *they* retire,
     and in *their* dens *they* crouch down.
23 <u>Human beings</u>, in turn, head out to <u>their</u> work,
     and to <u>their</u> labor [they are out] until evening.
24 How manifold are your works, YHWH!
     all of them in wisdom you have made.
        The earth is full of your ***creatures***.[95]
25 Over there is the sea, great and wide in both directions;
     there the *creeping things* are innumerable,
        living things both small and great.
26 There go the <u>ships</u>,
     and also *Leviathan,* which you fashioned for play.[96]
27 ***All of them*** place ***their*** hope in you
     to give ***them*** food in due season.
28 When you give to ***them,*** ***they*** gather;
     when you open your hand, ***they*** are satisfied with goodness.
29 When you hide your face, ***they*** are dismayed;
     when you take away ***their*** breath, ***they*** die and return to ***their*** dust.
30 But when you send forth your breath, ***they*** are (re)created;
     you make new the face of the ground.
31 May YHWH's glory endure forever;
     may YHWH rejoice in his works!
. . . .
35 Let <u>sinners</u> be finished off from the earth,
     and let the <u>wicked</u> be no more.
   Bless YHWH, O my soul.
   Hallelujah!
                              (104:10–31, 35, emphases added)

With the exception of Job 38–41, Psalm 104 revels in the wonder of earthly creation to a degree unmatched by any other creation text. By providing a veritable taxonomy of zoological species, Psalm 104 celebrates the manifold nature of life. Indeed, the psalm provides the most extensive treatment of *creatio continuata*—distinguished from *creatio prima*—in the Old Testament.[97] A veritable litany of life forms is punctuated by outbursts of rapturous praise over the rich biodiversity of the ecosystem and God's gracious provision (vv. 24, 31). Indeed, the prescriptive range of the psalmist's praise is so sweeping that God, too, is exhorted to rejoice (v. 31b)!

Even a cursory glance at vv. 10–31 reveals that human beings constitute only a small part of the psalm's cosmic purview. Moving in sections that deal with the basic constituents of creation (i.e., water [vv. 10–13], vegetation [vv. 14–15], habitation [vv. 16–18], time [vv. 19–23], and the sea [vv. 25–26]), the psalmist alternates between animals and humans, with humans occupying only three out of the five sections (vv. 14–15, 23, 26a). In the final section (vv. 27–30), as adumbrated in v. 24b, *both* animals and human beings are bound together as "creatures" dependent on and sustained by God. In short, the psalmist methodically moves from distinction to unity in the animal planet.

Far from bearing preeminent stature in a world fashioned (or conquered) to serve them, human beings are merely one species among many. The cosmos revolves not around humankind but around the earth, the medium of divine provision. Such a view carries significant ecological implications. The psalmist has made a decisive move away from the so-called "dominion model," which pervades much of biblical tradition about creation, including Gen 1:26–28; Psalm 8; and Wis 9:1–2. Psalm 104 has reinscribed the cosmos with an "integration model,"[98] one that positively assesses all of life as interdependent partners living off the earth. The planet constitutes nothing less than the hospitable household of life, the locus of God's blessing that accommodates life in all its various forms.[99] And in this household the wild animals are the first to occupy the living room (vv. 11–12)!

It is not until vv. 14–15 that human beings become the focus of attention. They, along with the cattle (*bĕhēmâ*), are supplied with plants. As grass is given to the cattle for consumption, so human beings receive grain for bread, grape for wine, and olive for oil, all for their sustenance *and* enjoyment (v. 15). The psalmist does not linger, however, in fascination over that which specifically sustains *human* life and culture, but quickly directs the reader's attention to the most magnificent form of botanical life, the towering cedars of Lebanon, the "trees of YHWH" (v. 16). In addition to their majestic stature, the wonder they evoke is rooted in what they provide for animal life. Trees, according to the psalmist, are literally for the birds! Like the rugged hills, which provide refuge for mountain goats and rock badgers, the towering cedars supply habitation for the creatures of the air (vv. 17–18; cf. v. 12).

In the next section (vv. 19–23), both animal and human share in the larger salutary order by inhabiting their separately assigned temporal domains. With sun and moon serving as temporal markers (cf. Gen 1:14–18), the animals of the forest, the young lions in particular, eke out their survival under the cover of darkness, while humans set out to "toil under the sun," to borrow an expression from another sage (Eccl 1:3). Night is for the wild animals to seek out their livelihood. But when the sun rises, they repair to their dens after a full night's work, while human beings punch their time cards, as it were, to begin their labors in the morning, working until evening. Every life form has its place, its home, reflecting the unsurpassed wisdom by which all creation is structured and continues to be sustained. Such is the fullness of creation (Ps 104:24b; cf. Genesis 1; Ps 24:1). This hymn, in sum, revels in the poetry of provision.[100]

As day follows night and vice versa, animals and humans operate within their respective timetables and domains. Although the lions carry the midnight shift, they are no different from human beings in at least one essential respect: they receive their livelihood from God (v. 21). Indeed, *all* creatures, animal and human alike, depend entirely on God's gracious provision (v. 28). But before a climactic affirmation of the unity of all creatures can be reached, the psalmist must overcome a considerable hurdle that has marred creation ever since the formation of the cosmogonic myth: the primordial division between chaos and order. The psalmist has saved for last this seemingly insurmountable challenge in his litany of creatures.

In a remarkable statement that counters much biblical and ancient Near Eastern tradition, the psalmist marshals the poetic imagination to redeem chaos itself, symbolized by the monstrous creature of the sea, Leviathan. In v. 26, attention is directed out toward the ocean, a threatening zone of habitation from the human standpoint (cf. vv. 6–9), where both ship and sea monster are observed. The image of the ship evokes humankind's ingenuity in reaping the ocean's harvest and conducting trade with distant lands. Leviathan, by contrast, symbolizes what is intractably hostile and untamable about creation.[101] But as the earth in its entirety is considered salutary, so must also be all denizens of sea and land, placed in their proper habitations and habits. At sea, God and monster meet, not in conflict but in play. The dreaded sea monster has become God's "rubber ducky."[102] Like all life, including the human variety, Leviathan is regarded as a thoroughly contingent creature. But the psalmist is not satisfied with a view that simply levels out the distinctions among the creatures in terms of a common denominator. Overturning the traditional depiction of Leviathan as an eminently fear-inspiring creature, the psalmist portrays God and Leviathan as playmates, rather than pitting them as mortal enemies, and in so doing has incorporated the sea monster into the fold of God's life-sustaining order.[103] To be sure, Leviathan retains the measure of fascination that it once held in the role of the *Chaosmonstrum,* but now in the role of God's special pet. The *mysterium tremendum* of chaos has been transformed into the *mysterium ludibundum* of creation.

The psalmist concludes the cosmic litany with all species, human and animal, both great and small, brought together as contingent creatures, sustained by and dependent on God (vv. 27–30). In this climactic section, God retakes center stage in the active role of provider who continually renews creation. The psalmist conceives God as sustainer, one who carefully delineates the domains and temporal rhythms of creation's diversity. The cessation and creation of life hinges on God's deployment and retrieval of "breath" (*rûaḥ*): breath "taken" entails death and the return to dust; breath "sent forth" generates life and renewal (vv. 29b–30a; cf. Gen 2:7; 3:19). In the psalmist's eyes, provision supplied in the midst of contingency reflects God's glory, the glory of God's gratuitousness made manifest as an effulgence of sustaining grace (Ps 104:31a). In v. 31b, whose central significance for the psalm has been largely overlooked by interpreters, the call for YHWH to rejoice in creation pointedly discloses the psalmist's purpose that has undergirded this rich litany of life: that God remain ever faithful in sustaining the order of life *as a labor of love,* as an act of unbounded joy, to match the delight of God's creatures, the recipients of grace (v. 34). Joyless toil has no place in the creative and sustaining activity of God, for if it did, all creation would cease from divine neglect (v. 29a). It is the psalmist's fervent wish that God not lose sight of the joy with which creation was fashioned and continues to be sustained, that even terror-inspiring Leviathan continue to play for heaven's sake, because all the world hangs in the balance.

Related to this exhortation is the petition that creation continue on its steady, sustainable course with the eradication of sinners from the face of the earth (v. 35), a dissonant note that is as jarring as it is discretely intoned within the concluding words of praise. Shock is elicited from even the most familiar reader of psalms, not because the language of imprecation raises its head, which is nothing new to Psalms, but because it has found its way precisely *here*, in a psalm that revels so wantonly in the wonder and diversity of God's creation. For all the goodness that characterizes creation, disruptive elements remain, the psalmist acknowledges. Yet, profoundly significant, the psalmist refuses to identify chaos and conflict, metaphorically or otherwise, with any animal, but lays the blame squarely on *human* shoulders. The psalmist has, in effect, thrown off the metaphorical cloak that the wicked have donned in so many psalms of imprecation and laments and exposed them for what they are, human beings. By redeeming the cosmos in praise, including Leviathan's fearsome stature, the psalmist has stripped the mythic veneer off chaos and lodged what is left of it within the Sturm und Drang of human relationships, a case of *reverse* transference or "demetaphorization," one might say. In so doing, the animals are freed from the guilt of association. They no longer serve as ciphers for the wicked, for they are themselves sustained and blessed by God. Indeed, they no longer *serve* at all. Like the towering cedars of Lebanon, the animals of the wild have gained standing within the psalmist's world.

CALL OF THE WILD: THE CONCLUSION OF THE PSALTER

As Psalm 104 concludes in praise, so also does the Psalter as a whole. The last five psalms, each of which lacks a superscription as well as opens and concludes with an identical command (*halĕlû yāh*), together constitute the Psalter's climactic paean of praise. Whereas many psalms address the basic existential needs for security and sustenance, these psalms in particular fulfill the need to praise.[104] As one moves through the sanctuary of the Psalter, hymns of praise turn into veritable praise choruses, while laments fade away. The reasons for praise given in these last psalms are varied, but the first reason, adumbrating the series of motivations that follow, makes reference to God, "who made heaven and earth, the sea, and all that is in them" (146:6) and moves effortlessly to God's role as provider of justice (v. 7). Thereafter, the reasons for praise come fast and furious, addressing in alternating fashion the realms of cosmos and culture: God "heals the broken-hearted" and "determines the number of the stars" (147:3–4); YHWH "lifts up the downtrodden; he casts the wicked to the ground" as well as "gives to the animals their food, and to the young ravens when they cry" (vv. 6, 9). Most signifi-

cant is the conclusion to Psalm 147, in which God's commanding word indivis-
ibly unites the cosmic and the constitutional.[105] God's word is initially profiled
in its cosmic role and concludes in identification with *tôrâ*. Like the sun, it "runs
swiftly," traversing the sky, and melts the frozen precipitation (vv. 15b, 18; cf.
19:6–7). It is the same word that prescribes moral conduct and constitution,
God's "statutes and ordinances," given exclusively to Israel. Both creative and prescriptive is God's *tôrâ*.

Psalm 148 warrants special attention for its sweeping roll call of participants
in praise of God. It is here, for the first and only time, that God's creatures are
given full, unmediated voice.

1 Hallelujah!
   Praise YHWH from the heavens;
      praise him in the heights!
2 Praise him, all his messengers;
      praise him all his hosts![106]
3 Praise him, sun and moon;
      praise him, all you stars of light!
4 Praise him, you highest heavens,
      and you waters above the heavens!
5 Let them praise the name of YHWH,
      for he commanded and they were created.
6 He established them forever and ever;
      he fixed an inviolable statute,[107]
7 Praise YHWH from the earth;
      you sea monsters (*tannînîm*) and all deeps (*tĕhōmôt*),
8 fire and hail, snow and frost,
      stormy wind fulfilling his word,
9 mountains and all hills,
      fruit trees and all cedars!
10 All animals, wild (*haḥayyâ*) and domestic (*bĕhēmâ*),
      creeping things (*remeś*) and flying birds (*ṣippôr*)!
11 Kings of the earth and all peoples,
      princes and all rulers of the earth!
12 Young men and women alike,
      the aged with the young!
13 Let them praise the name of YHWH,
      for his name alone is exalted;
         his glory is above earth and heaven.
14 He has raised[108] up a horn for his people,
      praise for all his faithful,
         for the people of Israel who are close to him.

   Hallelujah!

The psalm is essentially a catenation of exhortations that address the cosmos in
its entirety, a checklist of worshipers that proceeds from the heavenly sphere (vv.
1–6) to the earth with its various elements and inhabitants, including human
beings (vv. 7–12). With only minimal reference to particular motivations for
praise,[109] the psalm concludes with reference to the exalted position of God's

name and glory above *both* heaven and earth (v. 13) and, analogously, Israel's own elevation (v. 14a). The list of worshipers incorporated into this circle of praise is a veritable hodgepodge of natural phenomena, from meteorological elements (v. 8) to mountains and cedars (v. 9). Animals are also included: sea monsters, wild and domestic animals, "creeping things," and birds (vv. 7b, 10). From the inanimate to the animate, all are commanded to render praise to God; all are summoned to bear witness to God's majesty and glory as they are able, whether by fulfilling commands, as does the wind, or by expressing gratitude, as in Israel's case. Regardless of the particular context, however, all-encompassing praise constitutes the telos of creation's existence.

The enlistment of the animal kingdom, including the "sea monsters,"[110] to praise God marks a climactic turn in the Psalter's theological construal of life before God, best highlighted in comparison with the first creation psalm of the Psalter. In Psalm 8, all animals were placed "under the feet" of human beings, who by God's ordainment are to exercise dominion (8:6). As liturgist for the natural order, the author of Psalm 148 "fulfills" the exercise of dominion, not by subjugation and slaughter but by exhortation to praise. Dominion over the animals is redefined as the enablement to praise, the fulfillment for which the creature was created. In the Psalter's climactic call to praise, nature is finally and irrevocably given voice. Psalm 148 profiles the nonhuman world as "models of praise" for the human world to emulate.[111] At the psalmist's behest, the natural order and the human world are placed on equal footing. In the command (*halēlû*) lies the prescribed role and destiny of the natural order. In the exercise of dominion, the nonhuman world becomes integrated, rather than subjugated, into one unbroken circle of praise.

The particular focus on the animals at the conclusion of the Psalter is deliberate in another respect, pointing to an even more striking transformation. In Psalm 104, the wonder of creation's goodness was tempered only by the call to vengeance against the wicked in v. 35. In Psalm 148, the call to praise pervades every pore of the psalmist's exhortation. Suggestively absent is any hint of imprecation. Even the "rulers" and "kings of the earth," so often portrayed as the enemies of God who conspire to overthrow God's people (e.g., 2:2; 149:7–8), fall under the command to praise (148:11). Instead of vanquishing them with "a rod of iron" (2:9), the psalmist elicits their worship with a simple call. Alluded to in the universal call to praise is, moreover, the redemption of the wicked, the psalmist's stereotyped enemy. The metaphorical power of animal imagery that pulses throughout the Psalter finds its fitting conclusion in Psalm 148. As the nations join Israel in common worship, so the animals relinquish their enmity with human beings, and also, mutatis mutandis, the wicked vis-à-vis the psalmist. As the animals of the wild were made culpable by (metaphorical) association with the wicked throughout the Psalter, so now the wicked are implicated in the animals' praise of YHWH. Viewed from another angle: as chaos—metonymically represented by the "sea monsters" and Leviathan, on the one hand, and political conflict, on the other—is redeemed in praise and play, so also are the wicked from their wickedness. The psalmist's growing circle of praise, like expanding ripples in a pond, cannot stop short of incorporating all the world and claiming it as created for praise, not for conflict or conquest.

Although the global purview of Psalm 148 is all-inclusive, making it a fitting *theological* conclusion to the Psalter, it does not entirely represent the Psalter's *literary* conclusion, which includes two subsequent psalms. Similar to Psalm 148, Psalm 150 calls forth musical accompaniment to the words of praise that issue forth from "everything that breathes" (150:6). Whereas these two psalms scale the rapturous heights of cosmic praise, the psalm bracketed by them reenters the fray of conflict, in which kings are bound "with fetters . . . and chains of iron" and the wicked, presumably, are eradicated (149:6–9). And so the tension remains between the psalmist's cosmic perspective, in which redemption and reconciliation reign supreme, and the ongoing conflict that rages within the political fray. The clash between these two worlds, between vengeance and worship, gives praise its pathos. Yet within the tension, a vision is proffered: the household of life is remodeled into a cosmic setting for worship, in which human voices join the sounds of chirping birds, howling wind, raging seas, and babbling brooks. In this cosmic habitation, habits of conflict and disorder are stripped away, and all creatures find their true role and identity in worship. Even fearsome Leviathan has turned loquacious as it squeals with delight, giving thanks to God its maker and playmate.

Together, these psalms lay the foundation for a biblical "ecology of praise" that poses some pointed questions to modern readers: Can a stream poisoned by toxic waste praise God? Can trees destined for newsprint for tabloids clap for joy? Can the heavens adequately reflect God's glory when clouded by smog? What does it mean for nature to give praise to God?[112] In the psalmist's mandate of nature's praise lies nature's livelihood. Apart from the ecological issue, there is, moreover, another question to be considered that cuts to the heart of the Psalter's theological scope: What do all these animals have to do with the *practice of worship*? Why include a host of animal species, domestic and dangerous, on the hallowed ground of worship? Have the "gates of righteousness" collapsed?

It is the same question that can be posed to the mosaicists of ancient synagogues and churches in Jordan and Israel. From elephants to sea monsters, an illustrated encyclopedia of natural history is set on these carpets of stone.[113] The mosaics resonate fully with the Psalms. On the one hand, animals, both beasts of prey and beasts of burden, lie literally "under the feet" of the worshiper, fulfilling visually the model of dominion conveyed in Psalm 8. Hunting scenes of birds and wild game, for example, populate the mosaics of the al-Khadir church in Ma'dabā, the old Diakonikon-Baptistry in the Memorial of Moses on Mount Nebo, and the Church of Bishop Sergius at Umm al-Rasas.[114] On the other hand, the mosaics, for example, found at the Church of the Holy Apostles in the southeast corner of Ma'dabā, depict wild animals in situ, that is, free from human encroachment, such as stags and gazelles situated in a luxuriant grove of pomegranate and apple trees, most likely a depiction of paradise.

The center of this church's nave, moreover, features a medallion that contains a depiction of Sea personified, with the accompanying inscription: "O Lord God who has made the heavens and the earth, give life to Anastasius, to Thomas, and Theodora. [This is the work] of Salaman the mosaicist."[115] (See fig. 17.) Like Gen 1:21, the sea (and all therein) is included as a bona fide member of divinely wrought, life-sustaining creation. Such images welcome all creation into the domain of worship, a bold stroke of imagination that finds its precedent in the Psalter.[116]

In nature, the psalmists suggest, we recognize ourselves both as devouring lions and as meek doves. Like the sun that strides across the heavens, the tree that stands tall in the sanctuary, and the waters that sustain the righteous and render praise to God, the elements of nature find their own integrity and symbolic power in the Psalter's landscape. If all creation can be beckoned to glorify God, even the monsters of the deep, then what about the human species, those of differing race and ethnicity, differing sexual orientation, economic situation, and theological and political persuasion? The list, of course, can go on ad infinitum over the differences that divide one from another. But as inspiration for overcoming such divisions and discerning common bonds, the psalmists direct the reader's gaze to the denizens of churning seas and distant mountains, and claim even them among the company of worshipers.

Fig. 17: Floor mosaic of the personified sea from the Church of the Holy Apostles in Ma'dabā, Jordan. Adapted with permission from Michele Piccirillo, *The Mosaics of Jordan*, ed. Patricia M. Bikai and Thomas A Dailey (ACORP 1; Amman: American Center of Oriental Research, 1993), 96.

Chapter 7

"On You I Was Cast from My Birth"

The Anatomy of a Personal God

The providence we ascribe to God belongs not only to His eyes, but to His hands.

John Calvin[1]

While it is only fitting that this study conclude with a survey of metaphors for God in Psalms, these final chapters mark, at best, only a beginning. Space prohibits extended discussion of any one metaphor or cluster of metaphors. Moreover, the diversity of psalmic poetry preempts any attempt to achieve conceptual uniformity in the Psalter's mapping of the deity.[2] The most that can be hoped is that the ensuing discussion can serve as a point of departure for further exploration. But first the stage must be set to highlight the paradox that characterizes psalmic discourse about God and, indeed, all forms of God-talk, both ancient and (post)modern.

THE DISTINCTIVENESS OF DIVINITY

Though not cast in abstract terms, divinity in the ancient Near East is fundamentally distinguished from humanity and any other agency within the created order.[3] The prophet Hosea makes the metaphysical distinction in terms of pathos: "I will not execute my burning anger; I will never again destroy Ephraim, for God I am and not a mortal, the Holy One in your midst" (Hos 11:9).[4] Divinity, according to the prophet, involves the capacity of restraint, the resolve not to act on impulse as humans typically do.

The prayers and liturgies of the Psalms, too, draw a clear distinction metaphysically as well as functionally between God and the individual or community: "'God is great!' But I am poor and needy" is the lament in Ps 70:4b–5a. "[T]hough YHWH is high, he regards the lowly" conveys hope for the outcast (138:6a). "[A] thousand years in your sight are like yesterday when it is past, or like a watch in the night" exemplifies the superlative qualities of the deity (90:4). Frequently, as in the last example, the difference between the human and the divine is marked by a contrast in power: God exceeds in absolute fashion the finite and feeble capacities of human beings.[5] Moreover, the transcendent nature of the divine is embodied in the "awesome" and "wondrous" *acts* of God,[6] an object of concerted study and devotion for the psalmists (e.g., 111:2; 145:4–6). God's mighty acts, thus, indicate a property of divinity that cannot be shared by any deity other than Israel's God YHWH, let alone any part of creation: "[Y]ou are great and do wondrous things; you alone are God" (86:10).

The deity's incomparable nature is heightened all the more in the rhetorical question "YHWH, who is like you?" (35:10)[7] and the formulaic statement: "There is no one like you among the gods, O Lord, nor are there any works like yours" (86:8).[8] This theme resonates in various ways throughout the Psalter: God embodies unmatchable power (71:19b; 86:8), unsurpassable discernment (113:5–6), and uncompromising resolve to rescue the "weak and needy" (35:10). Examples of divine preeminence abound, from cosmic combat (89:9–11) and royal dominion (79:9) to deliverance of the oppressed (35:10; 113:7–9) and vindication of the individual (71:20–21). The language of theophany, too, highlights God's incommensurability with creation.[9] Only God can cause all creation to convulse by simply appearing or marching, accompanied by a mighty retinue, quite in contrast to the "sound of God strolling in the garden during the evening breeze" (Gen 3:8).

Pronouncements of divine incomparability, not surprisingly, lack explicit metaphorical application; indeed, they eschew all anthropomorphic associations. The "fear of YHWH" informs the nations that they—and not God—"are only human" (Ps 9:20). In those passages that intone God's transcendence over creation, the metaphors cluster at the latter side of the polarity. Before God human beings are "like a breath" and a "passing shadow,"[10] or "grass."[11] In the following "prayer of one afflicted," the metaphors are weighted toward the human rather than the divine:

> Long ago you founded the earth,
>   and the heavens are the work of your hands.
> They will perish, but you endure;
>   they will all wear out like a *garment*.
> You change them like *clothing*,
>   and they pass away.

> Yet you remain,
>   and your years have no end.
>   (102:25–27, emphasis added)

A metaphysical distinction is metaphorically drawn. The choice of textile imagery is telling: God's transcendence marks creation's transience (cf. vv. 11–12). The transcendent nature of the divine would seem to preclude all iconic references to the deity. Yet despite the prominent theme of divine incomparability, images that map the divine abound in the Psalter. Of all the books of Scripture, the Psalms provide the richest cache of metaphors for God. Moreover, of all the target domains in the Psalms, from pray-er to enemy, the figure of God enjoys the broadest range of figurative associations. While drawing an absolute distinction between creation and creator, even Psalm 102 casts a metaphorical cloak on the deity. God is one who "wears" creation as a garment that requires changing from time to time (v. 26). Although the focus is on nature's transience, the figure of the deity reflexively lends itself to metaphorical nuance. Not as body but as garment is creation metaphorically related to God. God has a body, the imagery suggests, but it is not the cosmos.[12]

DIVINE ANATOMY

The following discussion is at best only a sketch organized around two broad classifications of metaphorical source domains that pertain to the divine: personal (i.e., anthropomorphic) and impersonal or inanimate. Although instances of personal metaphors in the Psalter are widespread, impersonal images of the divine are equally evocative and theologically suggestive.

As is typical of ancient Near Eastern depictions of the deity, anthropomorphic language about God is traditional and commonplace in the Hebrew Scriptures. Although certain traditions appear to avoid, curtail, or modify anthropomorphic references to God, many tradents of Scripture, including its poets and narrators, refer to God as having a body, complete with limbs and senses. Given the complexity of the issue, one scholar observes that anthropomorphism is "both affirmed and relativized,"[13] while another refers to "transcendent anthropomorphism" as a way of capturing the paradoxical ways such language is used for the deity in biblical and extrabiblical traditions of the ancient Near East.[14] Regardless of how the general issue is to be cast, it is clear that the psalmists had a vested interest in deploying the metaphorical schema "God is person" in their prayers and liturgies, as the representative examples given below indicate.

The Senses

The Psalter is replete with references to God's "bodily" senses, particularly of sight and hearing, which serve to highlight God's perceptiveness and responsiveness to situations of distress. In Psalm 94, God is exhorted to wreak vengeance against the wicked who act with impunity and say: "YH[WH] does not see; the God of Jacob does not perceive" (vv. 6–7). The psalmist contravenes their words with the following argument from metaphor:

> The One who planted the ear, does he not hear?
> The One who formed the eye, does he not see?
> The One who disciplines the nations,
>   who teaches knowledge to humankind,
>   does he not chastise?
> YHWH knows that the thoughts of humankind
>   are fleeting (*hebel*).
>
> (94:9–11)

In a series of substantive participles (in Hebrew) that sound a distinctly hymnic tone, the psalm features various sensorial references aimed at countering the claim that God is indifferent, indeed senseless, to the conduct of the wicked. To counter the charge that God is blind (and deaf), the psalmist confidently claims that God is *acutely* perceptive of the judicial miscarriages committed against the innocent (v. 21). Amid the metaphorical flourish, a rational argument is unfolded whose linchpin is found in God's role as creator. The argument is driven by analogy: If the creator can fashion the creaturely senses of sight and hearing, then God is likewise capable of perception, even more so. *God has preeminent perspective* is the metaphysical claim of the psalmist's metaphorical inquiry. Indeed, God's perception affords a different perspective on human thoughts and activities: they are ultimately proved inefficacious, tantamount to nothing (*hebel*). With the divine senses, God is able to punish and protect.

As Psalm 94 well illustrates, the sensorial mapping of the divine serves to underscore God's perception and responsiveness to human need. To claim that God's "eyes have beheld my unformed substance" in the womb is to lay claim on God's beneficence and protection throughout all of life (139:16–18).[15] Psalm 34 renders thanksgiving by enlisting the metaphors of God's "eyes" and "ears":

> YHWH's eyes are upon the righteous;
>   his ears are open to their cry.
> YHWH's face is [directed] against evildoers,
>   to cut off their legacy from the land.
> When the righteous cry for help,
>   YHWH hears and rescues them from all their troubles.
> YHWH is near to the brokenhearted,
>   and saves the crushed in spirit.
>
> (34:15–18)

God's perception leads to "rescue" of the righteous (v. 17). Sensitivity to human need, moreover, underscores God's immanence: divine "nearness" offers refuge to those who seek it, particularly to the despondent and the downtrodden (vv. 18, 22). More prominently featured than sight in the Psalter, God's hearing is the divine sense par excellence:[16] "Give ear, YHWH, to my supplication" (86:6) is not only the characteristic cry of the psalmist;[17] it is the fundamental claim that governs the Psalter's prayers and praises. Without God's "ears" attuned to both the cry of the afflicted and praise from the delivered, the psalmist is literally without a prayer.

Elsewhere in the Psalter, the sensory mapping of the deity is resolutely challenged, but not by the psalmists. It is the wicked or unnamed enemies who proclaim that "YH[WH] does not see" (94:7) or that "[God] has hidden his face; he will never see it" (10:11), fostering the illusion of impunity. Such alleged lack of perception on the part of the deity leads the wicked to question God's very knowledge of their prosperity and pride:

> They say, "How can God know?
> Is there knowledge in the Most High?"
> Such are the wicked;
> always at ease, they increase in wealth.
> (73:11–12)

With equal audacity, the wicked in Psalm 64 pride themselves on their cunning and proclaim, "Who can see us?[18] Who can search out [our] evil acts?"[19] (64:5b–6a). The reason behind such brazen impunity is given an anthropological twist at the conclusion: "The human heart and mind are unfathomable (*ʿāmōq*)" (v. 6b). But not to God, the psalmist contends: as the wicked attack the innocent with verbal swords and arrows (vv. 3–4), so God, the divine archer, will swiftly kill them "because of their tongue" (vv. 7–8a). In short, to deprive the deity of the visual and auditory senses is to deny God's saving character and passion for justice. Indeed, to assert that "God will not seek it out" is tantamount to the claim "There is no God" (10:4; cf. 14:1; 53:1).

The metaphorical mapping of the divine "senses" in Psalm 115 touches on the larger issue of God's efficacious presence in contrast to the lifeless idols.

> Why should the nations say,
> "Where is their God?"
> Our God is in the heavens;
> he does whatever he pleases.
> Their idols are silver and gold,
> the work of human hands.
> They have mouths, but cannot speak;
> eyes, but cannot see.
> They have ears, but cannot hear;
> noses, but cannot smell;
> hands, but cannot feel;
> feet, but cannot walk;
> they cannot [even] produce noise in their throats.
> Those who make them are like them;
> so are all who trust in them.
> (115:2–8)[20]

Proclaiming YHWH's supremacy, the psalmist reduces the pagan gods to lifeless artifacts, mere idols,[21] and affirms God's active role in blessing (see vv. 12–15, 18). Speech, sight, hearing, smell, touch, even locomotion ("walk") are covered in this taxonomy of agency. Rather than delimiting the deity, the bodily senses highlight God's unbounded freedom (v. 2; see also 135:6): by virtue of the senses God remains free of manipulation as an utterly self-determined being. As sovereign, God's watchful, omniscient gaze renders all earthly affairs contingent and unpredictable, including military engagements (33:14, 15b–17). Divine freedom, moreover, is shared by those who cast their allegiance on God ("trust"), much in contrast to the idol worshipers, whose own senses are numbed to the point of death (115:8).

The sense of sight in psalmic God-talk also denotes the deity's adjudicative powers or, more broadly, moral discernment: "YHWH looks down from heaven on humankind to see if there are any who are wise, who seek after God" (14:2); "The boastful cannot stand before your eyes; you hate all evildoers" (5:5). Psalm 11 correlates God's "gaze" over all humankind with "testing" the righteous and the wicked (vv. 4–5; cf. 14:2). Conversely, to "see" suffering is to redress the wrongs committed against the victim by the wicked (9:13; 10:14). In comparable fashion, God's "ear" receives the desperate prayers of "the meek" (10:17) and the "sighing" (5:1–3). Ascribed to the divine, the senses ensure God's active perception and, in particular, attention to situations of suffering and persecution. Without the bodily senses, God would be indifferent to human plight and praise, indeed no God at all.

Face

The divine senses do not operate in isolation; they are graphically consolidated in the motif of God's "face" (*pānîm*), a conventional metaphor that in certain traditions outside the Psalter is theologically muted.[22] In the Psalms, however, there is more to God's face than the sum of God's perceptual and discursive faculties (eye, ear, mouth, nose). This distinctly expressive feature of God's "anatomy" serves to heighten the personal dimension of God's relationship to the individual and community. While the psalmist prays that God's "sight" toward the community be unhindered, it is God's "face" that is yearned for as an object of the *psalmist's* sight. More than any other part of God's "body," the face constitutes the effective and personal presence of the deity. The metaphor also functions as a synecdoche or *pars pro toto*: the singular "face" conveys the salutary *fullness* of God's presence, which sustains the psalmist amid conflict (41:12) and imparts joy and blessing (21:6).

As the human face can convey a variety of emotions, both positive and negative, so God's "face" conveys a range of divine activity, from favor and blessing to punishment and rebuke. First and foremost, God's face is something for which the psalmist yearns. It marks the personal God who is sought, but not necessarily found.

> Hear, YHWH, when I cry aloud;
>> be gracious to me and answer me!
> "As for you," my heart says, "seek his face!"[23]
>> Your face, YHWH, do I seek.
> Do not hide your face from me.
>
> (27:7–9a)

The psalmist seeks interface with the divine, an encounter that is efficacious for the psalmist's life and renders due honor to God. By no accident does the figure of the temple loom large in this psalm. In his longing to seek God's face, the psalmist concomitantly yearns "to live in the house of YHWH, to behold the beauty of YHWH, and to inquire in his temple" (v. 4). Similarly, the entrance liturgy of Psalm 24 identifies those who are admitted into the sanctuary as "the company of those who seek him, who seek the face of the God of Jacob" (24:6). Seeking God, thus, has a moral component: the psalmist identifies only those whose moral character is unassailable and worthy for admittance (vv. 3–4).

Worship constitutes the central setting in which the charge is given: "Seek YHWH and his strength; seek his face continually" (105:4). It is in the temple or, more broadly, in God's "sanctuary presence" that God's face is beheld. From one who seeks refuge comes the hopeful claim, "I shall behold your face in righteousness. When I awake, I shall be satisfied, beholding your likeness" (17:15). In this vigil psalm, the psalmist begins his prayer with the exhortation that God "give ear" to his cry; his supplication concludes with the prospect of seeing God's "face." Beholding God's face also concludes Psalm 11, which locates God in the heavenly temple examining humankind. The psalmist identifies those who "shall behold YWHW face" with the righteous who have taken refuge in YHWH (vv. 1, 7). The image of the face, in short, gives expressive nuance to God's protective presence.

The most common verbal predicates of the divine countenance in the psalms are "shine" and "hide." The former imbues God's presence with solar nuance and sanctuary setting (see chapter 4). God's face is luminous, bearing life-giving effulgence (89:15). God's "shining" connotes salvation and vindication (31:16), victory (44:3 ["light"]), restoration (80:3, 7, 19), blessing (67:1; cf. Num 6:25), and agricultural bounty (Ps 4:6). Psalm 119 gives the motif a pedagogical twist: "Make your face shine upon your servant, and teach me your statutes" (119:135). God's "shining" both saves and instructs.

As the object of desperate yearning and the subject of edifying import, the unveiled face of God also has its converse, namely, the "hiding" of the face, a prominent motif in the laments. Like the closed eye or the stopped ear, God's hidden face either connotes willful neglect or is perceived as incapacity and forgetfulness, which gives license for the wicked to act with impunity (10:11) and brings the psalmist to the brink of despair (13:1–2). Divine concealment, moreover, is consonant with the distancing of God's self from the psalmist's distress: "Why, YHWH, do you stand far off? Why do you hide yourself in times of trouble?" (10:1; cf. 22:1; 35:22).

With righteous indignation, the complainant of Psalm 44 associates the hidden face with a neglectful, indeed comatose, God (44:24). God's elusive countenance marks the opposite of divine favor (30:7), namely, wrath and rejection, as is also the case in the most despairing psalm of the Psalter:

> YHWH, why do you cast me off
> [and] hide your face from me?
> Wretched and close to death from my youth up,
>   I suffer your terrors. . . .
> Your wrath has swept over me;
>   your dread assaults destroy me.
>   (88:14–16)

Likened to watery inundation (v. 17) and military attack (v. 16b), God's punishing wrath is faceless. Salvation, in contrast, has a face, without which all creation reverts to dismay and dust (104:29), destined for the pit (143:7). The psalmist, in other words, attaches a Face to the blessing.

Yet, as several psalms make clear, God's face is not all favor and blessing. In an ironic twist, Ps 34:15–16 contrasts the divine senses and God's face (see above). Whereas God's senses are oriented positively to the righteous (also in v. 17), God's face is set, like a sharp sword, *against* those who promulgate evil. Janus-like, the divine countenance does double duty. That it can be directed in punishment as well as in benevolence is acknowledged in prayers that implore God's face to be hidden, as in the most well known penitential psalm:

> Purge me with hyssop, and I shall be clean;
>   wash me, and I shall be whiter than snow.
> . . . .
> Hide your face from my sins,
>   and blot out all my transgressions.
>   (51:7, 9)

By hiding the face, God disregards or casts out of sight the psalmist's sins. To bring about cleansing, God must look away. Conversely, the discerning power of God's face is literally brought to light in the communal lament of Psalm 90.

> For we are devoured by your fury;
>   by your wrath we are overwhelmed.
> You have set our transgressions before you,
>   our hidden sins in the light of your countenance.
>   (90:7–8)

The divine light of God's "face" not only exposes hidden sins; it consumes life itself. God's face is screwed up with wrath,[24] an anger so penetrating that it renders all human life fleeting like grass or a dream (vv. 5–6, 9–10).[25] The idiomatic expression "time of your face" in 21:9, like the prophetic "day of YHWH" (e.g., Joel 2:1–2; Amos 5:18–20; Zeph 1:14–16), refers to an act of retribution of theophanous proportions by which the wicked are destroyed or routed (Ps 21:10–12). The multiple expressions of God's face profiled in Psalm 80 invoke both divine "rebuke" against those who have "burned with fire" God's chosen "vine" (vv. 14–16) and, at the same time, appeal to God's shining face to restore the community (vv. 3, 7, 14). The versatility of God's "face" thus covers both blessing and judgment.[26]

Hand

While the metaphorical attributes of face and sense highlight the acuteness of God's perceptiveness, particularly in situations of distress, the image of God's hand stresses the efficacy of God's response:

> Arise, YHWH;
> O God, lift up your hand;
> do not forget the oppressed.
> Why do the wicked renounce God,
> and say in their hearts,
> "You will not seek [us] out"?
> But you do see!
> Indeed, you observe trouble and grief,
> so that you may take it into your hands.
> (10:12–14a)

Perception and response constitute the essential modes of divine activity.[27] God's lifted hand marks God's resolve to take action, whether in delivering the "helpless" (v. 14b) or punishing evildoers ("break the arm of the wicked," v. 15a). God's hand is the necessary metaphorical appendage to execute "justice for the orphan and the oppressed" (v. 18a).

As a human hand can perform various tasks, so God's "hand" reflects a variety of roles. In general, the hand targets God's power to effect certain consequences. First and foremost, it brings about victory against the psalmist's enemies: "[YHWH] will answer [his anointed] from his holy heaven with mighty victories by his right hand" (20:6).[28] "A strong hand and outstretched arm" facilitate Israel's passage through the Red Sea (136:12–14).[29] A withdrawn hand, kept in the "bosom," by contrast, permits the enemy to gain the upper hand (74:10–11) and accounts for Zion's decimation (vv. 3–8). Restoration, conversely, recalls God's primordial victories over chaos (vv. 12–15), which require decisive "hand action." God's outstretched hand signifies victory and the restoration of order, both cosmic and political. Reminiscent of the Song of the Sea in Exod 15:1b–18, Psalm 118 contains the tricolon of an ancient victory chorus, which could be called the "Song of the Hand":

> The right hand of YHWH does valiantly;
> the right hand of YHWH is exalted;
> the right hand of YHWH does valiantly.
> (118:15b–16)

The psalm adapts the ancient poem of Exodus 15,[30] which celebrates God's victory over the Egyptians, to bear witness to God's salvation of an individual, most likely the king, in the midst of battle. Similarly, God's hand in Psalm 136 is at work to bring about victory at sea over Egypt (vv. 10–13). In the context of conflict, this anatomical appendage also carries *perceptive* force: "Your hand will find out (*timṣā'*) all your enemies; your right hand will find out those who hate you" (21:8). Like the bodily senses, particularly that of sight, God's hand is as keenly discerning as it is consequential and decisive. God's hand blurs the line between perception and capacity for action.

It is not uncommon to find God bearing weapons such as bow and arrow, sword, spear, and javelin, in hand.[31] "By your sword deliver my life from the wicked, from mortals—by your hand, YHWH" is the confident cry of 17:13b–14a. "Your arrows have sunk into me, and your hand has come down upon me," complains the psalmist in 38:2. In both passages, hand and weapon are cast in parallel fashion. That God deftly handles the sword is presumed in 44:3. As is also the case in 144:6–7, the depiction of God's hand bearing arms highlights the warrior-king role typical of West Semitic iconography, which portrays particular deities, or so-called "smiting gods," with raised fists wielding weapons in aggressive postures, as in the famous but misnamed *Baal au foudre* ("Baal of the lightning") stela from Ugarit.[32] (See fig. 18.) The menacing posture of the deity, typically identified as Baal, is indicated by the raised right hand that brandishes a club or mace above the head. (The top is damaged.) The left hand holds a spear, whose top resembles a plant (not a lightning bolt).[33]

Another class of divine weaponry featured in psalmic poetry is cosmic in nature: "coals of fire and sulfur" and "scorching wind" (11:6), "burning coals" (140:10), "lightning," "whirlwind," and "thunder" (77:18) "hail" and "lightning" (105:32), "lightning" and "wind" (135:7), and "hail" and "wind" (147:17–18). Such meteorological phenomena, in some instances, serve as the target domain of the more metaphorically inspired images: God's "arrows" are "fiery shafts" or lightning bolts (7:13; cf. 77:17; 144:6). Frequently, however, the hand of God is itself considered sufficient in battle, "strong" and "high" (89:13), as well as outstretched (144:7), a hand "filled with victory" (48:10b). These instances, inter alia, possibly indicate a theological move to distinguish God's activity in effecting victory from human activity, which requires weapons.[34]

Coupled with military victory is a complementary mode of "hands on" activity, namely, that of "planting":

> You with your own hand drove out the nations,
>   but them you planted.
>
>   (44:2a)
>
> You brought a vine out of Egypt;
>   you drove out the nations and planted it.
> . . . .
> Have regard for this vine,
>   the stock that your right hand has planted.
>   (80:8, 14b–15)

Fig. 18: Stela of the god Baal from Ugarit, displayed in the Louvre, Paris. Copyright Réunion des Musées Nationaux / Art Resources, New York.

The hand is not only God's victorious weapon against Israel's enemies. It is also the instrument that "plants" a people on fertile soil. God can, as it were, wield a garden spade as effectively as a sword, for both modes of horticultural activity—clearing and cultivating—are deemed necessary for establishing Israel in the land.[35]

As in the exodus event, the enemy's defeat by God's "hand" also entails deliverance for both the psalmist and Israel: "Stretch out your hand from on high; set me free and rescue me from the mighty waters, from the hand of aliens" (144:7;

see also 31:15; 138:7). Refuge is hand-delivered (17:7). God's hand is also empowering, particularly for one engaged in battle, as in the case of the king: "Let your hand be upon the one at your right hand, the one whom you made strong for yourself" (80:17; cf. 89:21; 110:1).

God's hand can also be a "heavy" hand, however, one that renders judgment and affliction against the psalmist:[36] "For day and night your hand was heavy upon me; my strength was dried up as by the heat of summer" (32:4); "For your arrows have sunk into me, and your hand has come down upon me" (38:2); "I am destroyed by your hostile hand" (39:10).[37] God's unsparing affliction against the psalmist, too, is hand-delivered.[38]

Quite in contrast to the clenched fist of either victory or judgment, God's hand also has a salutary side: "When you open your hand, they are filled with good things" (104:28b); "You open your hand, satisfying the desire of every living thing" (145:16). God's open hand preserves life and provides for creation, as well as gives guidance. The hand that "remains with" betokens God's solidarity with the individual (139:10; 89:21). As for the king, God's hand will "set his hand" toward maintaining order, both social and cosmic (89:25). For the less than royal beneficiary, God's hand preserves and delivers "in the midst of trouble" (138:7); and so it is that the psalmist cries to God: "Do not forsake the work of your hands," the work of *ḥesed* or "faithful love" (v. 8b). It is in *ḥesed* that the work of God's hand is both creative and salvific (see 139:13–15).

Mouth and Voice

From eating to speaking, the mouth is a versatile organ whose image lends itself to poetic deployment in myriad ways. Like God's hand, the divine "mouth" is presupposed in certain imprecations against the enemy: "YHWH will swallow them (*yĕballĕʿēm*) in his wrath, and fire will devour them (*tōʾkĕlēm*)" (21:9b).[39] As an instrument of destruction, God takes on the role of the pit or Sheol, whose mouth swallows its victims whole. Yet unlike the watery abyss or the deep (69:15), God's "devouring" is more typically associated with fire: "Smoke went up from his nostrils, and devouring fire from his mouth; glowing coals flamed forth from him" (18:8). Whereas the pit is associated with death in general, God's consuming fire is associated inextricably with judgment against the enemy or the wicked. In later tradition, God's "devouring fire" becomes detached from anthropomorphic language: God is without "form" (*tĕmûnâ*), yet speaks from a "devouring fire" (Deut 4:12, 15, 24). In Psalm 18, however, mouth and nostril remain as essential "bodily" instruments of divine wrath.

The analogy of God's consumptive capacity finds its limit, however, in the psalmic critique of the sacrificial system. In Psalm 50, God declares judgment on those who rely insincerely on sacrifice to demonstrate their reverence:

> Even if I were hungry, I would not tell you,
> for the world and all that is in it is mine.

> Do I eat the flesh of bulls,
>   or drink the blood of goats?
> Offer to God a thanksgiving sacrifice,
>   and pay your vows to the Most High.
>   (50:12–14)

God is not one to suffer hunger pangs; no deity made in the image of man is God. The psalmist's indictment counters the popular conception that God consumes the offering (cf. Ezek 44:7, 15), despite the psalmist's reference to God's "devouring fire" in v. 3. In any case, satisfying God's hunger is not the rationale for worship. Rather, thanksgiving, praise, and discipline constitute genuine offerings (Ps 50:14, 17, 23). Anthropomorphic attribution, in turn, is relativized.[40]

As in Psalm 50, and throughout much of the Psalter, God's mouth is associated not so much with consumption and ingestion as with discourse and utterance. The psalms convey not only the cry from below,[41] but also a word from on high, the "word of the Lord." God's utterance is no alien word in the Psalter. The psalmists yearn for and receive the oracles and ordinances of the divine. Psalm 50, for example, contains an extended judgment oracle, a testimony against Israel that infuses worship with moral integrity (vv. 5, 7). In addition, a hymn for Sukkot features a divine oracle, a "voice . . . not known" that pleads, cajoles, indicts, and offers promise to the gathered community, recapitulating the essence of the first commandment (81:5b–16). It is the psalmist's fervent plea that the community "listen to [YHWH's] voice" (95:7b), and indeed a voice does come from above, one that admonishes worshipers for their disobedience (vv. 8–11). The psalmists exhort their audience to remember God's uttered judgments while declaring that God "is mindful of his covenant forever, of the word that he commanded for a thousand generations" (105:5, 8).

It is no coincidence that the Psalter opens with a decree from God, no less. In Psalm 2, God derisively laughs at those who attempt to supplant God's anointed, and assures the king of God's dominion (cf. 59:8). Given its placement in the Psalter, Psalm 2 relates all subsequent voices to Zion and to the divine (2:6, 7–9). As the Psalter opens with words of assurance from heaven, so it concludes with words of uninterrupted praise from below and above (e.g., 148:1–2). In a psalm that mixes judicial and royal motifs, God's word, for which the psalmist prays, counters the words of those who act with impunity: "You have seen, YHWH; do not be silent!" (35:22a). God is called on to give voice and, in turn, to stifle other voices, namely, those that utter deceit and violence against the supplicant, possibly the king (vv. 20, 25b). God's voice champions the psalmist's vindication (v. 27).

Similarly, a communal lament that appeals to God for help against a growing coalition of national enemies opens with the plea, "O God, do not keep silence; do not hold your peace or be still, O God!" (83:1). Divine speech marks the beginning point of God's sovereign response. Though unquoted in the psalm, God's utterance contravenes the speech of the hostile nations: "Come, let us wipe them out as a nation; let the name of Israel be remembered no more" (v. 4). The

parallel is unmistakable: as coalition-building speech—viewed as brazenly con-
spiratorial by the psalmist—leads to the nations' assault against Jerusalem, so
divine discourse subverts their cause and leads to their demise. By word alone,
"YHWH brings the counsel of the nations to naught; he frustrates the plans of
the peoples" (33:10). God's word testifies to God's power: "Once God has spoken; twice have I heard this: that power belongs to God" (62:11). Within the
international arena, God's sovereign word is sufficiently "persuasive" to elicit
praise from all the nations (138:4).

God's utterances throughout the Psalter are cast in differing forms and are designated in various ways: rebuke and admonition,[42] judgment,[43] covenant formulation[44] or oath,[45] *tôrâ* (and its equivalencies),[46] promise,[47] salvation,[48] and
peace.[49] In matters of prescription, God's voice commands obedience.[50] The
divinely uttered word also bears a creative component that reaches beyond individual, national, and international contexts.

> By the word (*dābār*) of YHWH, the heavens were made,
>   and by the breath (*rûaḥ*) of his mouth, so all their host.
> . . . .
> For he spoke, and it came to be;
>   he commanded, and it stood firm.
>
> (33:6, 9)

As in Genesis 1, God's commanding word is generative on a cosmic scale; God's
mouth is the instrument par excellence of creation. Like Marduk, the divine protagonist of the *Enūma eliš*, the sovereign voice of God *commands* creation into
existence and enlists the elements to do God's bidding.[51] "Stormy wind" in particular is poised to obey God's command or word (Pss 107:25; 148:8). Nevertheless, God's word, even given verbally, can also have the opposite outcome,
namely death: "Turn back [to dust], you mortals" is God's pronouncement on all
humanity (90:3).

God's mouth, in addition, receives a prominent role in the drama of theophany. God "thunders" and thereby sets the earth reeling (18:13). With equal
effect, Psalm 29 references the "voice of YHWH" seven times: it "thunders" (v.
3), "breaks cedars" (v. 5), "flashes forth flames of fire" (v. 7), "shakes the wilderness" (v. 8), and "strips the forest bare" (v. 9). Divine utterance either threatens
to unravel the cosmic order (77:18) or contains the forces of chaos that threaten
to do the same (104:7). In such contexts, God's "voice" is no barely audible whis-
per or still small voice (cf. 1 Kgs 19:12–13); it is the sound of majesty and power
over creation and chaos (Ps 68:33–34; 93:4).

The psalmist does not refrain from mixing two or more aspects of God's discourse within a single passage. In a portion of praise liturgy, God's creative word
and prescriptive decree are interchanged in the same breath:

> He sends out his speech (*'imrātô*) to the earth;
>   his word (*dĕbārô*) runs swiftly.

He gives snow like wool;
    he scatters frost like ashes.
He hurls down his hail like crumbs—
    who can stand[52] before his cold?
He sends out his word (*děbārô*), and melts them (*wěyamsēm*);
    he blows with his breath (*rûaḥ*),[53] and the waters flow.
He declares his word (*děbārô*[54]) to Jacob,
    his statutes and ordinances to Israel.
He has not dealt with any other nation in this way;
    they do not know his ordinances.
Hallelujah!

(147:15–20)

As in Psalm 19,[55] creation and constitution are tightly interrelated. The same word that governs the cosmos also constitutes Israel's national identity. God's word is deemed eminently precipitous in both the cosmic and constitutional realms: it causes the snow to fall and water to flow (cf. Isa 55:10–11), as well as marks Israel as God's chosen, distinct from the other nations (cf. Deut 4:7–8).

In summary, voice and mouth form an indispensable part of God's metaphorical profile. The divine voice in the psalms plays a crucial role in theophany and is found essential within the prescriptive realm of ethics and law. God's voice elicits awe, praise, and obedience, as well as counters voices of conspiracy among the nations and the roar of watery chaos. In Deuteronomy 4,[56] God's audible voice takes precedence over all other attributes to reconfigure the deity in disembodied form: the God of Horeb is formless yet has voice, specifically covenantal voice (vv. 12–13, 15).[57] In Psalms, the various patterns of divine discourse highlight the myriad roles, from king and lawgiver to judge and savior, that God assumes vis-à-vis Israel and creation (see "Roles of God," below). Without voice, God is a mere idol (115:7b).

Breath

Related to voice is God's breath, or wind. As noted above, Psalm 33:6 casts "breath" (*rûaḥ*) and "word" (*dābār*) in parallel relation.[58] "Breath" bears a narrower focus than "word," since it specifically highlights God's life-sustaining activity (104:27–30). God's "breath" creates and reinstates life (v. 30), while death is marked by the cessation of breath (v. 29b), literally the "taking away" (√ *ʾsp*) of breath—the opposite of "mouth-to-nose" resuscitation described in Gen 2:7. As breath is metonymic of earthly life, both human and animal (e.g., 76:12a; 104:29b; 146:4; 150:6), so it distinguishes divinity from idol: "There is no breath (*rûaḥ*) in their mouths," the psalmist observes about idols (135:17).

Equally vivid is the combative "breath" of God that injects itself into the fray of cosmic conflict.

Then the channels of the sea were exposed,
    and the foundations of the world laid bare,

at your rebuke, YHWH,
    at the blast of the breath (*nišmat rûaḥ*) from your nostrils.
                                                    (18:15)

YHWH's explosive blast (akin to a violent sneeze) routs the mighty waters that have assailed the psalmist (v. 16), a breath redolent of the "exodus exhale" that wards off and contains the waters of the Red Sea: "At the blast (*rûaḥ*) of your nostrils the waters piled up, the floods stood up in a heap" (Exod 15:8).

Other components of divine body language in the Psalter are rare and only indirectly made. A full taxonomy of anthropomorphic attribution is found in the contrast between lifeless idols and the living God in Psalm 115, which includes nose/smell (v. 6) and feet (v. 7). The divine sense of smell finds its home in the sacrificial system in which pleasing odors are sensed by the deity and found acceptable (e.g., Gen 8:21; Lev 1:9; Num 15:3; Ezek 6:13). The attribution of feet connotes independent movement on the part of God, in contrast to idols that must be borne aloft, as in a procession.[59]

In short, the poets behind the psalms were not reluctant to "map" the divine with some degree of physiological hyperbole as a way of highlighting God's active and efficacious nature, particularly within the fray of social and cosmic struggle. In addition to mapping the divine with organs of perception and action, the psalmists attributed a rich emotive life to the deity.

Pathos

The God of the ancient poet was no impassive, immutable force or Unmoved Mover. Quite the contrary—the psalmists characterized the God of Israel as bursting with pathos. To them, God exhibits an active, emotive life exemplified in the following dispositions and emotions, some more enduring than others.

Anger

Divine anger frequently serves as an instrument of judgment against the enemy, as in Ps 7:6–8, in which the psalmist appeals to God's anger (literally "flaring, burning nostril [*'ap*]") to counter the "fury" of his enemies and to have God execute judgment against them. In God, righteousness and rage are bound together: "God is a righteous judge (*šôpēṭ ṣaddîq*) and God of indignation (*'ēl zō'ēm*) every day" (v. 11). Divine indignation is no blind rage. God, rather, has the moral resolve and emotive wherewithal required to execute justice continually and without compromise. More akin to a disposition, God's "wrath" seeks redress for past crimes (56:6b–7), and it is out of God's justice that the psalmist appeals to God's anger to defeat the enemy: "[O God,] pour out your indignation (*za'am*) upon them, and let your burning anger (*ḥărôn 'ap*) overtake them" (69:24). The image is akin to boiling liquid "poured out" on the psalmist's enemies, elsewhere likened to fire (21:9b). In short, "anger" is no privatized, inward emotion but one that effects certain consequences, including judicial and historical outcomes. The "historical" Psalm 78, for example, narrates Israel's history from the standpoint of God's warranted wrath, which is sometimes exercised and other times restrained (vv. 21, 38, 49, 50, 58–59, 62b; cf. 106:29, 32).

God's anger can also be directed against, rather than on behalf of, the psalmist. In such cases, the psalmist finds divine wrath to be associated less with justice and more with unwarranted aggression. The opening plea of Psalm 38, for example, accuses God of exceeding the bounds of righteous indignation. The appeal that God cease and desist in the exercise of fury is not uncommon in the Psalter (e.g., 6:1; 27:9; 38:1). The lament "How long, YHWH? Will you be angry forever?" (79:5; cf. 80:4, 85:5) is a typical refrain. Anger and wrath, the psalmist admits, "leads only to evil" (37:8). At the very least, assurance is given that God's anger is not a permanent disposition, but is outweighed by divine favor: "For his anger is but for a moment; his favor is for a lifetime" (30:5). God's creedal confession in Exod 34:6 is echoed in the Psalms: "YHWH is merciful and gracious, slow to anger and abounding in faithful love" (103:8; 145:8).

Hatred

With anger is also hatred, a more enduring emotion. The language of hate found in the Psalter is typically reserved for the psalmist (139:21b–22) and the enemies (9:13; 21:8b; 69:4; 139:21a). Nevertheless, the language is occasionally attributed to God: "For forty years I loathed (*ʾāqûṭ*) that generation and said, 'They are a people whose hearts go astray, and they do not regard my ways'" (95:10). More intractable is God's stance toward the violent: "YHWH tests the righteous and the wicked, and he hates (*śānēʾâ*) the lover of violence"(11:5).[60] Like anger, YHWH's "hatred" is charged with moral potency, but is more categorical in nature than "wrath." Unlike anger, hatred enjoys no catharsis.

Love

References to divine "love" abound in Psalms.[61] Antithetically related, "love" and "hate" serve to define the moral will of Israel's God. As YHWH "hates the lover of violence," so "YHWH loves[62] those who hate[63] evil" (97:10a). The objects of God's "love," the righteous are included along with the lowly and the downcast as recipients of divine benevolence (146:8).

The scope of divine love is not only personally oriented. God's love also extends to more conceptual or institutional modes of conduct and policy: God "loves justice" (37:28),[64] "righteousness" (45:7), and "the gates of Zion" (87:2; cf. 78:68). The various objects of divine love are in some sense self-reflexive in that they also disclose the intrinsically moral qualities of God: "For YHWH is righteous (*ṣaddîq*); righteous deeds (*ṣĕdāqôt*) he loves" (11:7). The *object* of God's love indicates something of the *character* of God. Likeness attracts. To give further definition, God's love is bound up with *ḥesed* or faithful love: "He loves righteousness and justice; the earth is full of YHWH's faithful love" (33:5). Covenantal in scope,[65] God's "faithful love" identifies an enduring quality to which the psalmist confidently appeals for salvation and sustenance.[66] But whereas "love" is shared by both God and mortal, *ḥesed* is divinely initiated in Psalms.

Compassion

Like *ḥesed*, "compassion" (√*rḥm*) is unilaterally extended by God to mortals in the psalms, although it has analogical roots within the human, specifically familial, sphere: "As a father has compassion for his children, so YHWH has compassion for those who fear him" (103:13).[67] The familial is mapped onto the transcendent. God's compassion, the psalmist contends, is thoroughly parental and specifically paternal. But it can also be covenantal (106:45). Divine compassion keeps the continuing moral cycle of events (sin, punishment, and deliverance) from spiraling into disaster. Like the covenant that must be remembered by God in order to implement it, the psalmist exhorts God to "remember" compassion (25:6–7). It is precisely out of covenantal compassion that God resolves to disregard ("not remember") the psalmist's sins (v. 7). Compassion and *ḥesed* constitute the fundamental character of the covenanting God, evidenced in the long-standing history of gracious acts. The enduring nature of God's compassion is highlighted all the more when placed poetically alongside *ḥesed*.[68] As "faithful love" ceases, so compassion is "constricted" (*qāṣap*; 77:8–9).

Elsewhere, compassion is treated as something that bears its own presence, assuming nearly hypostatic status: "Let your compassion come speedily to meet us (*yĕqaddĕmûnû*), for we are brought very low" (79:8); "Let your compassion come to me (*yĕbōʾûnî*), so that I may live" (119:77). Divine compassion, like God's very self, advances with salutary effect. Conversely, it can be withheld: "Do not, YHWH, withhold (*tiklāʾ*) your compassion from me" (40:11). The psalmist prays that God's compassion be released or sent out, and practically in the same breath calls on God to "make haste to help me" (v. 13b). Divine compassion, thus, has a dynamic quality that signals God's own activity in behalf of the one who is "poor and needy" (v. 17), as well as all creation (145:9–10).

Delight/Pleasure

While the psalmists unabashedly expressed their personal delight in God (73:25),[69] they did not hesitate to ascribe personal pleasure to God. Identified objects of divine delight include the afflicted psalmist (18:19; 40:13; 41:11), Zion (51:18), Israel and its land (85:1; 106:4; 149:4), right sacrifice or offerings (51:19; 119:108), and right discourse (19:14). Wickedness, logically, has no place within the purview of God's pleasure (5:4). The language of delight sets in sharp relief God's *discriminating* nature. Divine pleasure, moreover, does not indicate a range of peripheral interests on the part of the deity. To the contrary, the metaphor of delight determines the very will and purpose of God, which can be taught: "Teach me to do your pleasure (*rāṣôn*, NRSV "will"), for you are my God" (143:10). Like "compassion," divine delight is antithetically related to wrathful anger (30:5; 77:7–9; 85:1, 5).

God's delight effects certain consequences. It has salutary import, as the psalmist's detractors declare, "Let [YHWH] rescue the one in whom he delights!" (22:8). Here, deliverance indicates delight.[70] Similar is the psalmist's affirmation:

"Great is YHWH, the one who delights (*ḥeḥāpēṣ*) in the well-being (*šālôm*) of his servant" (35:27). Psalm 5 highlights the protective nature of God's delight or favor:

> Spread your protection over them,
>   so that those who love your name may exult in you.
> For you bless the righteous, YHWH;
>   you cover them with favor (*rāṣôn*) as with a shield (*ṣinnâ*).
>   (5:11b–12)

The image of the shield, elsewhere connoting divine presence, lends protective nuance to God's favor, extended to those who "take refuge in" God (v. 11a). God's favor or delight also confers strength (30:7a).

All in all, the God of the ancient poet is one whose desire is eminently discriminating:

> He gives to the animals their food,
>   and to the young ravens when they cry.
> He delights (*yeḥpāṣ*) not in the strength of the horse,
>   nor takes (*yirṣeh*) pleasure in the speed of an athlete.[71]
> Rather, YHWH takes pleasure (*rôṣeh*) in those who fear him,
>   in those who hope in his faithful love.
>   (147:9–11)

Although a measure of satisfaction is reflected in God's care of creation, supreme delight is reserved not for the physically agile but for those who revere God and hope in *ḥesed*. Yet God's delight, determined as it is morally and salvifically, also preserves God's sovereign freedom: "Our God is in the heavens; he can do whatever he pleases (*ḥāpēṣ*)" (115:3). Divinity is, in part, measured by the degree of freedom that underlies the nexus between delight and action.

Remembering

Remembrance constitutes a special attribution in the psalmist's repertoire of metaphors that target the active life of God. As a testimony of faith, the psalmist confidently professes or exhorts remembrance of God,[72] God's "wonders of old,"[73] covenant,[74] and God's power and *ḥesed*.[75] Even the earth, including all its peoples, is charged to "remember" God (22:27). In remembrance, God's renown is ensured (111:4).

Reciprocally, God is said or exhorted to "remember." Divine remembrance ensures life; forgetfulness entails death. The dead are defined as "those whom you remember no more, for they are cut off from your hand" (88:5b; cf. 83:4). The objects of God's remembrance are varied. The psalmist proclaims God's benevolent "remembrance" of human beings (8:4),[76] Zion (74:2), the afflicted (9:12; 136:23), the psalmist (106:4), covenant (105:8; 106:45; 111:5), David (132:1), *ḥesed* and faithfulness (98:3), promise (105:42), sacrifice (20:3), divine word (119:49), and certain acts or conditions that demand redress from God (74:18, 22; 89:50; 137:7). The act of divine remembrance clearly entails more than recollection; it marks God's orientation toward the psalmist and the community.

Divine remembrance also serves to maintain coherence with God's true nature; it enables God to "keep in touch," as it were, with divine self-identity and relationship to the community:

> Remember your compassion (*raḥămêkā*), YHWH,
>   and your faithful love (*ḥesed*),
>   for they have been from of old.
> Do not remember the sins of my youth or my transgressions;
>   according to your faithful love remember me,
>   for your goodness' sake, YHWH.
>
> (25:6–7)

Because God's benevolence is demonstrated in certain primal acts, remembrance is requisite for salvation (vv. 16–21). The psalmist grounds his petition in the precedent of the past, when God established God's reputation or acted true to God's nature. Similar petition occurs in a hymn extolling divine kingship: victory over political or cosmic conflict is achieved through remembrance of God's special, unilateral relationship to Israel (98:3).

As a frequent object of God's remembrance, "covenant" provides a constitutional framework and precedent for God's providential care over Israel and creation. In Psalm 105, the psalmist exhorts remembrance of God's past deeds while proclaiming the deity's remembrance of the covenantal promises made to Abraham (vv. 5, 8–11; see also v. 42). In the penitential counterpart to this psalm, the following psalm rehearses Israel's defiance of God, yet concludes with the theme of God's forbearance, formalized in remembrance of covenant (106:44–45). By remembering covenant, God refrains from destroying Israel, despite sufficient warrant, and in turn ensures sustenance and salvation (111:4–5). Covenantal remembrance ensures continuity between past salvation and assurance for the future.

Yet it is not uncommon that the psalmists charge God with forgetfulness: "I say to God, my rock, 'Why have you forgotten me?'" (42:9). Having proclaimed her own remembrance of God (v. 6), the psalmist laments her dereliction. God's forgetfulness, thus, is not so much a sign of senility as betrayal, a matter of will rather than incapacity (see also 77:9). The language of remembrance preserves a level of euphemistic diplomacy between the psalmist and God by which the former feels free to take up the task of reminding God of God's true nature without charging God with duplicity.

An ironic variation on this theme is found in the psalmist's exhortation to forget, even within an exhortation to remembrance! God is enjoined to forget the "sins of my youth" (25:7) and "the iniquities of our ancestors" (79:8). God is encouraged to remember *selectively*, which necessarily involves disregarding other matters of the past that would prompt the saving God to different action. Hence, the psalmist is not reluctant to direct God's attention to particular grievances in the language of remembrance: "Remember this, YHWH, how the enemy scoffs, and an impious people reviles your name" (74:18, 20, 22). God is exhorted to attend to the razed temple (v. 7). The temple's destruction and the continuing havoc wrought by Israel's enemies are submitted as incontrovertible evidence worth remembering. They are, as it were, "for the record." It is in remembrance that redress is warranted. With equal fervor, another psalmist enjoins God to "remember . . . against the Edomites the day of Jerusalem's fall" (137:7a). To remember the trauma of such devastation is to remember not just for the sake of the victim but also "against" the perpetrators.

From wrath to compassion, the psalmist cannot avoid metaphors of emotion and disposition when speaking of God's character. Remembrance, in particular, gives God coherence of character as well as historical grounding. The psalmist's plea for God to "remember" marks the retrieval of the God of the past, the God of the established covenant, for the present. It also binds God to covenantal conduct, which ensures Israel's preservation amid crisis. For Israel, whose historical consciousness was unmatched by its surrounding cultures, the language of remembrance is bound up with God's very nature.

ROLES OF GOD

Whereas the above list of metaphors reference God's "body" and personal attributes, those given below profile the various roles God assumes in the Psalter. Of course, much could be said of God as creator,[77] provider,[78] redeemer/savior,[79] and healer[80]—roles prominently featured in the psalms—but they lack the measure of iconic content evident in those listed below.

King

As is often noted, God's royal profile pervades much of Scripture, including the Psalter.[81] The ringing proclamation "YHWH reigns" (*yhwh mālak*) of the enthronement psalms indicates God's incontestable dominion over Israel, the nations, and the cosmos,[82] a staple of psalmic theology. Psalm 47 serves as a poetic précis: God's subjection of the nations (v. 3), the granting of Jacob's "heritage" or special possession (v. 4), God's enthronement (vv. 5–7), and the imperial extent of God's reign, which requires tribute from the nations (vv. 8–9). A cosmic counterpart to Psalm 47 is found in Psalm 29, which proclaims YHWH's enthronement over the "flood" (v. 10).[83] The role of creator is given specific iconic significance from this root metaphor or schema.[84] The metaphor maps God's sovereignty as universally cosmic, eliciting praise even from the sea.[85] Indeed, God creates by command (see above).[86] The royal ascription, moreover, attests God's sovereignty over the gods (95:3). Crafting a clever word pun, Psalm

96 relegates the "gods" (*'ĕlōhîm*) to "idols," or literally "nothings" (*'ĕlîlîm*), in the face of the Suzerain's universal reign (vv. 4–5; cf. 97:7).[87]

Other metaphorical images and roles are incorporated into the royal schema. Though drawn from the pastoral setting, God as Israel's *shepherd* has its home in the royal context.[88] God's role as cosmic *judge*, too, is intrinsically related to the royal metaphor.[89] As king, God executes justice par excellence (9:7; 72:1–3; 99:4). "Father of orphans and protector of widows is God in his holy habitation" (68:5). Psalm 99 lifts up God's justice, rather than military strength, to highlight royal divinity (v. 4). As the upholder of justice, the divine king is also lawgiver (93:5), as also exemplified in the exodus-Sinai episode of 99:7. God in the role of gardener also has deep roots in the royal schema.[90] The language of theophany, moreover, frequently accompanies the royal profile,[91] which points to another metaphorical profile that is intimately related to, if not indistinguishable from, the royal domain: God as divine warrior (see below).

The kingship metaphor generates additional poetic reflection in the Psalter: "Righteousness and justice are the foundation of your throne; faithful love and faithfulness go before you" (89:14). The psalmist deploys the images of throne and royal entourage or vanguard to highlight the values of just rule and covenantal promise (*ḥesed*) as fundamental and enduring. They are also, not coincidentally, emblematic of the earthly king's rule. The royal metaphor, thus, establishes an indissoluble link between King and king. While the incomparable God rules "the raging of the sea" (89:8–9), God also raises "the highest of the kings of the earth" (89:27), from whom divine *ḥesed* shall not depart (vv. 24, 33). God's sovereign rule is made manifest through the earthly king (2:7–12). As God's righteous rule ensures equitable treatment of the most vulnerable, so does the king's reign (72:12–14).

Finally, the royal metaphor packs a powerful illocutionary force: worship and praise are designated the proper responses to God's sovereign rule, as prescribed in Psalm 96.[92]

> Honor and majesty are before him;
>   strength and beauty are in his sanctuary.
> Ascribe to YHWH, O families of the peoples;
>   ascribe to YHWH glory and strength.
> Ascribe to YHWH the glory due his name;
>   bring an offering and come into his courts.
> Worship YHWH in holy splendor;
>   tremble before him, all the earth.
> (96:6–9)

A nearly identical series of commands opens Psalm 29, in which the members of the divine assembly ("sons of God") are commanded to acknowledge God's sovereignty (vv. 1–2). Worship, thus, is the consummate sign of fealty to the Sovereign.

That the royal metaphor is one of the most prominent metaphors in the Psalter is due in no small measure to its integrative and generative power: it incorporates a myriad of other roles and profiles (e.g., judge, warrior, protector, creator, savior, redeemer, lawgiver) into a coherent metaphorical schema. Moreover, the royal metaphor serves to cement a political connection with Israel's own form of governance. God's palace stands on Zion, the "city of the great King" (48:2b), the locus of cosmic rule (74:2; 76:1–2), and God's anointed is God's "son," the king (2:7; cf. 110:3). Yet even with the dismantling of Israel's monarchy, God's royal status is in no way compromised in the psalmist's eyes. To the contrary, the enthronement psalms (Psalms 93; 95–97; 99) testify to the enduring power of the metaphor apart from any human correlate. As king, God's presence is commanding and compelling.

Warrior

Warrior imagery serves in part to disclose the salvific side of God's royal profile. Indeed, it is well-nigh impossible to separate out the warrior from the royal schemas. Kings go to war, and wars are won by kings (or by usurpers to the throne). As king, God is also warrior of cosmic proportions:

> God my King is from of old,
> working salvation in the earth.
> You divided the sea by your might;
> you broke the heads of the dragons in the waters.
> You crushed the heads of Leviathan.
>
> (74:12–14a)

In this psalm, the profiles of creator and warrior are bound together. But there is more: while God enters into the thick of battle to drive away enemies "as smoke" (68:2), the valiant "rider upon the heavens" also founds homes for the desolate and acts as "father of orphans and protector of widows" (v. 5). Battle prowess and magnanimity both befit the King.

Nevertheless, there are examples among the psalms in which battle imagery commands central stage *without* explicit reference to God's royal profile. God bears and uses weapons such as sword, arrow, and javelin to vanquish the enemy and afflict the psalmist (7:12, 13; 35:3; 38:2; 64:7).[93] Divine prowess on the battlefield neutralizes all weapons of destruction (46:9; 76:3). God wages war on a cosmic scale (18:7–15; 29:1–10) as well as on a national and personal scale (64:7), frequently within the same text (18:7–19). God's military retinue comprises both "mighty chariotry" (68:17) and natural elements (104:3b–4). God's warrior status is so thoroughly presupposed in psalmic theology that one suppliant complains, "You do not go out . . . with our armies" (60:10), a sure sign of divine rejection.

Also distinct from the explicit rhetoric of royal imagery is the terse formulaic imperative addressed to the warrior deity: "Rise up!"[94] and "Wake up!" or "Rouse yourself!"[95] From one hunted down like prey by unnamed enemies comes the cry: "Rise up, YHWH, confront them. Overthrow them! By your sword deliver my life from the wicked" (17:13; cf. vv. 8–12). The psalmist's cry is a call to battle (35:2–3) and, metaphorically, an alarm for the "slumbering" Warrior:

> Then the Lord awoke as from sleep,
>   like a warrior shouting because of wine.
> He struck his foes from behind;[96]
>   he delivered them to everlasting disgrace.
>   (78:65–66)

The imagery is daring but not unprecedented: the psalmist depicts the deity in a wine-induced stupor, aroused not a moment too soon to defeat Israel's adversaries. "Why do you sleep, O Lord?" is part of the repertoire of accusations leveled against God (44:23). The metaphor of the sleeping or drunken warrior accounts for the period of inactivity on the part of the deity when action is most needed.[97]

The alarm cry, however, is directed not only to the divine warrior but also to God the judge: "Rise up, O judge of the earth; give to the proud what they deserve!" (94:2; cf. 7:6–8). The epithet transforms the battleground into a law court and casts the enemies' defeat as "restitution" (94:23). Psalm 7 thoroughly mixes battle and judicial imagery. God is not only armed with sword and bow (v. 12); the deity also conveys judgment from the high seat in the "assembly" (vv. 7–8). The psalm's order of presentation is deliberate: God first acts as judge (vv. 6b–11) before executing judgment as an armed warrior (vv. 12–13), and the drama of battle turns on whether the enemy repents (v. 12).

The mixing of military and judicial metaphors significantly nuances the rhetoric of divine conquest:

> If one does not repent, [God] will whet his sword;
>   he has bent and strung his bow.
> He has prepared his deadly weapons,
>   making his arrows fiery shafts.
> See how they devise evil,
>   and are pregnant with mischief and deliver lies.
> They make a pit, digging it out,
>   and fall into the hole of their own making.
> Their mischief returns upon their own heads,
>   and on their own heads their violence descends.
>   (7:12–16)

The language moves from military imagery to that of self-inflicted demise ("make a pit"). The former complex of metaphors, namely weapons of war, gives way to images that target immoral conduct ("evil, mischief"), whose outcome is revealed to be self-defeating. Psalm 10, on the one hand, calls on God: "Rise up, YHWH; O God, lift up your hand; do not forget the oppressed" (v. 12), and "Break the arm of the wicked and evildoers; seek out their wickedness until you find none" (v. 15). On the other hand, the psalm opens with the prayer that the wicked "be caught in the schemes they themselves have devised" (v. 2b). In Psalm 59, the psalmist exhorts God, "Rouse yourself, come to my help. . . . Wake up to punish all the nations" (59:4b–5b), yet at the same time commands God, "Do not kill them, lest my people forget. . . . For the sin of their mouths, the words of their lips, let them be trapped in their pride" (vv. 11–12a). The psalmist's plea that God take on the role of warrior slides into an exhortation for the wicked to trap themselves. Divine conquest leads to *self-inflicted* defeat of the wicked.

Perhaps the most graphic portrayal of the wicked and their demise at their own hands is found in Psalm 37:

> The wicked draw the sword and bend their bows
> to bring down the poor and needy,
> to kill those who walk uprightly.
> Yet their sword shall enter their own heart,
> and their bows shall be broken.
> (37:14–15)

Though littered with corpses, the scenario lacks any reference to God assuming the role of warrior. At most is the reference to the "arms of the wicked" being "broken" (v. 17). But lacking is any reference to active engagement on the deity's part, as if to suggest that God's weapons are displaced by weaponry deployed by the wicked *against themselves*. Nowhere does the psalmist call on God to vanquish the enemy; rather, his audience is exhorted to "be still before YHWH and wait patiently for him" (v. 7). Refuge, not warrior, is the defining metaphor for the saving God of Psalm 37 (v. 39; cf. vv. 23, 31).

The juxtaposition of combat imagery and moral consequence within the warrior schema highlights the active engagement of the deity in bringing about the *just* deserts of the wicked. The battlefield and the courtroom become coextensive. Furthermore, in some psalms the metaphor of divine weaponry "targets" the self-inflicted consequences of wicked conduct. As warrior, God ensures that the wicked fall victim to their own machinations. God's "weapons" uphold the moral order, an order in which the wicked do indeed receive self-prescribed retribution.[98] Call it poetic justice.

Parent

Parental imagery is not eschewed in biblical poetry, and the psalms are no exception. The psalmists develop both paternal and maternal metaphors to highlight the power and poignancy of God's providential care.[99] The paternal relationship, for example, specifically targets the relationship between God and king:

> I will tell of the decree of YHWH:
> He said to me, "You are my son;
> today I have begotten you."
> (2:7)

> I will set his hand on the sea
> and his right hand on the rivers.
> He shall cry to me, "You are my Father,
> My God, and the Rock of my salvation!"
> (89:25–26)

Both texts commemorate the intrinsic link between God and king or "son." Indicating much more than simply adoption, paternal imagery connotes inviolable solidarity, a "genetic" relationship that confers power amid threat (2:8–9) and ensures uninterrupted lineage (89:29–37).[100] The latter psalm in particular naturalizes the royal covenantal relationship through parental imagery (89:28).

The psalmists by no means confine paternal imagery to the earthly king, however. As king and warrior, God is also the "father of orphans and protector of widows" (68:5). As the paterfamilias, God safeguards the most socially vulnerable. More broadly, paternal imagery is well suited to convey God's benevolent orientation to the community as a whole:

> As a father has compassion (*kĕraḥēm*) for his children,
>   so YHWH has compassion (*riḥam*) for those who fear him.
> For he knows how we were made;
>   he remembers that we are dust.
>
> (103:13–14)

The paternal imagery not only heightens the tender and unwavering nature of God's compassion but also deepens the sense of absolute dependence on God shared by mortals. God, moreover, "knows" and, thus, is intimately aware of, if not involved in, the work of human genesis (cf. Gen 4:1). Such knowledge sets a precedent for continued care (see Psalm 139 in the conclusion).

Although more subtle and indirect than paternal imagery, *maternal* imagery is also deployed by the psalmists.[101] Psalm 131, likely composed by a woman, casts trust in the serene terms of a child comforted by its mother:

> I have calmed and quieted my soul,
>   like a weaned child with its mother;
>   my soul is like the weaned child that is with me.
> O Israel, hope in YHWH,
>   from this time on and forevermore.
>
> (131:2–3)

One of the shortest psalms in the Psalter, this prayer opens confessionally on a note of humble trust and concludes with an exhortation to hope (v. 3). Refusing to ascend the heights of rapturous reflection on God's marvelous deeds (v. 1), the psalmist likens herself to a maternally comforted child whom she herself holds. The last line of v. 2 signals a remarkable shift in perspective while preserving the metaphorical relationship: likening herself to a child, the pray-er identifies herself as a mother. Yet the prayer concludes in a way that provokes, however subtly, an even more suggestive shift. The psalmist's exhortation in v. 3 to "hope in YHWH . . . forevermore" casts Israel in the role of child and God as comforting mother. Hope in God, thus, takes on the palpable sense of maternal tenderness.

Elsewhere, maternal imagery finds a more explicitly divine target. Psalm 22 conjoins two related metaphorical schemas, the mother and the midwife.

> Yet it was you who took me from the womb;
>   you kept me secure on my mother's breast.
> On you I was cast from my birth,
>   and from my mother's womb you have been my God.
> Do not be far from me,
>   for trouble is near and there is no one to help.
>   (22:9–11)

As deliverer (in the obstetrical sense), God acts as midwife to bring to birth the psalmist's life and hope.[102] The visual parallel of the infant sustained on the mother's breast and the psalmist "cast" on God "from . . . birth" marks God's protection as one of maternal compassion. Metonymically expressed by the *imago mammae* (cf. Gen 49:25), maternal love effectively conveys the intimacy of God's caring presence, so palpably real in the psalmist's past but jarringly absent in the present (Ps 22:1–21a). The imagery only heightens the horrifying incongruity.

As a concluding example, Psalm 27 extends God's care beyond the metaphorical limitations of parental love:

> Do not turn your servant away in anger,
>   you who have been my help.
> Do not turn cast me off;
>   do not forsake me, O God of my salvation.
> If my father and mother forsake me,
>   YHWH will take me in.
>   (27:9b–10)

In this prayer for refuge in the temple, the psalmist appeals to the past in order to invoke God's salutary presence for the present. God's love is parental in nature yet found to be more enduring and reliable than human parenting.[103]

Teacher

The psalmists frequently exhort God to teach. Divine instruction has a metaphorically dynamic, even peripatetic dimension. Frequently, the request for understanding is infused with the desire to be led on a "level path" (e.g., 27:11; 143:10).[104] In addition, the psalmists pray to be taught God's "statutes" and "ordinances,"[105] *tôrâ*,[106] knowledge,[107] skill in combat,[108] and the litany of God's "wonderful deeds."[109] Even in Psalm 119,[110] these prayerful requests are frequently expressed in situations of distress rather than within a secure educational setting.[111]

> Make known to me your ways, YHWH;
>   teach me your paths.

> Lead me in your truth and teach me,
>   for you are the God of my salvation.
> . . . .
> Good and upright is YHWH;
>   therefore he teaches sinners in the way.
> He leads the humble in what is right,
>   and teaches the humble his way.
> All the paths of YHWH are faithful love and faithfulness,
>   for those who keep his covenant and his decrees.
>   (25:4–5a, 8–10)

On its own, this passage seems suspended above the fray of crisis, but in fact it is accompanied by a plea for forgiveness (vv. 11, 18) and deliverance from unnamed enemies (vv. 19–20). What, then, does the metaphor of God as teacher have to do with God's saving work, to which the psalmist urgently appeals? A clue is evident at the psalm's conclusion: "May integrity and uprightness preserve me, for I wait for you" (v. 21). God as teacher and God as savior are effectively integrated into the psalmist's final petition. Through God's teaching, the psalmist appropriates moral integrity and thereby preserves his life. Moreover, the psalmist's receptivity to God's teaching signals genuine repentance. As the formative outcomes of divine instruction, "integrity" and "uprightness" serve as the psalmist's guardians (cf. Prov 2:11). God's role as teacher, in short, imbues the language of salvation with a distinctly moral nuance.

Psalm 32 features a divine oracle that conveys another dimension of God's pedagogical profile vis-à-vis the psalmist:

> I will instruct you and teach you the way you should go;
>   I will counsel you with my eye upon you.
> Do not be like a horse or a mule without understanding,
>   whose gallop[112] must be curbed with bit and bridle,
>   else it will not stay near you.
>   (32:8–9)

The psalmist is exhorted to be receptive to divine instruction, which is qualitatively distinguished from the brute force required to train a beast of burden. The psalmist is warned to be compliant and self-restrained (see vv. 7, 11). But the decision to appropriate such instruction is left with the psalmist. "He will teach them the way they should choose" (25:12b). God's pedagogy does not coerce; it in fact offers protection along with enlightenment:

> How fortunate are those whom you discipline, YH[WH],
>   and whom you teach from your tôrâ,
> giving them respite (lĕhašqît) from the days of trouble,
>   until a pit is dug for the wicked.
>   (94:12–13)

God's teaching is itself a refuge, a "respite" from danger posed by the wicked. God's role as teacher, thus, forms an essential part of the psalmist's repertoire of metaphors. It preserves a sense of divine transcendence apart from God's role as warrior or king, and yet, at the same time, bears salutary, even saving, consequences.[113] While not governed by images of royal might or combat prowess, the metaphor enhances God's authoritative claim on the psalmist and community. Though not as vividly prevalent as the royal or warrior imagery among the psalms, the teacher metaphor is fundamental to the final coherence of the Psalter as a source of instruction, indeed, as the *tôrâ* of YHWH (Ps 1:2–3).

Chapter 8

"As the Mountains Surround Jerusalem"

Mapping the Divine

*I do not know much about gods; but I think that the river
Is a strong brown god—sullen, untamed, and intractable.*

T. S. Eliot[1]

In addition to featuring a plethora of metaphors that profile God as person, the psalms are replete with impersonal or inanimate metaphors: images drawn from source domains that bear no relation to God's personhood or *embodied* Agency. In this category, the language of aesthetics takes a front seat. "One thing I asked of YHWH, . . . to behold the beauty of YHWH and to inquire in his temple" (27:4). As with the refuge metaphor, holy beauty is commonly associated with Zion or the temple (48:1, 12–14; 50:2; 84:1; 96:6). God's presence is in one instance associated with the sense of taste, in addition to sight: "O taste and see how good is YHWH" (34:8).[2] Out of such aesthetic revelry emerge several iconic metaphors for God that are distinctly impersonal in nature yet equal in significance to the host of personal metaphors that populate the psalms.[3]

LIGHT

The metaphor of light, as applied to the deity, draws much of its source from solar imagery, itself rich in associations (see chapter 4). Most generally, light signifies flourishing life, "the light of life" (56:13),[4] and, thus, shares special affinity with the Author of life. To ascribe light to God is to acknowledge the fullness of life that God imparts to creation. In a royal thanksgiving psalm, the king likens himself to a lamp whose light is provided by God, who "lights up my darkness" (18:28). As in Genesis 1, light is the first element of creation designated in the Psalter's preeminent creation text: "[Y]ou wrap yourself in light as with a garment" (104:2). Unmatched in theological significance by any other element or part of creation, light bears an intrinsic connection to God. Indeed, the psalms frequently cast theophany in terms of a heliophany bursting with divine effulgence that reestablishes justice in the world (50:1–4; cf. 80:1–2).

The metaphor conveys a wide range of connotations. The light of God's face guides the psalmist in his or her path (89:15; cf. 119:105), as well as exposes hidden sins (90:8), brings about victory (44:3), and conveys agricultural bounty (4:6–7). Apart from its reference to God's countenance, divine light imparts joy to the righteous (97:11) and makes possible human perception: "In your light we see light" (36:9). Where there is perception, there also is life (13:3). Darkness, in turn, signifies distress and death.[5]

The metaphor, moreover, points to the need for guidance. As pedagogue and light bearer, God illumines pathways and renders guidance for those who seek security and wholeness.

> Send out your light and your truth;
>   let them lead me;
>   let them bring me to your holy hill and to your dwelling.
>   (43:3)

Personified as God's emissaries or guardians, "light" and "truth" serve to guide the psalmist on her sojourn to God's sanctuary (see 42:4). Such language also enhances the formative power of divine discourse: "Your word is a lamp to my feet and a light to my path" (119:105). Transmitted by authoritative word, light enlightens the uneducated (v. 130).[6]

Finally, God's effulgence highlights the salvific side of divine activity: "YHWH is my light and my salvation, whom shall I fear?" (27:1; cf. 56:13). By the light of God's countenance, comparable to God's mighty arm and right hand (44:3), victory is won. The break of dawn signals the in-breaking of divinely wrought deliverance (46:5b).[7] Light so thoroughly pervades divine imagery in the Psalter that it may appear surprising to find references to divine darkness, as in the following descriptions:

> YHWH reigns! Let the earth rejoice;
>   let the many coastlands exult!
> Clouds and thick darkness (*ǎrāpel*) surround him on all sides;[8]
>   righteousness and justice are the foundation of his throne.
> Fire (*'ēš*) goes before him,
>   and consumes his adversaries on every side.
>   (97:1–3)

Smoke went up from his nostrils,
and devouring fire (*'ēš*) from his mouth;
glowing coals flamed forth from him.
He bowed the heavens, and came down;
thick darkness (*'ărāpel*) was under his feet.
He rode on a cherub, and flew;
he came swiftly on the wings of the wind.
He made darkness (*ḥōšek*) his covering all around him,
his canopy thick clouds dark (*ḥeškat*) with water.
Out of the brightness (*nōgah*) before him,
there broke through his clouds hailstones and coals of fire (*'ēš*).
(18:8–12)

Both texts combine sharply contrasting images to convey the fearsome power of God's theophanous presence. Darkness constitutes an essential element in the constellation of storm images (clouds, wind, water) that highlight God's role as warrior-king. Yet fire imagery, including lightning (97:4), also plays a significant role: God's attack against the land or enemy is literally a *Blitzkrieg*.

Darkness ensures God's elusive, fearsome presence, whether on the battlefield or in the sanctuary (1 Kgs 8:12–13). Light, however, is more multifaceted in its connotations. In addition to playing an indispensable role in cosmic conflict, light also conveys God's salutary, public presence, beheld by the worshiper (e.g., 27:1; 56:13). Both sets of images or metaphorical schemas are essential in preserving God's formidable otherness and saving grace.

METAPHORS OF PROTECTION

The protective activity of God is a prominent theme in the Psalter. "I will place them in the safety for which they long," says YHWH (12:5b). As the psalmist's "keeper" (121:5, 7–8), God "watches over" or "guards" (√*šmr*, 12:7; 17:8; 146:9), and the psalmist, in turn, is the "apple of [God's] eye" (17:8), who reposes in safety, assured of protection (4:8; 23:2). This schema is densely populated with various metaphors that fill it with a powerfully iconic content. Most prominent is the metaphor of *refuge,* already discussed in chapter 1.

Shield

Of all the references to instruments of war in the psalms, the shield is the most common. Deeply embedded in the rhetoric of salvation, the image highlights the protection God affords both the psalmist and the community. So central and evocative is the image that it serves as an epithet or part of a formulaic declaration of trust: "O Lord, our shield" (59:11b); "[YHWH] is our help and shield" (33:20; cf. 115:9, 10, 11); "God is my shield, who saves the upright in heart" (7:10); "YHWH is my strength and my shield; in him my heart trusts" (28:7a). Psalm 18 refers to God's gift as "the shield of your salvation" (v. 35). The image connotes encompassing protection: "But you, YHWH, are a shield around me"

(3:3a); "For you bless the righteous, YHWH; you cover them with favor as with a shield" (5:12). By developing the common motif of "covering," Psalm 91 revels in mixed metaphor without apology:

> He will cover you with his pinions,
>   and under his wings you will find refuge.
> His faithfulness is a shield and buckler (*ṣinnâ wĕsōḥērâ*).
>   (91:4)

As God actively protects with outstretched wings,[9] God's faithfulness is deemed protective and unwavering, a shield. Similarly, in a call for God to "rise up" and "fight" with various weapons, the opening stanza of Psalm 35 enlists two kinds of shields to illustrate God's combat on behalf of the psalmist: the smaller, round kind used in military engagement (*māgēn*) and the larger variety designed to protect the full body against assault (*ṣinnâ*, v. 2).

Typical is the correspondence between shield and refuge or shelter: "You are my hiding place and my shield" (119:114a). Psalm 144 lists the shield within a catalog of terms that constitutes much of the "refuge" word field:

> My rock and my fortress,
>   my stronghold and my deliverer,
> my shield (*māginî*), in whom I take refuge,
>   that subdues the peoples under me.
>   (144:2)

Refuge is achieved by God's shield, which not only provides a sure defense but also actively "subdues." An iconographic parallel is found, for example, in the bronze representations of the Canaanite god Reshef, a menacing yet benevolent deity who typically wields *both* weapon and shield.[10] (See fig. 19.)

Finally, shield imagery is shared by both earthly and divine kings as providers of protection and blessing (84:9, 11a). In sum, the shield establishes a zone of safety and security, a fitting image for God's protective activity.

Shade/Shadow.

God's "shadow" is consistently construed as a positive, rather than negative, image. Drawn from ornithological imagery, for example, is reference to the "shadow" of God's "wings," under which the psalmist or community is granted safety (17:8; 36:7; 57:1; 63:7).[11] In a psalm that fully develops such imagery, the "shadow of *Shaddai*" (NRSV "Almighty") is equated with God's shelter or refuge (91:1; cf. v. 4).

A significantly different source domain for this metaphor, however, is found in Psalm 121, in which God is likened to "shade":

> YHWH is your protector;
>   YHWH is your shade (*ṣillĕkā*) at your right hand.
> The sun will not strike you by day,
>   nor the moon by night.
>   (121:5–6)

Fig. 19: Bronze statue of Resheph from Megiddo. Courtesy of the Oriental Institute of the University of Chicago.

God provides "shade" from the scorching heat of the sun (sunstroke?)[12] and from the "assault" of the moon (moonstruck?).[13] The poetic hyperbole, however, need not be taken literally. The juxtaposition of sun and moon may serve as a merism to indicate the total reach of God's protection. "Shade at your right hand" suggests unfailing protection in all of one's endeavors, both day and night. Moreover, it is difficult to ascertain whether the deity is depicted as a tree or cloud or some other entity that effectively protects the psalmist from danger. In any case, set against the blazing sun, the shadow of protection is cast toward those who trust in God.

Mountain

Connoting both stability and awe, mountain imagery has a home in the profile of divine protection. As a conduit between the earthly and the heavenly realms, mountains afforded the ancients an acute awareness of God's formidable presence and unsurpassed majesty. In the Psalter, towering summits can signify God's strength as creator (65:6). The "mighty mountains," as well as the "great deep," highlight the vastness of God's righteousness, a universal order in which God "save[s] humans and animals alike" (36:6). In addition to its commanding physical presence, the mountain's lofty profile conveys a primordial sense of age. As with the roaring deep (93:4), God's incomparable majesty is measured against the "everlasting mountains" (76:4 [LXX]), made relative by God's eternal reign (90:2). Indeed, the mountains become animated, "skip[ping] like rams" (114:4, 6), before God's presence or in the turmoil of chaos (46:2–3).

As further background for the use of such poetic imagery, the mountain provides a natural setting for God's abode, specifically Mount Zion, "his holy mountain" (48:1), won in victory (78:54).[14] Its location "in the remote [parts of the] north" (*yarkětê ṣāpôn*, 48:2) suggests metaphorical affinity with the Canaanite portrayal of Ba'al's palatial abode on Mount Sapan, near Ugarit.[15] God's mountainous home base, rising above all others, is immovable (125:1b), for on it is situated "the city" (87:1).

In the psalms, the mountain metaphor is employed to convey divine protection against external threat:

> Those who trust in YHWH are like Mount Zion,
>   immovable and abiding forever.
> As the mountains surround (*sābîb*) Jerusalem,
>   so YHWH surrounds (*sābîb*) his people,
>   from this time on and forevermore.
>   (125:1–2)

In a remarkable twist, the people, not God, are likened to Mount Zion, while the deity is profiled as the mountains that surround the holy hill. Topographically, the metaphorical scenario is vividly realistic. Jerusalem does not rest on the highest mountain within visual proximity. Geopolitically, the psalmist looks to the surrounding hills, not just the temple on the summit, to situate Zion's security (cf. 121:1).[16] The mountains convey a sense of all-encompassing protection, of protection in perpetuity. Similarly, another psalm likens the speaker to a mountain:

> As for me, I said in my prosperity,
>   "I shall never be moved."
> By your favor, YHWH,
>   you had established me as a strong mountain;[17]
> [But when] you hid your face,
>   I was dismayed.
>   (30:6–7)

Set in granite, so it seemed, the psalmist's former prosperity becomes quickly dismantled in the face of God's absence. Like the mountains that "tumble into the heart of the sea" (46:2), the psalmist's security crumbles before the vicissitudes of God's sovereign purposes. Even the imagery of bedrock stability is shown to be inadequate in accounting for the psalmist's experience of divine favor and absence, a journey from prosperity to Sheol (30:3) and back again. Flux rather than stability is the norm before God's sovereign freedom. The mountain metaphor, in short, serves as both foundation and foil for divine activity.

FOUNTAIN

Twice in the Psalter God is related to a fountain or water source.[18] The precedent for such attribution is clearly given in Jeremianic poetry, where the divine epithet "the fountain of living water" (*mĕqôr mayim ḥayyîm*) is well attested (Jer 2:13; 17:13[19]). The iconic background of this metaphor holds a venerable position in the ancient Near East. The motif of poured water is, for example, dramatically portrayed in the wall painting of the Old Babylonian palace of King Zimri-Lim at Mari.[20] (See the middle, lower panel of fig. 7 in chapter 3.) In this lush garden setting, two goddesses are depicted pouring four streams of water—an iconic precursor to Eden's primordial rivers described in Gen 2:10–14.

Another well-known example, also from Mari, is the statue of a goddess holding a vase poised to pour out life-giving water. (See fig. 20.) The chiseled ripples and fish on her gown identify her as a water goddess. Male deities, too, were used to depict water's life-giving power, as in a thirteenth-century B.C.E. ivory inlay from Assur (see fig. 21), which depicts a mountain god holding a vase from which four streams of water flow into four pots, presumably representing the four ends of the earth.

The numinous nature of water, particularly water's source, is vividly described in the Psalter. The "fountain of life" is lodged squarely in God's abode, the temple:

> They are well filled from the richness (*dešen*[21]) of your house,
>   and from the river of your
>   abundant provisions (*naḥal 'ădānêkā*)[22]
>   you give them drink.
> For with you is the fountain of life (*mĕqôr ḥayyîm*);
>   in your light we see light.
>
> (36:8–9)

The expressed setting for such poetic praise is the temple, south of which lies the Gihon spring, Jerusalem's underground water source. Whether the psalmist has the physical parameters of the temple distinctly in mind is, however, moot. Unequivocally affirmed is that the source of life, parallel to Eden's primordial rivers (cf. Gen 2:10–14), flows from God's abode, providing abundant blessings for all who take refuge. Another example of comparable imagery also depicts the setting of temple worship.

> "Bless God in the assemblies;[23]
>   [bless] YHWH, you who are
>   of Israel's fountain (*mimmĕqôr yiśrā'ēl*)!"
>
> (Ps 68:26)

Fig. 20: Water-goddess with vase. Mari, Syria. Copyright Erich Lessing / Art Resource, New York.

Although presented as a public address, likely sung by an accompanied choir (v. 25), the verse is difficult. The above translation suggests that the worshiping congregation is identified as being from "Israel's fountain." In God's abode, specifically its "fountain," the congregation finds its source and sustenance, both identity and well-being. If God is not explicitly targeted by the metaphor, then at least an essential feature of God's dwelling place, the temple, is designated. In any case, the metaphor highlights God's sustaining provision for both Israel and creation.

POSSESSION: "PORTION" AND "CUP"

Offensive perhaps to modern theological sensibilities, references to God as one's "portion" and "cup" indicate an essential dimension to psalmic piety. Unwavering confidence in God, for example, is conveyed by the following passage from a song of trust:

YHWH is my chosen portion (*ḥelqî*) and my cup (*kôsî*);
   you hold my lot (*gôrālî*).
The boundary lines have fallen for me in pleasant places;
   I have a goodly heritage (*naḥălāt*).

                                                              (16:5–6)

Connoting immediate accessibility to God, the imagery seems to run counter to any notion of divine transcendence. Elsewhere, the reference to "portion" corresponds to the protection God extends to the psalmist: "I say, 'You are my refuge, my portion (*ḥelqî*) in the land of the living'" (142:5). As often noted, references to "portion" and "heritage" are drawn from the settlement of the land traditions,[24] specifically in connection with the Levites, who received no allotment of land but only God as their inheritance and portion.[25] However, land is not the issue in Psalm 16. This passage forms part of a declaration of allegiance to YHWH; choosing "another god" is denounced (v. 4). "I keep YHWH always before me" is the psalmist's profession of faith and conduct (v. 8a) (cf. Exod 20:3). With equal fervor, the psalmist of the law proclaims, "YHWH is my portion; I promise to keep your words" (119:57). To pronounce God as one's portion is to declare one's allegiance to God through obedience and proper worship. More valuable than land, God is the psalmist's most prized possession, which, like land, provides security and identity.

In comparable fashion, the reference to God as "cup" in the psalms designates both allegiance and sustenance. As the wicked suffer a burning wind from the "portion of their cup," the cup of judgment (11:6; cf. 17:14b; 75:8), so the

Fig. 21: Ivory inlay of a water god from Assur. Reprinted with permission from Othmar Keel, *Song of Songs: A Continental Commentary* (Minneapolis: Fortress, 1994), 144 (#81). Courtesy of the Department of Biblical Studies, University of Fribourg.

speaker in Psalm 16 declares God's salvific blessings granted him (vv. 2b, 6, 10–11), a cup of sustenance (v. 5; cf. 23:5).[26] One delivers judgment, this "cup of staggering" and "of horror and desolation" (so Isa 51:22; Ezek 23:33); the other offers salvation (Ps 116:13).

The above discussion by no means exhausts the plethora of metaphors, both personal and impersonal, that designate the deity. Only the most common (and a few less common) have been considered. But even this modest survey demonstrates that the Psalter proudly showcases a bewildering variety of images, cast as metaphors, for God. Any psalm that depicts or directs itself to God in any extended fashion cannot avoid employing imagery. Reveling in both conventional and innovative images, the poetry of the psalms is anything but aniconic. On the other hand, the breadth and diversity of imagery alone would seem to mitigate against the temptation to represent the deity materially, that is, with any "graven image." By way of example, this study concludes with an examination of the iconic contours of Psalm 139.

Conclusion

In Defense of
Iconic Reflection
The Case of Psalm 139

Just as we taste food with the mouth,
so we taste the psalm with the heart.

Bernard of Clairvaux[1]

Owing to its emotive depth and vivid imagery, Psalm 139 has stirred the imagination of readers throughout the ages. Its universal appeal derives from the innovative yet interrelated ways both God and the self are profiled, ways that pull at the heart and stimulate theological reflection. The poet proves to be a master of iconic manipulation, taking the reader seemingly down one path while, all along, forging another. Significant, too, is the psalm's social setting, which seems to belie its iconic artistry. The psalm is no serene meditation on the nature of God and humankind's place. Rather, it is a desperate plea to God and a defense against false accusation.[2] The psalm operates metaphorically on two levels, the personal and the judicial, and therein lie its complexity and power.

THE METAPHORICAL CONTOURS OF PSALM 139

For all its sublime rhetoric, Psalm 139 defers its true aim and motive until the end: to clear the self of all charges of illicit conduct, including idolatry (v. 24),[3] by laying claim to God's personal knowledge and support (vv. 1–6; 23–24).

Beneath the poetic elegance lies an urgent, if not defiant, juridical appeal that God test the psalmist's moral mettle for the sake of his acquittal.[4] Unlike other appeals for vindication, this psalm avoids the bitter rhetoric of lament.[5] Praise, rather, sets the norm.[6] Moreover, as a defense of the psalmist's integrity the psalm lacks a litany of righteous deeds, as found in Psalm 26. Instead, the psalmist fixes his gaze resolutely on the mystery of God's beneficence, albeit viewed through the prism of the self. The psalm's overriding theme is knowledge, both of self and of God,[7] and it is within this noetic context that the psalm's numerous tropes are given full play, marking this psalm as one of the most evocative in the Psalter. Indeed, the density of iconic metaphors is even more striking in light of the fact that the psalm serves as a defense against the charge of idolatry.

The Nearness of Knowledge

As the basis of the psalmist's self-knowledge, God's tender yet totalizing knowledge pervades the first four verses.

> YHWH, you have searched me and known [me].
> You have known my sitting and my rising;
> > you have perceived my purpose (*rē'î*) from far away.
> My path and my stay you determine (*zērîtā*);[8]
> > with all my ways you are familiar.
> Before a word is on my tongue,
> > YHWH, you know it completely.
>
> (139:1–4)

The psalmist views God as a preeminently discerning power that achieves an intimacy of familiarity even "from far away" (v. 2b). The reference to God's distance in this context is suggestive. Whereas other psalmists decry God's detachment from their distress as a sign of abandonment,[9] Psalm 139 effortlessly holds together divine distance and intimacy. God is neither the psalmist's "cup" nor his "portion," but the subject of totalizing discernment. God "searches" (√*ḥqr*) and "discerns" (√*byn,* √*yd',* √*skn*),[10] and the psalmist enjoys being the object of knowledge that bridges the distance between creator and creation. For the first four verses, such noetic activity governs God's relationship with the psalmist. The psalmist's pathways (v. 3), desires (v. 2), and discourse (v. 4) are all brought under divine scrutiny, a determining knowledge. The deity is more than "Perry Mason."[11] God's investigation of the psalmist is imbued with poignancy and warmth. A sense of serenity controls the rhetoric: God is the psalmist's intimate yet transcendent partner. Such "knowledge" comes with the passion of solidarity.

In the following two verses, however, the language turns violently physical and explicitly metaphorical:

> Behind and before [me] you besiege (*ṣartānî*) me;
> and you lay your palm upon me.

> Such knowledge is too wonderful for me;
> too high for me to attain.
>
> (vv. 5–6)

The metaphor of God's hand or palm (*kap*) takes center stage and generates considerable ambiguity. The language of combat in v. 5 stresses the thoroughness with which God knows the psalmist: God "besieges" (√*ṣwr*) him from all sides, "behind and before," and lays down the hand from above. Such rhetoric leads the reader to expect a cry of protest or despair over God's oppressive treatment.[12] But no such response is to be found from this psalmist's lips, only adulation (v. 6). Riveting the reader's attention, the change to explicitly figurative language in v. 5 pitches the psalmist's message to a new level. God's knowledge of the self is not just comprehensive; it is overpowering. God's discerning power is considered invasive, a force so totalizing that it can only be welcomed, indeed petitioned (v. 23). The hand metaphor, thus, receives an iconic twist. Deployed as if to crush, the palm serves to discern, sustain, and vindicate. Besiegement by God's hand renders the exercise of divine discernment with irresistible force. In short, the psalmist's testimony paradoxically transfers the language of battle into the realm of divine beneficence. The psalmist is overwhelmed with God's knowledge of the self: God's knowledge is claimed as "too wonderful" and too "high" because it is, the psalmist affirms, *too near*.

In the Grip of Guidance

The next section (vv. 7–12) is arguably the most evocative portion of the psalm. The first two verses set the stage:

> Where can I go away from your spirit?
> Where can I flee from your face?
> Were I to ascend to heaven, you would be there,
> or to lie down in Sheol, there you would be.
>
> (vv. 7–8)

As God remains "far away" yet immanently discerning (v. 2), so the psalmist transports himself to the farthest reaches of creation, including the netherworld. Yet his far-flung journeys do not take him *in search of* God. To the contrary, the psalmist is in "flight" (v. 7b) and affirms, in effect, that neither depth nor height nor breadth can hide the psalmist. Like v. 5, the opening question of this section and the subsequent protases maintain a level of ambiguity: Is the psalmist, like Jonah in his flight, seeking to flee from God's punishing presence? From a judicial standpoint, is he trying to escape God, the Bounty Hunter?

> Were I to take the wings of the dawn (*kanpê šāḥar*),
> [and] land at the farthest limits of the sea,
> also there your hand would guide me (*tanḥēnî*),
> and your right hand grip me (*tōʾḥăzēnî*).
>
> (vv. 9–10)

Another surprise, borne by metaphor, hits the reader. Rather than fleeing from a God in hot pursuit, the psalmist is guided by divine agency. The discursive result is a thoroughly positive testimony of God's pervasive presence, even in Sheol, where God has no business being.[13] The language further nuances the profile of God's hand, described as seizing or gripping the psalmist (√ʾḥz), akin to being leveled against him (v. 5b). But the verb in v. 10a (√nḥh) achieves a striking shift in perspective: far from being a death grip, God's hand serves to *guide* the psalmist (v. 10; cf. v. 24; 23:4). God's searching presence is not the outstretched hand of judgment poised to snatch the psalmist in flight. Rather, the metaphor of the hand comes to connote divine guidance and unwavering support. God's powerful "grip" highlights the all-encompassing protection the psalmist enjoys. God's protective care holds the psalmist tight and secure. The level of poetic innovation is matched only by another psalmic profession of trust that identifies God's "goodness and kindness" with enemies in hot pursuit (23:6). Through metaphor, both psalms transform mortal threat into protective blessing.

The image of God's hand is not the only punch thrown by the psalmist. The "wings of the dawn" is part of a repertoire of solar images widely attested in the Psalter and elsewhere.[14] Iconographically, the metaphorical expression draws from the common depiction of the deity as a winged disk. Without necessarily identifying God with the sun, the psalmist does develop an inextricable connection. The imaginative journey to the margins of creation *presupposes* divine aid. The psalmist envisions himself catching a ride on the sun as it is dawning (and thus accessible from ground level, as it were) and transported across the domed sky. Verse 9, thus, leads the reader to another level of association: God's guiding hand is solarized. The psalmist's very mode of transport across the heavens is "winged," as it were, by God's providential care.

The psalmist's journey with the sun does not end, however, at the western horizon over the Mediterranean. The following two verses carry this metaphorically inspired voyage into the land of gloom, Sheol:

> Were I to say, "Surely, the darkness will cover me up,[15]
>   and the light around me become night,"
> even the darkness would not be dark to you,
>   and the night as bright as day.
> For darkness is as light [to you].
>
> (vv. 11–12)

The order of presentation in vv. 9–12, adumbrated in v. 8b, has affinities with the mythological "plot" of the Egyptian hymns to the sun, which depict the sun rising, setting, and descending into the netherworld to illuminate the abode of the dead.[16] From dawn to darkness made radiant, the journey is metaphorically vivid and dramatically rendered. The conclusion of this section corresponds to the theme of the first section. Stripped of its mythological trappings, solar imagery serves to highlight the penetrating nature of God's discerning presence, and God's "hand" serves to link God's omniscience with omnipresence.

From Tomb to Womb

The third section dramatically shifts the frame of reference, but in a remarkably interrelated way: the darkness is no longer Sheol. Now the psalmist recalls the darkness of the womb in which he was conceived and fashioned.

> Indeed, it was you who formed my kidneys (*kilyōtāy*);[17]
>   you wove me (*tĕsukkēnî*)[18] in my mother's womb.
> I praise you, for I am exquisitely awesome (*niplêtî*).[19]
> Wonderful are your works;
>   that I know quite well.
> My skeletal frame was not hidden from you,
>   when I was being made in secret,
>   skillfully woven (*ruqqamtî*)[20] in the depths of the earth.
> Your eyes beheld my shapeless being (*gōlem*).[21]
> In your scroll were written all of them,
>   the days that were fashioned [for me]
>   before any of them had occurred.

(vv. 13–16)

The change in perspective is abrupt yet maintains congruence with the previous section: the "depths of the earth," or Sheol, metaphorically deployed in this section, maps the "mother's womb." The psalmist's own genesis, as a result, corresponds to the genesis of humankind from the earth.[22] The maternal womb becomes the chthonic womb, and darkness is transfigured into the light of life. The psalmist's own creation replicates the primal genesis of humanity from the earth's "womb."

The shift from tomb to womb is accompanied by a concomitant shift in God's character. No longer as sun to illumine the darkness (cf. v. 16a), God takes on the active role of creator in utero through a particularly vivid metaphor: God is weaver, an image that targets God's (pro)creative activity. The iconic metaphor is novel. In antiquity, textile production was traditionally associated with women's activity,[23] while the power of procreation was lodged almost exclusively with the male.[24] The psalmist, in turn, construes himself as handwoven material and praises God for the masterful handiwork he knows so well—himself! Yet the psalmist is no egoist; the intricacy of his physical structure bears direct witness to the Weaver's care. He is a work of wonder as well as a work in progress. Through his testimony, the formation of the human self, physically and morally, is rendered comparable to the divine acts of deliverance, covenant, and conquest, those "wonderful deeds" that elicit corporate praise and covenantal obedience.[25] This new role for the deity is attested elsewhere only in Job 10:11, which likely draws from Psalm 139,[26] and in Prov 8:23.[27] Nevertheless, the image of God's "hand" remains presupposed. The psalmist attributes the mystery of his gestation in the womb not to the active role of semen and most certainly not to the fertilization of the ovum—a discovery only of modern science—but to God's handiwork in the womb.

The Path of Orthodoxy

Lastly, God assumes the role of scribe. Registered in the scroll are all the psalmist's days of life.[28] To highlight God's omniscience, the psalmist conjoins the divine act of recording with God's work in creation. As God weaves the psalmist in the womb, so God also wields a pen[29] to record a life, foreordaining it. God excels in the scribal profession as much as in weaving and gynecology.

Moving through a series of metaphors and images, the psalmist aptly concludes his praise with an adoration of divine mystery:

> How inestimable ($yāqĕrû$[30]) are your purposes ($rē'êkā$), O God!
> How vast they are in their totality!
> I [try to] count them, but they are more than the sand.
> I come to the end,[31] yet I am still with you.
>
> (vv. 17–18)

As in v. 6, the psalmist has reached a limit to his ruminations. The only metaphor to marshal for God is the sand with its innumerable grains, so infinitely vast are God's purposes (cf. v. 2b).

Following an imprecation against his enemies (vv. 19–22), the psalmist concludes as he began, but on a note of added urgency:

> Search me, God, and know my heart;
> test me and know my anxious thoughts ($śar'appāy$).
> See if there is any idolatrous ($'ōṣeb$)[32] way within me,
> and lead me in the orthodox ($'ôlām$)[33] way.
>
> (v. 23–24)

God is invoked, in the end, as tester, the one to test the psalmist's moral and religious mettle. Here, for the first and only time, the psalmist registers a modicum of doubt regarding his integrity. But admission of guilt is far from the psalmist's purview. Resolution, rather, is presented as a divinely guided return to the established path of proper worship.

In sum, a storehouse of metaphors both target the deity and tease the reader. In the judicial arena, God is judge, advocate, scribe, and bounty hunter, as well as attacker. From a more personal, poignant standpoint, God is guide and partner, as well as sun, weaver, and procreator. Other metaphorical associations can be discerned, but linking many of them is the pervasive image of God's hand. Beheld and handwoven, the psalmist, in turn, is the beneficiary of God's discerning favor and (pro)creative blessing. Yet for all the iconic characteristics ascribed to the divine, the psalmist, even though an accused idolater, never loses sight of God's unattainable transcendence. Indeed, the very fluidity with which the psalmist moves from metaphor to metaphor serves his defense well. He is not fixed on any one image. But regardless of the final verdict, through metaphor a person's plea of innocence becomes a map of life's journey, from womb to tomb, *coram deo*.

POSTSCRIPT: A THEOLOGY OF PRAYER AND *POESIS*

The speaker of Psalm 139 relishes every opportunity to target the divine with metaphor, fashioning verbal icons while, paradoxically, presenting a defense against the charge of idolatry. In light of its originating setting and function, the poetry illustrates a fundamental law of Newtonian physics: For every action there is a reaction. In renouncing the veneration of material *images,* the psalmist pushes the imagination to discern the mystery of God's providential care in all its *iconic* fullness and diversity. His defense marshals various metaphorical profiles of the deity, without which the cry of praise and prayer, indeed theological discourse in general, would be impoverished to the point of silence. While fully acknowledging God's incomparability, the psalmist does not resort to silence or apophatic reflection. To the contrary, it is reveling in the sheer variety of metaphors that bolsters his defense.

If the raw and vivid rhetoric of the psalms is at all formative for theological reflection, then the traditional dictum that *lex orandi* ("the rule of prayer") be the norm for *lex credendi* ("the rule of faith") pertains all the more. By its very nature, prayer invokes metaphor and exercises the imagination. The pray-er is one who imagines in the fullest sense. More than a recitation of words, prayer "imagines" the One who is addressed and the person(s) on behalf of whom prayer is given. Moreover, authentic prayer boldly claims to bear ontological power, regardless of the empirical outcome. Prayer marks the imagination in its most potent form, transforming the realm of pure possibility into the realm of potentiality, leading possibly to that of the actual. It is no accident, then, that the majority of psalms, given their rich imagery, are prayers.

If prayer is the stuff of theology, then theology must find its home within the fray of life. Like its sapiential counterpart in Scripture, the Psalter draws from the full range of human experience. From the cry of dereliction to the shout of jubilation, pathos pulses throughout the psalms. An all-encompassing immediacy, even "facticity," pertains to the poetry of Psalms that is unmatched elsewhere in Scripture. The psalms respond viscerally to both the corporate crises of history and the personal traumas of the individual. The interconnection between the community and the individual, between the corporate and the personal, embraces a holistic view of human experience: God is trusted to remain active on all levels of experience and existence.

And it is on the anvil of experience that metaphor is forged. The poetic metaphor draws on a stock of common, immediate, and sometimes controversial images and events and transforms them into icons, into intimations of divine activity and reflections of human character. Metaphor knits together the jumbled elements of experience into an intricate web of relationships whose center is the God who creates, redeems, and sustains within the fray of human existence. "Every metaphor . . . points to the shared existence of beings and things."[34] But every metaphor also has its limit, and it is the task of theology to adjudicate these images according to their contextual worth and veracity.

Word and image coalesce in Psalms. Sound and sight are set on equal footing. Far from dogmatic or abstract, the language of the Psalter is palpably incarnational. It breathes with pain and glory, and thereby remains remarkably alive, resurrected for every generation of readers. Throughout its long history, both compositional and interpretive, the Psalter has remained a book in season because it continues to perform evocatively, owing in no small measure to its masterful deployment of metaphor. By generating novel associations that open up new vistas of interpretation and application, the metaphor makes the Psalter eminently appropriable for readers in various settings and circumstances. Through the performance of metaphors, the reader becomes the psalmist.

The power of the metaphor, moreover, lies in its ability (and its manipulability) to inspire new theological vision. Under the psalmist's green thumb, the figure of the tree in Psalm 1 and elsewhere is transplanted to cultivate a more rigorous monotheism. Uprooted from the rocky soil of questionable worship, the tree is planted squarely within the sanctuary grounds. No longer does the arboreal image connote goddess, consort or otherwise, or even divine power per se; it has, rather, become a cipher for embodied righteousness. Likewise, the sun in Psalm 19 radiates not so much divine effulgence as the ethos of *tôrâ*-piety. While the sun sprints its ordained path across the heavens, bursting with virility and joy, the reader of psalms appropriates the commandments of *tôrâ* and "runs" with them in the pace of life. In both psalms, a common image that has flourished in the transcendent realm has been brought down to earth, so to speak, to take on human flesh and blood. Such symbols traditionally associated with the divine are incarnated, new associations are forged, and flesh becomes word. Elsewhere, mundane images such as rock, bird, flowing streams, fountain, shepherd's staff, lamp, and oil intimate some aspect of the transcendent. In all cases, things are not only what they seem to be.

When its target is transcendent, the metaphor does its work by both *broadening* the horizons of the moral self and *familiarizing* the realm of the Other. Through metaphor, the parameters of the macrocosm become associated with the microcosm of the perceiving self in community. Most dramatic is the conclusion to the book of Job. God's answer to Job is populated with various exotic creatures, denizens of the wild, which serve to explode Job's provincial world. At the same time, these alien figures of awe and otherness become intimately related to Job's own self and experience, prompting him toward self-discovery.[35] Through metaphor, the Psalter also moves in this direction. The animals of the wild, made culpable through metaphorical association with the wicked, are "redeemed," and so also the wicked. The denizens of chaos, affirmed in their fear-inspiring otherness, are in the end brought into the circle of worship as models of praise, no less, for the human community. On the one hand, the psalmist beholds the vastness of the universe and wonders what role, if any, human beings play in it (Ps 8:3–4). On the other hand, the universe bears, according to the same psalmist, a certain domesticity in which human beings have been granted the divine role of steward (vv. 5–8). In short, new horizons turn out to bear an "uncanny familiarity," and familiar horizons take on cosmic, providential signif-icance. The metaphor facilitates such reflection.

Through metaphor, a unifying vision of the Psalter is forged, one that is wrought in *movement*. By fits and starts, the pray-er of psalms is taken from trench to temple, from lament to praise, from "pathway" to "refuge." In so doing, the book of Psalms addresses most directly human need: the need for sustenance and protection, the need for refuge and health, and, perhaps most importantly, the need for praising God. While the psalmists fully acknowledge that strife and sin wreak mortal havoc in the world, they find them in the end to be of only penultimate status: palpably real but ultimately impermanent. From lament to praise, the psalmist is vindicated and enemies are reconciled before the banquet that God, as host, has set (23:5). From lament to praise, community is strength-ened and celebrated, like "precious oil . . . running down upon the beard" (133:2). From lament to praise, the cry for vengeance is left behind, and through such movement, the world is made whole.

Through metaphor, the psalms paint a world of possible impossibility wherein conflict is resolved and shalom reigns, a world in which deliverance is experienced and sustenance is gained. Any vision that falls short of encompass-ing the world in toto is, thus, deemed deficient theologically. If the psalms can be taken as foundational, then the primary task of theology is to envision a *world*, not an enclave, a world that continues to be a work in progress, blessed and redeemed, a world in which metaphors serve as pointers. Nevertheless, accom-modation to the world as it stands is not an option. The God of the Psalter comes to judge and implement justice in order to reconfigure the world. In justice and blessing, the psalmist anticipates a world in which all living forms find their voice in giving praise to God in holy refuge. If unobstructed praise is the ultimate aim of theology, then metaphors help clear the way.

Notes

Introduction

1. Kenneth Schmitz, "World and Word in Theophany," *Faith and Philosophy* 1 (1984): 56.
2. See James Samuel Preuss, *From Shadow to Promise: Old Testament Interpretation from Augustine to the Young Luther* (Cambridge, Mass.: Belknap Press of Harvard University Press, 1969), esp. 153–271.
3. The designation is found in Luther's 1528 "Preface to the Psalter" (*Luther's Works*, vol. 35, ed. E. Theodore Bachman [Philadelphia: Muhlenberg, 1960], 254). James L. Crenshaw, however, objects to Luther's claim by noting that the Psalter consists primarily of prayer and praise, literature that "originated from below" (*The Psalms: An Introduction* [Grand Rapids: Eerdmans, 2001], ix, 14). Granted, the Psalms are generically distinct from most biblical literature. However, Luther's claim addresses the *theological* cadences sounded elsewhere in Scripture that are also found in ample supply in the Psalter. Crenshaw's issue is generic; Luther's was theological. Indeed, Luther acknowledged the distinction of genre in the very next paragraph: "Other books have much ado about the works of the saints; but say very little about their words. The Psalter is a gem in this respect. . . . [I]t relates not only the *works* of the saints, but also *their words, how they* spoke with God and *prayed*" (Luther, "Preface" [emphasis added]). Luther's sweeping claim is matched in historical critical research by the observation that "the historical setting of the psalms can be said to be the *entire*

history of Israel's religion" (James L. Mays, *Psalms* [IBC; Louisville, Ky.: John Knox, 1994], 9 [emphasis added]).

4. So Harold Fisch, *Poetry with a Purpose: Biblical Poetics and Interpretation* (ISBL; Bloomington / Indianapolis: Indiana University Press, 1988), 106.

5. See, e.g., Gary Rendsburg, *Linguistic Evidence for the Northern Origin of Selected Psalms* (SBLMS 42; Atlanta: Scholars Press, 1990), who argues for the northern origin of various psalms, including those of Asaph and Korah; and Harry P. Nasuti, *Tradition History and the Psalms of Asaph* (SBLDS 88; Atlanta: Scholars Press, 1988).

6. See the functional (as opposed to generic) classifications proposed by Walter Brueggemann, *The Message of the Psalms: A Theological Commentary* (Augsburg Old Testament Studies; Minneapolis: Augsburg, 1984), 19 and passim.

7. Paul Ricoeur, "Toward a Hermeneutic of the Idea of Revelation," in his *Essays on Biblical Interpretation* (Philadelphia: Fortress, 1980), 90 (emphasis added).

8. E.g., Pss 5:1; 19:14; 49:3; 104:34.

9. According to Ricoeur, "Everyday reality is metamorphosed by . . . imaginative variations that [fiction and poetry] work *on the real*" ("Philosophy and Religious Language," *JR* 54 [1974]: 80 [emphasis added]).

10. Represented by Johann Gottfried von Herder. See his *The Spirit of Hebrew Poetry,* 2 vols., trans. James Marsh (1922; reprint, Naperville, Ill.: Aleph Press, 1971).

11. E.g., Paul Avis, *God and the Creative Imagination: Metaphor, Symbol and Myth in Religion and Theology* (London / New York: Routledge, 1999); Garrett Green, *Theology, Hermeneutics, and Imagination: The Crisis of Intepretation at the End of Modernity* (Cambridge: Cambridge University Press, 2000); and idem, *Imagining God: Theology and the Religious Imagination,* 2d ed. (Grand Rapids: Eerdmans, 1998).

12. The "epic" is considered to be represented, in part, by the oldest poems of the Hebrew Scriptures (e.g., Exod 15:1–18; Judg 5:2–31; Hab 3:2–19).

13. See, e.g., William Foxwell Albright, *Archaeology, Historical Analogy and Early Biblical Tradition* (Rockwell Lectures Series; Baton Rouge: Louisiana State University Press, 1966), 11; and Frank Moore Cross, "The Epic Tradition of Early Israel: Epic Narrative and the Reconstruction of Early Israelite Institutions," in *The Poet and the Historian,* ed. Richard E. Freidman (HSS 26; Chico, Calif.: Scholars Press, 1983), 20. See also the critique in Yehoshua Gitay, "W. F. Albright and the Question of Early Hebrew Poetry," in *History and Interpretation: Essays in Honour of John H. Hayes,* ed. M. Patrick Graham et al. (JSOTSup 173; Sheffield: JSOT Press, 1993), 192–202.

14. Quoted by Amos Wilder from a paper Robert Funk delivered in Washington under the auspices of the Church Society for College in October 1967 (*Theopoetic: Theology and the Religious Imagination* [Philadelphia: Fortress, 1976], 88).

15. Luis Alonso Schökel, *A Manual of Hebrew Poetics,* trans. Adrian Graffy (Subsidia Biblica 11; Rome: Editrice Pontificio Istituto Biblico, 1988), 98.

16. Ibid., 102, 104.

17. See the assessment of the current theological enterprise in Douglas F. Ottati, *Hopeful Realism: Reclaiming the Poetry of Theology* (Cleveland: Pilgrim Press, 1999), 26–31. I am not saying, however, that biblical theology must abandon its critical focus on the historical background of the text. Far from it—the cultural and historical background of texts is essential for interpretive understanding.

18. Ellen F. Davis, "Exploding the Limits: Form and Function in Psalm 22," *JSOT* 53 (1992): 93.

19. Schökel, *Manual of Hebrew Poetics,* 95.

20. Gerhard von Rad, *Theology of the Old Testament,* vol. 1, trans. D. M. G. Stalker (1957; reprint, New York / Evanston: Harper & Row, 1962), 218 (emphasis added). Cf. Moshe Barasch, *Icon: Studies in the History of an Idea* (New York: New York University Press, 1992), 19.

21. E.g., Exod 20:3–6, 22–23; 34:17; Lev 19:4; 26:1; Deut 4:15–19; 5:8–10; 27:15. See Tryggve N. D. Mettinger's definition of programmatic aniconism (as opposed to its tolerant de facto form) in *No Graven Image? Israelite Aniconism in Its Ancient Near Eastern Context* (ConBOT 42; Stockholm: Almqvist & Wiksell, 1995), 18–20. For other representative studies on the developmental background behind ancient Israel's polemic against cult images, see Tryggve N. D. Mettinger, "Israelite Aniconism: Developments and Origins," in *The Image and the Book: Iconic Cults, Aniconism, and the Rise of Book Religion in Israel and the Ancient Near East*, ed. Karel van der Toorn (Leuven: Peeters, 1997), 173–204; Angelika Berlejung, *Die Theologie der Bilder: Herstellung und Einweihung von Kultbildern in Mesopotamian und die alttestamentliche Bilderpolemik* (OBO 162; Freiburg: Universitätsverlag / Göttingen: Vandenhoeck & Ruprecht, 1998), esp. 315–411; and Ronald S. Hendel, "Aniconism and Anthropomorphism in Ancient Israel," in *The Image and the Book*, 205–28.
22. See Mettinger, *No Graven Image?* 15.
23. See the Conclusion of this book.
24. To borrow (and misapply) an expression from Paul Ricoeur. Ricoeur's assessment was directed against the focus on the isolated "noun or name" to the exclusion of the "sentence as the primary unity of meaning" (*The Rule of Metaphor: Multi-Disciplinary Studies of the Creation of Meaning in Language,* trans. Robert Czerny with Kathleen McLaughlin and John Costello, S.J. [London: Routledge & Kegan Paul, 1978], 44).
25. Athanasius, *The Life of Antony and the Letter to Marcellinus,* trans. Robert C. Gregg (Classics of Western Spirituality; New York: Paulist, 1980), 108, par. 10 (emphasis added). See the broader discussion given by Harry P. Nasuti, *Defining the Sacred Songs: Genre, Tradition and the Post-Critical Interpretation of the Psalms* (JSOTSup 218; Sheffield: Sheffield Academic Press, 1999), 111–16.
26. Athanasius, *Letter to Marcellinus,* 112, par. 14.
27. Ibid., 111, par. 12.
28. See the discussion in Nasuti, *Defining the Sacred Songs,* 108–16.
29. Ibid., 111.
30. Jan Assmann, *Egyptian Solar Religion in the New Kingdom: Re, Amun and the Crisis of Polytheism,* trans. Anthony Alcock (London / New York: Kegan Paul International, 1995), 38 (emphasis added).
31. Ibid., 65.
32. Earl R. MacCormac, *A Cognitive Theory of Metaphor* (Cambridge / London: Massachusetts Institute of Technology, 1985), 192–93.
33. Cf. Aristotle, *Poetics* 21 (1457^{b}6–32); *Rhetoric* 3.10 (1410^{b}13–36).
34. Janet Martin Soskice, *Metaphor and Religious Language* (Oxford: Clarendon Press / New York: Oxford University Press, 1985), 15.
35. Ivor Armstrong Richards, *The Philosophy of Rhetoric* (The Mary Flexner Lectures on the Humanities 3; New York: Oxford University Press, 1965), 96.
36. Ibid., 96–97.
37. Avis, *God and the Creative Imagination,* 94.
38. Max Black, "More about Metaphor," in *Metaphor and Thought,* ed. Andrew Ortony (Cambridge: Cambridge University Press, 1979), 28.
39. See the critique of the "emotive theories" of metaphor in Soskice, *Metaphor and Religious Language,* 26–31.
40. George Lakoff and Mark Turner, *More than Cool Reason: A Field Guide to Poetic Metaphor* (Chicago / London: University of Chicago Press, 1989), 38–39.
41. Lakoff and Turner's theory of metaphor runs counter to the more traditional "interaction theory" of I. A. Richards and Max Black, who considered metaphorical movement to be "bidirectional," that is, from target to source *and* from source to target. However, the universal metaphor "Life is a journey" in no way construes journeys *as*

lives (Lakoff and Turner, *More than Cool Reason,* 131–32). The metaphorical mapping is only one way. Yet the "interaction theory" remains the theory of choice in theological and biblical studies: e.g., Soskice, *Metaphor and Religious Language,* 43–51; MacCormac, *A Cognitive Theory of Metaphor,* 5; and, most recently in biblical studies, Markus Philipp Zehnder, *Wegmetaphorik im Alten Testament: Eine semantische Untersuchung der alttestamentlichen und altorientalischen Weg-Lexeme mit besonderer Berüchsichtigung ihrer metaphorischen Verwendung* (BZAW 268; Berlin / New York: de Gruyter, 1999), 38–46.

42. But not necessarily the *source* domain; see note above. Soskice adopts a modified "interactive" theory of metaphor, specifically an "interanimation" theory (*Metaphor and Religious Language,* 43–51). MacCormac, too, adopts an interactive theory in which he erroneously claims that the metaphorical statement "computers think" draws the implication that human beings "take on the attributes of computers" (*A Cognitive Theory of Metaphor,* 10; cf. 33).

43. Lakoff and Turner, *More than Cool Reason,* 50–51.

44. See MacCormac, *A Cognitive Theory of Metaphor,* 37–38.

45. Such a cognitive view of metaphor requires focus on the literary context, including the "beliefs held mutually by both hearer and speaker, and the patterns of inference the hearer employs in determining the speaker's meaning" (Soskice, *Metaphor and Religious Language,* 44).

46. Lakoff and Turner, *More than Cool Reason,* 62.

47. The "dead metaphor" is devoid of figurative connections and has become literal: e.g., "the leg of a chair," the "flow of electricity." See Soskice's nuanced discussion of the "dead metaphor" in *Metaphor and Religious Language,* 71–83.

48. See also George Lakoff and Mark Johnson, *The Metaphors We Live By* (Chicago: University of Chicago Press, 1980); and idem, "Conceptual Metaphor in Everyday Language," *The Journal of Philosophy* 77 (1980): 453–86, who argue that much of language considered literal is in fact metaphorical. See, however, the corrective given in MacCormac, *A Cognitive Theory of Metaphor,* 57–78.

49. See MacCormac's definition of metaphor in *A Cognitive Theory of Metaphor,* 1, 5.

50. Schökel, *Manual of Hebrew Poetics,* 99, cf. 114.

51. Soskice, *Metaphor and Religious Language,* 16.

52. Soskice, *Metaphor and Religious Language,* 57–58.

53. Avis, *God and the Creative Imagination,* 94.

54. Richards, *The Philosophy of Rhetoric,* 94 (emphasis original).

55. Soskice, *Metaphor and Religious Language,* 26.

56. See Sallie McFague, *Speaking in Parables: A Study in Metaphor and Theology* (Philadelphia: Fortress, 1975), 43–44; and Earl R. MacCormac, *Metaphor and Myth in Science and Religion* (Durham, N.C.: Duke University Press, 1976), 93–94.

57. Soskice, *Metaphor and Religious Language,* 73.

58. Richard Kearney, *Poetics of Imagining: Modern to Post-Modern* (New York: Fordham University Press, 1998), 148.

59. See MacCormac, *A Cognitive Theory of Metaphor,* 5, 10, where he distinguishes metaphor from analogy by the degree to which metaphor conveys "strangeness" (p. 10).

60. So Robert J. Fogelin, *Figuratively Speaking* (New Haven / London: Yale University Press, 1988), 25.

61. Avis, *God and the Creative Imagination,* 97.

62. *BHS* suggests that the comparative preposition *kĕ* be inserted, due presumably to haplography of the consonantal *kaph,* but without textual warrant. Furthermore, the MT is the *lectio difficilior.*

63. See Robert Kysar, *Stumbling in the Light: New Testament Images for a Changing*

Church (St. Louis: Chalice, 1999), 30, where he classifies the simile as a particular "kind of metaphor."

64. Soskice, *Metaphor and Religious Language,* 59.
65. Lakoff and Turner, *More than Cool Reason,* 133.
66. The term is borrowed from Johann Georg Hamann, a critic of Immanuel Kant, as quoted from Green, *Theology, Hermeneutics, and Imagination,* 21.
67. Kysar, *Stumbling in the Light,* 31.
68. Assmann, *Egyptian Solar Religion,* 66.
69. In modern biblical studies, the methodological foundation for deriving a word's lexicographical meaning is set in the classic work of James Barr, *The Semantics of Biblical Language* (1961; reprint, London: SCM Press, 1983). Although helpful as a cautionary guide, Barr nowhere discusses the semantic value of metaphors, but rather restricts his discussion to more conceptually laden terms such as "faithfulness" and "truth" (pp. 161–205; cf. Barr's cautious approach to identifying metaphors in Hebrew lexicographical tradition in his "Scope and Problems in the Semantics of Classical Hebrew," *ZAH* 6 [1993]: 13). Barr is no doubt correct when he insists "that lexicographic research should be directed towards the semantics of words *in their particular occurrences* and not towards the assembly of a stock of pervasive and distinctive terms which could be regarded as a linguistic reflection of the theological realities" (*Semantics,* 274). One particular mistake that has plagued biblical research, as monumentalized in Kittel's *Theologisches Wörterbuch zum Neuen Testament,* is what Barr calls the "illegitimate totality transfer," the error that arises "when the 'meaning' of a word (understood as the total series of relations in which it is used in the literature) is read into a particular case as its sense and implication there" (p. 218). Nevertheless, in view of its "imagistic" nature, the iconic metaphor generates associations that extend beyond its purely semantic value and achieves greater conceptual coherence than lexical analysis alone permits. In understanding the metaphor within its context, the interpreter is compelled to move "beyond the bare utterance into a network of implications, . . . beyond the words one is given" (Soskice, *Metaphor and Religious Language,* 18). A metaphor, as metaphor, can broaden its own lexical scope and fill lexical gaps.
70. C. H. Dodd, *The Parables of the Kingdom,* 2d ed. (New York: Charles Scribner's Sons, 1961), 5.
71. See Kearney, *Poetics of Imagining,* 164, 224.
72. Schökel, *Manual of Hebrew Poetics,* 120.
73. So Mary Warnock, *Imagination* (Berkeley / Los Angeles: University of California Press, 1976), 182.
74. See Kearney's discussion of Bachelard's reflections on the "poetical imagination" in his *Poetics of Imagining,* 100 (emphasis original).
75. Ricoeur observes that the "linguistic imagination . . . generates and regenerates meaning through the living powers of metaphoricity" (quoted in Richard Kearney, *Poetics of Imagining,* 158).
76. Kearney, *Poetics of Imagining,* 145.
77. Avis identifies the metaphor as one of three genres of the imagination, including symbol and myth (*God and the Creative Imagination,* vii). See also David Tracy, *The Analogical Imagination: Christian Theology and the Culture of Pluralism* (1981; reprint, New York: Crossroad, 1987), 129.
78. T. S. Eliot, *Four Quartets,* "East Coker," V (New York: Harcourt, Brace, 1943), 16.
79. Susan E. Gillingham, *The Poems and Psalms of the Hebrew Bible* (Oxford Bible Series; Oxford: Oxford University Press, 1994), 15–16.
80. Ibid., 15.
81. Paul Ricoeur, *The Rule of Metaphor,* 303.

82. Brian Gerrish, *The Pilgrim Road: Sermons on Christian Life*, ed. Mary T. Stimming (Louisville, Ky.: Westminster, 2000), 1. Or as Gaston Bachelard observes, "The image has touched the depths before it stirs the surface" (cited in Gillingham, *The Poems and Psalms of the Hebrew Bible*, 277).
83. Paul Ricoeur, *Time and Narrative* (Chicago: University of Chicago Press, 1984), 80.
84. Gillingham, *The Poems and Psalms of the Hebrew Bible*, 4.
85. Ibid.
86. Philosopher Edward S. Casey talks about the "educability" of the imagination (*Imagining: A Phenomenological Study* [Bloomington: Indiana University Press, 1976], 83–84).
87. Gillingham, *The Poems and Psalms of the Hebrew Bible*, 4, 188. Unfortunately, Gillingham tends to pit these two options against each other.
88. Ibid., 16.
89. From a Reformed Protestant perspective, such forays into biblical poetics recall John Calvin's comparison of Scripture to a new set of spectacles (*Institutes of the Christian Religion*, ed. John T. McNeill, trans. Ford Lewis Battle [LCC; Philadelphia: Westminster, 1960], 1.6.1 [p. 70]). For Calvin, through the lens of Scripture the world is disclosed as the "theater of God's glory" (ibid., 1.5.1–2, 8.10; 1.6.2–4; 1.14.20; *Consensus Genevensis* in *Calvini opera*, 8:294). For a trenchant analysis of Calvin's view of nature, see Susan E. Schreiner, *The Theater of His Glory: Nature and the Natural Order in the Thought of John Calvin* (Grand Rapids: Baker Books, 1991).
90. Calvin, *Institutes*, 1.11.5 (p. 105).
91. See, e.g., Rosemary Radford Ruether, *Sexism and God: Toward a Feminist Theology* (Boston: Beacon, 1983), 66–69; Sallie McFague, *Metaphorical Theology: Models of God in Religious Language* (Philadelphia: Fortress, 1982), 145–76; Anna Case-Winters, *God's Power: Traditional Understandings and Contemporary Challenges* (Louisville, Ky.: Westminster / John Knox, 1990), 219–20.
92. See Paul Tillich, *Dynamics of Faith*, ed. Ruth Nanda Anshen (World Perspectives 10; New York: Harper, 1958), 97; idem, *Systematic Theology* (Chicago: University of Chicago, 1963), 3.206; Schubert Ogden, *The Reality of God and Other Essays* (New York: Harper & Row, 1966), 49; Grace M. Jantzen, *God's World, God's Body* (London: Darton, Longman & Todd, 1984), 12.
93. E.g., *fons omnium bonorum* or "the fountain of all good" (*Institutes* 1.2.1 [p. 41]; see also 1.1.1 [p. 36]), "the intense light of the sun" (1.1.2 [p. 38]); father (1.2.1 [p. 41]), "mother" (Commentary on Isaiah 49:15 [*Calvini opera* 37:204]). See Brian A. Gerrish, *Grace and Gratitude: The Eucharistic Theology of John Calvin* (Philadelphia: Fortress, 1993), 21–49.
94. See Kearney's discussion of Gaston Bachelard in *Poetics of Imagining*, 100.
95. See, e.g., Eric Donald Hirsch Jr., *Validity in Interpretation* (New Haven, Conn. / London: Yale University Press, 1967), 68–126. For an integrative study of the function of genre in psalmic research, see Nasuti, *Defining the Sacred Songs*, 82–220. Nasuti opts for a "constructive view of genre," one that involves the reader's interaction with the text (ibid., 52–53).
96. Richard L. Eslinger talks of "archetypal imagining," whereby "some universal is evoked in the particularity of the poetic image" (*Narrative and Imagination: Preaching the Worlds That Shape Us* [Minneapolis; Fortress, 1995], 65).
97. Avis, *God and the Creative Imagination*, 50. In support, Avis misconstrues the meaning of Ezek 20:49, which records Ezekiel's lament over the people's *misinterpretation* of his prophetic message!
98. Luke T. Johnson, "Imagining the World Scripture Imagines," in *Theology and Scriptural Imagination*, ed. L. Gregory Jones and James J. Buckley (Directions in Modern Theology; Oxford / Malden, Mass.: Blackwell, 1998), 3.

99. See the discussion in Schökel, *Manual of Hebrew Poetics*, 100.
100. Ibid.
101. Ibid., 10.
102. G. D. Kaufman, *God—Mystery—Diversity: Christian Theology in a Pluralistic World* (Minneapolis: Fortress, 1996), 6.
103. Johnson, "Imagining the World," 13.
104. See James K. A. Smith, *The Fall of Interpretation: Philosophical Foundations for a Creational Hermeneutic* (Downers Grove, Ill.: InterVarsity, 2000), 175, who prefers the ethical over the epistemological in the hermeneutical enterprise.
105. Augustine, *De doctrina christiana*, 1.36.40.
106. Ibid., 3.15.23. Translation from D. W. Robertson Jr., *Saint Augustine: On Christian Doctrine* (The Library of Liberal Arts 80; New York: Liberal Arts Press, 1958), 93.
107. For general discussion, see Kearney, *Poetics of Imagining*, 233–34. Kearney notes that various strands of postmodern reflections on hermeneutics give pride of place to ethics, specifically the presence of the other (ibid., 185–255). For theological discussion, see William Stacy Johnson, "Rethinking Theology: A Postmodern, Post-Holocaust, Post-Christendom Endeavor," *Int* 55 (2001): 5–18.
108. See Benedict M. Guevin, "The Moral Imagination and the Shaping Power of the Parables," *JRE* 17 (1989): 64, who draws from the work of Kathleen Fischer.
109. Kathleen Norris, "Incarnational Language," *Christian Century* 114/22 (July 30–August 6, 1997): 699.
110. In their widely regarded introduction to biblical interpretation, Robert Morgan and John Barton observe that interpreters are the only "active subjects in the act of interpretation," whereas the texts they interpret are "like dead men and women, [who] have no rights, no aims, no interests" (*Biblical Interpretation* [Oxford Bible Series; Oxford: Oxford University Press, 1988], 7). The interpreter, in short, is sovereign, and the text is nothing more than a corpse. In a rarified, academic sense, Morgan and Barton are right. On a material level, all texts are nothing more than artifacts waiting to be read. The situation is analogous to the philosophical conundrum: Does a falling tree make a sound when there is no one to hear it? Does a text generate its own interpretation when there is no one to read it? Clearly not, but so what? Focusing on the text's physical "inertness" misses the mark entirely when it comes to describing the interpreter's *engagement* with the text. Perhaps the time has come to declare the resurrection of the text and the receptivity of the reader. If postmodern thought has shown us anything, it is the necessary "deflation of the sovereign subject," which is to say that humility has a prominent place in the hermeneutical enterprise (Kearney, *Poetics of Imagining*, 235).
111. One notable work in homiletics that attempts to recapture in a systematic way the significance of the image, and more broadly the imagination, in preaching is Eslinger, *Narrative and Imagination*.
112. Quoted from Edward Hirsch, "Octavio Paz: In Defense of Poetry," *New York Times: Book Review*, June 7, 1998.
113. Walter Brueggemann has aptly noted how the praise psalms in particular both deconstruct and reconstruct the world (e.g., "Praise and the Psalms: The Politics of Glad Abandonment," in *The Psalms and the Life of Faith*, ed. Patrick D. Miller [Minneapolis: Fortress, 1995], 112–32; and idem, *Israel's Praise: Doxology against Idolatry and Ideology* [Philadelphia: Fortress, 1988]). See also the similar points made by Rolf Jacobson, "The Costly Loss of Praise," *ThT* 57 (2000): 375–85.
114. Thomas G. Long, *Preaching and the Literary Forms of the Bible* (Philadelphia: Fortress, 1989), 47.
115. To quote refrain from the wonderful redheaded character in Lucy Maud Montgomery's novel, *Anne of Green Gables*.

116. Along with the "discourse of consumption" is another form of corporate-sponsored rhetoric that constitutes part of the American cultural fabric: what theologian Douglas Ottati calls "leadership-speak," discourse that promulgates the "social Darwinist–*laissez faire* myth of ceaseless competition" (Ottati, *Hopeful Realism,* 17).

117. Paul Griffiths, *Religious Reading: The Place of Reading in the Practice of Religion* (New York: Oxford University Press 1999), ix.

118. Ibid.

119. Kearney, *Poetics of Imagining,* 222.

Chapter 1: "In the Shadow of *Shaddai*"

1. For a sociological analysis of such stock language, particularly the language of justice and poverty, in the Psalter, see J. David Pleins, *The Social Visions of the Hebrew Bible: A Theological Introduction* (Louisville, Ky.: Westminster John Knox, 2001), 419–37.

2. James L. Mays, "The Question of Context in Psalm Interpretation," in *The Shape and the Shaping of the Psalter,* ed. J. Clinton McCann (JSOTSup 159; Sheffield: Sheffield Academic Press, 1993), 17.

3. For extended discussion on this matter, see Harry P. Nasuti, *Defining the Sacred Songs: Genre, Tradition and Post-Critical Interpretation of the Psalms* (JSOTSup 218; Sheffield: Sheffield Academic Press, 1999), 52–81.

4. Ibid., 18.

5. I use "wisdom" reservedly, since the literary status of the so-called "wisdom psalms" is hotly debated. I note only a family resemblance between certain psalms and the didactic literature one finds outside the Psalter—e.g., Psalms 1, 19, 119 ("Torah" psalms) and Psalms 32, 34, 49, 111, 112 ("wisdom" psalms). See the foundational study by Roland E. Murphy, "A Consideration of the Classification of the 'Wisdom Psalms,'" in *Congress Volume: Bonn, 1962* (VTSup 9; Leiden: Brill, 1963), 156–67. Cf. James L. Crenshaw's critique in *The Psalms: An Introduction* (Grand Rapids: Eerdmans, 2001), 87–95, whose criteria, if rigorously implemented, would also place much of the wisdom literature into question. My intent is to focus more on function ("didactic") than genre.

6. Psalms 1–41 (I); 42–72 (II); 73–89 (III); 90–106 (IV); 107–150 (V).

7. Joseph Reindel, "Weisheitliche Bearbeitung von Psalmen: Ein Beitrag zum Verständnis der Sammlung des Psalter," in *Congress Volume: Vienna, 1980,* ed. J. A. Emerton (VTSup 32; Leiden: Brill, 1981), 340. See also the important essays of James L. Mays, "The Place of the Torah-Psalms in the Psalter," *JBL* 106 (1987): 3–12; and J. Clinton McCann Jr., "The Psalms as Instruction," *Int* 46 (1992): 117–28.

8. See n. 13 below.

9. Gerald H. Wilson, *The Editing of the Hebrew Psalter* (SBLDS 76; Chico, Calif.: Scholars Press, 1985).

10. Ibid., 207–8. See also Gerald H. Wilson, "The Use of Royal Psalms at the 'Seams' of the Psalter," *JSOT* 35 (1986): 91–92.

11. Wilson, *Editing of the Hebrew Psalter,* 214–28.

12. Gerald H. Wilson, "The Shape of the Book of Psalms," *Int* 46 (1992): 133–34.

13. Gerald H. Wilson, "Shaping the Psalter: A Consideration of Editorial Linkage in the Book of Psalms," in *The Shape and the Shaping of the Psalter,* ed. J. Clinton McCann (JSOTSup 159; Sheffield: Sheffield Academic Press, 1993), 81. The "tension" between private meditation and public performance prompts Wilson to critique the common assumption that the Psalter was essentially a hymnbook: "Rather than a hymnbook, the Psalter is a symphony with many movements, or better yet an oratorio in which a multitude of voices—singly and in concert—rise in a crescendo of

praise" (ibid., 81–82; cf. his earlier comments about the Psalter's nonhymnic status in light of Psalm 1 in his *Editing of the Hebrew Psalter*, 206).

14. Gerald T. Sheppard, *Wisdom as a Hermeneutical Construct: A Study in the Sapientializing of the Old Testament* (BZAW 151; New York: de Gruyter, 1980), 138–42; see also idem, "Theology and the Book of Psalms," *Int* 46 (1992): 143–55. In an earlier study, Walther Zimmerli referred to Psalms 1 and 2 as "twin psalms" ("Zwillingspsalmen," in *Wort, Leid, und Gottesspruch: Beiträge zu Psalmen und Propheten* [Festschrift für Joseph Ziegler], ed. Josef Schreiner [Forschung zur Bibel 2; Würzburg: Echter Verlag Katholisches Bibelwerk, 1972], 106).

15. Reindel argues that Psalm 1 signals the sapiential editing of the Psalter, as indicated also by wisdom glosses in certain psalms and in the strategic positioning of Psalms 90–92 ("Weisheitliche Bearbeitung von Psalmen," 333–56).

16. It is doubtful, however, that Psalm 118 can be classified as a royal psalm. See the most recent classification of royal psalms in Scott R. A. Starbuck, *Court Oracles in the Psalms: The So-called Royal Psalms in Their Ancient Near Eastern Context* (SBLDS 172; Atlanta: Society of Biblical Literature, 1999), 205.

17. Mays, "The Place of the Torah-Psalms," 3, 10.

18. Walter Brueggemann, "Bounded by Obedience and Praise: The Psalms as Canon," *JSOT* 50 (1991): 63–92 (reprinted in *The Psalms and the Life of Faith*, ed. Patrick D. Miller [Minneapolis: Fortress, 1995], 189–213).

19. Ibid., 205–9.

20. Brueggemann, "Response to Mays, 'The Question of Context,'" in *The Shape and the Shaping of the Psalter*, ed. J. Clinton McCann, 41.

21. See the discussion in Nasuti, *Defining the Sacred Songs*, 194–97.

22. Wilson, "Shaping the Psalter," 81.

23. Jerome F. D. Creach, *Yahweh as Refuge and the Editing of the Hebrew Psalter* (JSOTSup 217; Sheffield: Sheffield Academic Press, 1996).

24. Creach's program is sparked by Sheppard's earlier essay, "Theology and the Book of Psalms," esp. 149–52, in which he confines his survey to the *term* "refuge," which limits him primarily to Books 1–3 (Psalms 2–89).

25. Creach, *Yahweh as Refuge*, 50.

26. Ibid., 17.

27. Ibid., 18.

28. Ibid., 18; cf. pp. 50–73.

29. Ibid., 51 n. 6.

30. Ibid., 51–52.

31. For an analysis of the significance of the macarism or *'ašrê* saying in Hebrew, see Waldemar Janzen, "*'Ašrê* in the Old Testament," *HTR* 58 (1965): 215–26. His observation that the term connotes a "touch of envy" remains pertinent.

32. For a discussion of the metaphorical "schema," see George Lakoff and Mark Turner, *More than Cool Reason: A Field Guide to the Poetic Metaphor* (Chicago / London: University of Chicago Press, 1989), 61–62. In their language, a "schema" is filled in with the "slots" of particular metaphorical images.

33. See also Ps 144:2.

34. For further discussion on this metaphor in its various attestations in the Psalter, see Peter Riede, *Im Netz des Jägers: Studien zur Feindmetaphorik der Individualpsalmen* (WMANT 85; Neukirchen-Vluyn: Neukirchener Verlag, 2000), 355–63.

35. See chapter 8; also Riede, *Im Netz des Jägers*, 363.

36. See, e.g., the falcon figure of Horus or Behedet perched behind the head of King Khaf-Re (*ANEP*, #377). For discussion, see Othmar Keel, *The Symbolism of the Biblical World: Ancient Near Eastern Iconography and the Book of Psalms*, trans. T. J. Hallet (New York: Seabury, 1978), 191–92. For wing imagery in Syro-Palestinian

iconography, particularly in the Egyptian style, see Othmar Keel and Christoph Uehlinger, *Gods, Goddesses, and Images of God in Ancient Israel,* trans. Thomas H. Trapp (Minneapolis: Fortress, 1998), 195–98, 250–62.

37. E.g., Horus, Isis, Nephthys, Amon, and the vulture-goddess Nekhbet, the protectress of the king of Upper Egypt. The sun or sky god was often depicted with outstretched wings over the king (e.g., Re-Harakhte), a motif by no means limited to Egypt. See chapter 4.

38. See also the sarcophagus of Tutankhamun, which features both Isis and Nephthys embracing their respective corners with outstretched wings and arms (Barbara Watterson, *The Gods of Ancient Egypt* [New York: Facts on File, 1988], plate # 17).

39. Keel speaks of it as "a kind of hieroglyph" (*Symbolism of the Biblical World,* 192).

40. Literally, "oil."

41. In a forthcoming paper, P. Kyle McCarter ties the meaning of √*'dn* with the sense of "to make rich/plentiful/abundant" (Colloquium for Biblical Research, August 19, 2001, Duke University). The parallelism in the psalm, moreover, suggests such a sense. See also Gen 18:12; Neh 9:25; Jer 31:12; 51:34.

42. Usually translated "Most High." For discussion, see Tryggve N. D. Mettinger, *In Search of God: The Meaning and Message of the Everlasting Names,* trans. Frederick H. Cryer (Philadelphia: Fortress, 1988), 122.

43. Usually translated "Almighty." The etymology of *šadday* is likely derived from the Akkadian *šadû,* meaning "mountain" (see Mettinger, *In Search of God,* 70–71).

44. Read *maḥsekā* for MT *maḥsî,* in line with the parallelism (so *BHS*).

45. See Paul Joüon, *Ruth: Commentaire philologique et exégétique* (Rome: Institut Biblique Pontifical, 1953), 55–56.

46. The parallelism favors slight emendation of the MT in line with the Samaritan Pentateuch.

47. Or "griffon vulture" (*nešer*). In both Egypt and Mesopotamia, the vulture was considered a symbol of royalty and divinity. See Oded Borowski, *Every Living Thing: Daily Use of Animals in Ancient Israel* (Walnut Creek, Calif.: AltaMira, 1998), 150–51.

48. Read plural object with the Peshitta or the MT's singular suffix as a collective.

49. Related to the use of this metaphor is Deutero-Isaiah's portrayal of the exiles themselves "as raptors" (*kannĕšārîm*) in flight from Babylonian captivity, a second exodus (Isa 40:31). From the exilic perspective of Isaiah, the metaphor of choice to describe God's leading is not raptor but "shepherd" (40:11).

50. See the survey of opinions regarding the origin of such imagery in Riede, *Im Netz des Jägers,* 328–31; Creach, *Yahweh as Refuge,* 62–63. Psalm 91:3–4, in particular, suggests that ornithological imagery applied to God is drawn directly from the animal world, specifically the image of the mother bird protecting her brood, and not from the cherubim iconographically represented in the temple's adytum (contra J. A. Wharton, "Refuge," *IDB,* 4.24; and Hans-Joachim Kraus, *Psalms 60–150: A Commentary,* trans. Hilton C. Oswald [Minneapolis: Augsburg, 1989], 222–23). Reference to wings in the Psalter is ascribed to God, not to the cherubim, which constitute part of God's throne or footstool (Keel, *Symbolism of the Biblical World,* 190).

51. See J. J. Schmitt, "The Motherhood of God and Zion as Mother," *RB* 92 (1985): 564.

52. Read *ḥêlāh* with feminine suffix.

53. The rhetorical force of this last section of the psalm is perhaps matched only by the climax of the Gilgamesh Epic, in which the protagonist, the beaten and despairing king, enjoins his companion (and readers of the epic) to marvel at the enduring testimony of the walls of Uruk, ending the tale as it began (Tablet XI).

54. The Masoretic pointing of the adjective (as a construct) carries superlative force.

55. The form could be taken as a plural of amplification and thus translated as a singular. Perfect sense, however, can be made by retaining it as a semantic plural, which acknowledges the existence of other sanctuaries in the land while asserting Jerusalem's primacy.

56. See chapter 2.

57. Eating on God's holy mountain is a common image in biblical literature: e.g., Gen 31:54; Exod 24:9–11; Judg 21:19–21; 2 Sam 6:5; Isa 25:6–8.

58. Hans-Joachim Kraus, *Theology of the Psalms*, trans. Keith Crim (Minneapolis: Fortress, 1992), 159.

59. Possibly read with LXX "stronghold" (*mā'ôz*), although it is difficult to determine which final letter represents the graphic confusion of the other.

60. See also Ps 16:1, 9–10.

61. See *KTU* 1.4.8–1.6.2.

62. See Pss 27:5; 31:21; 32:7; 61:4; 91:1; 119:114.

63. See also Pss 22:24; 69:17; 88:13–14; 102:2; 143:7.

64. Given the context, the verbal root is more likely derived from *'wz* ("to seek protection") in its preterit form, not *'zz* ("to be strong"). The form is explainable through haplography of the preceding "waw."

65. See also Pss 49:5–6; 115:8–9; 135:18 for other forms of misplaced trust.

66. I.e., the *people's* grain.

67. In the Pentateuchal and Deuteronomistic traditions, as well as in rabbinic tradition, the reverse is also true: the tabernacle is cast as a microcosm of creation. See Jon D. Levenson, *Creation and the Persistence of Evil: The Jewish Drama of Divine Omnipotence* (San Francisco: Harper & Row, 1988), 78–99.

68. The connection between king and creator is conventional. The king as temple builder is a common motif in biblical and ancient Near Eastern literature. See Marc Zvi Brettler, *God Is King: Understanding an Israelite Metaphor* (JSOTSup 76; Sheffield: Sheffield Academic Press, 1989), 116–18.

69. See, in particular, James L. Mays, *The Lord Reigns: A Theological Handbook to the Psalms* (Louisville, Ky.: Westminster John Knox, 1994), esp. 12–22; idem, "The Language of the Reign of God," *Int* 47 (1993): 117–26; and Mettinger, *In Search of God*, 92–122. For further treatment, see chapter 7.

Chapter 2: "I Shall Walk in Freedom"

1. See Jerome F. D. Creach, *Yahweh as Refuge and the Editing of the Hebrew Psalter* (JSOTSup 217; Sheffield: Sheffield Academic Press, 1996), 36; P. Hugger, *Jahwe meine Zuflucht: Gestalt und Theologie des 91. Psalms* (Münsterschwarzacher Studien 13; Würzburg: Vier-Turme-Verlag, 1971), 37.

2. Creach, *Yahweh as Refuge*, 36–37; see also 47–48.

3. Ibid., 69.

4. Creach admits this: "Granted, in the examples above it is not said that '*tôrâ* is a refuge'; neither *ḥāsâ* nor the nominal forms that designate 'shelter' appear in direct connection with the word *tôrâ*" (ibid., 72).

5. Literally, "in a broad space" (*bārĕḥābâ*).

6. See the discussion in Jon D. Levenson, "The Sources of Torah: Psalm 119 and the Modes of Revelation in Second Temple Judaism," in *Ancient Israelite Religion: Essays in Honor of Frank Moore Cross,* ed. Patrick D. Miller, Paul D. Hanson, and S. Dean McBride (Philadelphia: Fortress, 1987), 562.

7. E.g., *dābār, 'imrâ, mišpāṭîm, ḥuqqîm, miṣwôt, 'ēdôt, piqqûdîm*.

8. I.e., God's instructive word, teaching, commandment, statute, precept.

9. James L. Mays contends that the metaphor gets only "marginal use" in the psalm, a problematic conclusion in light of the various examples cited above ("The Place of the Torah-Psalms in the Psalter," *JBL* 106 [1987]: 7). Granted, the term and its semantic equivalents do not occur as frequently as the legal terms related to *tôrâ* do, but that does not diminish its power as a metaphor for *tôrâ*-piety.

10. For an extensive study of the wide-ranging metaphorical nuances of *derek* (and related words) in the Old Testament and ancient Near Eastern Literature, see Markus Philipp Zehnder, *Wegmetaphorik im Alten Testament: Eine semantische Untersuchung der alttestamentlichen und altorientalischen Weg-Lexeme mit besonderer Berüchsichtigung ihrer metaphorischen Verwendung* (BZAW 268; Berlin/New York: de Gruyter, 1999), esp. 117–613. Zehnder broadly distinguishes the host of metaphorical nuances of the "way" motif between "Ethic" and "History (*Geschichte*)" (pp. 483–528).

11. Jean-Pierre Prévost, *A Short Dictionary of the Psalms,* trans. Mary Misrahi (Collegeville, Minn.: Liturgical Press, 1997), 72–74.

12. For translation, see chapter 3.

13. See also Pss 78:1, 5, 10; 81:4; 89:30.

14. E.g., Pss 49:3–4; 51:6; 105:22; 111:10.

15. E.g., Pss 25:4; 32:8; 51:13; 86:11.

16. E.g., Pss 119:33; see also 119:12, 26, 64, 108, 124, 135; 94:12.

17. E.g., Pss 104:24; 136:5.

18. E.g., Pss 19:6; 119:89–90.

19. Read with a conjunctive "waw," according to several Hebrew manuscripts, LXX, and Peshitta.

20. See, e.g, Psalm 119, in which the psalmist affirms *tôrâ*-righteousness as both morally prescriptive and life sustaining (e.g., vv. 3, 33, 35, 37, 40, 50, 92, 94), even in the face of those who "have dug pitfalls" (v. 85) and "lie in wait to destroy" (v. 95).

21. For this idiomatic expression, see also Amos 2:14; Jer 25:35; and Job 11:20.

22. For a classic, but overly wrought, statement of this moral dynamic (i.e., the "deeds-consequences" construct) in Old Testament theology, see Klaus Koch, "Is There a Doctrine of Retribution in the Old Testament?" in *Theodicy in the Old Testament,* ed. James L. Crenshaw (IRT 4; Philadelphia: Fortress, 1983), 57–87. Cf. the important refinement of this thesis in Patrick D. Miller, *Sin and Judgment in the Prophets: A Stylistic and Theological Analysis* (Chico, Calif.: Scholars Press, 1982).

23. Gerald T. Sheppard, in particular, observes that "seeking refuge" is found primarily in laments ("Theology and the Book of Psalms," *Int* 46 [1992]: 149–52). But as a metaphor, the expression focuses more on the destination than on the plight.

24. Erich Zenger, *A God of Vengeance: Understanding the Psalms of Divine Wrath,* trans. Linda M. Maloney (Louisville, Ky.: Westminster John Knox, 1996), 11.

25. Read *'ōraḥ* or *derek* with some Hebrew manuscripts (so also Peshitta). MT has *'ereṣ* ("land").

26. A difficult word, whose meaning is disputed. For this translation, based on an Arabic cognate, see A. A. Macintosh, "A Third Root *'dh* in Biblical Hebrew?" *VT* 24 (1974): 454–73.

27. See the comparable analysis by Reuben Ahroni, who finds the tranquil, pastoral imagery deceptive ("The Unity of Psalm 23," *HAR* 6 [1982]: 21–34).

28. Mark S. Smith, "The Psalms as a Book for Pilgrims," *Int* 46 (1992): 164. See also idem, "Setting and Rhetoric in Psalm 23," *JSOT* 41 (1988): 66.

29. The reference to "name" serves as a metonym for God's character. It is out of God's very integrity, the psalmist affirms, that God guides him.

30. Again, the loaded term *ṣedeq* serves double duty to designate both protection and righteousness (see above).

31. The translation for *'ak* is debatable ("surely" NRSV). For the restrictive sense ("only"), see, e.g., 1 Sam 18:8; Isa 45:14; Pss 37:8; 62:6.

32. The verbal form in Hebrew (√*rdp*) exhibits an ironic intensity that most English translations fail to acknowledge (e.g., NRSV "follow").

33. The verb is likely a "precative perfect" and thus should not be repointed as an infinitive construct (so Michael L. Barré, "An Unrecognized Precative Construction in Phoenician and Hebrew," *Biblica* 64 [1983]: 416. Cf. Pss 27:4b; 61:8).

34. This concluding reference to the temple indicates priestly rather than domestic provenance, contra James L. Crenshaw, *The Psalms: an Introduction* (Grand Rapids: Eerdmans, 2001), 61–62. I am intrigued with the possibility that this so-called "pilgrimage psalm" has an even more specific provenance and function. The reference to the pursuit of enemies and the psalmist's vindication suggests a scenario comparable to that of one falsely accused of murder fleeing the "avenger of blood" while seeking asylum in the sanctuary or a city of refuge (cf. Exod 21:12–14; Num 35:9–28; Deut 19:1–13; Josh 20:1–9). For the sanctuary, specifically the altar, as a locus of asylum, see 1 Kgs 1:49–53; 2:28–35.

35. Literally, "for length of days" (cf. Deut 30:20; Job 12:12; Pss 21:4; 91:16; Prov 3:2, 16).

36. The term *měsillôt* literally refers to public access roads. LXX reads "ascents" (*ma'ălôt*).

37. Literally, "they make it a spring."

38. Given the problematic nature of this stich, only a tentative translation is possible. Moreover, the line appears to be a gloss that mitigates the metaphorical nuance of the previous line.

39. MT has "the God of gods will be seen in Zion." As in 42:2 (so a few Hebrew manuscripts, as well as Peshitta and Targum), the niphal pointing of the verb suggests a scribal correction that avoids any implication that God's face can be seen.

40. See Smith, "The Psalms as a Book for Pilgrims," 156–66.

41. Compare LXX and MT on v. 8b.

42. So Qere; Ketib is plural.

43. Literally, "were not known."

44. See Emil Fackenheim, *God's Presence in History: Jewish Affirmations and Philosophical Reflections* (New York: Harper & Row, 1972), 9–14.

45. See the emendation proposed by BHS.

46. For this image's place within the "pathway" word field, see Zehnder, *Wegmetaphorik*, 414. For further discussion on translation, see chapter 7.

47. See chapter 7.

48. NRSV, "at liberty."

49. Johann Gottfried von Herder, *The Spirit of Hebrew Poetry*, trans. James Marsh (1922; reprint, Naperville, Ill.: Aleph Press, 1971), 1.37.

50. Beyond the limits of this study, see Zehnder's survey of the "historical" usage of the "way" lexeme throughout Old Testament literature in *Wegmetaphorik*, 503–28.

51. E.g., Pss 18:17–18 [=2 Sam 22:17–18]; 32:6; 42:7; 69:2–3, 15; Jonah 2:5. See chapter 5.

52. Read plural; the singular verb in Hebrew, in view of the parallelism, is to be taken as a collective.

53. The final phrase may allude to an afterlife. See Crenshaw, *The Psalms*, 126.

54. Book 4 includes, with one exception, the enthronement psalms (Psalms 93, 95–99; cf. 47). See James L. Mays, *The Lord Reigns: A Theological Handbook to the Psalms* (Louisville, Ky.: Westminster John Knox, 1994), 12–22; Gerald H. Wilson, "The Use of Royal Psalms at the 'Seams' of the Hebrew Psalter," *JSOT* 35 (1986): 92. The phrase YHWH *mālak* ("The LORD reigns") occurs only in Psalms 93, 96, 97, and 99.

55. Patrick D. Miller, "The Beginning of the Psalter," in *The Shape and the Shaping of the Psalter,* ed. J. Clinton McCann Jr. (JSOTSup 159; Sheffield: Sheffield Academic Press, 1993), 91–92.

56. See James L. Mays, *Psalms* (IBC; Louisville, Ky.: John Knox, 1994), 14, 36; J. Clinton McCann Jr., "The Psalms as Instruction," *Int* 46 (1992): 117–28.

57. See, e.g., Isa 55:6 and Jer 29:12–13, both calls to repentance.

58. See Gerald H. Wilson, "Shaping the Psalter: A Consideration of Editorial Linkage in the Book of Psalms," in *The Shape and the Shaping of the Psalter,* ed. J. Clinton McCann Jr., 80–81; and James L. Mays, "The Question of Context," in ibid., 18–19. Cf. Brueggemann's critique of the alleged contrast between "ritual accompaniment" and "instruction" in his "Response to James L. Mays, 'The Question of Context,'" in ibid., 31–32.

59. For the relationship between wisdom and *tôrâ,* see William P. Brown, "The Law and the Sages: A Reexamination of *Tôrâ* in Proverbs" (forthcoming).

60. For Proverbs, see Norman C. Habel, "The Symbolism of Wisdom in Proverbs 1–9," *Int* 26 (1972): 131–57.

61. References to "refuge" and its semantic field, however, can be found in the older, "Solomonic" collection of Proverbs (see 10:29; 11:28; 14:26, 32; 18:10–11).

62. Indeed, wisdom herself is found out and about on the streets and public areas (Prov 1:20–21; 8:2–3).

63. The plural form in Hebrew indicates the collective modes of conduct.

64. See the discussion of Ps 1:2b in chapter 3.

65. Tom F. Driver, *Liberating Rites: Understanding the Transformative Power of Ritual* (Boulder, Colo.: Westview, 1998), 16–17 (originally published as *The Magic of Ritual: Our Need for Liberating Rites That Transform Our Lives and Our Communities* (San Francisco: HarperSanFrancisco, 1991), emphasis added.

66. See Creach, *Yahweh as Refuge,* 69.

67. As Driver points out, "The path-making character of ritual performance has . . . become world-making. We glimpse ourselves as the inhabitants of a cosmos that is put in place and held firm around us through ritual performance" (*Liberating Rites,* 149).

68. See chapter 6.

69. See Driver's discussion of Arnold Van Gennep's notion of "rite of passage" and Victor Turner's expansion of it in Driver, *Liberating Rites,* 157–65.

70. E.g., Pss 1:5; 22:22, 25; 35:18; 40:9; 111:1; 149:1.

71. Driver, *Liberating Rites,* 190.

72. Ibid., 147.

73. The dual prominence of "refuge" and "pathway" is especially striking in Johannine Christology, as conveyed in John 14:1–7. The convergence of "place" and "way" is found, the evangelist asserts, in Christ, the incarnate Word. In a different vein, Matthew's Gospel casts Jesus as a refuge in which one finds respite *and* continued growth in faith, paradoxically represented in the metaphor of "yoke" (Matt 11:28–30).

Chapter 3: The Transplanted Tree

1. Quoted from P. Ackroyd, *Blake* (London: Sinclair-Stevenson, 1995), 209.

2. See, e.g., Brevard Childs, *Old Testament Theology in a Canonical Context* (Philadelphia: Fortress, 1985), 207–8; and Gerald H. Wilson, *The Editing of the Hebrew Psalter* (SBLDS 76; Chico, Calif.: Scholars Press, 1985), 207, who observes that this psalm defines the Psalter's literary context qua "Word of God" and, hence, establishes the "hermeneutical principles for the correct approach" to the psalms. I do not agree, however, with Wilson's claim that nothing of the *content* of the Psalter is addressed

in this initial psalm. The orienting power of Psalm 1 has all to do with understanding the Psalter's content (see below).

3. See, representatively, Patrick D. Miller, "The Beginning of the Psalter," in *The Shape and Shaping of the Psalter*, ed. J. Clinton McCann Jr. (JSOTSup 159; Sheffield: Sheffield Academic Press, 1993), 84–92; idem, *Interpreting the Psalms* (Philadelphia: Fortress, 1986), 87–88. I agree with Jerome Creach's balanced assessment that although Psalms 1 and 2 do not constitute a literary unity, much less bear the same provenance, they do exhibit suggestive verbal and thematic points of correspondence to warrant their juxtaposition and pride of place in the Psalter ("Like a Tree Planted by the Temple Stream: The Portrait of the Righteous in Psalm 1:3," *CBQ* 71 [1999]: 34–46; see also Gerald T. Sheppard, *Wisdom as a Hermeneutical Construct: A Study in the Sapientializing of the Old Testament* [BZAW 151; New York: de Gruyter, 1980], 139–40).

4. The exclamatory term *'ašrê*, which introduces a macarism and is distinguishable from *bārûk* ("blessed"), commends the virtuous conduct and character of the one who enjoys God's support rather than invokes God's blessing. As Waldemar Janzen has pointed out, the term is imbued with a hint of envy ("*'Ašrê* in the Old Testament," *HTR* 58 [1965]: 226). Examples include Pss 32:1; 40:4; 41:1; 84:5; 89:15; 94:12; 112:1; 119:1; 128:1 (cf. Prov 3:13; 8:32, 34; 28:14; Job 5:17). For more extensive discussion, see E. Lipinski, "Macarismes et Psaumes de congratulation," *RB* 75 (1968): 321–67. It is no accident that Psalm 1 opens with a word that begins with the first letter of the Hebrew alphabet, while the last word of the psalm begins with the last letter of the alphabet. Within the psalm's structure, *'ašrê* designates the good fortune the righteous enjoy, represented by the flourishing "tree," much in contrast to the wicked's demise as "chaff."

5. The term *tôrâ*, frequently translated as "law," suggests the more general sense of divine teaching or instruction, which likely includes the ethos of Pentateuchal legislation, particularly in light of the Psalter's fivefold division. Psalm 1, thus, boldly claims the Psalter as a reflection of the Torah.

6. The verb *hgh* exhibits a deliberative and discursive sense that is not reflected in the typical translation "meditate" (so NRSV).

7. The consecutive verbal form (*wĕhāyâ*) indicates incomplete aspect or future tense in this case.

8. Nahum M. Sarna, *On the Book of Psalms* (New York: Schocken House, 1993), 42, translates the passive construction *šātûl* as "well-rooted." The translation given above, however, does not rule out this sense (cf. Ps 92:13; Ezek 17:22, 23; 19:10, 12–13), but the primary nuance of "transplant" cannot be gainsaid. See Carey Ellen Walsh, *The Fruit of the Vine: Viticulture in Ancient Israel* (HSM 60; Winona Lake, Ind.: Eisenbrauns, 2001), 100, 105; and Mitchell Dahood, *Psalms I* (AB 16; Garden City, N.Y.: Doubleday, 1965), 3–4.

9. For this peculiar translation of *'al-kēn*, I take my cue from Wilhelm Rudolph's translation of Hos 4:3, which begins with the identical construction: "Kein Wunder, daß das Land vertrocknet" (*Hosea* [KAT 13, 1; Gütersloh: Gütersloher Verlagshaus Gerd Mohn, 1966], 93, 101–2). As a rule, this compound particle establishes a tighter, more natural connection between the previous material and what follows than the more generic *lākēn*, both of which are usually translated "therefore." See Ehud Ben Zvi, Maxine Hancock, Richard Beinert, *Readings in Biblical Hebrew: An Intermediate Textbook* (New Haven, Conn.: Yale University Press, 1993), 90; and H. Lenhard, "Über den Unterschied zwischen *lkn* und *'l-kn*," *ZAW* 95 (1983): 269–72, who argues that the compound conjunction indicates already progressing consequences, whereas *lākēn* refers only to future activity. For a broader analysis, see Ernest Jenni, "Eine hebräische Abtönungspartikel: *'al-ken*," in *Prophetie und Psalmen: Festschrift*

für Klaus Seybold zum 65. Geburtstag, ed. Beat Huwyler, Hans-Peter Mathys, and Beat Weber (Munich: Ugarit-Verlag, 2001), 201–16.

10. The emphatic rather than causal use of *kî* is preferable, since it signals conclusive corroboration.

11. Robert Alter, *The Art of Biblical Poetry* (New York: Basic Books, 1985), 116

12. Thomas G. Long, *Preaching and the Literary Forms of the Bible* (Minneapolis: Fortress, 1989), 51.

13. The outline is a modified from David L. Petersen and Kent Harold Richards, *Interpreting Hebrew Poetry* (Guides to Biblical Scholarship, Old Testament Series; Minneapolis: Fortress, 1992), 96.

14. James L. Crenshaw suggests that Psalm 1 is "simplistic, even Pollyanish" vis-à-vis the preponderance of laments that populate the Psalter (*The Psalms: An Introduction* [Grand Rapids: Eerdmans, 2001], 58). The psalmist, however, does not deny the bona fide expressions of pain and suffering conveyed in many of the psalms, but claims them as formative for righteousness.

15. Cf. 119:92. "Delight" is also associated with the consummate desire for wisdom in Prov 3:15 and 8:11.

16. Indeed, it is associated with the channeled streams of water (see below and chapter 5).

17. See Psalm 19 and chapter 4.

18. Harold Fisch, *Poetry with a Purpose: Biblical Poetics and Interpretation* (ISBL; Bloomington / Indianapolis: Indiana University Press, 1988), 108.

19. For the instructional dimension, see James L. Mays, *Psalms* (IBC; Louisville, Ky.: John Knox, 1994), 42–43; Patrick D. Miller, *Interpreting the Psalms* (Philadelphia: Fortress, 1986), 86.

20. Knowing the right time is a prominent sapiential theme: "To make an apt answer is a joy to anyone; and a word in season, how good it is!" (Prov 15:23; cf. 25:11; Eccl 3:1–8).

21. In later Jewish Hellenistic literature, the Torah is given the epithet "the tree of life" (Michael V. Fox, *Proverbs 1–9* [AB 18A; New York: Doubleday, 2000], 159). For further discussion of the metaphor of water in association with *tôrâ,* see chapter 5.

22. Because the text is corrupt at the beginning of v. 3 (cf. v. 2), it is unclear whether Pharaoh or Assyria serves as the specific target of the following metaphor.

23. Read *hōlîkâ* (hiphil).

24. Literally, "many waters," which often designates watery chaos instead of sustenance.

25. See Dexter E. Callender Jr., *Adam in Myth and History: Ancient Israelite Perspectives on the Primal Human* (HSS 48; Winona Lake, Ind.: Eisenbrauns, 2000), 50–54, who discusses Ps 36:8–10; Jer 17:12–13; Ezekiel 47; and the book of Jubilees.

26. See n. 20 above.

27. See Michael D. Coogan, "Canaanite Origins and Lineage: Reflections on the Religion of Ancient Israel," in *Ancient Israelite Religion: Essays in Honor of Frank Moore Cross,* ed. Patrick D. Miller Jr., Paul D. Hanson, S. Dean McBride (Philadelphia: Fortress, 1987), 118–20. In contending that the goddess Asherah constitutes the mythological antecedent of wisdom in Proverbs, Coogan curiously overlooks this important text for support. For a related argument, see Judith M. Hadley, "Wisdom and the Goddess," in *Wisdom in Ancient Israel: Essays in Honour of J. A. Emerton,* ed. John Day, Robert P. Gordon, and H. G. M. Williamson (Cambridge: University of Cambridge Press, 1995), 234–43.

28. Read plural instead of MT singular form.

29. Tablet XI.6.

30. For a classic synopsis and psychological analysis of this epic, see Thorkild Jacobson, *The Treasures of Darkness: A History of Mesopotamian Religion* (New Haven, Conn.: Yale University Press, 1976), 193–219.

31. Tablet IX, lines 175–78. For discussion, see Callender, *Adam in Myth and History,* 47; Geo Widengren, *The King and the Tree of Life in Ancient Near Eastern Religion* (Uppsala Universitets Årsskrift 4; Wiesbaden: Otto Harrassowitz / Upssala: A.-B. Lundequistska Bohkhandeln, 1951), 7–8.

32. See the discussion in Widengren, *The King and the Tree of Life,* 5–9.

33. Ibid., 10.

34. See the most recent survey by Othmar Keel, *Goddesses and Trees, New Moon and Yahweh: Ancient Near Eastern Art and the Hebrew Bible* (JSOTSup 61; Sheffield: Sheffield Academic Press, 1998), 16–57.

35. Dated to the Early Dynastic III of Ur (ca. twenty-fifth century), these statues feature he-goats standing on their hind legs, with forelegs fastened to the branches of a tree. It is hypothesized that the two animals flanked a sacred tree (*ANEP,* #667–668 [pp. 218, 329]).

36. For the connection between the tree image and the epigraphic reference to "his *'ăšērâ,*" see Ruth Hestrin, "Understanding Asherah: Exploring Semitic Iconography," *BAR* 17/5 (September/October 1991): 50–59, esp. 57.

37. For further examples, see Othmar Keel and Christoph Uehlinger, *God, Goddesses, and Images of God in Ancient Israel,* trans. Thomas H. Trapp (Minneapolis: Fortress, 1998), 215–17. Also striking are Akkadian seals from Syria that depict stalks and leafy branches sprouting from a female figure emerging from the earth or, in the case of a Mari seal, from flowing streams issuing out of the foot of a mountain on which a god is enthroned. See Keel, *Goddesses and Trees,* 20–21 (particularly fig. 7 among the representations at the back of Keel's survey). See also *ANET,* #672 (p. 219), which dates from the Uruk period.

38. Keel, *Goddesses and Trees,* 25.

39. See ibid., 34–36, figure 52, with accompanying discussion. The drawing is a reconstruction from three fragments.

40. In the words of Susan Ackerman, the two registers are "permeated with the imagery of Asherah" (*Under Every Green Tree: Popular Religion in Sixth-Century Judah* [HSM 46; Atlanta: Scholars Press, 1992], 191. See below.

41. Keel, *Goddesses and Trees,* 48. The depiction of the goddess in connection with the stylized tree during the Iron Age, Keel notes, is occasionally replaced with a male figure. Curious is a bone handle from Hazor attributed to Iron Age II B (930–730 B.C.E.) that shows a "youthful four-winged god holding a small palm tree in each hand" (ibid., 43). Also, a male figure seated or enthroned before the tree, sometimes depicted holding a vessel for liquids in his hand, is also attested. In these cases, Keel guesses, the tree signifies sacred space or "the presence of a divine power, namely of prosperity and blessing, which ultimately resides in the earth" (ibid., 46).

42. Ibid., 41–42.

43. 1 Kgs 7:21; 2 Kgs 25:16–17; 2 Chr 3:15–17. For discussion, see E. O. James, *The Tree of Life: An Archaeological Study* (Studies in the History of Religions XI; Leiden: E. J. Brill, 1966), 37–38, who refers to them, perhaps too confidently, as "cult posts of the *asherah* type." In any case, the inscribed pillars that flanked the temple's entrance, such as at Jerusalem, 'Ain Dara in Northwest Syria, and Tianat, have their precursor in the stylized tree representations (Elizabeth Bloch-Smith, " 'Who Is the King of Glory?': Solomon's Temple and Its Symbolism," in *Scripture and Other Artifacts: Essays on the Bible and Archaeology in Honor of Philip J. King,* ed. M. D. Coogan, J. C. Exum, L. E. Stager [Louisville, Ky.: Westminster John Knox, 1994], 23).

44. The latter, if repointed as in the LXX, could be translated "in strength." For discussion, see R. B. Y. Scott, "The Pillars Jachin and Boaz," *JBL* 58 (1939): 143–49. Victor A. Hurowitz suggests that the names are comparable to Mesopotamian temple inscriptions that convey blessings or wishes for the king (*I Have Built You an Exalted*

House: Temple Building in the Bible in Light of Mesopotamian and Northwest Semitic Writings [JSOTSup 115; Sheffield: Sheffield Academic Press, 1992], 257 n. 2).

45. Carol Meyers, "Jachin and Boaz in Religious and Political Perspective," *CBQ* 45 (1983): 173.

46. Keel, *Goddesses and Trees*, 42.

47. For general discussion, see Bloch-Smith, "'Who Is the King of Glory?'" 22–23; Lawrence Stager, "Jerusalem as Eden," *BAR* 26/3 (2000): 38–39. For more technical analysis, see the original publication of the scene, complete with illustrations, in André Parrot, *Mission Archéologique de Mari*, vol II, *Le Palais: Peintures Murales* (Institut Français d'Archéologie de Beyrouth, Bibliothèque et historique 59; Paris: Paul Geuthner, 1958), 53–64; Abraham Malamat, *Mari and the Early Israelite Experience* (The Schweich Lectures of the British Academy, 1984; Oxford: Oxford University Press, 1989), 22–23; Jean-Claude Margueron, "Mari: A Portrait in Art of a Mesopotamian City-State," in *Civilizations of the Ancient Near East*, ed. Jack M. Sasson (New York: Charles Scribner's Sons, 1995), 2.892–93.

48. Margueron, "Mari," 2.892–93.

49. For a brief sampling of the annalistic records from Egypt and Assyria, see William P. Brown, *The Ethos of the Cosmos: The Genesis of Moral Imagination in the Bible* (Grand Rapids: Eerdmans, 1999), 248–52; Callender, *Adam in Myth and History*, 59–61; A. L. Oppenheim, "On Royal Gardens in Mesopotamia," *JNES* 24 (1965): 328–33; Donald J. Wiseman, "Mesopotamian Gardens," *Anatolian Studies* (1983): 137–44.

50. *AR* 2.290 (A.0.87.1.vii.17–27).

51. *AR* 2.26 (A.0.87.1.vii.17–27). See also *AR* 2.55 (A.0.87.10.71–74) and *AR* 2.27 (A.0.87.1.vii.17–27).

52. For example, *ARAB* 2, §§ 402, 403.

53. For the picture and brief description, see Stager, "Jerusalem as Eden," 45; *ANEP*, 155 (#451).

54. *ARE* 4.115n.e., 264 n.a.

55. *ARE* 4, §272.

56. See Ackerman, *Under Every Green Tree*, 187.

57. *šadmôt qidrôn* (2 Kgs 23:4; Jer 31:40). So Lawrence E. Stager, "Jerusalem and the Garden of Eden," *Eretz Israel* 26 (1999): 183*; idem, "The Archaeology of the East Slope of Jerusalem," *JNES* 41 (1982): 113–17.

58. Steven Tuell argues that the Gihon of Eden in Genesis 2 is Zion's Gihon spring writ mythically large ("The Rivers of Paradise: Ezekiel 47:1–12 and Genesis 2:10–14," in *God Who Creates: Essays in Honor of W. Sibley Towner*, ed. William P. Brown and S. Dean McBride Jr. [Grand Rapids: Eerdmans, 2000], 178–79).

59. For discussion, see Callender, *Adam in Myth and History*, 63; Widengren, *The King and the Tree of Life*, 19

60. *ANET*, 267.

61. Widengren, *The King and the Tree of Life*, 42.

62. Ibid.

63. For discussion concerning the precise nuance of the term, see Carol L. Meyers and Eric M. Meyers, *Haggai, Zechariah 1–8* (AB 25B; Garden City, N.Y.: Doubleday, 1987), 202–3; S. E. Loewenstamm, *Comparative Studies in Biblical and Ancient Oriental Literature* (AOAT 204; Kevelaer: Butzon & Bercker / Neukirchen-Vluyn: Neukirchener Verlag, 1980), 212–13; Moshe Weinfeld, *Social Justice in Ancient Israel and in the Ancient Near East* (Minneapolis: Fortress, 1995), 60.

64. E.g., Gen 1:26–29; Isa 55:3–5.

65. For further discussion, see Brown, *The Ethos of the Cosmos*, 241–48.

66. Cf. Pss 44:2; 80:8–9.

67. Regarding the patriarchal narratives of the Yahwist, see Theodore Hiebert, *The Yah-*

wist's Landscape: Nature and Religion in Early Israel (New York / Oxford: Oxford University Press, 1996), 107–9.

68. See Callender, *Adam in Myth and History,* 43.

69. Emphasis added. For more extended discussion, see Elizabeth C. LaRocca-Pitts, *"Of Wood and Stone": The Significance of Israelite Cultic Items in the Bible and Its Early Interpreters* (HSM 61; Winona Lake, Ind.: Eisenbrauns, 2001), 175–80.

70. For this etymology, see William Foxwell Albright, *Yahweh and the Gods of Canaan: A Historical Analysis of Two Contrasting Faiths* (Winona Lake, Ind.: Eisenbrauns, 1968), 189. Noteworthy is the word *'lt* ('Elat or "goddess"?), an epithet for Asherah, found on a thirteen-century ewer from Lachish, which likely bears a connection to the drawing of a stylized tree flanked by two ibexes. See Ruth Hestrin, "The Lachish Ewer and the Asherah," *IEJ* 37 (1987): 212–23; Judith M. Hadley, *The Cult of Asherah in Ancient Israel and Judah: Evidence for a Hebrew Goddess* (University of Cambridge Oriental Publications 57; Cambridge: University of Cambridge Press, 2000), 156–61; Keel, *Goddesses and Trees,* 33–34.

71. This text suggests that Deuteronomy, at least, regarded the *'ăšērâ* as a live tree (LaRocca-Pitts, *"Of Wood and Stone,"* 100, 174).

72. See the survey of the verbs used in connection with *'ăšērâ* in Hadley, *The Cult of Asherah,* 54–55.

73. Compare, for example, 1 Kgs 15:13 and 16:33. For a survey of scholarly opinion, see Hadley, *The Cult of Asherah,* 11–36 and passim.

74. See John Day, "Asherah in the Hebrew Bible and Northwest Semitic Literature," *JBL* 105 (1986): 387; and Hadley, *The Cult of Asherah,* 43.

75. In addition to the iconographic survey conducted by Keel, see Hadley's discussion of Kuntillet 'Ajrud and the thirteenth-century B.C.E. Late Bronze Age ewer from Lachish (*The Cult of Asherah,* 106–60). Her survey of the extant evidence suggests that the goddess Asherah was worshiped in Palestine by the thirteen century B.C.E. (at least in Lachish) and "her symbol was a stylized tree flanked by ibexes and associated with lions" (ibid., 187).

76. E.g., Judg 3:7 (plural); 1 Kgs 14:15, 23; 15:13; 16:33; 2 Kgs 13:6; 17:10, 16; 18:4, 19; 21:3, 7; 23:4, 6–7, 14–15; see also 2 Chr 15:16.

77. See also Isa 17:8; 27:9; Jer 17:2; Mic 5:14. Ackerman argues that Asherah worship also lies behind the "image of jealousy" in Ezek 8:3 (*Under Every Green Tree,* 60–62).

78. Discussion on this issue is voluminous. For recent representative treatments, see Ackerman, *Under Every Green Tree,* 62–66; Keel and Uehlinger, *Gods, Goddesses, and Images of God,* 210–48; Tilde Binger, *Asherah: Goddesses in Ugaritic, Israel and the Old Testament* (Copenhagen International Seminar 2 / JSOTSup 232; Sheffield: Sheffield Academic Press, 1997); Hadley, *The Cult of Asherah,* 206–9; and LaRocca-Pitts, *"Of Wood and Stone,"* 161–204. I am inclined to agree with William Dever and others that the most straightforward solution to the problem regarding the range of symbolic power borne by the a/Asherah references at Kuntillet 'Ajrud and Khirbet el-Qôm lies in their connection to Canaanite religion. In "popular religion," YHWH, like 'El in Ugaritic mythology, was considered to have a divine consort. Thus, "one cannot separate the symbol from the goddess, either conceptually or existentially" (William G. Dever, "Archaeology and the Ancient Israelite Cult: How the Kh. El-Qôm and Kuntillet 'Ajrud 'Ashera' Texts Have Changed the Picture," *Eretz-Israel* 26 [1999]: 11*).

79. Contrary to many interpreters who contend that the possessive suffix precludes any connection to the goddess, it need only be noted that the expression of one deity "possessing" another is not to be expected within the limited word field of biblical Hebrew, even though it is attested in certain cognate languages. For a balanced but inconclusive discussion regarding the complexities of the issue, see Mark S. Smith,

The Origins of Biblical Monotheism: Israel's Polytheistic Background and the Ugaritic Texts (Oxford: Oxford University Press, 2001), 72–74, 236–38. Elsewhere, Smith seems to grant that Asherah became YHWH's consort as a result of "his identification with El," and together they represented a transitional "ditheistic" model in the development of Israelite monotheism, hinted in Gen 1:27 (ibid., 90, 142, 155).

80. I favor the latter alternative, since it is the most economical explanation. See Christoph Uehlinger, "Anthropomorphic Cult Statuary in Iron Age Palestine and the Search for Yahweh's Cult Images," in *The Image and the Book: Iconic Cults, Aniconism, and the Rise of Book Religion in Israel and the Ancient Near East,* ed. Karel van der Toorn (Contributions to Biblical Exegesis and Theology 21; Leuven: Uitgeverig Peters, 1997), 140–52.

81. See Judg 3:7 (plural); 1 Kgs 15:13; 18:19; 2 Kgs 21:7; 23:4, 7; 2 Chr 15:16; and Dever, "Archaeology and the Ancient Israelite Cult," 14*.

82. 2 Kgs 17:16; 21:3; and 23:15. So LaRocca-Pitts, *"Of Wood and Stone,"* 68. Elsewhere, she finds 1 Kgs 15:13; 2 Kgs 21:7; 23:4, 7; and 2 Chr 15:16 to suggest that the cult items are "the possessions of someone, namely the goddess" (ibid., 190).

83. See also Ackerman, *Under Every Green Tree,* 65.

84. LaRocca-Pitts, "Of Wood and Stone," 82.

85. Christoph Uehlinger has tentatively proposed that a recently discovered terracotta object from the late Iron Age sanctuary of Sarepta and published by Jörg Jeremias features "Yahweh and his Asherah" sitting together on a throne (Uehlinger, "Anthropomorphic Cult Statuary in Iron Age Palestine," 149–51). For lack of supporting epigraphic evidence, such an identification is, of course, entirely conjectural.

86. Note the helpful distinction made by John S. Holladay Jr. between official or "established worship" and "tolerated nonconformist worship" on the popular level ("Religion in Israel and Judah under the Monarch: An Explicitly Archaeological Approach," in *Ancient Israelite Religion: Essays in Honor of Frank Moore Cross,* ed. Patrick D. Miller, Paul D. Hanson, and S. Dean McBride Jr. [Philadelphia: Fortress, 1987], 268–75).

87. See also Isa 30:25; 32:2.

88. As Creach points out, Isa 30:25 and 32:2 also employ the term *peleg* to designate water channels that flow from the holy mountain ("Like a Tree Planted by the Temple Stream," 41–42). In Ugaritic literature, moreover, El's dwelling or sanctuary is said to be *mbk nhrm qrb 'apq thmtm* ("at the sources of the Rivers, at the streams of the Deeps" [*KTU* 1.3.v.6–7; 1.4.iv.21–22; 1.6.i.33–34; 1.17.vi.47–47; cf. 1.100.3; Job 38:16]). In Mesopotamian lore, the great Utnapishtim (or Sumerian Ziusudra), the forerunner of Noah in biblical tradition, resided in the abode of the gods at the head of the rivers (Gilgamesh XI.202–5; *ANET,* 44). The often-noted Egyptian parallel in the *Instruction of Amenemope* 4.6.1–12 also assumes some connection to the temple: the "heated man in the temple" is compared to a "tree growing in the open," whose demise is certain. In constrast, the "silent man" is "like a tree growing in a garden," which "stands in front of its lord" (*ANET,* 422; *AEL,* 2.150–51).

89. But cf. Pss 52:8; 92:13–14 (see below).

90. The specific reference to grain in relation to Zion's stream in Ps 65:9 is suggestive of the alleged origin of the temple as the former threshing floor of the Jebusite Araunah, bought by David (2 Sam 24:18–25).

91. See the reference to "oaks of righteousness" in Isa 61:3.

92. E.g., Pss 35:4–6; 37:1–2; 72:15a, 16–17a; 83:113–15; 90:3, 5–8; 102:3–4, 11; 103:15–18; 129:5–6.

93. E.g., 128:1–6; 144:12–13a, 14b–15.

94. The root *qwh* can mean either to hope or to call out.

95. E.g., Deut 12:1; 1 Kgs 14:23; 2 Kgs 16:4; 17:10; Jer 2:20; 3:6, 13; Isa 57:5; Ezek 6:13; cf. Ps 92:12. See LaRocca-Pitts, *"Of Wood and Stone,"* 122.

96. See n. 9.
97. The psalmist refers specifically to the (re)empowerment of the king to bring about Israel's restoration in the land (v. 17).
98. For historical descriptions, see Psalms 78, 105–106, 135–136.
99. See also chapter 6.
100. The assonantal bond of these two terms may not be entirely accidental.

Chapter 4: The Sun of Righteousness

1. C. S. Lewis, *Reflections on the Psalms* (New York: Harcourt, Brace, Jovanovich, 1958), 63.
2. The meaning of *qawwām* is disputed. Poetic parallelism suggests that it refers in some sense to discourse ("their words"; *millēhem*). As often suggested, the form could be due to textual corruption of an original *qōlām* ("their voice," so LXX). However, the elision of the *lamed* is difficult to explain textually. Mitchell Dahood, following Jacob Barth (1893), reconstructs the meaning from the root *qwh* (II), "to call, collect," but the resulting sense is far from clear (*Psalm I* [AB 16; Garden City, N.Y.: Doubleday, 1965], 122). The normal meaning of *qaw* is "measuring line," used for construction or demarcation (e.g., 1 Kgs 7:23; Job 38:5; Isa 44:13). Sense can be made of this literal meaning by recognizing that the psalmist is couching a *visual* image in the language of verbal discourse, as is done with the sun in the subsequent lines. In other words, this enigmatic term could refer either to the designated paths or circuits that the celestial bodies follow (cf. the sun's "rising" [*môṣā'û*] in v. 6) or, more likely, to beams or rays emanating from the astral bodies themselves, particularly the sun—a widespread motif in ancient Near Eastern iconography (see below).
3. If the sense of the grammatical subject is akin to a light beam, then the generic verb would have the more focused meaning of "emanate."
4. The Hebrew *zēdîm* can also be translated "presumptuous ones" (so Dahood, *Psalm I*, 124) or "the insolent" (so NRSV). I consider the following petition ('*al-yimšĕlû-bî*) to be an allusion to Gen 4:7, in which YHWH challenges Cain to resist "sin" (*ḥaṭṭā't*): "and if you do not do well, sin is lurking at the door; its desire is for you, but you must master it (*wĕ'attâ timšol-bô*)." As Cain fails to master the impulse to engage in fratricide, the psalmist pleads to God that sin not overtake him. The psalmist's interior side, moreover, is maintained in vv. 12 and 13, suggesting that sins, and not sinful persons or idols, are of utmost concern. If so, then vv. 12–13a reflect a dual petition that God purge the psalmist of any faults unknowingly committed and spare him of any future offenses.
5. From √*tmm*, "to be whole, complete."
6. Hermann Gunkel, e.g., treats vv. 1–6 and 7–14 as entirely unrelated sections (*Die Psalmen* [1897; reprint, Göttingen: Vandenhoeck & Ruprecht, 1968], 74–81). See also Hans-Joachim Kraus, *Psalms 1–59: A Commentary*, trans. H. C. Oswald (Minneapolis: Augsburg, 1988), 268–69.
7. For a brief summary of the history of research, see J. Glen Taylor, *Yahweh and the Sun: Biblical and Archaeological Evidence for Sun Worship in Ancient Israel* (JSOTSup 111; Sheffield: Sheffield Academic Press, 1993), 220–21. For representative studies on the psalm's coherence, see Michael Fishbane, "Psalm 19: Creation, Torah, and Hope," in *Text and Texture* (New York: Schocken Books, 1979), 84–90; and David J. A. Clines, "The Tree of Knowledge and the Law of Yahweh (Psalm XIX)," *VT* 24 (1974): 8–14.
8. Karl Löning and Erich Zenger rightly refer to the psalm's "metaphorical coherence," but solely from a traditio-historical perspective (*To Begin with, God Created . . . :Biblical Theologies of Creation*, trans. Omar Kaste [Collegeville, Minn.: Liturgical Press, 2000], 138–40).

9. A comparable case of cosmic speech can be found in Hos 2:21–22, which depicts a chain of discourse (*ʿānāh*, "answer") from God to heavens, earth, and the Jezreel valley. Such "speech" refers to each domain's creative force: divine command, precipitation from the sky, and agricultural produce from the land.

10. Mark S. Smith, *Psalms: The Divine Journey* (New York: Paulist, 1987), 52–53. For technical discussions of the traditio-historical background behind the use of such imagery, see idem, "The Near Eastern Background of Solar Language for Yahweh," *JBL* 109 (1990): 29–39; Hans-Peter Stähli, *Solare Elemente im Jahweglauben des alten Testaments* (OBO 66; Freibourg: Universitätsverlag / Göttingen: Vandenhoeck & Ruprecht, 1985); Bernd Janowski, "JHWH und der Sonnengott. Aspekte der Solarisierung JHWHs in vorexilischer Zeit," in *Pluralismus und Identität*, ed. Joachim Melhausen (Veröffentlichungen der Wissenschaftlichen Gesellscahft für Theologie 8; Gütersloh: Chr. Kaiser / Gütersloher Verlagshaus, 1995), 214–41; Othmar Keel and Christoph Uehlinger, "Yahweh und die Sonnengottheit von Jerusalem," in *Ein Gott allein? JHWH-Verehrung und biblischer Monotheismus im Kontext der israelitischen und altorientalischen Religionsgeschichte*, ed. Walter Dietrich and Martin A. Klopfenstein (OBO 139; Freibourg: Universitätsverlag / Göttingen: Vandenhoeck & Ruprecht, 1994), 269–306; Martin Arneth, *"Sonne der Gerechtigkeit": Studien zur Solarisierung der Jahwe-Religion im Lichte von Psalm 72* (Beihefte zur Zeitschrift für altorientische und biblische Rechtsgeschichte 1; Wiesbaden: Harrasowitz, 2000).

11. See, e.g., Pss 11:7; 17:15; 42:2b. For a full discussion, see Mark S. Smith, "'Seeing God' in the Psalms: The Background to the Beatific Vision in the Hebrew Bible," *CBQ* 50 (1988): 171–83.

12. E.g., Pss 4:6; 31:16; 90:8, and in the refrain of 80:3, 9, 19.

13. E.g., Pss 18:7–19; 68:7–9. Storm and solar imagery appear to have separate traditio-historical roots, West Semitic and Egyptian respectively, which converged in both Israel and Phoenicia at least by Iron Age II B. Biblical texts that combine both schemas include Hos 6:3; Ezek 43:1–5; Pss 50:1–3; 104:3–4, 7, 26, and 19–30 (Othmar Keel and Christoph Uehlinger, *Gods, Goddesses, and Images of God in Ancient Israel*, trans. Thomas H. Trapp [Minneapolis: Fortress, 1998], 261; Paul E. Dion, "YHWH as Storm-God and Sun-God: The Double Legacy of Egypt and Canaan as Reflected in Ps 104," *ZAW* 103 [1991]: 43–71; Smith, "Solar Language for Yahweh," 33–34).

14. See Anthony R. Ceresko, "A Note on Psalm 63: A Psalm of Vigil," *ZAW* 92 (1980): 435–36.

15. So Smith, *Psalms*, 53. Nevertheless, the same verb is used in 78:34 without such connotations.

16. For a text-critical discussion of this most difficult verse, see William P. Brown, "A Royal Performance: Critical Notes on Psalm 110:3aγ-b," *JBL* 117 (1998): 93–96.

17. *KTU* 2.16.6–10. For discussion, see Smith, "The Near Eastern Background of Solar Language," 35, who also notes parallels in the Amarna letters.

18. For biblical parallels of solar imagery applied to the king, see 2 Sam 23:3b–4 and Ps 72:5–6. As Smith notes, Isa 58:8 describes the "theophany of the righteous" with solar imagery (Smith, "Solar Language for Yahweh," 37).

19. Cf. Pss 88:14; 90:14; 143:8; Isa 17:14; 33:2. For a discussion of this motif in the Hebrew Scriptures, see Bernd Janowski, *Rettungsgewißheit und Epiphanie des Heils* (WMANT 59; Neukirchen-Vluyn: Neukirchener Verlag, 1989), esp. 2–3, 185–91.

20. Cf. Zeph 3:5, where solar imagery is used to convey divine *judgment* (see below).

21. LXX reconstrues the line as "I shall be satisfied when your glory appears."

22. Indeed, some were evidently used by pilgrims in vigils at the temple (e.g., Psalms 17, 27, 63). See J. W. McKay, "Psalms of Vigil," *ZAW* 91 (1979): 229–47.

23. Cf. 1 Kgs 8:12–13, which reads, "YHWH said that he would dwell in thick dark-

ness. I have built for you an exalted house, a place for you to indwell forever." With the LXX, which includes reference to God's setting of the sun in heaven prior to the divine pronouncement, a reconstruction of this Deuteronomistic text suggests a *constructive correlation* between the heavenly and earthly realms, between sunlight and darkness (Janowski, "JHWH und der Sonnengott," 223–26).

24. For similar attestations of this verb, see Ps 94:1; Deut 33:2; Job 3:4; 10:3, 22; 37:15; 50:2. Its Ugaritic cognate suggests battle imagery (e.g., *KTU* 1.3.iii.37).

25. For discussion of this unique passage, along with a survey of opinions, see Stähli, *Solare Elemente*, 42–43. In Israelite warfare and ornamentation, the *māgēn* was a small circular shield, distinct from the larger, and likely rectangular, *ṣinnâ*, which was designed to protect the whole body. Both kinds of shield were made from "beaten gold" (cf. 1 Kgs 10:16–17).

26. That there were indigenous solar cults in Canaan is evident from the proper names given to places and persons in the biblical traditions: *bêt šemeš* ("Sun-house," Josh 15:10; 21:16; 1 Sam 6:9–19; 1 Kgs 4:9; Judg 1:33), *ʿên šemeš* ("Sun-source," Josh 15:7; 18:17), *har-ḥeres* ("Sun-mountain," Judg 1:35), *maʿălēh ḥeres** ("Sun-ascent," Judg 8:13), and *timnat ḥeres* ("Sun-portion," Judg 2:9). For complete references, see Stähli, *Solare Elemente*, 12–17.

27. The dating for the beginning of Josiah's reforms is given greater precision in 2 Chr 34:3 (628 B.C.E.) than in 2 Kgs 22:3 (622 B.C.E.).

28. 2 Kgs 2:11–12; cf. 6:17; 13:14; Sir 48:9. See Edouard Lipinsky, "Shemesh" in *Dictionary of Deities and Demons in the Bible*, ed. Karel van der Toorn et al., 2d ed. (Leiden: Brill / Grand Rapids: Eerdmans, 1999), 765.

29. T. A. Holland, "A Study of Palestinian Iron Age Baked Clay Figurines with Special Reference to Jerusalem: Cave 1," *Levant* 9 (1977): 149–51; Smith, "'Seeing God,'" 178–79; Taylor, *Yahweh and the Sun*, 58–66. Othmar Keel and Christoph Uehlinger, however, interpret the disk as merely an ornamental feature (*Gods, Goddesses, and Images of God in Ancient Israel*, trans. Thomas H. Trapp [Minneapolis: Fortress, 1998], 343).

30. See Keel and Uehlinger, *Gods, Goddesses, and Images of God*, 157–58; and Taylor, *Yahweh and the Sun*, 24–40.

31. Keel and Uehlinger, *Gods, Goddesses, and Images of God*, 158.

32. Among the *lmlk* seals, the motif of the winged sun-disk appears to be more widespread than that of the four-winged and, more typical in Palestine, two-winged scarab. For drawings and discussion, along with representative examples, see Keel and Uehlinger, "Jahwe und die Sonnengottheit von Jerusalem," 294, 297a; and idem, *Gods, Goddesses, and Images of God*, 262–64. See also Benjamin Sass, "The Pre-Exilic Hebrew Seals: Iconism vs. Aniconism," in *Studies in the Iconography of Northwest Semitic Inscribed Seals*, ed. Benjamin Sass and Christoph Uehlinger (OBO 125; Fribourg: University of Fribourg Press / Göttingen: Vandenhoeck & Ruprecht, 1993), 238–39. For a discussion of a two-winged scarab featured on a bulla attributed to Hezekiah, along with comparable Egyptian examples, see Meir Lubetski, "King Hezekiah's Seal Revisited," *BAR* 27/4 (July/August 2001): 44–51, 59. Frank Moore Cross observes from this bulla that, given the lack of solar iconography among the royal seal impressions in the late seventh century B.C.E., Josiah's reforms were more stringent than Hezekiah's ("A Bulla of Hezekiah, King of Judah," in *Realia Dei: Essays in Archeology and Biblical Interpretation in Honor of Edward F. Campbell, Jr. at His Retirement*, ed. P. H. Williams, Jr., and T. Hiebert [Scholars Press Homage Series 23; Atlanta: Scholars Press, 1999], 62–66).

33. See, e.g., *ANEP*, # 281 (Zinjirli), 486 ('Amrit), 493 (Ugarit), 531 and 532 (Til-Barsib), and 534–536 (Assur); Keel and Uehlinger, *Gods, Goddesses, and Images of God*, #258a–c (Samaria and Shechem); R. Mayer-Opificius, "Die geflügelte Sonne:

Himmels- und Regendarstellung im Alten Vorderasien," *UF* 16 (1984): 189–236, who discusses various pictorial representations from Syria, Assyria, and Babylonia.

34. *ANEP,* 180 (#156). See Smith, "Solar Language for Yahweh," 33; Mayer-Opificius, "Die geflügelte Sonne," 200, 233 (#25); E. D. van Buren, *Symbols of the Gods in Mesopotamian Art* (AnOr 23; Rome: Pontificium Institutum Biblicum, 1945), 89–90.

35. See chapter 1.

36. More direct attestation to the winged sun is found in the evocative reference in Mal 4:2a [3:20a, Heb.] (see below).

37. See Janowski, "JHWH und der Sonnengott," 220, 223–26. The evidence is too meager, however, to claim that the temple, given its geographical orientation, was designed as a solar cult site (contra Julian Morgenstern, "The Gates of Righteousness," *HUCA* 6 [1929]: 1–37). See also the mixed caveat provided by Taylor, *Yahweh and the Sun,* 66–86, who points out that the archaeological evidence is, at best, ambiguous, or in the case of the Jerusalem temple, nonexistent. The biblical evidence, Taylor concedes, is more decisive (pp. 161–64).

38. Keel and Uehlinger, "Jahwe und die Sonnengottheit von Jerusalem," 286.

39. For an overview of the material remains, see Morton Smith, "Helios in Palestine," *Eretz Israel* 16 (1982): 205*–206*; Keel and Uehlinger, *God, Goddesses, and Images of God,* 249–60.

40. For a survey of relevant Egyptian texts that highlight the soteriological nature of other solar deities, particularly Amun and Re, see Janowski, *Rettungsgewißheit,* 112–64. Solar religion in Mesopotamian ritual prayers and hymns between 1500 and 1000 B.C.E. also ascribes to the sun god Šamaš the power to "revive the moribund" (see the texts cited in Benjamin R. Foster, *Before the Muses: An Anthology of Akkadian Literature,* 2d ed. (Bethesda, Md.: CDL Press, 1996], 2.634, 638, 645–46).

41. So Jan Assmann, *Egyptian Solar Religion in the New Kingdom: Re, Amun and the Crisis of Polytheism,* trans. Anthony Alcock (London / New York: Kegan Paul International, 1995), 42.

42. This new iconographic depiction of the sun is simply a large-scale version of the hieroglyph for "light." The sun's "penetrating rays" are described in at least two hymns of this period (Assmann, *Egyptian Solar Religion,* 71, 73).

43. For various photographs, see *ANET,* 141–43 (# 405, 408, 409, 411).

44. See the discussion in Assmann, *Egyptian Solar Religion,* 80–86, who employs the less appropriate technical expression *creatio continua.* Biblical scholars have typically compared the Egyptian hymn to Psalm 104 (see chapter 6).

45. "Your rays, they embrace the lands of the earth as far as the end of your whole creation. As Re you penetrate to its limits and subject them to your beloved son" (lines 22–24; translated in Assmann, *Egyptian Solar Religion,* 96). For a complete translation of the hymn, see Erik Hornung, *Akhenaton and the Religion of Light,* trans. David Lorton (Ithaca / London: Cornell University Press, 1995), 79–83; *AEL,* 2.96–100; *ANET,* 369–70.

46. Much discussion over the years has focused on the way Akhenaton's physiognomy is depicted in a new art form, one that allegedly casts Pharaoh as "grotesque" and "feminine" (see Hornung, *Akhenaton and the Religion of Light,* 42–46). My own impression is that such artistic renderings of Akhenaton attempt to depict him as a child (e.g., thin arms, sunken chest, and soft physique), in light of the rejuvenating power of the Aten.

47. Hornung, *Akhenaton and the Religion of Light,* 50.

48. Translated in Assmann, *Egyptian Solar Religion,* 97. For complete translation, see Jan Assmann, *Ägyptische Hymnen und Gebete,* 2d ed. (OBO; Freiburg: Universitätsver-

lag / Göttingen: Vandenhoeck & Ruprecht, 1999), 327. See also the Suty-Hor hymn ("A Universalist Hymn to the Sun" in *ANET,* 367–68) composed during the reign of Amenhotep III: "The day is short, your journey is long, millions and hundreds of thousands of miles. Every day that you bring is a moment" (Assmann, *Egyptian Solar Religion,* 98). Later in the hymn, the deity is called "runner, racer, courser" (*ANET,* 368). In the sun, movement and time are one and the same.

49. Assmann, *Egyptian Solar Religion,* 98.

50. Egyptian liturgical literature also attributes communicative significance to the sun: "Light is the medium of communication between creator and creation. The gaze of the created at the sun is met in turn by the gaze of the creator, who animates their hearts and fills them with joy" (Assmann, *Egyptian Solar Religion,* 75).

51. See J. Eaton, "Some Questions of Philology and Exegesis in the Psalms," *JTS* 19 (1968): 604–5.

52. E.g., Ps 24:4; Job 11:4; Prov 14:4 (MT).

53. E.g., Gen 7:2, 8; Lev 14:4; 20:25; Deut 14:11, 20; Ps 51:10; Prov 30:12.

54. E.g., Exod 25:11, 17; 31:8; Lev 24:6. See the cognates listed in Eaton, "Some Questions of Philology," 605.

55. BDB, 263–64; *HALOT,* 1.265; Eaton, "Some Questions of Philology," 605.

56. The association of youthful vigor and "wedding canopy" in the psalm finds a parallel in a Sumerian/Akkadian bilingual prayer that refers to Šamaš as a "youthful warrior" who retires to his chamber with his wife, Aya, the goddess of dawn (see n. 79). From a royal ritual comes the following prayer for the king's protection: "O warrior Shamash, young hero, when you come forth from the pure heavens . . . Anu and Enlil greet you with joy" (Foster, *Before the Muses,* 2.648). Moreover, the exceptional prowess of the sun god Šamaš is acknowledged in lines 45–46 of the Akkadian Šamaš Hymn: "Among all the Igigi-gods there is none who does such wearisome toil but you, nor among the sum total of the gods one who does so much as you!" (Foster, *Before the Muses,* 2.533).

57. An interesting, albeit indirect, parallel is found among a number of Egyptian-styled ivories and seals of the eighth century in Palestine, both of northern and southern provenance, that profile the sun god as a child, sometimes combined with the image of the lotus plant, the traditional symbol of regeneration. The image of the "sun child," which achieved predominant status in the New Kingdom, may lie behind the claim of *tôrâ's* restorative capacities insofar as the "law" reflects the sun's renewing force. For a discussion of the seals, see Keel and Uehlinger, *God, Goddesses, and Images of God,* 249–51, 259.

58. For a selective survey of Akkadian texts, see Janowski, *Rettungsgewißheit,* 84–98.

59. *ANEP,* 246, 515; *ANET,* 163–180; *LCMA,* 71–142.

60. XLVII.85–89; *ANET,* 178; *LCMA,* 134.

61. XLVIII.95–99; *ANET,* 178; *LCMA,* 135; see also XLIX.12–17.

62. V.2–8; *ANET,* 165; *LCMA,* 80. Cf. Hammurabi's self-reference in the Epilogue: "I caused light to rise on them (*nūram ušēṣišinašim*)" (XLVII.21–22; *ANET,* 165; *LCMA,* 133).

63. I.38–40; *ANET,* 164; *LCMA,* 76–77.

64. V.19; *ANET,* 165.

65. For background and second literature, see Foster, *Before the Muses,* 2.679 n. 4.

66. Foster, *Before the Muses,* 645–46 (lines 40, 93–94).

67. Ibid., 637 (lines 2, 10). Elsewhere, the "destitute, widow, waif," and "female companion" are named (line 6).

68. II.129–133 in Erica Reiner, *Šurpu: A Collection of Sumerian and Akkadian Incantations* (AfOB 11; Osnabrück: Biblio Verlag, 1970 [1958]), 16.

69. Keel and Uehlinger, "Jahweh und die Sonnengottheit von Jerusalem," 279.

70. See the fourth strophe of the Chester Beatty Paprus IV (11.8–12.14).
71. See Janowski, *Rettungsgewißheit*, 169.
72. Jan Assmann, *Re und Amun: Die Krise des polytheistischen Weltbilds im Ägypten der 18.–20. Dynastie* (OBO 28; Freiburg: Universitätsverlag / Göttingen: Vandenhoeck & Ruprecht, 1983), 77.
73. *AEL*, 2.111.
74. Janowski, *Rettungsgewßheit*, 164–74, 178.
75. E.g., Hos 6:5 ("[God's] judgment goes forth as the light"). See the extended discussion in Janowski, "JHWH und der Sonnengott," 228–34.
76. *ANEP*, 178 (#529); André Parrot, *The Arts of Assyria*, trans. Stuart Gilbert and James Emmons (New York: Golden, 1961) 168, #215. For a discussion of the iconography and epigraphy, see Thorkild Jacobsen, "The Graven Image," in *Ancient Israelite Religion: Essays in Honor of Frank Moore Cross*, ed. Patrick D. Miller, Paul D. Hanson, S. Dean McBride (Philadelphia: Fortress, 1987), 20–23; Tryggve N. D. Mettinger, *No Graven Image? Israelite Aniconism in Its Ancient Near Eastern Context* (ConBOT 42; Stockholm: Almqvist & Wiksell International, 1995), 47–48.
77. Löning and Zenger, *To Begin with . . .*, 140.
78. See Joel 2:16, where *ḥuppâ* is set in parallel with *ḥeder* (cf. Song 1:4).
79. Hermann Gunkel points out that Šamaš is sometimes called "bridegroom" in Akkadian literature and discerns an allusion to a myth of the sun's marriage (Gunkel, *Die Psalmen*, 75). In the so-called "Prayer to the Gods of the Night," written in the first half of the second millennium B.C.E., one reads of Šamaš, Sin, Adad, and Ishtar having their regular sleep period, with Šamaš in particular sleeping in "his chamber" (*ANET*, 390–91). More vivid is a Sumerian/Akkadian bilingual prayer that portrays the sun coming home at the end of the day to his abode, Ebabbar, to meet Aya, the goddess of dawn:

> O Shamash, when you enter innermost heaven.
> . . . .
> Show your splendor to the Ebabbar, your lordly dwelling.
> May Aya, your beloved wife, meet you happily;
> May she make you relax.
> (Foster, *Before the Muses*, 2.660)

See also the conclusion of the Šamaš Hymn, lines 192–93, 200 (ibid., 2.539). For further examples that refer to Šamaš retiring to his holy chamber (*kummu*) during the night, see Janowski, *Rettungsgewißheit*, 40 n. 108. Of note in all the Akkadian examples is the motif of the sun's repose *at dusk*. The psalm's focus, by contrast, is on the dawn, the sun's *exit* from its cosmic "tent."

80. Or from "mountain of the deep" (*šad naqbi*). See, e.g., the ritual prayer of the king cited in Foster, *Before the Muses*, 2.644, as well as the numerous cylinder seals that depict the deity ascending a mountain. For discussion, see Janowski, *Rettungsgewißheit*, 41–42, 48–54.
81. E.g., Num 9:15; 17:22, 23.
82. See, e.g., Ps 119:15; Prov 2:8, 13, 19; 9:15; 17:23; Isa 2:3=Mic 4:2; cf. Deut 9:12, 16; 10:12 and passim. For further exploration of the "path" motif in the Psalter, see chapter 2.
83. Neither does it fly with wings, contrary to a standard iconographic motif (see above), nor traverse by barque, the ship that carried the sun god Re in early Egyptian lore.
84. Foster, *Before the Muses*, 2.641 (line 2).
85. Ibid., 2.644 (lines 11–16).
86. See the extensive list of victims delineated in lines 17–39 (ibid., 2.644–45).

87. Line 176 from the "Šamaš Hymn" (ibid., 2.538).
88. See line 3 of the prayer drawn from the "washing-of-the-mouth" ritual cited in Foster, *Before the Muses,* 651. The "Šamaš Hymn," moreover, refers to the deity's radiance spreading "out like a net over the world" (line 5; Ibid., 2.532).
89. Line 10; ibid., 2.532.
90. Line 50; ibid., 2.533.
91. Tzvi Abusch, "Mesopotamian Anti-Witchcraft Literature: Texts and Studies; Part I: The Nature of *Maqlû:* Its Character, Divisions, and Calendrical Setting," *JNES* 33 (1971): 258 n. 25. See Foster, *Before the Muses,* 2.633–34,
92. This series was concerned with warding off the effects of black magic through burning or melting figurines (see Foster, *Before the Muses,* 2.679).
93. I.e., the sun.
94. Reconstructed as *ētelil ina napaḫ ᵈŠamašᵛ* (*UTU*). Lines 153–58, translated in Abusch, "Mesopotamian Anti-Witchcraft Literature," 257–58.
95. Foster, *Before the Muses,* 679. See the collection in Reiner, *Šurpu,* 7–53.
96. Appendix rev. 10–13, 24–28 (Reiner, *Šurpu,* 53), translation by Foster, *Before the Muses,* 2.568.
97. Tablet I.10–23; Tablet V–VI.60–142 (Reiner, *Šurpu,* 11, 31–34).
98. Tablet V–VI.185–186 (Ibid., 35).
99. See Tablet VII.80/81: "May this man, son of his god, become pure, clean, resplendent" (Ibid., 38).
100. The abrupt change in imagery from gold's luster to honey's sweetness in the psalm suggests a deliberate shift from sight to taste, indicating the individual's *appropriation* of authoritative teaching.
101. For possible intertextual allusion to Gen 4:7, see n. 4.
102. The closest parallel in the *Šurpu* incantations is found in Tablet III.183: "[the s]in he knows and the sin he does not know," but it occurs in the context of sins committed by one's family and friends, dead or living (Reiner, *Šurpu,* 24).
103. See, e.g., Nahum M. Sarna, "Psalm XIX and the Near Eastern Sun-God Literature," in *Fourth World Congress of Jewish Studies. Papers,* vol. 1 (Jerusalem: World Union of Jewish Studies, 1967), 171–75; Stähli, *Solare Elemente,* 17–20.
104. J. Ross Wagner, "From the Heavens to the Heart: The Dynamics of Psalm 19 as Prayer," *CBQ* 61 (1999): 255.
105. So also Löning and Zenger, *To Begin with . . . ,* 133–34.
106. Taylor, *Yahweh and the Sun,* 222–23.
107. See Jon D. Levenson's treatment in "The Sources of Torah: Psalm 119 and the Modes of Revelation in Second Temple Judaism," in *Ancient Israelite Religion: Essays in Honor of Frank Moore Cross,* ed. Patrick D. Miller, Paul D. Hanson, and S. Dean McBride (Philadelphia: Fortress, 1987), 559–74.
108. Other examples of synagogue iconography that feature both the zodiac, or specifically Helios, and the Torah shrine include Naʾaneh (Helios without the zodiac), Jericho, and possibly Khirbet Susiya. While numerous synagogues feature the Torah shrine (e.g., Kokhav Ha-Yarden, Nabratein, Peqi-in, Beth She'an [fifth century], Capernaum, and Naʿaran), only Japhia, Husaifah, and possibly Khirbet Marus feature the zodiac without an accompanying depiction of the Torah shrine (based on and supplemented from the list developed by Andrew G. Vaughn and revised by James F. Strange in Jacob Neusner, *Symbol and Theology in Early Judaism* [Minneapolis: Fortress, 1991], 145–58).
109. For discussion of the design and symbolism of the zodiac depictions, see Rachel Hachlili, *Ancient Jewish Art and Archaeology in the Land of Israel* (HO 7; Leiden: Brill, 1988), 301–9.
110. E.g., two lulabs (palm branches) and ethrogs (citrus fruit tied to the lulab), which were used to commemorate the Feast of Tabernacles (Sukkot).

111. Joseph M. Baumgarten, "Art in the Synagogue: Some Talmudic Views," in *Jews, Christians, and Polytheists in the Ancient Synagogue: Cultural Interaction during the Greco-Roman Period,* ed. Steven Fine (London / New York: Routledge, 1999), 73.

112. Baumgarten observes that such archaeological findings reveal that a "considerable number of synagogues of the Amoraic period were built by Jews strongly influenced by contemporary Hellenism" (ibid., 75). He also notes that some rabbis (e.g., Rabbi Yohanan and Rabbi Abun) held a remarkably permissive position regarding the use of murals and mosaics in synagogues, whose driving impulse came from wealthy Jewish patrons "who viewed the synagogue not only as a source of salvation but as a means of displaying their acculturation in the Hellenistic world" (ibid., 82).

113. See Asher Ovadiah, *Mosaic Art in the Ancient Synagogues in Israel* (Tel Aviv: Genia Schreiber University Art Gallery, 1993), 61; idem, "Art of the Ancient Synagogues in Israel," in *Ancient Synagogues: Historical Analysis and Archaeological Discovery,* vol. 2, ed. Dan Urman and Paul Flesher (Studia Post-Biblical 47, 2; Leiden / New York / Cologne: Brill, 1995), 301–18, esp. 308. Ovadiah finds the *Sol Invictus* imagery to be the product of solar personification. For a different perspective, see Erwin R. Goodenough, *Jewish Symbols in the Greco-Roman Period,* abridged and ed. Jacob Neusner (Princeton: Princeton University Press, 1988), 135, 151–52, 168–73, who uses Philo as the interpretive lens to argue that Helios is symbolic of God. Hachlili, on the other hand, argues that the zodiac's primary function was calendrical (*Ancient Jewish Art,* 309).

114. Neusner, *Symbol and Theology in Early Judaism,* 181.

115. Indirect confirmation of such pre-Hellenistic association is given in *Numbers Rabbah* 12:4, which refers to the chariot mentioned in Song of Solomon 3:10 as symbolic of the "sun which is set on high and rides on a chariot, lighting up the world, as it is written (Psalm 19:6–7, Heb.): 'and he is a bridegroom coming out of his canopy'" (quoted in Ovadiah, *Mosaic Art,* 61 [misquoted on p. 81]. Ovadiah also quotes *Pirqei de Rabbi Eliezer VI*: "The sun is riding on a chariot and rises with a crown as a bridegroom, . . . and he is as a bridegroom coming out of his canopy" [ibid.]).

116. See Levenson's discussion in *The Death and Resurrection of the Beloved Son: The Transformation of Child Sacrifice in Judaism and Christianity* (New Haven, Conn. / London: Yale University Press, 1993), 73–74.

117. In the Torah alcove of the Dura-Europos synagogue in Syria (built in the third century C.E.), the same biblical scene flanks the Torah shrine opposite an elaborate menorah. See plate 21 in Ida Huberman, *Living Symbols: Symbols in Jewish Art and Tradition* (Tel Aviv: Massada, 1988).

118. An analogous case of the cosmic and the constitutional coexisting, albeit in separate positions, can be found in the two starkly different treatments of the so-called Davidic covenant: 2 Sam 7:1–29 and 2 Sam 23:1–7. The former is subsumed under the larger ethos of Israel's covenant, mediated by Moses. The latter speaks of a covenant that is cosmic in scope (and solarized in part) and hyperbolically ascribes to David nothing short of divine attributes (cf. Ps 72:5–7, 17). Canonically, one perspective does not shortchange the other. Rather, the vertical and the horizontal, a theology from above and one from below, complement each other. They coexist happily in the received text, as they did throughout much of Israel's history.

119. It is no accident, then, that Martin Luther saw in the image of the sun bursting forth from its wedding canopy a distinctly missiological message, namely, the gospel's spread across the world. See *Luther's Works,* vol. 18: *Lectures on the Minor Prophets,* ed. Hilton C. Oswald (St. Louis: Concordia, 1975), 31–32; *Luther's Works,* vol. 14: *Selected Psalms III,* ed. Jaroslav Pelikan (St. Louis: Concordia, 1958), 9–10. In his "Personal Prayer Book," Luther links Ps 19:5 with Jesus' commissioning of the dis-

ciples in Mark 16:15–16 (*Luther's Works*, vol. 43: *Devotional Writings*, ed. Gustav K. Wiencke [Philadelphia: Fortress, 1968], 45).

120. See the Introduction to this book.

Chapter 5: The Voice of Many Waters

1. Quoted by Kathleen Norris of a Benedictine sister, "Why the Psalms Scare Us," *Christianity Today* 40/8 (July 15, 1996): 22.

2. Craig Childs, *The Secret Knowledge of Water: Discovering the Essence of the American Desert* (Boston / New York / London: Little, Brown, 2000), xiv.

3. See the well-known indictment against Israel's worship practice in Amos 5:24: "Let justice roll down (*wĕyiggal*) as the waters (*mayim*), and righteousness like a perennial torrent (*naḥal 'êtān*)." The water imagery targets both the inundation of judgment against the upper class and the outpouring of righteousness in behalf of the poor. By means of this powerful metaphor, the prophet is able to say two things at once: God's justice destroys as much as it provides. See Jon L. Berquist, "Dangerous Waters of Justice and Righteousness: Amos 5:18–27," *BTB* 23 (1993): 54–63, esp. 61.

4. For a general description of the topography and climate of Palestine, see J. Maxwell Miller and John H. Hayes, *A History of Ancient Israel and Judah* (Philadelphia: Westminster, 1986), 40–52.

5. David C. Hopkins, *The Highlands of Canaan: Agricultural Life in the Early Iron Age* (SWBA 3; Decatur, Ga.: Almond, 1985), 86–87. Hopkins also notes that the rainfall of highland Canaan tends to "seal pores in the surface of the soil and, thus, reduce infiltration" (p. 91).

6. Hopkins, *Highlands of Canaan*, 95.

7. See *Atlas of Israel: Cartography, Physical Geography, Human and Economic Geography, History* (Jerusalem: Survey of Israel, Ministry of Labour / Amsterdam: Elsevier Publishing Co., 1970), sheets 12 and 13.

8. That is, the sea's waves; see v. 23.

9. Literally, "souls" (*nepeš*).

10. See n. 8.

11. See the same verb in Jonah 1:11–12.

12. So LXX, Vulgate, Peshitta; see Rykle Borger, "Weitere Ugaritologische Kleinigkeiten (III-V): III. Hebäisch MḤWZ (Psalm 107,30)," *UF* 1 (1969): 1–3.

13. The expression is drawn from the title of Sebastian Junger's gripping account of the monster gale that destroyed the *Andrea Gail* south of Nova Scotia on October 28, 1991, during a routine fishing expedition (*The Perfect Storm: A True Story of Men against the Sea* [New York: Norton, 1997]).

14. Thorkild Jacobsen, "The Battle between Marduk and Tiamat," *JAOS* 88 (1968): 104–08; Mark S. Smith, *The Ugaritic Baal Cycle*, vol. 1: *Introduction with Text, Translation and Commentary of KTU 1.1–1.2* (Leiden: Brill, 1994), 106–14. For Egyptian counterparts to this tradition, see Otto Kaiser, *Die Mythische Bedeutung des Meeres in Ägypten, Ugarit und Israel* (BZAW 78; Berlin: Töpelmann, 1959).

15. For the complete account, see the translation by Stephanie Dalley in *Myths from Mesopotamia: Creation, The Flood, Gilgamesh, and Others* (Oxford / New York: Oxford University Press, 1989), 254–55.

16. Ibid., 257.

17. *KTU* 1.2.ii.25; 1.3.iii.40–42; 1.5.i.1–3, 28–30. Translations are based on Mark S. Smith, *Ugaritic Narrative Poetry*, ed. Simon B. Parker (SBLWAWS 9; Atlanta: Scholars Press, 1997), 104, 111, 141–42, passim.

18. Translation by Smith, *Ugaritic Narrative Poetry*, 104.

19. So Smith, *Ugaritic Narrative Poetry,* 104. The enigmatic verb *yšt* may derive from the common root *šty,* "to drink," suggesting that Yamm's demise is by ingestion.

20. See the account in a letter to Zimri-Lim of Mari in which the West Semitic storm god, "Adad" (cognate to Baal's title, Haddu ["thunderer"]), and Tiamat are featured. For discussion see, Smith, *Ugaritic Narrative Poetry,* 84–86.

21. See Mark. S. Smith, *The Origins of Biblical Monotheism: Israel's Polytheistic Background and the Ugaritic Texts* (Oxford: Oxford University Press, 2001), 35.

22. For a synopsis of the ancient Near Eastern background and theological context of these two psalms, see Jon D. Levenson, *Creation and the Persistence of Evil: The Jewish Drama of Divine Omnipotence* (San Francisco: Harper & Row, 1988), 18–23.

23. Cf. 1 Kgs 8:65; 2 Kgs 24:7; Ps 80:11; Isa 7:20; Ezek 47:19.

24. So NJPS. The Hebrew literally reads "for the people, desert-dwellers [or hyenas?] (*lě'ām ṣiyîm*)." The expression is corrupt and defies textual reconstruction. For the various possibilities, see Marvin E. Tate, *Psalms 51–100* (WBC 20; Dallas: Word, 1990), 243–44.

25. For comparable imagery outside the Psalter, see also Isa 51:9–11; Job 26:12–13.

26. The tricolon of v. 3 is of special note, exhibiting both parallelism and ellipsis, whereby the middle segment clarifies the way in which the divine voice is set "over" the waters, namely as thunder: A [a:b] / B [a'] / A'[a:b'] //. Cf. 93:4.

27. Herbert G. May suggests that the verb *gʿr* be translated "roar" rather than "rebuke" in the context of the storm-god conflict with the sea dragon ("Some Cosmic Connotations of *Mayim Rabbîm,* 'Many Waters,'" *JBL* 74 [1955]: 17 n. 32). At any rate, envisioned is God's thunderous utterance.

28. So also Smith, *The Origins of Biblical Monotheism,* 37.

29. A comparable example of such a transition can be found in Pss 65:7–10; 78:13–14.

30. Levenson describes Psalm 104 as depicting "creation without opposition" (*Creation and the Persistence of Evil,* 53–65).

31. For an analysis of the distinctly mythological contours of the Red Sea, see Bernard F. Batto, "The Reed Sea: *Requiescat in Pace,*" *JBL* 102 (1983): 27–35; and idem, *Slaying the Dragon: Mythmaking in the Biblical Tradition* (Louisville, Ky.: Westminster/John Knox, 1992), 115–16.

32. In other psalmic accounts of the wilderness period, kings are defeated (78:55; 136:17–22).

33. The language of the second colon is nearly identical to the earliest poetic account of the exodus event, which also features highly mythologized language: Exod 15:8aβ.

34. See also Ps 136:13 ("who divided [*gōzēr*] the Red Sea into two").

35. A comparable reversal can be found in Isa 43:16–21, in which the new exodus from exile is described as a reversal of the old. The "path in the many waters" (v. 16) is now "rivers in the desert" (vv. 19, 20).

36. Literally "gave voice" (cf. next verse).

37. Reading Qere; Ketib features the plural form.

38. Literally, "were imperceptible" (*lō' nōdā'û*).

39. The shift in aspect from perfect to imperfect is significant, implying continued reign and conflict in creation.

40. Literally, "crushing" (√*dkh*).

41. The term indicates expansive glory, both divine (Ps 67:5) and watery (Exod 15:10).

42. For general discussion of its genre and its implications with regards to creation theology, see Karl Löning and Erich Zenger, *To Begin with, God Created . . . : Biblical Theologies of Creation,* trans. Omar Kaste (Collegeville, Minn.: Liturgical Press, 2000 [1997]), 33–34.

43. For discussion of this poetic technique, see Wilfred G. E. Watson, *Classical Hebrew Poetry: A Guide to Its Techniques* (JSOTSup 26; Sheffield: Sheffield Academic Press, 1986), 150–56.

44. The verb is frequently governed by the subject "hand" (e.g., Amos 5:19; Num 27:18, 23; Deut 34:9; Exod 29:10, 15, 19; Lev 1:4).
45. See the use of *yāwēn* in Ps 40:2, which is paired with "pit of tumult."
46. Read *mîyaḥēl* (see LXX and Targum) for MT's *mĕyaḥēl*. The psalmist's eyes are clouded with tears from weeping (cf. Lam 2:11; Ps 119:28, 123).
47. The poetic alliteration is unmistakably frightful: *'āṣĕmû maṣmîtay*.
48. The concluding colon is a complaint, not a question (contra NRSV). For the deictic force of the temporal adverb *'āz*, see *IBHS* 39.3.1h (p. 658) and Tate, *Psalms 51–100*, 189.
49. *BHS* suggests emending the social reference to *miššô'â* ("devastation, waste"), but without textual support.
50. As is well known, the allusion to death has its parallel in the Ugaritic deity of death, Mot, whose mouth swallows up Baal (*KTU* 1.5.ii.2–6; 1.6.ii.21–23).
51. Elsewhere, the terms are used interchangeably: the "roaring" of the seas can indicate the din of international threat and battle (e.g., Isa 17:12–13; Jer 48:45; 51:55; Hos 10:14; Amos 2:2; Ps 74:23). "Tumult," in turn, is applied to nature: approaching storm (1 Kgs 18:41) and, through the cognate *hămôt*, the seas (Isa 17:12).
52. The Masoretic pointing of the adjective as a construct carries superlative force.
53. The form could be taken as a plural of amplification, and thus translated as a singular. Perfect sense, however, can be made from the semantic plural, which acknowledges the existence of other sanctuaries in the land, while asserting Jerusalem's primacy.
54. See, e.g., Isa 8:6. For its mythical allusions, see Steven Tuell, "The Rivers of Paradise: Ezekiel 47:1–12 and Genesis 2:10–14," in *God Who Creates: Essays in Honor of W. Sibley Towner*, ed. William P. Brown and S. Dean McBride Jr. (Grand Rapids: Eerdmans, 2000), 178–79.
55. See 2 Chr 32:30 (cf. vv. 2–3).
56. MT has "shatter" (*mḥṣ*), as in the preceding verse. The context requires slight emendation in favor of the root *rḥṣ*("wash"). See Ps 58:10 and the textual versions.
57. Such imagery is intimately associated with the pit elsewhere (see chapter 1).
58. For comparable imagery, see Ps 58:10; Isa 63:1–6.
59. See Isa 25:11 for the use of √*śḥḥ* and its nominal cognate *śāḥû* in Ezek 47:5.
60. See Peshitta; MT has "strife" (*mādôn*).
61. If the term is derived from the verbal root *nwd* ("move to and fro, flutter"), which in the hiphil and hitpolel can denote physical "shaking," then the above meaning is rendered (e.g., Jer 22:10; Isa 51:19; Nah 3:7). The other possibility is "flask" or "skin bottle," equivalent to the final word in v. 8aβ in this psalm (√*n'd; "flask"), which makes little sense. The similarity of roots indicates a provocative wordplay.
62. Josh 9:4, 13; 1 Sam 16:20.
63. It has been argued that the reference to stumbling feet in Ps 56:13 is a gloss inspired by 116:8 (so *BHS*). If so, a case can be made that reference to tears in Psalm 116 is a gloss inspired by 56:8. Indeed, in light of some Hebrew and Syriac textual evidence, the reference to tears in Psalm 116 may be secondary.
64. The MT ("bearing the sowing of seed") contains an extra verb (*nōśē'*) inadvertently reduplicated from the following verse.
65. Read *ḥikkî* for MT's *kōḥî* ("strength").
66. See Deut 34:7, which literally reads "Moses was one hundred twenty years old when he died; his sight was unimpaired and his moisture (*lēḥōh*) had not left." See also Ezek 37:11.
67. It is the "rebellious [who] live in a parched land," another psalmist observes (68:6b; cf. 107:34).
68. The expression is elliptical in Hebrew. The following verb in v. 7aβ (*kālĕtāh*), perhaps misplaced in its present context, fills the gap nicely.

69. In a forthcoming paper, P. Kyle McCarter ties the meaning of √'dn with the sense of "to make rich/plentiful/abundant" (Colloquium for Biblical Research, August 19, 2001, Duke University). The parallelism in the psalm, moreover, suggests such a sense. See also Gen 18:12; Neh 9:25; Jer 31:12; 51:34.

70. Exilic and postexilic prophetic literature taps river imagery to highlight the eschatological restoration of God's people (Ezek 47:1–2; Joel 3:18; Zech 14:8).

71. See also chapter 8.

72. Derived from the root *qhl*, the term is a hapax that most likely refers to various groups within the worshiping community, delineated along tribal lines in v. 27.

73. Parallelism suggests the emendation proposed by *BHS* (*mĕqôr* > *miqrā'ê* ["convocations"]), but without adequate textual support. (See the plural featured in the LXX ["fountains"].)

74. For further discussion, see chapter 8.

75. The term *nĕdābôt*, in the form of an abstract plural, can also connote voluntary generosity (cf. Hos 14:4; Ps 54:6; Deut 23:23) and, within a cultic context, freewill offerings (e.g., Exod 35:29; Ezra 1:4; 8:28).

76. The verb √*nwp* (hiphil) literally means to "wave, move to and fro," such as a hand (2 Kgs 5:11), a tool (Exod 20:25; Deut 27:5), or the priestly "wave-offering" before the temple altar (Exod 29:26; Lev 7:30; 23:11).

77. To be emended as *rōkēb be'ăbôt* or *rōkēb ba'ărāpôt* from *rōkēb ba'ărābôt* ("rider of deserts"), in light of the Ugaritic epithet for Baal, *rkb 'rpt*, "cloud rider" (*KTU* 1.4.iii.18). Cf. v. 33.

78. Cf. Isa 41:17–20, which opens with a similar statement that leads directly into God's provision for the exiles, transforming them into a veritable garden of Eden. For discussion, see William P. Brown, *The Ethos of the Cosmos: The Genesis of Moral Imagination in the Bible* (Grand Rapids: Eerdmans, 1999), 241–48.

79. E.g., Pss 78:15–16; 105:41; 114:8; cf. Exod 17:6; Num 20:11.

80. See n. 76.

81. The root is *šwq*.

82. Literally, "their grain."

83. See the use of *'ăgālâ* in Amos 2:13; Gen 45:19, 21, 27; Num 7:3, 6–8. The imagery may also recall the story of the ark of the covenant, which tells of the ark carried by cart in 1 Sam 6:7–14 and 2 Sam 6:3. In one important instance, the term appears to designate a war chariot (Ps 46:9), though the text is disputed (LXX reads *'ăgîlôt* ["shields"] for *'ăgālôt* ["chariots"]). The RSV renders the term in 65:11b as "tracks of thy chariots." David A. Dorsey has cast doubt on the etymological connection between *'ăgālâ* and *ma'gāl* (*The Roads and Highways of Ancient Israel* [ASOR Library of Biblical and Near Eastern Archaeology; Baltimore: Johns Hopkins University Press, 1991], 234–36). However, the case of Psalm 65 is not taken up in his discussion.

84. See n. 77.

85. *BHS* suggests *mayim ya'ămōdû* ("the waters stand"), an ingenious proposal lacking textual support.

86. Reading Ketib; Qere reads plural.

87. Read LXX (which apparently reads *ya'ărîk*) instead of MT ("may they fear you" [*yîrā'ûkā*]), which makes little sense in context.

88. Cf. Amos 7:1, which makes specific reference to the king's field.

89. The hapax likely means to "drip" in Qal.

90. Read with the versions the abstract *ṣedeq* instead of the substantive adjective *ṣaddîq*, "righteous one."

91. Literally "sprout."

92. The word is corrupt and requires only slight emendation to make good sense: *geber*

rāš > *geber rōš* (=*rō'š*), meaning "head," hence, "leader" (so also William McKane, *Proverbs: A New Approach* [OTL; Philadelphia: Westminster, 1970], 628–29).

93. For a more general description of the scourge of monarchic rule, see 1 Sam 8:10–17.

94. Pss 6; 32; 38; 51; 102; 130; 143. For discussion of the generic contours of these psalms, see Harry P. Nasuti, *Defining the Sacred Songs: Genre, Tradition and the Post-Critical Interpretation of the Psalms* (JSOTSup 218; Sheffield: Sheffield Academic Press, 1999), 30–52.

95. To cite just one example, water as cleanser is found in the Sumerian and Akkadian *Šurpu* ritual incantations (see chapter 4 for background discussion). A striking but natural convergence of watery chaos and cleansing is found in the concluding incantation of Tablet IX: "High waters! Flowing straight from the high mountains, waters, flowing out straight from the pure Euphrates, born of the Apsû . . . have touched the body of (this) man, son of his god, made him clean, made him pure" (lines 119–127*; trans. Erica Reiner, *Šurpu: A Collection of Sumerian and Akkadian Incantations* [1958; reprint, AfOB 11; Osnabrück: Biblio Verlag, 1970], 49).

96. This striking shift within an identical image has prompted *BHS* to propose, without textual support, its deletion.

97. Mount Hermon lies north of Bashan and broaches territory traditionally held by Syria in biblical times.

98. For translation issues and discussion of structure, see chapter 3.

99. For textual issues and discussion of the first strophe, see chapter 6.

100. The text is corrupt; read *běsōk 'addirim,* as proposed by *BHS*. The psalmist evidently recalls a time in which she eluded or escaped from unnamed enemies and found refuge. "Covert" can also designate the lair of lions (Pss 27:5; 76:3).

101. The term can refer to either multitude (so NRSV) or tumult, as of the sea (Isa 60:5; Jer 51:55). The parallelism suggests *joyous* clamor.

102. The root *hmh* exhibits a wide range of significance. It refers frequently to the tumult of the sea or flood (Isa 17:12; 51:15; Jer 5:22; 6:23; 31:35; 50:42; 51:55; Ps 46:3), the bark of a dog (Ps 59:6, 14), and the sound of musical instruments (Isa 16:11; Jer 48:36), as well as the moans of inner distress (e.g., Isa 16:11; Jer 31:20; Song 5:4; Pss 55:8; 77:4).

103. Read *pinê 'ělôhay* (cf. v. 11), which includes the first word in the next verse (so also Peter C. Craigie, *Psalms 1–50* [WBC 19; Waco, Tex.: Word, 1983], 323–24).

104. The epithet is found elsewhere in the context of water imagery: Josh 3:10 (Jordan River); Hos 1:10 ("the sand of the sea"); 84:2 (see vv. 5–7).

105. In addition to Psalm 42, God is frequently cast as the object of longing and hope elsewhere in the Psalter (e.g., 27:14; 33:20; 37:7–8; 62:1; 63:1, 5; 130:5–6).

106. See vv. 3–4.

107. The Jordan is formed by three headstreams supplied by the snow waters that seep from the top of Mount Hermon: Nahal Snir (Wadi Hatzbani), Nahal Dan, and Nahal Hermon (Wadi Bāniyās). Mizar, whose location is unknown, stands presumably in the vicinity.

108. Scholars have typically found these two scenes to be incompatible, if not mutually exclusive: the latter scene conveying the terror of primeval chaos; the other depicting an uplifting context of worship. See, e.g., Craigie, *Psalms 1–50, 326–27*; Hans-Joachim Kraus, *Psalms 1–59,* trans. Hilton C. Oswald (Minneapolis: Augsburg, 1988), 440; Peter Riede, *Im Netz des Jägers: Studien zur Feindmetaphorik der Individualpsalmen* (WMANT 85; Neukirchen-Vluyn: Neukirchener Verlag, 2000), 317; and Luis Alsonso Schökel, "The Poetic Structure of Psalm 42–43," *JSOT* 1 (1976): 4–8.

109. For a haunting account of how running water in a wadi can imitate human voices, see Childs, *The Secret Knowledge of Water,* xiv–xv.

Chapter 6: The Song of Leviathan

1. Quoted in Richard Kearney, *Poetics of Imagining: Modern to Post-Modern* (New York: Fordham University Press, 1998), 235.
2. 1 Cor 15:32a.
3. See Patrick D. Miller, "Animal Names as Designations in Ugaritic and Hebrew," *UF* 2 (1970): 177–86. Miller limits his survey to animal names used as designations or titles, or to what he later refers to as animal imagery that "is not developed in any [metaphorical] way" (pp. 177, 183). For a fuller treatment that incorporates the iconographic and further epigraphic evidence, see Peter Riede, *Im Netz des Jägers: Studien zur Feindmetaphorik der Individualpsalmen* (WMANT 85; Neukirchen-Vluyn: Neukirchener Verlag, 2000), esp. 150–278. Riede, however, does not address the Psalter's theological shape.
4. The image of "bees" in Psalm 118 is cast as a simile in reference to the nations that surround the king. For discussion, see Riede, *Im Netz des Jägers*, 256–66.
5. The "boar" in Psalm 80 symbolizes the nations, perhaps Babylon in particular, that "ravage" the vine transplanted from Egypt by YHWH.
6. The one predatory animal not mentioned in the psalms but indicated elsewhere in biblical tradition is the bear (see Hos 13:8; Amos 5:19; 1 Sam 17:34, 37; Prov 28:15; Lam 3:10). For discussion, see Riede, *Im Netz des Jägers*, 267–77.
7. See, e.g., Prov 30:30; Hos 13:7; Amos 3:8; Isa 31:4; Mic 5:8; Job 38:39–40.
8. See, e.g., Isa 31:4; Mic 5:8; Nah 2:11–12. See also Gen 49:9–10, where the figure of the lion designates political Judah, and Ezek 19:2–9, in which the "young lion" (*kĕpîr*) targets two proud and predatory princes/kings of Judah, both of whom "devoured" people yet became caught in a pit set by the nations.
9. The singular verb maintains the metaphorical image of the single lion yet denotes collective sense in light of the previous verse.
10. For the translation possibilities, see Norbert Lohfink, "Ps 7, 2–6—vom Löwen gejagt," in *Die Freude an Gott—Unsere Kraft: Festschrift für Otto Bernhard Knoch zum 65. Geburtstag,* ed. Johannes Joachim Degenhardt (Stuttgart: Verlag Katholisches Bibelwerk 1991), 62–63; Riede, *Netz des Jägers,* 164–66. Although *nepeš* can denote "life" or serve as the personal object ("me"), the psalmist graphically conveys the way lions kill their prey, as portrayed in the Nimrud ivory relief dated to the late eighth/early seventh century B.C.E., shown here (see Riede, *Netz des Jägers,* 160 [#16]), and in an eighth-century ivory from Samaria (see Othmar Keel and Christoph Uehlinger, *Gods, Goddesses, and Images of God in Ancient Israel,* trans. Thomas H. Trapp [Minneapolis: Fortress, 1998], 189 [#203]; Riede, *Netz des Jägers,* 160 [#15]).
11. Contrary to the Masoretic correction, read with Ketib (*ḥelkā'îm*) as the plural form for the noun in v. 8 (so also Riede, *Netz des Jägers,* 176 n. 184).
12. For an analysis of the mythological and exegetical background of this passage, see Riede, *Netz des Jägers,* 215–30.
13. See, e.g., Prov 10:6, 11, 18, 32; 11:12; 12:18–19; 26:18, 22–25, 28.
14. Peshitta reads "dogs" (*klb'*), a case of dittography.
15. Textual emendation is unnecessary. The participial form of the root *lhṭ* ("to flame") can denote consuming wrath (e.g., Isa 42:25).
16. Read *nokrîm* instead of the hapax *nēkîm* ("smitten"?).
17. Several passages outside the Psalter cast God in the role of lion: Job 10:16; 16:9; Lam 3:10b–11; Isa 38:13. For detailed discussion, see Riede, *Netz des Jägers,* 187–93.
18. LXX reads "snake," which breaks the parallelism that follows in the next colon (Riede, *Netz des Jägers,* 186 n. 253).
19. For extended discussion, see Riede, *Netz des Jägers,* 247–53.
20. It is no coincidence that the Yahwist identifies a word-bearing serpent as the provo-

cateur of disruption in the pristine garden of creation (Gen 3:1–5). Garrett Green aptly refers to the wily serpent as the first interpreter of Scripture (*Theology, Hermeneutics, and Imagination: The Crisis of Interpretation at the End of Modernity* [Cambridge: Cambridge University Press, 2000], 1).

21. E.g., 1 Sam 17:43; Prov 26:11; Eccl 9:4; Matt 15:26–27; 2 Pet 2:22.

22. This abrupt citation indicates the brazen attitude of impunity shared by the "bellowing" enemies.

23. See the reference to the enemies' "pride" in v. 12.

24. Literally, "from the paw of the dog."

25. It is rare to find in ancient Near Eastern literature outside the Bible, a rapprochement between human and beast; see Enkidu's habitation in the wild recounted in the Epic of Gilgamesh, Tablet I.

26. So Mark S. Smith, *Psalms: The Divine Journey* (New York: Paulist, 1987), 73 n. 36.

27. One notable exception is found in Ps 18:23, 34–42; see below.

28. For a sampling of animal portrayals in the royal annals, see William P. Brown, *The Ethos of the Cosmos: The Genesis of Moral Imagination in the Bible* (Grand Rapids: Eerdmans, 1999), 352–54.

29. The construct form is most likely epexegetical or appositional in function.

30. Read *hitrappēs* (imperative) for MT *mitrappēs* (participle). The Masoretic rendering is attributable to a combination of dittography of the *mem* with the preceding word and graphic confusion (resulting in haplography) with the subsequent letter (*taw*).

31. Read *běrōṣê* for MT *běraṣṣê* ("in [silver] bars"?).

32. I.e., tribute.

33. Read the imperative form *bazzēr* instead of the perfect form.

34. So Miller, "Animal Names," 180–81. For the plethora of suggestions, see Marvin E. Tate, *Psalms 51–100* (WBC 20; Dallas: Word, 1990), 183–84.

35. See the proposal of M. Dahood, *Psalms II* (AB 16; Garden City, N.Y.: Doubleday, 1968), 150.

36. So NJPS. The Hebrew literally reads "for the people, desert dwellers [or hyenas?]" (*lĕ'ām ṣiyîm*). The expression is likely corrupt. For the various possibilities, see Tate, *Psalms 51–100,* 243–44.

37. See chapter 5.

38. In Jer 51:34, Tannin represents Babylon.

39. Read *hārîm kĕṣippôr* in light of LXX.

40. LXX consistently renders the term as *pelekan,* which is improbable in Isa 34:11; Zeph 2:14; and here. G. R. Driver suggests "scops-owl" ("Birds in the Old Testament. II. Birds in Life," *PEQ* 87 [1955]: 131).

41. Oded Borowski, *Every Living Thing: Daily Use of Animals in Ancient Israel* (Walnut Creek, Calif.: AltaMira, 1998), 150–51.

42. See the thorough syntactical study in Riede, *Netz des Jägers,* 300–305. The verb reflects a root attested in nominal form in Ezek 2:10 and in verbal form in Isa 16:2; 26:17. See also Driver, "Birds II," 131 n. 4; and *The Dictionary of Classical Hebrew,* ed. David J. A. Clines (Sheffield: Sheffield Academic Press, 1995), 2.540, which identifies a *hyh* III ("to bewail"), citing Isa 16:2; 26:17; Ps 102:8.

43. The expected participial form is feminine; the verb points back to the psalmist's own identity (Riede, *Netz des Jägers,* 304).

44. Lev 11:17–18; Deut 14:16–17.

45. E.g., Zeph 2:13–14; Isa 34:11.

46. Riede, *Netz des Jägers,* 293.

47. Cf. Solomon's prayer of dedication for the completed temple in 1 Kgs 8:38, 42–43, 44–45, 48–49, in which prayer is oriented toward the temple for it to be heard and

acted on by God, not unlike the Muslim practice of qibla, or praying in the direction of Mecca.

48. Borowski, *Every Living Thing*, 150–51. See chapter 1.
49. Outside the Psalter, God is envisioned as a predatory animal, either bear or lion, in Job 10:16; 16:9; Lam 3:10–11; and Isa 38:13.
50. See the ancient Near Eastern antecedents for the theriomorphic portrayals of deities in Mark S. Smith, *The Origins of Biblical Monotheism: Israel's Polytheistic Background and the Ugaritic Texts* (Oxford: Oxford University Press, 2001), 32–35. Well known is the depiction of the warrior-goddess Anat as a bird.
51. E.g., Pss 17:8b; 36:7b; 57:1b; 61:4; 63:7; 91:1–4.
52. Literally, "the scorn of humans."
53. Cf. Job 17:14; 25:6.
54. See, e.g., Job 21:26; Isa 14:11. Cf. Isa 41:14.
55. See, particularly, the so-called psalms of Asaph (Psalms 50, 73–83). For discussion, see James L. Crenshaw, *The Psalms: An Introduction* (Grand Rapids: Eerdmans, 2001), 23–26.
56. The MT, as it stands, features the more difficult text compared to one Hebrew manuscript and other versions that feature the singular form.
57. Dependent on the context, the same preposition denotes two different meanings.
58. Crenshaw, *The Psalms*, 126.
59. Read *'ayyelet* instead of MT's *'ayyāl* ("buck"). The form is feminine, owing to haplography with the following verbal form.
60. So a few Hebrew manuscripts, Peshitta, and Targum. Most Masoretic texts attest "appear," which avoids reference to perceiving God directly, a later exegetical move reflected elsewhere in the LXX (see A. T. Hanson, "The Treatment in the LXX of the Theme of Seeing God," in *Septuagint, Scrolls and Cognate Writings: Papers Presented to the International Symposium on the Septuagint and Its Relations to the Dead Sea Scrolls and Other Writings [Manchester, 1990]*, ed. George J. Brooke and Barnabs Lindars, S.S.F. [SCSS 33; Atlanta: Scholars, 1992], 557–68).
61. Cf. reference to "rock" in v. 9. For the use of water imagery in this psalm, see chapter 5.
62. See Othmar Keel and Christoph Uehlinger, *God, Goddesses, and Images of God*, 185–86. Moreover, among the inscribed West Semitic seals, the image of the grazing doe appears to be exclusively Hebrew (Benjamin Sass, "The Pre-Exilic Hebrew Seals: Iconism vs. Aniconism," in *Studies in the Iconography of Northwest Semitic Inscribed Seals*, ed. Benjamin Sass and Christoph Uehlinger [OBO 125; Fribourg: University of Fribourg Press / Göttingen: Vandehoeck & Ruprecht, 1993], 224).
63. See chapter 1.
64. The superscription identifies the psalm with David in conflict with his enemies, including Saul (cf. vv. 43–44).
65. Read without the Masoretic suffix ("my"), which could have occurred through dittography.
66. Read, most likely, *'ezrātĕkā*, instead of Masoretic *'anwatkā* ("your humility"?); cf. 2 Sam 22:36 ("your answering").
67. See the discussion of 2 Sam 23:20 in Miller, "Animal Names," 185.
68. See n. 28 above.
69. But cf. the metaphorical use of such imagery to designate national and royal entities: Gen 49:9 (Judah); Deut 33:22 (Dan); Jer 4:7 (Babylon?); 50:17 (Assyria and King Nebuchadrezzar); Ezek 19:1–9 (Judah, Jehoahaz, and Jehoiachin or Zedekiah).
70. Flight does not figure in the metaphorical context of this psalm.
71. For examples, see Brown, *The Ethos of the Cosmos*, 356–59.
72. Read Qere; Ketib reads, "It is he who made us, not ourselves."

73. Iran Stele I A.27; see Hayim Tadmor, *The Inscriptions of Tiglath-Pileser III* (Jerusalem: Israel Academy of Sciences and Humanities, 1994), 97.
74. *AR* 1.234 [A.0.78.1.i.29–31]; see also *AR* 2.13 [A.0.87.1.i.34]; 2.194 [A.0.101.1.i.13].
75. Cf. the pseudepigraphical Psalms 151–153, which focus specifically on David's protection of the flock as a shepherd boy (*The Old Testament Pseudepigrapha*, ed. James H. Charlesworth [Garden City, N.Y.: Doubleday, 1985] 2.612–17).
76. See below. For a brief introduction to creation theology in the Psalter, see James L. Mays, "'Maker of Heaven and Earth': Creation in the Psalms," in *God Who Creates: Essays in Honor of W. Sibley Towner*, ed. William P. Brown and S. Dean McBride Jr. (Grand Rapids: Eerdmans, 2000), 75–86.
77. Pss 7:2; 10:9; 22:13, 21; see also 35:17.
78. There is no compelling reason for textual emendation despite the LXX.
79. Read with LXX, Peshitta, and Targum; MT has "mountains."
80. The text is hopelessly corrupt. For a review of the proposals with a new solution, see Mark S. Smith, "Psalm 8:2b–3: New Proposals for Old Problems," *CBQ* 59 (1997): 637–41, who reconstructs two first-person cohortatives as *'ašîrâ 'etĕnâ*, resulting in the following translation: "*I will sing [and] celebrate* your splendor over the heavens." Based on Smith's reconstruction, I propose to translate the verbs as a hendiadys.
81. The synonymous, appositional arrangement of *'ŏlĕlîm wĕyōnĕqîm* (literally "infants and nurslings") constitutes a hendiadys. Citing the "suckers" (*ynqm*) in *KTU* 1.23.59, 61, Helmut Ringgren views the "infants" of Psalm 8 as cosmic enemies or "evil forces in the world" that God must vanquish, in parallel with the "avenging enemy" at the end of v. 2 ("Some Observations on the Text of the Psalms," *Maarav* 5–6 [Spring, 1990]: 308). The possible mythological overtones, however, do not cohere with the poetic context. First, Ps 73:9, an alleged parallel cited by Ringgren, fails to indicate familiarity with this myth, since it is the wicked, not infantile figures, who are identified as having set their mouths "against heaven" and "over the earth." Moreover, in parallel with the previous line, the reference to the "mouth" of infants can refer only to the discourse of praise, not to devouring mouths.
82. The root of *'ōz* should be identified with *'wz* ("to take refuge") rather from *'zz* ("to be strong"), although some semantic overlap may be intended. See Ps 104:5, 8. Cf. Ringgren, "Some Observations on the Text of the Psalms," 308.
83. Smith suggests that the Masoretic *ṣôrĕrêkā* be repointed to **ṣûrĕrêkā*, "stronghold," an attractive, though speculative, proposal ("Psalm 8:2b–3," 640–41). For similar use of the preposition with identical or similar objects, see Pss 5:8; 27:11; 69:19.
84. The parallelism suggests that the Masoretically pointed hiphil infinitive construct was originally a finite form of the stem with a proclitic asseverative use of *l-*, as attested frequently in Ugaritic. See Daniel Sivan, *A Grammar of the Ugaritic Language* (Leiden / New York / Cologne: Brill, 1997), 191–92; Smith, "Psalm 8:2b–3," 640.
85. The appositional conjunction of *'ôyēb ûmitnaqqēm* constitutes a hendiadys.
86. Hebrew *'ĕlōhîm* refers here to the divine beings that form the divine council. In Job 1–2, they are referred to as "sons of God" (*bĕnê hā'ĕlōhîm*, 1:6; 2:1; cf. Ps 82:1).
87. For the background behind humanity's cultic role vis-à-vis the deity in Genesis 1, see S. Dean McBride Jr., "Divine Protocol: Genesis 1:1–2:3 as Prologue to the Pentateuch," in *God Who Creates: Essays in Honor of W. Sibley Towner*, ed. William P. Brown and S. Dean McBride Jr. (Grand Rapids: Eerdmans, 2000), 15–18.
88. See chapter 5.
89. See Walter Harrelson, "Psalm 8 on the Power and Mystery of Speech," in *Tehillah le-Moshe: Biblical and Judaic Studies in Honor of Moshe Greenberg*, ed. Mordechai Cogan et al. (Winona Lake, Ind.: Eisenbrauns, 1997), 69–72.

90. So Erich Zenger, "'Du kannst das Angesicht der Erde erneuern' (Ps 104, 30)," *Bibel und Liturgie* 64 (1991): 77.
91. See Rüdiger Bartelmus, "Die Tierwelt in der Bible I: Exegetische Beobachtungen zu einem Teilaspekt der Diskussion um eine Theologie der Natur," in *Gefährten und Feinde des Menschen: Das Tier in der Lebenswelt des alten Israel,* ed. Bernd Janowski, Ute Neumann-Gorsolke, Uwe Glessmer (Neukirchen-Vluyn: Neukirchener Verlag, 1993), 269.
92. Or "wild donkeys" (*pĕrā'îm*).
93. *ḥăsîdâ.*
94. Or "rock badgers" (*šĕpannîm*).
95. *qinyānekā;* read plural with many Hebrew manuscripts. In any case, the Masoretic singular spelling conveys collective sense.
96. *lĕśaḥeq-bô.* The antecedent of the preposition in the final clause is Leviathan, not the sea (see below).
97. See, particularly, v. 30, which enlists the verb √*br'* to designate renewal and restoration. Jon D. Levenson appropriately claims that the psalm is "not a depiction of the process of creation" but a "panorama of the natural world" (*Creation and the Persistence of Evil: The Jewish Drama of Divine Omnipotence* [San Francisco: Harper & Row, 1988], 57).
98. Erhard Gerstenberger, "Versöhnung mit der Natur? Anfragen an gottesdienstliche Texte des Alten Testaments (Ps 8 und 104)," in *Versöhnung mit der Natur?,* ed. Jürgen Moltmann (Munich: Chr. Kaiser Verlag, 1986), 141–49. See also James Limburg, "Down to Earth Theology: Psalm 104 and the Environment," *Currents in Theology and Mission* 21 (1994): 344–45. Mining its ecological implications, Erich Zenger observes that the psalm is "no kitschy-idyllic music-meditation, but a critical utopian song, which today calls for ecological change" (Zenger, "'Du kannst das Angesicht der Erde erneuern,'"84).
99. See Zenger, "'Du kannst das Angesicht der Erde erneuern,'"80.
100. See also Patrick D. Miller, "The Poetry of Creation: Psalm 104," in *God Who Creates: Essays in Honor of W. Sibley Towner,* ed. William P. Brown and S. Dean McBride Jr. (Grand Rapids: Eerdmans, 2000), 87–103.
101. Cf. Isa 27:1; Ps 74:14; Job 3:8; 41 [40:25–41:26, Heb.].
102. Cited in Levenson, *Creation and the Persistence of Evil,* 17. This felicitous designation by one of Jon Levenson's students is rejected by Levenson himself in view of the alleged parallel he cites from Job 41:1–2 [40:25–26, Heb.], which indicates to him the conflict and captivity of this erstwhile agent of chaos (but cf. Brown, *The Ethos of the Cosmos,* 350–75). Nevertheless, wonder over creation's order is the norm in Psalm 104. As with all the creatures enumerated in the psalm, Leviathan is a creature sustained and blessed, and yet carries the special distinction of being God's playmate. The psalmist replaces the language of captivity and bondage with the language of *creation.* Leviathan is neither captured nor tamed.
103. As Mark Smith points out, the "kindly attitude toward cosmic monsters" is not unique to Israelite religion, but is attested in Mesopotamian and Ugaritic literature (*The Origins of Biblical Monotheism,* 33–35).
104. See Rolf Jacobsen, "The Costly Loss of Praise," *ThT* 57 (2000): 375–85.
105. For translation, see chapter 7.
106. Read Qere.
107. Literally, "a law that cannot be transgressed." The verb is likely passive.
108. MT pointing indicates completed action, in contrast to LXX and Peshitta, suggesting a causal connection with the universal praise prescribed earlier.
109. See the *kî* clauses in vv. 5b–6, 13b.
110. The Hebrew name is identical with the reference in Gen 1:21, which depicts the *tannînîm* as bona fide creations of God on the fifth day.

111. So Terence E. Fretheim, "Nature's Praise of God in the Psalms," *Ex Auditu* 3 (1987): 28.
112. See also ibid., 27–30.
113. See Michele Piccirillo's introductory discussion in *The Mosaics of Jordan*, ed. P. M. Bikai and T. A. Dailey (ACORP 1; Amman, Jordan: American Center of Oriental Research / Jordan Press Foundation, 1993), 41. For a sample survey of animal images in the early synagogues of Palestine (e.g., Ma'on/Nirim, Gaza Maiumas, and Beth Shean), see Asher Ovadiah, *Mosaic Art in the Ancient Synagogues in Israel* (Tel Aviv: Genia Schreiber University Art Gallery, 1993), 58–59. See also chapter 4.
114. Piccirillo, *Mosaics of Jordan*, 129–31, 146, 234–35.
115. Ibid., 106–7. The picture is on pp. 96 and 98.
116. By way of personal reflection, I cannot help but point out that the Psalter exposes how the first question of the Larger Catechism of the Presbyterian *Book of Confessions* is incorrectly framed. It should read: What is the chief and highest end of *all creation*? To glorify God, and to enjoy God's presence forever.

Chapter 7: "On You I Was Cast from My Birth"

1. John Calvin, *Concerning the Eternal Predestination of God*, trans. J. K. S. Reid (Cambridge: James Clarke, 1961), 162.
2. For one attempt to achieve some degree of coherence among a limited number of psalmic images ("power and justice"), see Mary E. Mills, *Images of God in the Old Testament* (Collegeville, Minn.: Liturgical Press, 1998), 109–21.
3. On the marks of divinity vis-à-vis the human in the Hebrew Scriptures, see Mark S. Smith, *The Origins of Biblical Monotheism: Israel's Polytheistic Background and the Ugaritic Texts* (Oxford: Oxford University Press, 2001), 6–7, 83–103.
4. See also 1 Sam 15:29; Isa 31:3a; Ezek 28:2; Job 9:32.
5. A notable exception is Psalm 45, a royal wedding song, that addresses the king as "God" (v. 6).
6. E.g., Pss 66:3; 92:5; 96:4–5; 105:1–6; 106:2, 7–8; 126:2–3.
7. See also Pss 71:19b; 89:8; 113:5.
8. See also Exod 15:11; cf. Deut 4:32–34.
9. E.g., Pss 18:6–15; 29:3–10; 68:7–9, 17; 97:2–5; 144:5–6.
10. Ps 144:4; cf. 39:5–6; 109:23.
11. Ps 102:11.
12. See, e.g., the exploration of the cosmos as God's body in Grace M. Jantzen, *God's World, God's Body* (London: Darton, Longman & Todd, 1984). Such, however, would not be the psalmist's claim.
13. Smith, *Origins of Biblical Monotheism*, 88.
14. Ronald S. Hendel, "Aniconism and Anthropomorphism in Ancient Israel," in *The Image and the Book: Iconic Cults, Aniconism, and the Rise of Book Religion in Israel and the Ancient Near East*, ed. Karel van der Toorn (Leuven: Peeters, 1997), 208.
15. See below and William P. Brown, "*Creatio Corporis* and the Rhetoric of Defense in Job 10 and Psalm 139," in *God Who Creates: Essays in Honor of W. Sibley Towner*, ed. William P. Brown and S. Dean McBride Jr. (Grand Rapids: Eerdmans, 2000), 107–24.
16. In 39:13, the psalmist petitions that God's chastising gaze be averted, while exhorting God to "give ear" to his cry (v. 12).
17. E.g., Pss 6:9; 18:6; 28:2, 6; 31:22; 55:17; 116:1; 130:2; 140:6; 141:1.
18. Read *lānû* for *lāmô* ("them"), as attested in the Peshitta and Vulgate.
19. The Hebrew of v. 6a is difficult. The MT literally reads, "They search out evil acts." The parallelism of v. 6a, however, suggests another interrogative construction.

20. This section is replicated in abbreviated form in Ps 135:15–18, preceded by a recitation of God's saving and creative deeds (vv. 5–14).
21. Cf. Ps 82:1–7, in which a heavenly trial is conducted against the gods ("sons of Elyon" in Hebrew) by YHWH, which results in a death sentence.
22. The aniconic tenor of Deuteronomy 4, for example, eschews *concrete* reference to God's "face" (Deut 4:12, 15; cf. v. 37).
23. See the emendation proposed by *BHS*.
24. Divine wrath is frequently indicated by the metonym of the (inflamed) nostril (*'ap*). See, e.g., 18:8; 90:7.
25. The poet's profile of human life as fleeting and toilsome (v. 10) is similar to Qoheleth's depiction of life and human activity (e.g., Eccl 1:3, 8, 13; 2:11, 18–19). But whereas the sage attributes the human condition to God's inscrutable ways, the psalmist is quick to attribute it to God's wrath.
26. Divine grief or weeping, however, is not featured in the Psalms as in, e.g., Jer 12:7–13. See J. J. M. Roberts, "The Motif of the Weeping God in Jeremiah and Its Background in the Lament Tradition of the Ancient Near East," *Old Testament Essays* 5 (1992): 361–74.
27. See also Ps 10:17–18, which identifies God's hearing as requisite for implementing justice on behalf of the helpless.
28. See also Pss 60:5; 78:54; 98:1; 118:15–16.
29. For the motif of God's hand in connection with the plague and exodus traditions, see Karen Martens, "'With a Strong Hand and Outstretched Arm': The Meaning of the Expression *byd ḥzqh wbzrw' nṭwyh*," *SJOT* 15 (2001): 123–41.
30. Compare Ps 118:14–16 with Exod 15:2, 6.
31. In addition to the examples listed below, see also Pss 35:2–3; 64:7.
32. For early bibliography, see *ANEP*, 307 (#490). Of note also is the discovery in the City of David in Jerusalem (stratum 14, tenth century) of a 4-cm-long bronze model of a clenched fist with a hole bored through it to hold a weapon, which derived from a statue that stood ca. 38 cm in height. See the discussion in Othmar Keel and Christoph Uehlinger, *Gods, Goddesses, and Images of God in Ancient Israel*, trans. Thomas H. Trapp (Minneapolis: Fortress, 1998), 135–36.
33. For discussion, see Izak Cornelius, *The Iconography of the Canaanite Gods Reshef and Ba'al: Late Bronze and Iron Age I Periods (c 1500–1000 BCE)* (OBO 140; Fribourg: University of Fribourg Press / Göttingen: Vandenhoeck & Ruprecht, 1994), 135–38. The other prominent type of "smiting god" is identified as Reshef, who carries a shield, apparently in contrast to Baal (ibid., 125–33).
34. The Song of the Sea, e.g., refers only to God's hand (Exod 15:6, 12, 16–17) and breath or wind (vv. 8, 10) in effecting victory. Enlisted also are the "floods" (v. 5) or "sea" (v. 10), driven by God's nostril blast (v. 8), the "earth," which swallows the army (v. 12), and God's consuming "fury" (v. 7b). The enemy is "thrown" or "cast into the sea" (v. 1b, 4). The only mention of a hand-wielded weapon is found in the *enemy's* declaration: "I will draw my sword, my hand shall destroy them" (v. 9b).
35. Note again the above portrayal of Baal, whose left hand holds a plant spear.
36. The redirection of the metaphor has its prophetic parallel in the turn of God's "strong hand" *against* Israel in Jer 21:5–6 and Ezek 20:33–34.
37. Literally, "hostility (*tigrat*) of your hand." The term in question evidently corresponds to the Aramaic *tigrā'*.
38. Outside the biblical tradition, the deity's hand on the individual causes plagues and illness as well as violence (Martens, "'With a Strong Hand and an Outstretched Arm,'" 137–38; J. J. M. Roberts, "The Hand of Yahweh," *VT* [1971]: 244–51).
39. Cf. Ps 59:12b–13a.
40. See Smith, *The Origins of Biblical Monotheism*, 89.

41. Cf. James Crenshaw, *The Psalms: An Introduction* (Grand Rapids: Eerdmans, 2001), 1, 14.
42. E.g., Pss 6:1; 46:10; 50:21b; 95:8–11; 104:7; 105:14b–15.
43. E.g., against the gods in Ps 82:2–4, 6–7 and against Israel in 50:7–23.
44. E.g., Pss 89:3–4, 19–37; 105:10–11.
45. E.g., Pss 110:4; 132:11–12, 14–18.
46. E.g., Pss 81:9–10a; 119:13, 43, 72, 88.
47. E.g., Ps 60:6–8=108:7–9.
48. E.g., Ps 62:11–12.
49. E.g., Ps 85:8.
50. E.g., Pss 103:20; 106:25.
51. Tablet V of the *Enūma eliš*. See also Ps 148:5, 8.
52. *BHS* suggests *mayim ya'ămōdû* ("the waters stand"), an ingenious proposal lacking textual support.
53. For similar imagery, see Isa 40:7.
54. Reading Ketib; Qere reads plural.
55. See chapter 4.
56. Deuteronomy 4 can be considered the theological summit of the book as a whole.
57. Smith notes the tension among priestly texts in Numbers regarding an "older anthropomorphism" and the tendencies in the tradition to present God in more disembodied form (Smith, *The Origins of Biblical Monotheism*, 89).
58. "Breath" (*nišāmâ*) and exhaled "wind" (*rûaḥ*) need to be distinguished from other uses of *rûaḥ* that designate, e.g., "soul" or personal being (Pss 31:6; 77:4; 142:4), wind (18:11; 83:13; 104:3–4; 135:7), "spirit" (e.g., 51:13; 143:10), and demeanor or conduct (32:2; 51:12, 17; 78:8; 106:33). Although the same word is used, different source domains are presupposed.
59. Note, for example, the four three–foot-long footprints impressed in the limestone slabs of the temple portico at 'Ain Dara in northern Syria, denoting the entrance of a striding deity (Ba'al-Hadad or Ishtar) into the temple's main hall (John Monson, "The New 'Ain Dara Temple: Closest Solomonic Parallel," *BAR* 26/3 [May/June, 2000]: 27–28).
60. Cf. Ps 45:7 ("you love righteousness and hate wickedness"). It is unclear, however, whether God or the king is the subject.
61. Contra James L. Crenshaw, who curiously claims that the "psalmists rarely allude to love . . . by God" (*The Psalms,* 69). References to human love for God, moreover, are well attested (e.g., 31:23; 69:36; 116:1; 119:132; cf. 40:17; 122:6).
62. Read *'ōhēb.* The following colon suggests that YHWH is the subject rather than the object of the verb. The MT likely reflects a dittograph of the yod.
63. A few Hebrew manuscripts, along with the Peshitta, attest the participle rather than the imperative form of the verb. The context requires the former.
64. See also the epithet in Ps 99:4 ("Mighty King, lover of justice"). The translation is questionable, but requires little emendation. The MT has "and the king's strength, he loves justice," which with slight repointing can read "strong is the king who loves justice." In either case, however, the broader context requires God as the subject rather than an earthly king. Translating the clause as an extended title makes the best sense.
65. See, e.g., Ps 106:46.
66. E.g., Pss 5:8; 26:3; 33:22; 36:6; the refrain in Ps 136.
67. The same metaphorical schema can be found in Prov 3:11–12, but with a different target domain, discipline.
68. E.g., Pss 25:6; 40:11; 51:1; 69:16; 103:4.
69. Cf. 1:2; 40:8; 111:2; 112:1; 119:35.

70. See also 40:13; 44:3; 77:7; 106:4; 149:4.
71. Literally, "legs of a person."
72. Pss 42:6; 63:6; 78:35 (as "rock").
73. Pss 77:11; 105:5; 143:5.
74. Ps 103:18.
75. Pss 78:42; 106:4.
76. In addition to denoting benevolent care, divine "remembrance" of humanity is evinced in God's "crowning" of human beings over creation, granting them dominion within the created order (Ps 8:5–8).
77. E.g., Pss 8:3, 5; 33:6; 46:8; 95:5; 96:5; 100:3; 104:24; 115:15; 119:73; 121:2; 124:8; 134:3; 136:5; 139:14–15; 146:6; 149:2.
78. E.g., Pss 3:5; 78:18–20; 81:16; 104:10–23; 107:9; 111:5; 136:25; 145:15–16; 146:7; 147:9.
79. E.g., Pss 6:4; 19:14; 25:22; 26:11; 31:5; 37:40; 44:26; 49:15 (cf. v. 7); 69:18; 71:23; 72:14; 74:2; 77:15; 78:35; 106:10; 107:2; 130:8.
80. E.g., Pss 6:2; 30:2; 103:3; 147:2–3. For an extensive study of this metaphorical role in the Hebrew Bible, see Michael L. Brown, *Israel's Divine Healer* (Studies in Old Testament Biblical Theology; Grand Rapids: Zondervan, 1995).
81. See, e.g., James L. Mays, *The Lord Reigns: A Theological Handbook to the Psalms* (Louisville, Ky.: Westminster John Knox, 1994), esp. 12–22. For broader analysis, see Mark Z. Brettler, *God Is King* (JSOTSup 76; Sheffield: Sheffield Academic Press, 1989); Horst Dietrich Preuss, *Old Testament Theology,* 2 vols. (Louisville, Ky.: Westminster John Knox, 1995), 1.152–59; Tryggve N. D. Mettinger, *In Search of God: The Meaning and Message of the Everlasting Names,* trans. Frederick H. Cryer (Philadelphia: Fortress, 1988), 92–122.
82. See *yhwh mālak* in Pss 93:1; 96:10; 97:1; 99:1; 146:10; and *'ĕlōhîm mālak* in 47:8. See also Pss 22:28; 47:2b.
83. See also Ps 93:3–4.
84. E.g., Pss 93:1–4; 95:4–5, 6b; 96:10–13.
85. E.g., Pss 95:5; 96:11; 98:7–8.
86. This would also include Gen 1:1–2:3.
87. See Smith, *The Origins of Biblical Monotheism,* 152.
88. E.g., Pss 23:1; 28:9; 74:1; 78:52, 71; 79:13; 80:1; 95:7; 100:3; cf. 119:176. For a well-known extrabiblical example from the legal literature, see Hammurabi's self-presentation as "shepherd" in both the Prologue and Epilogue of his law code (I.49–50; IV.41; reverse 24.41–42).
89. E.g., Pss 7:1; 9:4, 8; 75:2, 7; 96:10–13; 98:9; cf. 58:1; 82:1–7; 138:1b.
90. See chapter 3. For a listing of the ancient Near Eastern evidence, see William P. Brown, *The Ethos of the Cosmos: The Genesis of Moral Imagination in the Bible* (Grand Rapids: Eerdmans, 1999), 248–52.
91. E.g., Pss 29:3–9; 68:7–8; 97:2–5.
92. See also Pss 47:1–2; 95:1–2; 96:1–3; 98:1.
93. See above in connection with God's hand.
94. *qûmâ;* e.g., Pss 7:6a; 17:13; 35:2; 44:26; 59:5; 94:2.
95. *'ûrâ, hā'îrâ, hāqîṣâ;* e.g., Pss 7:6b; 35:23; 44:23; 59:4b; cf. the Song of the Ark in Num 10:35–36.
96. Or "in the rump." In any case, a decisive rout is depicted.
97. The imagery runs counter to Ps 121:4 and Isa 40:28, which depict God's protective vigilance.
98. For the classic statement of this moral dynamic, see Klaus Koch, "Is There a Doctrine of Retribution in the Old Testament?" in *Theodicy in the Old Testament,* ed. James L. Crenshaw (IRT 4; Philadelphia: Fortress, 1983), 57–87. Cf. the important

refinement of this thesis in Patrick D. Miller, *Sin and Judgment in the Prophets: A Stylistic and Theological Analysis* (Chico, Calif.: Scholars Press, 1982).

99. For paternal imagery, see Exod 4:22; Deut 32:6; Isa 63:16; 64:8; Jer 3:4, 19; 31:9; Hos 11:1; Mal 1:6; 2:10.

100. On the language of birth in the royal rhetoric of Isaiah 9, see J. J. M. Roberts, "Whose Child Is This? Reflections on the Speaking Voice in Isaiah 9:5," *HTR* 90 (1997): 115–29.

101. Maternal or female imagery is found in Deut 32:18; Isa 42:14; 46:3; 49:14–15; cf. 45:10–11; 66:9, 13; Jer 12:7–13. For ancient Near Eastern parallels of feminine imagery attributed to male deities, see Smith, *The Origins of Biblical Monotheism*, 90–91.

102. For similar imagery, see Pss 71:6; 139:13, 15.

103. Mark Smith notes an ancient parallel in a prayer of Gudea, the *ensi* of Lagash, to the city-goddess Gatumdug:

> I have no mother—you are my mother.
> I have no father—you are my father.
> You implanted in the womb the germ of me;
>   you gave birth to me from out of the vulva (too).
> Sweet, O Gatumdug, is your holy name!

(Translation adapted from Smith, *The Biblical Origins of Monotheism,* 91)

104. See chapter 2. See, e.g., Pss 32:8; 51:13; 86:11; 143:8b.

105. E.g., Ps 119:12, 26, 64, 68, 108, 124, 135, 171.

106. Ps 94:12.

107. Ps 94:10.

108. Pss 18:34; 144:1.

109. Ps 71:17.

110. See Ps 119:23, 61, 84–88, 110, 115, 150.

111. E.g., Pss 27:11; 34:11; 86:11; 94:10; 143:10.

112. A difficult word, whose meaning is disputed. For this translation, based on an Arabic cognate, see A. A. Macintosh, "A Third Root *'dh* in Biblical Hebrew?" *VT* 24 (1974): 454–73.

113. An extension, as well as flip side, of the teacher metaphor is God as tester, which presupposes the deity's pedagogical role while highlighting more sharply God's recourse to power in the form of punishment (e.g., Pss 11:4–7; 26:2; 66:10–12; 139:23).

Chapter 8: "As the Mountains Surround Jerusalem"

1. *Four Quartets,* "The Dry Salvages" I.1–2.

2. "Taste" refers metaphorically to the abundant provision supplied to those "who seek YHWH," presumably in the context of a sacrificial meal such as the communal "well-being offering" (*zebaḥ šĕlāmîm;* Lev 3; 7:11–36). In contrast to the worshiper, "young lions" suffer hunger pangs (Ps 34:10).

3. Many of these metaphors are discussed more fully in previous chapters.

4. Cf. Pss 13:3; 36:9; 38:10.

5. E.g., Pss 88:6, 12, 18; 105:28 [plague in Egypt]; 107:10, 14; 139:11–12; 143:3.

6. The light of guidance is also manifested in the historical recounting of the exodus and wilderness wandering, in which God's "fiery light" leads Israel on the way (78:14; cf. 105:39).

7. For a survey of ancient Near Eastern roots, see Bernd Janowski, *Rettungsgewißheit und Epiphanie des Heils: Das Motiv der Hilfe Gottes "am Morgen" im Alten Orient und*

im Alten Altestament, Band 1: Alter Orient (WMANT 59; Neukirchen-Vluyn: Neukirchener Verlag, 1989), as well as additional bibliography listed in chapter 4.

8. Cf., by contrast, Ps 104:2.

9. For ornithological imagery applied to God, see chapter 1.

10. Reshef was a chthonic deity, as well as a god of battle and diseases, as confirmed in Ugaritic ritual texts and the Amarna Letters. For discussion of the various iconographic examples, see Izak Cornelius, *The Iconography of the Canaanite Gods Reshef and Ba'al: Late Bronze and Iron Age I Periods (c 1500–1000 BCE)* (OBO 140, Fribourg: University of Fribourg Press / Göttingen: Vandenhoeck & Ruprecht, 1994), 125–33. Cornelius argues that the shield is the primary distinguishing feature of this deity, setting it apart from the Baal type of Syrian iconography.

11. See chapter 1.

12. Cf. 2 Kgs 4:19; Jonah 4:8.

13. I.e., possessed by demons or rendered a "lunatic" (cf. Matt 17:15)? In any case, a wealth of evidence indicates a thriving moon cult in ancient Israel (Deut 4:19; 17:3; 2 Kgs 23:5; cf. Jer 8:2; Job 31:26; Wis 13:2). See Brian B. Schmidt, "Moon," in *Dictionary of Deities and Demons in the Bible,* ed. Karel van der Toorn, Bob Pecking, and Pieter W. Van der Horst (2d ed.; Leiden: Brill; Grand Rapids: Eerdmans, 1999), 589–91.

14. Mount Sinai shares this distinction to a lesser degree in the Psalter (68:8, 17; cf. Exod 19:16–25).

15. *KTU* 1.4.v.56.

16. The author of Psalm 121 polemicaly claims that his "help" comes *not* from the hills but from YHWH (cf. 1 Kgs 20:23, 28).

17. The text is corrupt (literally, "my mountain, strength"), likely owing to a misplaced suffix.

18. For water imagery, see chapter 5.

19. The first text is an indictment against Israel for its apostasy; the latter functions doxologically.

20. For further detail on the mural, see chapter 3.

21. Literally, "oil."

22. In a forthcoming paper, P. Kyle McCarter ties the meaning of √*'dn* with the sense of "to make rich/plentiful/abundant" (Colloquium for Biblical Research, August 19, 2001, Duke University). The parallelism in the psalm, moreover, suggests such a sense. See also Gen 18:12; Neh 9:25; Jer 31:12; 51:34.

23. Derived from the root *qhl,* the term is a hapax that most likely refers to various groups within the worshiping community, delineated along tribal lines (v. 27).

24. See Deut 4:21; Josh 13:23; 14:4; 15:13; 17:5; Num 18:21.

25. See Num 18:20; Deut 10:9; Josh 13:14. For discussion, see Hans-Joachim Kraus, *Theology of the Psalms,* trans. Keith Crim (Minneapolis: Fortress, 1992), 160.

26. For the metaphor of cup as God's judgment on Israel and/or the nations, see Isa 51:17, 22; Jer 25:15–29; Ezek 23:31–34; Hab 2:16; cf. Obad 16. The "target domain" of divine judgment for the metaphor occurs twice in the Psalter: 11:6 and 75:8. Elsewhere, the image connotes hospitality (Ps 23:5), YHWH (16:5, "my chosen portion and my cup"), and "salvation" (116:13). See Tuviah Friedman, "The Origin and Transformation of a Biblical Image" (in Hebrew), *Beit Mikra* 33 (1987/88): 135–38.

Conclusion

1. Cited from Mark S. Burrows, "'To Taste with the Heart': Allegory, Poetics, and the Deep Reading of Scripture," *Int* 56 (2002): 172 (Sermon 67.ii.3 on the Song of Songs).

2. For a sociopolitical perspective, see Robert B. Coote, "Psalm 139," in *The Bible and the Politics of Exegesis: Essays in Honor of Norman K. Gottwald on His Sixty-Fifth Birthday,* ed. David Jobling et al. (Cleveland: Pilgrim Press, 1991), 33–38.

3. The final verse suggests that the speaker has been charged with the sin of idolatry (see below).

4. For more on the rhetoric of Psalm 139, see William P. Brown, "*Creatio Corporis* and the Rhetoric of Defense in Job 10 and Psalm 139," in *God Who Creates: Essays in Honor of W. Sibley Towner,* ed. William P. Brown and S. Dean McBride Jr. (Grand Rapids: Eerdmans, 1999), 107–24.

5. Cf. Psalms 10, 13, 22, 44, 89.

6. The exception is found in the psalmist's imprecation against his enemies in 139:19–22. God, however, is not charged.

7. God's knowledge of the (psalmist's) self opens and concludes the psalm (139:1–4; 23–24), whereas the unattainable knowledge of God is featured within the thematic envelope (vv. 6, 17–18).

8. The verb is best taken as a denominative of *zrt* ("span") to mean "measure off" (*HALOT,* 280).

9. See, e.g., Pss 10:1; 35:22.

10. Cf. 1 Chr 28:9, which casts God as the One who "searches every mind" but also desires to "be found."

11. So Coote, "Psalm 139," 36.

12. See, e.g., Pss 32:4; 38:2; 39:10.

13. See, e.g., Pss 88:5–6; 115:17.

14. See chapter 4.

15. The verb as it stands in the MT makes little sense ("bruise" from *šwp;* cf. Gen 3:15) and should be emended in accordance with Symmachus and Jerome to read "cover" (*šwk,* so *BHS*).

16. See chapter 4 and Jan Assmann, *Egyptian Solar Religion in the New Kingdom: Re, Amun and the Crisis of Polytheism,* trans. Anthony Alcock (London / New York: Kegan Paul International, 1995), 57–65.

17. The kidneys were considered the most secret, innermost organ of the human anatomy (see Jer 11:20; 20:2; Pss 7:10; 26:2), as well as the seat of moral conscience and self-knowledge (Ps 16:7; Prov 23:16; Jer 12:2). See Hans Walter Wolff, *Anthropology of the Old Testament,* trans. Margaret Kohl (Philadelphia: Fortress, 1974), 65–66, 96.

18. NRSV "knit me." But clearly the use of needles and yarn is not envisioned here. Since the verb √*skk* is etymologically related to "booth" (*sukkâ*), Mary P. Boyd speculates that the verb designates plaiting as in mat weaving or basketry (personal communication).

19. So MT. LXX, Peshitta, and Targum evidently read *niplêtā* ("you are [awesomely] wonderful"), in accordance with the following stich (cf. 11QPsᵃ). Despite the majority of textual witnesses, the MT represents the more difficult, and likely original, rendering.

20. Outside of this psalm, the verb (√*rqm*) is exclusively found in relation to the multicolored, embroidered curtains of the tabernacle and priestly tunics (Exod 26:23; 27:16; 28:39; 35:35; 36:37; 38:18, 23; 39:29).

21. I.e., embryo (so Talmudic Hebrew). Various emendations have been suggested in order to bring the second colon in parallel with the first and to make sense of the antecedent for *kullām* ("all of them"): *kol-yāmay* ("all my days" [KBL, 185]), *gĕmulay* ("all my deeds" [Gunkel, *Die Psalmen* {1897; reprint, Göttingen: Vandenhoeck & Ruprecht, 1968}, 591]), and *gilay-mî* ("my life stages" with enclitic mem [Dahood, *Psalms III,* 101–50 {AB 17A; Garden City, N.Y.: Doubleday, 1970}, 295]).

With the above translation, the temporal phrase in v. 16a must be taken proleptically.

22. See Gen 2:7; 3:19; Ps 90:3; Eccl 3:20; 5:15; 12:7; Job 1:21; Sir 16:30; 40:1; 2 Esd 5:48; 10:9–14. The psalmist strategically transfers the secrecy of his genesis to the corporate sphere of humanity's genesis. His "genesis of secrecy" is made public.

23. See, e.g., Prov 31:13, 18–19, 21–22.

24. For a discussion of the limitations of gynecological knowledge in ancient Mesopotamia, see R. D. Briggs, "Conception, Contraception, and Abortion in Ancient Mesopotamia," in *Wisdom, Gods, and Literature: Studies in Assyriology in Honor of W. G. Lambert,* ed. A. R. George and I. L. Finkel (Winona Lake, Ind.: Eisenbrauns, 2000), 1–13. The ancients attributed the power of procreation to semen.

25. Cf. Exod 3:20; 34:10; Deut 10:21; Judg 6:13; 2 Sam 7:23; Isa 64:2–3; Jer 21:2; Pss 9:1b; 26:7; 96:3–4; 106:22; 145:5–6.

26. See Brown, *"Creatio Corporis,"* 117–24.

27. Read *nisakkōtî* for *nissaktî.* See Gale A. Yee, "The Theology of Creation in Proverbs 8:22–31," in *Creation in the Biblical Traditions,* ed. Richard J. Clifford and John J. Collins (CBQMS 24; Washington, D.C.: Catholic Biblical Association of America, 1992), 89 n. 8.

28. Cf. Pss 40:7; 56:8; 69:28; Mal 3:16.

29. Hebrew *'ēṭ;* cf. 45:1b.

30. The Hebrew verb can mean "be precious" as well as the Aramaic sense of "difficult"; hence, the translation offered above captures this double sense. The point is that God's purposes are unattainable for the psalmist (cf. v. 6).

31. The MT reads "I awoke (*hĕqîṣōtî*)," which makes little sense in context. Slight revocalization to *hăqiṣṣōtî,* also attested in three Hebrew manuscripts, necessitates the postulation of an otherwise unattested stem for √*qṣṣ* (hiphil) in the MT.

32. The term can either denote agony or hardship (e.g., 1 Chr 4:9; Isa 14:3), or imply idolatry, the worship of false gods (Isa 48:5; see also the cognate *'āṣāb* ["idol"] in Pss 106:38; 135:15). The latter makes better sense, for the psalmist asks God to assay his integrity (so, e.g., Ernst Wurthwein, "Erwägungen zu Psalm 139," *VT* [1957]: 165–82; Albert A. Anderson, *Psalms: Volume 2 [73–150],* NCB [London: Marshall Pickering / Grand Rapids: Eerdmans, 1972], 904–5; Leslie C. Allen, *Psalms 101–150* [WBC 21; Waco, Tex.: Word, 1983], 250, 253).

33. Or "ancient" way. Comparable use of this metaphor is found in Jer 6:16 and 18:15, in which idolatry is also at issue. The old, established way vividly designates the reputedly well-worn path of orthodoxy.

34. Jane Hirshfield, *Nine Gates: Entering the Mind of Poetry* (San Francisco: HarperCollins, 1997), 99.

35. See William P. Brown, *The Ethos of the Cosmos: The Genesis of Moral Imagination in the Bible* (Grand Rapids: Eerdmans, 1999), 317–80.

Scripture and Ancient Source Index

(Biblical citations correspond to NRSV versification.)

Author/Subject Index